The Man Who Stole Rock 'n' Roll

'It's rock 'n' roll plagiarism… only this time the songs are stolen from the future'

Bob Lawton

Copyright © Bob Lawton 2015

This book is sold subject to the condition that it shall not, by way of trade or otherwise, be lent, resold, hired out, or otherwise circulated without the publisher's prior consent in any form of binding or cover other than that in which it is published and without a similar condition including this condition being imposed on the subsequent publisher.

The moral right of Bob Lawton has been asserted.

ISBN-13: 978-1508729228

ISBN-10: 1508729220

DEDICATION

To Cynthia.

CONTENTS

ACKNOWLEDGMENTS i
Chapter 1. 'Rock 'n' Roll Music' 1
Chapter 2. 'So You Wanna Be A Rock 'n' Roll Star' 13
Chapter 3. 'Let's Stay Together' 33
Chapter 4. 'Drivin' In My Car' 45
Chapter 5. 'The Stranger' 65
Chapter 6. 'Signed, Sealed, Delivered' 76
Chapter 7. 'My Heart Belongs To Daddy' 89
Chapter 8. 'The Joker' 109
Chapter 9. 'Wayward Wind' 122
Chapter 10. 'We Gotta Get Out Of This Place' 128
Chapter 11. 'Listen To The Music' 145
Chapter 12. 'New Kid In Town' 157
Chapter 13. 'Seven Days Is Too Long' 168
Chapter 14. 'Like I've Never Been Gone' 189
Chapter 15. '18 With A Bullet' 200
Chapter 16. 'Let's Have A Party' 222
Chapter 17. 'Here Come The Judge' 243
Chapter 18. 'Route 66' 258
Chapter 19. 'Travellin' Band' 277
Chapter 20. 'Road To Nowhere' 295
Chapter 21. 'Don't Believe A Word' 312
Chapter 22. 'Wondrous Stories' 326
Chapter 23. 'Living In The Past' 352
Chapter 24. 'Back Together Again' 368
Chapter 25. 'A Day In The Life' 387
Chapter 26. 'Can I Get A Witness' 404
Chapter 27. 'On The Road Again' 420
Chapter 28. 'News Of The World' 434
Chapter 29. 'Yesterday Once More' 453

ACKNOWLEDGMENTS

Elaine Bane, Rick Price. All Swingin' Chimes and Rockin' Berries past and present.

CHAPTER 1
'ROCK 'N' ROLL MUSIC'

Chuck Berry

The lounge bar of the Crown and Anchor was almost deserted, but with the rain and wind gusting outside that was hardly surprising. On the far side of the lounge, where the maroon carpet finished and the wood grain vinyl flooring began, three guys were playing darts; or rather two guys were playing darts whilst a third was chalking up the scores.

On the opposite side, a vintage Rock-Ola jukebox stood silent. It bubbled and blinked away. Orange, to yellow, to green, to blue, and then back to orange to start again. The colours changed endlessly, or at least until someone unplugged the beast at closing time.

Perched on a stool at the bar, Frank watched them from behind his sunglasses whilst he waited his turn to be served.

'There you are, Walter,' said the blonde barmaid as she handed the old chap his change. 'Careful how you go, don't get spilling it.'

'Thankee Gloria,' said Walter as he grasped his change, his arthritic fingers making it difficult as he slipped the coins into his jacket pocket. He picked up his pint of bitter with a slight wobble and looked to make sure he wasn't going to trip over his dog's leash. 'Get from under me feet, Monty and forget 'bart crisps, thou's gettin' too fat.'

They made their way over to the bay window that overlooked Market Square. Old Walter put his pint on the table and sat down next to the coat and trilby he'd left drying on the upholstered seating that curved around the inside of the bay. Monty, a little black and tan Yorkshire terrier, took a disinterested sniff at a well chewed rubber bone lying under the table and sprawled himself full length, his head cocked slightly to one side as one of the dart players, wearing an Aston Villa top, shouted, 'One hundred and twenty!' pumping the air with both fists.

Frank Richards had arrived in the village by train and got a good soaking whilst making his way to the pub where he'd arranged to meet Stan and Bodkin. He'd peeled off his dripping Burberry trench coat, hung it on the coat rack next to the door to the gents, and sat himself on one of the stools that stood in front of the long, polished bar.

'What can I get for you?' Gloria smiled sweetly as she stepped towards him.

'Have you a house red?'

'I've got Shiraz or Rioja.'

'Shiraz would be great; can you make it a large one, please?'

South African Shiraz, Frank read to himself from the label as Gloria poured it.

'That'll be four fifty, please.' Gloria placed the glass of

wine on the bar.

'Sorry I've got nothing smaller,' apologised Frank as he peeled a twenty off a wad that would have choked a horse.

'Not a problem.' Gloria was still smiling sweetly as she returned with his change. Then she went back to filling the shelves.

Frank sat there for the next ten minutes studying, in turn, the Dartboard Three, old Walter and Monty, the glimmering, shifting colours of the jukebox and Gloria's bottom as she bent to place the glasses under the counter.

He also watched himself in the mirror that ran the length of the bar as he drained his wine glass; he studied his reflection with a sardonic eye. His black wavy hair from the halcyon days of youth was now replaced by a ponytail stretched tight to the back of his skull, and, without doubt, becoming a whiter shade of pale. He inwardly groaned as he recognised he was starting to look as fatigued as his expensively distressed denim jacket and as washed out as his faded T-shirt. He put his glass down, took two hands to straighten his jacket collar in the mirror, and sat up straight. That made him feel better.

'Same again?' Gloria broke his thoughts, offering the bottle across the bar.

'Yes please,' he answered, nodding his head and pushing his empty glass towards her.

She caught her reflection in his sunglasses and he caught a glimpse of her cleavage as she took a fresh glass from beneath the counter. Frank may have thought he'd had a sneaky peek at the top of her tits from behind those sunglasses, but Gloria was quite aware; in fact maybe she stooped a little lower for him. As she poured his wine, a particularly foul piece of industrial language came winging its way over from the dartboard. Frank frowned as he looked at Gloria, putting a hand on the counter to get up off his stool.

'No, don't get involved.' Gloria put her hand on his to stop him. 'If it gets any worse I'll deal with it. That's Curly and Chopper Mottershead, or the Meathead Brothers as they're known locally, and their gormless mate Pimples. You don't want to mess with them, believe me. If there's trouble in the village it's a pretty good bet that they'll be up to their tattooed necks in it.'

Frank bit his lip and glowered towards them.

Gloria put her elbow on the counter and spoke quietly. 'Curly's the bald headed one in the Villa shirt, Chopper's in the black AC/DC T-shirt, he's Curly's older brother and particularly nasty. Pimples is the one in the camouflage jacket with the hoodie up.'

Frank could see that Pimples had, at some time, had a really bad case of acne that had left him with a badly scarred face. Despite him being inside in the warm and dry, Frank guessed he wore the hoodie up to try and hide his moonscape complexion. Somehow it only seemed to emphasise it. 'Why Pimples? Seems a little harsh,' said Frank, trying desperately not to smirk.

'No idea,' shrugged Gloria. 'Don't even know his real name, it's always been Pimples. That's Curly and Chopper Meathead for you; they take no prisoners, friend or foe.'

***

Gloria had worked at the Crown and Anchor since she arrived in the thriving Worcestershire village of Fordrough in late 1999. She'd got a day job nearby, not best paid, so to begin with she took a temporary evening job to help her finances, collecting glasses and doing a bit of serving when it got busy, but during those crazy days celebrating the millennium she became more and more invaluable to old Dennis Jenkinson, the landlord. He soon realised she was good at her job, knew how to serve drinks, had a quick brain and that the customers loved her. Two years to the day after her first glass collection, Dennis made her manager of the Crown and Anchor.

Gloria was a pretty girl who wasn't shy to show a little bit of leg where necessary with a skirt just short enough to keep the menfolk of Fordrough drinking and the womenfolk of Fordrough at arm's length. The bar staff all wore sky blue tops and Gloria always made sure she left that extra button undone on her frilly sky blue blouse. In the years since the millennium, Gloria had grown into an attractive thirty-something who was priceless to the Crown and Anchor, as far as old Dennis was concerned.

She worked full-time running the show. She organised the bar staff, waitresses and cleaners, re-ordered stock, cashed up and looked after a busy kitchen and what seemed like a succession of chefs, some with their eye on the big chance, others whose ambitions stopped at microwaving lasagne or chicken Madras. Then there were sous-chefs, waitresses and bottle-washers. Dennis still took a pride in his cellar, but his appearances behind the bar were rare. His wife Mildred looked after their four B&B guest rooms. Otherwise the pair of them watched a lot of DVDs and Jeremy Kyle.

***

'You must be Frankie Atom,' said Gloria.

Frank raised his eyebrows in surprise. 'Blimey! Didn't expect to be recognised in the village, it's been a long time.' He paused to check himself in the mirror again. 'Looking a bit dog-eared these days, I'm afraid.'

'I didn't recognise you, I just guessed it must be you. Stan Ravenscroft was telling everyone last night just before last orders, that he was meeting you and your drummer here this afternoon to talk about a reunion.' Gloria glanced at her watch. 'About now, in fact. Some of the older folks got quite excited I can tell you, especially one or two of the ladies. Mind you they'd had a few drinks by then,' she laughed.

Frank's look of surprise turned to one of annoyance as he half turned away, shaking his head. 'Stan couldn't keep his trap shut, could he?' He turned back to Gloria. 'Sorry, I'm being rude. My name's Frank Richards. Frankie Atom and The Bombastics was our stage name. I expect Stan has already told you that he was our bass player.' He held out a hand to her.

'Hi, Frank, I'm Gloria.' She took his hand and Frank leant forward to gently peck her on the cheek. 'Yes he did, he was full of it last night, was our Stan.'

Frank slid his sunglasses up and perched them on top of his forehead. 'I can see I don't need these, not that I was expecting to be chased across Market Square by screaming teenage girls, more like grannies with shopping trollies, I suppose. Fordrough was where it all started for us all those years ago; though I have to say in those days it was the village hall rather than the Crown and Anchor, just young lads who hadn't yet discovered the evils of wine, women and song.' He paused and grinned. 'Well one out of three ain't bad. When it all began happening and the hits started, we came under a lot of pressure to move down to London, but we just never got round to it. Stan in particular, was adamant he was staying around here, but Barry, Bodkin and me too, even Carol didn't want to move in those rock 'n' roll days. I guess we were all home birds. We even had our fan club run from the village.'

'Yes, by Mavis and Marion Meredith,' interrupted Gloria. 'They were in here last night. What was it Stan called them? The Dither Sisters, was that it?'

'Uh huh! That was Barry's name for them in the sixties,' smiled Frank. 'Mind you, he was the ditherer not them; could never make his mind up which one to share his Kit Kat with. I think they both got a finger in the end.'

Gloria didn't bat an eyelid.

Just then the wind gusted heavy rain against the leaded light window with that much force it startled old Walter. It made Monty jump up and growl at the window. Frank noticed he wasn't on his leash anymore.

'It looks like it's gonna be a quiet one in here tonight,' said Gloria, nodding towards a wet and windy Market Square where the light was fading fast. 'I can't see many venturing abroad in this lot.'

'Just as long as Stan and Bodkin make it,' said Frank. 'You can't blame people wanting to stay at home in the warm and dry watching TV. You gotta be some kind of loony to be out in that. Like me – or them lot.' He nodded towards one man and his dog, and the Dartboard Three.

Chopper was searching through his pockets, looking for money no doubt. They were preparing to refuel.

'Three Peronis and three sambucas, please Gloria!' Chopper shouted as he made his way over to the bar followed by Pimples.

Gloria took the tops off three bottles and put three shot glasses on the counter. She then turned and pulled out the sambuca from an assortment of multi-coloured bottles that stood under the back mirror.

'Are you the geezer what's had the hit records?' Chopper turned to ask Frank.

'Er, yes – I am,' Frank replied, noticeably taken aback.

'Trying to make some sort of comeback, ain't yer? So the old geezer was telling everyone in the bar last night.'

Exasperated, Frank blew loudly through his teeth and stared at Gloria in silence for a few seconds. 'I'll swing for that Stanley Ravenscroft, just how many people has he told?'

Gloria shrugged.

'What sort of stuff do you play, then?' asked Chopper, tossing a crumpled ten pound note onto the bar.

'Not exactly yer bleedin' hip hop, I'll bet,' butted in Pimples. He'd dropped a handful of loose change onto the bar next to Chopper's tenner and was searching through it with his forefinger.

Frank and Gloria detected a sneer in his voice.

'We play rock 'n' roll,' said Frank, taking his sunglasses off his head and pushing them into his breast pocket. 'It's the music that started it all.'

'Music to die of old age to,' scoffed Pimples, making no eye contact with Frank.

'Don't be a twat, Pimps.' Chopper gave him a sharp nudge. 'We got a lot to thank that old rock 'n' roll music for. Without it there wouldn't have been no AC/DC, no Led Zeppelin, nor no Iron Maiden.'

Frank smiled.

'Chopper knows his music,' said Gloria taking the ten pounds and picking up the correct change, clearly too much of a challenge for Pimples.

'Still play all me old man's stuff.' Chopper pulled his smart phone out of the pocket of his jeans, pressed a couple of buttons and scrolled through it with his thumb. 'Listen, I got some Buddy Holly and the Crickets here.' He held it up and Frank could hear 'That'll Be the Day' hissing from it.

'I ain't never heard of no Buddy 'olly and the Cricketers and I wouldn't like 'em if I had,' grumbled Pimples, turning away to scoop up the loose change left over on the bar and slipping it into the side pocket of his hoodie.

Still arguing about their tastes in music, Chopper and Pimples picked up the bottles and shots between them and ambled their way back to their darts, the crotches of their jeans hung low between their legs, revealing bum cracks and tomorrow's washing.

Frank looked at Gloria and they both sniggered.

'It may be haute-couture in Sing Sing, but why the hell would three cool cats wander around Worcestershire with their arses hanging out?'

Villa Top was idly tossing darts into the board awaiting their return, completely oblivious to the conversation that had just taken place between his big brother, his gormless mate and former teenage idol Frankie Atom. Monty had wandered across to Frank and was sniffing at the legs of his bar stool.

'You don't often see dogs in pubs these days,' he said to Gloria.

'There's only two or three of the villagers bring them in,' she replied. 'We only allow dogs in when there's no food being served. Old Walter will know he has to take Monty home by six-thirty. We've had no little accidents up until now, although Monty can be a bit of a pest if somebody has crisps.'

The whooping and fist pumping had begun again over on the oche. War had restarted. Monty had worked his way to the far end of the bar and was sniffing at the tables and chairs that stood near to the game of darts.

'Come 'ere, Monty, you daft little bugger,' snapped Walter. 'You'll be coppin' one o' them arrows up yer jacksie.'

Monty took no notice and carried on sniffing.

Frank looked at his watch, took his iPhone out of his breast pocket and impatiently punched out a text message to Stan. He then put his phone down on the bar. 'Let's see where the hell he's got to.' He sat back on his stool and pushed his empty wine glass towards Gloria. 'Give me another of your finest reds, please, Gloria.'

'At your service O mighty rock star.' She mock curtsied, pretending to hold her skirts each side twixt finger and thumb, then took his glass and re-filled it.

'Tell me, Gloria.' Frank's eyes had wandered over to the jukebox. 'How come you've got an old vintage Rock-Ola like that? Most pubs these days have flat screens playing wall to wall MTV or Premiership football.'

'It was Dennis, the gaffer's idea; he felt the Fordrough villagers, well most of them,' she glanced over at the Dartboard Three, 'are of a more mature generation. At least the ones that come in the Crown and Anchor are, so he thought he'd try bringing back a jukebox. It works too. Today's an exception, it's normally putting in overtime. Not too loud, you understand. Dennis likes his customers to have a bit of chit chat in his pub whilst they're downing a few pints and it's far enough away from the diners not to cause a problem.'

Frank moved over to the Rock-Ola and Gloria could see him studying the playlist.

'There's all sorts on there, rock, pop, punk, new wave, country, you name it. You'll definitely find Frankie Atom and The Bombastics somewhere on there,' she added.

'Bet it ain't got no Buddy 'olly and the Cricketers,' Frank mimicked, in a pretty decent Pimples voice, as he dropped a pound coin into the slot and pressed the buttons.

As he returned to his bar stool and picked up his glass the driving guitar of Chuck Berry filled the bar. Frank was just lifting the glass to his mouth when there was an almighty shout.

'Yeeeeesssss! Double five, that's it – game set and match.' This time Chopper was pumping his fists in victory.

Frank couldn't believe his eyes as he saw Pimples stoop

quickly and grab Monty, pick him up, and use him to wipe the scoreboard clean.

'You bastard!' screamed old Walter jumping to his feet and knocking over his table, spilling his beer across the Axminster. 'You evil bastard!'

Curly and Chopper were doubled up laughing as Pimples dropped Monty to the floor and they watched him scramble back over to his master, slipping and sliding on the vinyl, yelping pitifully, his fur on one side covered in blue chalk.

Frank got off his stool to confront the three of them but Gloria caught hold of his arm. 'Like I said, Frank, leave this to me.'

She strode over to them, tossing a bar towel over to old Walter to sop up his beer and maybe get the chalk dust off his dog, as she went. She stood arms akimbo, hands on shapely hips, looking fishwife fierce. 'There was no need for that, you frightened the living daylights out of the poor little creature and you've spilt Walter's beer. You should be ashamed!'

Frank was worried what might happen next and stood to alert, conscious that he was clenching his fists. He pictured himself piling into them, right hook, left hook, saving Gloria. Then reality dawned. *You're nearly seventy, you silly old sod.*

As it turned out he needn't have worried, Gloria wasn't one to be messed with and she certainly wouldn't kowtow to this lot, bad reputation or not.

'Sorry Gloria, it was only a bit of a laugh,' said Pimples. 'I didn't hurt him.'

'Get Walter another pint, Gloria,' said Chopper, reaching into his pocket. 'I'll pay for it.'

Old Walter was sat down again, still scowling, and Monty's eyes shone from the darkness underneath the safety of the table. Gloria poured Old Walter another pint and took it over to him, along with a packet of cheese and onion crisps for Monty.

Frank settled down again and took a sip of his Shiraz. Chuck Berry was still playing 'Rock and Roll Music' any old way you choose it, which seemed appropriate, whilst Frankie Atom waited to parley with his drummer and bass player.

CHAPTER 2
'SO YOU WANNA BE A ROCK 'N' ROLL STAR'

The Byrds

Elsie Ravenscroft sat up in bed, rollers bulging from under her hair net, and sipping at a cup of tea hubby Stan had brought up for her. Bertie, their black and white mongrel lay sprawled across the bottom of the bed with a look of complete disinterest, any expectation of bickies long gone. He'd been told so many times not to jump up on the bed, but he kept doing so after they'd fallen asleep until eventually they gave up.

The previous night Elsie had got fed up with waiting for Stan to come home from the Crown and Anchor, flicked through the channels and started to watch yet another repeat of Midsomer Murders, then finally gone to bed around eleven o'clock. Stan came in about half an hour later full of Anchor bitter, kicked off his shoes, peeled off his socks, let his shirt and trousers fall to the floor, pushed Bertie to one side, flopped his head back on the pillow and then remembered he hadn't taken his tablets. Too late, he'd take them in the morning.

***

Stan tried to remember whilst making the early morning tea. He had a half-remembered conversation with someone in the pub last night.

Did I tell someone about meeting up with Frank and Bodkin? About a reunion? I'm sure I told someone, maybe more than someone.

He caught his reflection in the veranda window.

One thing's for certain, if there's to be a Bombastics' reunion I'm going to have to do something about the size of this belly. More time at the gym and less time at the Crown and Anchor. You'll just have to be single-minded and resolute Stanley Ravenscroft!

As he plodded his way up the stairs, carefully balancing a cup of tea on a saucer in each hand, he remembered that they were both exactly the same New Year resolutions he'd made nine months ago. Neither of them had even got past February. *Oh dear!* He nudged the bedroom door ajar with his foot and stood by the bedside offering Elsie her cup of tea.

'Stan, do you remember all those years ago,' asked Elsie, taking her tea, 'when the travelling fair used to come round to the village every October?'

Stan was now posing in front of the full-length wardrobe mirrors. First turning this way and then turning that, he took in a deep breath and pushed his chin outwards and upwards. His spare tyre poked out from under his vest and spilled down over his Y-fronts. Stan was no stranger to a kebab and double chips.

'Remember the Hall of Mirrors that made us all go funny shapes?'

'I dooooooo.' Stan exhaled, raised his arms to shoulder height and flexed his biceps like some 1950s Charles Atlas advert.

'The one that really made us laugh, you know, the one that made you look like the Michelin Man?'

Stan turned to look at Elsie.

'Well that mirror's not one of them.' Elsie clapped her hand over her mouth and began snorting though her fingers. Shaking with the giggles she filled her saucer with hot tea as she struggled to place it, and the cup, on the bedside table.

Bertie buried his snout between his front paws. *God, was the bloody dog laughing too?*

Stan slumped down on the end of the bed next to Bertie.

'That just isn't funny, our Elsie,' despaired Stan. 'I always wore my Fender bass slung low like a gunslinger, it was my image, the way my fans remember me. Trouble is with all this blubber up front,' he clasped his hands around his belly, 'I won't be able to see what I'm playing.'

Elsie was wringing the corner of one of her pillows, holding it up to her mouth trying hard to stop sniggering. 'Listen to me John Wayne, you'll just have to wear it above your bikini line.' At this point she could stifle the giggles no longer, collapsed sideways into the pillow and threw the bedclothes over her head.

'I could forget the exercise and diet malarkey if you treated me to a double bass.'

Elsie's head shot back up from beneath the duvet. 'What?' She'd stopped giggling. 'And just how much is one of those double bass thingies going to cost?'

'A thousand, maybe fifteen hundred.' Stan waved his hand vaguely. 'I could pick up a decent second hand one for eight hundred.'

'You can forget that crap.' Elsie spoke poker-faced. 'I've got some second hand Weight Watchers books you can have for free.'

***

Stan had first met Frank in 1962.

Frontman Marty Spilsbury had walked out on The Bombastics and cleared off to Germany to join another band. In the early sixties night clubs in German cities like Hamburg, Dusseldorf and Munich wanted British rock groups, mainly because they attracted British and American troops stationed over there and that meant Deutschmarks; and plenty of them. The hours were long, but Marty was told the money was good and the Fräuleins were willing. Marty had been a good lead guitarist and singer, but he felt at the distinctly decrepit age of twenty-six that fame might be passing him by. Like all the kids, in all the groups, he dreamed of being a star and maybe he thought a residency in a Hamburg nightclub might be the right step.

It wasn't.

Ten years later Marty was driving DREAM-EEZY mattress lorries up and down the M6.

So back in Birmingham of 1962, Stan, Barry and Bodkin were on a mission to find a replacement as quickly as possible, rather than lose any more of the work they had in their diary. They got the cash together to put a small ad in the Music and Entertainments section of the *Birmingham Mail*.

'Wanted; Lead guitarist/singer for Bombastics Rock Band Phone KIN 1932' (the home number of Stan's mom and dad).

They trimmed the number of words down as much as they could to save on the cost. Because of Marty's hasty departure they'd already had to cancel three gigs at fifteen quid each, so they didn't have money to throw about. Stan and Barry had to keep up the monthly payments on their guitars, plus the two VOX amps, an echo chamber and an assortment of mics and stands, on which they were paying hire purchase. Bodkin had a similar commitment on his drums. Barry, the group's self-styled ladies man, tried to chat up the girl in the ads department to give them a free ad on Saturday if they paid for the rest of the week, but she was having none of it, and certainly didn't want a free ticket for their September gig at The Cosmos in Wolverhampton. Anyway, she'd added very snootily, she and her boyfriend were into modern jazz.

The ad ran from Monday for five nights. There were only two other ads in their section. One for Mrs Kimberley offering violin lessons and the other for a children's entertainer called Mr Bubbles.

The size of the Music and Entertainments section was so tiny it concerned them. Would people have even seen their three-line ad?

They needn't have worried, the response was amazing. Stan and his mom seemed to be taking calls for most of the week. Nine guitarists wanted a chance to join The Bombastics and become a rock 'n' roll star.

They'd already got Fordrough village hall booked on Saturday morning for their usual practice session and as it was school half term and the ballet classes were not due to meet that week, Mrs Morris, the caretaker, said they could go on into the afternoon as long as they weren't too loud.

Stan recalled it was a bright sunny morning and that they'd got there early to unload the gear. Rather than lug it all up the side steps that led to the stage, they set it up in front of the stage on the wooden floor of the main hall. Whilst Bodkin was busy setting up his drum kit and cymbals, Barry and Stan wired up the amps, echo chamber and three microphones on stands at the front. Barry was such an untidy worker, it annoyed Stan.

'Just look at the way you've powered up this plug board; I just don't believe that tangle of leads and wires. You'll get us all electrocuted, you bloody dimwit.'

Stan took control and one by one he untangled the leads and got them lying neat and tidy, secured to the floor with gaffer tape. Stan liked neat and tidy. After a bit of fiddling around getting tuned up, they did a brief sound check and waited for guitarist number one. It was Roger. Stan had slightly cringed when he'd introduced himself on the phone as Rockin' Roger.

Rockin' Roger was right on time and he looked old enough to be Stan's father. This was not going to be a good start. He had a comb-over hairstyle that seemed to start behind his left ear. Somehow he'd managed to tease it into a kiss curl on his forehead, but it refused to stay in curl and half way through 'Rock Around the Clock' it was in his eyes, bobbing about from one eye to the other, finally dangling down his left cheek. It looked ludicrous. He was not destined to become a Bombastic. Stan took his number and thanked him for turning up. When he'd gone Barry started to sing 'See You Later Alligator', and Bodkin joined in on drums.

'Shut up, you two. He'll hear you, he's only outside.'

Next through the door was worse, if that was possible. Stan tried to remember, he'd called himself either Big Lonnie or Big Ronnie. He definitely wore a loose-fitting beige woolly jumper with large black musical notes and a treble clef embroidered on the front, along with what looked like this morning's soft-boiled egg. In a ponderous and faltering style he strummed his way through 'Rock Island Line', and if that wasn't bad enough, whilst he played it in D, he sang it in something that sounded more like A sharp. By the time he'd finished Barry and Bodkin had given up, only Stan plodded gamely on.

He then started the intro to 'Cumberland Gap'. Stan cut him short. 'Sorry mate, but we left skiffle behind a few years ago, and you really do need to practice that guitar a bit more.'

Big Ronnie, or Big Lonnie, was not a happy man.

'Practice my guitar? That's rich coming from you.' He started finger pointing angrily in their general direction. 'I seen you lot down the Phantom Coach and you was rubbish. No wonder that guitarist of yours pissed off.'

Big Lonnie, or Big Ronnie, then noticed how big Bodkin was when he stood up. He swiftly departed, looking over his shoulder to give one last scowl from the safety of the exit door.

Bodkin disappeared into the kitchen at the far end of the hall and reappeared carrying three empty teacups and a bottle of Dandelion and Burdock. He placed them on the stage and poured. 'What's the betting a bleedin' Cliff Richard look-a-like is the next to walk through that door. Just wait and see.'

Bodkin raised his eyes to the heavens when a kid, who looked no more than twelve, swaggered in with a jacket that looked like it belonged to an older and much bigger brother, black drainpipe trousers and fluorescent pink socks. He introduced himself as Kevin Turner.

'You're Slash Turner's little brother, right?' said Barry.

'Yeah,' he replied, with a carefully practised pout. He had all the lyrics to 'Livin' Doll' and 'Move It' written down in a school exercise book which he opened up and placed on one of the chairs near to him. Barry and Stan could barely contain themselves. He took his acoustic guitar, looped the strap over his shoulder and moved over to the nearest mic, which Stan had to lower for him. He hesitated whilst he carefully formed the chord of A with his fingers on the fret board. He started strumming and to everyone's amazement started to pick his way through Lionel Bart's lyrics in a shrill boy soprano voice; stopping and carefully changing to the chord of E7, then stopping again and carefully changing back to the A chord shape...

'Hold on, Kevin,' said Barry, holding up a hand. 'You've obviously been practising hard and you seem to be progressing well, but we're looking for somebody that can start right away, so we're just gonna have to ask you to come back when you're ready for us and we'll be ready for you.'

Barry collected up the book of lyrics whilst Kevin put his guitar back in its cover. He then put a sympathetic arm round his shoulder and walked a disappointed Kevin to the door. 'You be sure to give Slash our best, now.' Kevin left.

'What the bleedin' hell were you on about?' asked Stan. '"You've been practising hard", "we'll be ready for you"? He sounded like Cliff with his balls cut off!'

'Listen Stan, Slash Turner was two years above us at school before he was expelled.' Barry's voice was flinty. 'You must remember he was one evil Teddy Boy, he used to pull the legs off first years for fun. Believe me I do not want a homicidal Slash Turner turning up on my front door with his little brother wailing and pointing an accusing finger at me.'

They were interrupted by Nigel and his mother. Mother came in first, carrying a music stand and satchel, followed by a tall gangly teenager in a green corduroy jacket and sharply creased grey flannels. He had a guitar case tucked underneath his arm.

Mrs Kimberley introduced herself. 'I'm Constance Kimberley, I teach violin. My little advert was next to yours in the *Birmingham Mail*; you may have seen it.'

'We did,' smiled Stan. 'I trust this young gentleman has a guitar in that case and not a Stradivarius.'

'Oh, it's a guitar, alright,' answered Mrs K, completely straight-faced. Even with Bodkin and Barry laughing that one had gone right over her head. 'This is my son, Nigel. He's been playing guitar for over a year now, and I've been teaching him to read music.'

Mrs Kimberley was a busy little woman in rimless glasses; she had her hair pulled back into a grey bun. She soon had Nigel's guitar out and then proceeded to fuss about straightening the strap as he put it over his shoulder, plugged his lead in and started to tune up. Mother then took sheet music out of the satchel and arranged it on the music stand in front of Nigel. She whispered some final instructions into his ear, flicked away some specks of dandruff on his jacket and sat down on one of the chairs that stood around the perimeter of the hall.

Nigel wasn't bad. He played a couple of Shadows instrumentals pretty much note perfect. He did break a string near the end of 'Wonderful Land', but with Mother's help pulling a replacement out of his case, he was soon re-strung and tuned up.

The problem was his personality. He was clearly shy and very nervous; he never made eye contact with any of them and hardly spoke a word. He had two goes at singing 'Halfway to Paradise', but forgot the words and got completely flummoxed. Ironically he got about halfway on both attempts. Everyone could see he was on the verge of tears. Mother came to his rescue with a clean, pressed handkerchief out of her handbag.

They could all see he wasn't yet ready for his public. Mother smiled, but her eyes told a different story as she whispered admonishments from the corner of her mouth. 'We practised this, Nigel, over and over it we went, you really have to start concentrating.'

He slowly packed away his guitar, whilst she folded up the sheet music and collapsed his music stand. She took a business card out of her handbag. Stan took it and glanced quickly at it. It read, 'Constance Kimberley *BMus*. Violin lessons', in embossed blue lettering.

'Give me a ring when you've made your decision. Nigel's only seventeen. I shall make sure he keeps up his lessons.'

'Thank you Mrs Kimberley, thank you Nigel,' said a very polite Stan.

'Nigel needs to get out more,' whispered Bodkin, just out of earshot as they trooped sadly out of the door.

Elvis with the gammy leg came next, in full character; greased back hair, sideburns, collar turned up. 'Good afternoon, boys,' he chirped.

'At least he spared us the Mississippi drawl and a quivering top lip,' Barry said later.

'You must be Simon Pollock,' asked Stan, reading from his list of applicants, now starting to run worryingly low.

'That's me.' He strapped his guitar on and moseyed on over to the microphone.

His guitar picking on 'Wooden Heart' was pretty mean, but when he opened his mouth to sing the timbre of his voice was totally wrong. Stan, Barry and Bodkin daren't look at each other; he sounded more like the Chipmunks than the king of rock 'n' roll. Also the boys couldn't help noticing that when he gyrated his pelvis during his guitar solos, his gammy leg forced him round in half circles, so to finish up in the same place as the microphone stand, he had to keep doing a quick shoe shuffle to be ready for the next verse.

After he'd gone Barry joked, 'Instead of singing "but I don't have a wooden heart", he should change it to "but I do have a wooden leg".'

'You're a sick man Barry Harper,' said Stan, but they all laughed.

Bodkin picked up his cup of Dandelion and Burdock, took a long slug and belched, loudly. 'Don't know why we're laughing, this is a waste of time, they've all been a pile of shite so far, surely we gotta get someone decent soon.'

Stan was sat on his VOX amp looking disconsolate. Barry shrugged and offered his cup to Bodkin for a top-up.

It became even gloomier in Fordrough Village Hall when number six didn't bother to turn up... but things were about to change.

Barry lit up a Park Drive and offered one to Bodkin. They waited. The next couple of hours would change their lives forever.

A young kid with black wavy hair carrying a guitar case strutted in and asked if this was where the Bombastic auditions were being held. Barry was tempted to ask if he thought it was the Women's Institute Knitting Circle having a stitch and bitch session, thought better of it and asked him who he was and how old he was.

'I'm Frank Richards and I'm fifteen.'

He was a good-looking kid. He had a smooth complexion, no sign of acne, but a growth of bum fluff round his mouth and on his chin. He was wearing the sort of white shirt and grey flannel trousers he'd wear to school. He rested his guitar case on the stage, opened it and took out a magnificent Gibson guitar.

'Bugger me,' spluttered Barry. 'That's some guitar you've got there!'

Stan gazed in wonder. 'It must have cost you a fortune.'

'Not a penny,' grinned young Frank. He slung a woven leather strap around his neck and walked over to them, jack-plug and lead in hand. 'Where shall I stick this?' he asked.

Bodkin nearly choked on his Dandelion and Burdock and thought, *If you're as bad as the lot we've had to listen to so far, I just might tell you.*

Frank fiddled around with his volume and tone knobs, adjusted the tuning on a couple of strings and then looked up.

'Okay, let's try 'Roll Over Beethoven', we'll do it in A.' Without hesitation he powered his way into the classic Chuck Berry intro, hitting it note for note. At the same time he moved slowly over to the nearest microphone stand and started belting out the lyric.

Stan reacted first, following Frank's lead and Bodkin soon followed, picking up the rhythm on his bass pedal, hi-hat and snare.

Barry stood open-mouthed until well into the first chorus. By the time they got to the end, the whole sound was not just good, it was great. They all knew it.

Frank gave them a cheeky grin as he changed the tone on his guitar. 'What about a bit of Eddie Cochran?' he suggested. "C'mon Everybody' in E.' The sound he produced on the opening chord sequence was spot on, you'd have thought somebody had put the record on.

There were looks of disbelief on all their faces. They were all thinking, *Where on Earth did a fifteen-year-old kid learn to play like this and what was he doing with a Gibson guitar like that?*

His singing voice too, perfect pitch, and he really knew how to rock.

There was no stopping him now. He laughed as he threw in a bit of Hank Marvin, complete with tremolo arm and Shadows steps. Not a word was said, but they all knew that this kid was special.

Stan spoke up first. 'That was very good Frank, but there are a number of things to discuss, like you being only fifteen years old and still at school.'

Frank didn't come up short in the confidence department. 'Not a problem, I'm sixteen in two weeks' time and I left school at the end of last term.'

'What about your parents?' asked Barry. 'We travel about a fair bit and there are a lot of late nights involved. What are they going to think about you rolling in at two o'clock in the morning?'

'Again, no problem. It was my old man who saw your advert in the paper and it was him who said I should phone for an audition,' grinned Frank. 'He said it was about time I started to earn my keep. I mean five weeks out of school and he wants to stop my pocket money!'

'You've done really well, I think I can speak for the others,' said Stan, not wanting to lose this kid but at the same time trying not to sound too over eager. 'Look, Frank we got two more auditions to hear and we must be fair to these two guys, they deserve their chance. Can you stick around for another hour or so?' He looked at Barry and Bodkin, 'Right, chaps?' They both nodded.

'Not a problem; it's only fair, they may have travelled some distance. Tell you what, I've got a mate who lives in the village, haven't seen him since school broke up, I'll go and knock on his door.'

'One question I must ask you before you go, Frank,' said Stan. 'What's the story with the Gibson, how come it didn't cost you anything?'

Frank had that grin on his face again. 'My dad used to tell me and my big sister, Suzie, that it was down to a Halifax Town fullback named Albert Arkwright, who, in 1955, scored a last minute own goal to give Accrington Stanley a 1-1 draw in a Division Three North football match. That gave my dad 8 draws on the Treble Chance and Littlewoods gave Jack Richards, that's my dad, a cheque for £75,000.

'Unlike some woman named Viv Nicolson five years later, who told the world she was going to "spend, spend, spend" my dad took his prize anonymously. He and mom bought a detached bungalow in Little Barnham and put a Jaguar XK140 on the drive. He bought my sister Suzie the Lambretta motor scooter she'd been saving up for, and he bought me this Gibson. I'd seen it in a magazine and told him it was time to replace my old acoustic.'

'Lucky boy, it's one hell of an axe.' Barry got down on his haunches to take a closer look.

'Okay, I'd best get from under your feet,' continued Frank. 'That old schoolmate I mentioned, Dougie Short, lives in the village, somewhere along Station Road. He borrowed some of my records ages ago and never gave them back. A whole box of 45s, Jerry Lee Lewis, Gene Vincent and stuff like that.' He laid his guitar carefully in its case and snapped the clip fasteners shut. 'Any chance of leaving this here, save lugging it around the village?'

'Sure,' answered Stan. 'You're very trusting, leaving a two hundred quid guitar with a bunch of strangers, especially these two reprobates.'

Frank laughed. 'Me dad's got your phone number, remember?' With that he gave another cheeky grin and half waved as he disappeared through the door and into the Market Square.

Barry gasped. 'Bugger me, where in God's name did he come from?'

Bodkin nodded in agreement. 'He's a cocky little bleeder, but I tell you what, he can play that thing.'

Stan looked at both of them. 'Get him out of that school clobber and I think we just found ourselves a new front man.'

There was another short silence, then they broke into spontaneous laughter, and how they laughed.

The next poor blighter didn't really stand a chance. Vince somebody or other. He was quite good too, played some rock-a-billy, played some blues and sang in tune. Stan recalled he wore a purple mohair suit and white winkle picker shoes, had sideburns and a lot of Brylcreem in his hair. Stan took his name and telephone number, but really only out of politeness, telling him they had others to listen to.

As he disappeared through the door which led to the square they heard him stop and acknowledge someone as he let them pass.

A young girl's face peered round the door. She had a blonde ponytail, and as she entered the room three testosterone-laden teenagers saw she was wearing a tight turtleneck red sweater, a dark grey pencil skirt with a slit to the side of her right knee and a pair of red high-heeled sling-backs. She was carrying what was clearly a musical instrument case, but certainly not the shape that would hold a guitar.

'I've come for an audition with The Bombastics,' she said.

Now there were a few girl singers around the scene, some quite good, but no girl guitarists that any of them could think of, anyway.

'Listen boys,' she said, somewhat coyly. 'We told a bit of a white lie on the telephone when we spoke to one of you.'

'That'd be me,' replied Stan, looking at his list. 'I'm Stan, and I'm guessing from where I'm standing you're not Dennis Meadowsweet, then?'

'No, that's my dad, I'm Carol Meadowsweet,' she

continued. 'I don't play guitar, well not very well anyway, but I love rock 'n' roll. I came to your gig at the Phantom Coach last month and I thought you were great. I think I have something to offer you.'

They were intrigued.

'What's this something you think you can offer The Bombastics then, Carol?' asked Bodkin.

She put her instrument case down on the stage, unfastened the clips, lifted the lid and took out a tenor saxophone and joined them at a mic Stan had adjusted for her. The smell of some tantalising perfume wafted their way.

'When I left Lordsfield High School last year I was playing first clarinet in the school band and my music teacher, Mrs Fanshaw, wanted me to audition for The Birmingham Symphony Orchestra.'

If any of them had been tempted to tell Carol that clarinets don't fit into a rock 'n' roll band and maybe a jazz band was a better idea for her, the outline of her figure in the afternoon sun streaming through the west window and the tenor sax she had in her hands, shut them up. Any coyness had gone as she continued with aplomb.

'My dad's a musician, plays clarinet in a dance band. He also plays clarinet and sax in a jazz band, so from a very young age I've been playing both, too. Dad also collects records. Swing, jazz, classical, rock 'n' roll, you name it, he's got it. I've grown up listening to some of the great sax players.'

She slipped the threaded leather strap round her neck, clipped her sax onto the end of it and blew a few tenuous notes. 'Can I play you something?'

'Go ahead,' said Stan, lowering a mic head for her.

She moved towards it, licked the reed on her sax to dampen it, ran up and down a couple of scales, gathered herself and then burst into a medley of sax solos which they recognised were taken from Little Richard hits. The girl was good, more than good, and all three would be liars if they said they hadn't enjoyed her wailing sax and the rise and fall of her pert young bosom in that tight red sweater.

She then launched into 'Yakety Sax', which Stan, then Bodkin and finally Barry picked up and followed. By the time they finished it sounded pretty damned decent.

A loud clapping came from the doorway. It was Frank Richards.

'Blimey, that sounds great. Can I join in the jam?' He walked across the hall, took out his guitar and plugged in. The five of them were soon jamming and enjoying themselves.

When they'd finished Frank apologised. 'Sorry to be back so soon but my mate Dougie wasn't in. I waited around for a bit, but the place was deserted, so I guess Jerry Lee and the rest of my records will just have to wait.' He turned to face Carol. 'Do you know any Johnny and the Hurricanes? 'Red River Rock'?'

'Hang on.' Stan raised the palm of his right hand, fingers outstretched. 'Can you give us five?' He gestured to Barry and Bodkin with a sideways jerk of his head towards the door at the side of the stage. He turned back to Frank and Carol. 'Stick around folks, we just need to have a chat in the committee room underneath the stage. We shouldn't be long.'

Stan and Barry unplugged their guitars and leant them against the Vox amps. Bodkin stepped from behind his drum kit and led the way as they disappeared downstairs, Barry with his Park Drive and matches, Bodkin with three teacups and the rest of the Dandelion and Burdock.

Stan closed the committee room door. Bodkin put down the teacups, unscrewed the bottle and poured.

'Bugger me, after all that crap we had to put up with, I

just don't believe what's happened in the last two hours,' said Barry, pausing to light a cigarette. He offered the packet to Stan who rarely smoked, but this time took one.

'I need something to calm me down.' Stan caught the matches that Barry tossed him and lit up. 'We need to get these two on board.' He cocked his ear towards the ceiling. 'Just listen to that.'

'Blue Moon' drifted down from the hall above. Frank and Carol were jamming the old Rodgers and Hart classic. Carol's sax was haunting.

'Just hold on a minute.' Bodkin put down his pop and wiped his mouth on his shirt sleeve. 'We've never been a five piece. It's bad enough having to split fifteen quid four ways after buying petrol, especially when I do most of the driving and now you want *five* Bombastics – and one a girl too!'

'We definitely need young Frank with us,' said Barry. 'Get rid of that bum fluff and he's absolutely perfect.'

'Are you saying you don't want Carol?' There was a moment's pause. 'Just hark at that now.' Stan directed his gaze upwards as 'Blue Moon' was replaced by some jazz riff which Stan didn't recognise, but sounded smooth. The way the two of them blended the melody so easily was quite stunning.

'No, I'm not saying that at all. She's fantastic on that sax, really gets that wailing rock 'n' roll sound. Nice tits too,' smirked Barry lasciviously.

'You've got a one-track mind Barry Harper,' frowned Stan. 'Keep your mind on what we're here for. Anyway, she's only a kid. What is she, sixteen?'

'Old enough,' leered Barry. Then turning towards Bodkin he said, 'Any road up, it looks like old Four-skins over there, is putting the kibosh on it – right, Mr Tight Arse?'

They'd been talking in hushed tones so as not to be overheard. So when Stan lowered his voice still further they listened even more intently. 'Lads, I get most of our work, I'll just have to tell the agents we're now a five piece and we need to be paid more. Most of them know we pull in a good crowd. I've also been thinking for some time now that we need to broaden our horizons. At the moment we're stuck to the Midlands and it tends to be the same gigs, month after month. We need to get work in London, you only have to look in the music papers to see the amount of places with live music. I bet they pay a lot more down there as well.'

'Yeah, but don't forget we gotta buy petrol to get there, and muggins here has to do all the bleedin' driving,' said Bodkin. 'Always me behind the wheel doing all those miles, your own personal chauffeur, whilst you lot are snoring and farting in the back.'

'The M1 makes things a lot easier, mind,' continued Stan. 'We need to get a few of these Cockney agents together; when they hear us they're bound to give us work. Having a fantastic sax player will help too, especially when they see her. As Barry put it so succinctly, she's got a bostin' figure, very pretty too. We can't afford to miss out on either of these two, they are going places with or without us. Trust me, they'll be an absolute knockout, I feel it in me water.'

There was a pause.

'Okay, okay, I'll run with it.' There was a shrug of acceptance from Bodkin. 'Just make sure you get those bleedin' fees up.'

'On the question of getting more work,' he continued. 'Why don't we hire some dance hall nearer to the Smoke and do our own thing? Invite yer Cockney agents, we're more likely to get them to come along if it's closer to home. We should work on the frozen north too,

Manchester and Leeds.'

'Bugger me, that's brilliant; old Four-skins strikes again.' Barry punched Bodkin playfully on the shoulder causing him to spill Dandelion and Burdock down his sleeve. He snarled.

'Agreed then?' Stan held out his hand to Barry and Bodkin and both grabbed it for a team handshake and a team smile for a job well done.

'Let's go and sign them up.'

CHAPTER 3
'LET'S STAY TOGETHER'

Al Green

'What the devil are you smirking at?' Elsie woke Stan from his daydream.

'Oh nothing, just remembering The Bombastics auditions all those years ago.' He went to drain the last of the tea in the mug he was holding, grimaced as he realised it was stone cold and got up to pour it down the sink.

'We haven't got time for daydreaming we got a busy day in front of us. We got groceries to get in and then we need to call at B&Q to get that boarding you need for the roof space. Remember it's twenty per cent off on Wednesdays for us pensioners.'

'Does she never stop?' mumbled Stan.

'I heard that, Stanley Ravenscroft. You need to start

pulling your weight. Get the car keys and bring our raincoats too,' she looked into the distance through the kitchen window. 'Something's brewing, it's as black as your hat over the village.' She locked the back door and shut Bertie in the utility to prevent any little accidents on the lounge carpet.

***

Stan and Elsie had been childhood sweethearts. She was a fourth generation village girl and she met Stan at the local school when they were both eleven years old. He had moved into Fordrough with his parents when the company his dad worked for, a builder's merchants, opened a branch in Bromsgrove and installed him as manager.

There really hadn't been anyone else for either of them, despite the temptations that come the way of big bad rock stars, Stan never bothered. They married in 1967 at the village church of St. Bartholomew's. It was supposed to have been a quiet wedding but The Bombastics were hot news at that time and when word got out, Fordrough got swamped. It was the summer of love, but that didn't stop mods and rockers fighting in the graveyard. Neither did it stop Barry getting into a tussle with one of Elsie's extended family at the reception. The trouble started when Barry polished off the last of the wine on his table and then took a bottle of sparkling wine off another table when he thought nobody was looking. Elsie's cousin tried to snatch it back and for a moment they whirled like dervishes around the dance floor, finally crashing into the three-tier wedding cake. Elsie was distraught when she saw the little bride and groom from the top of the cake had been split asunder amongst the marzipan and icing on the parquet.

Despite her worries of a bad omen for the newlyweds, here they were on the brink of a Golden Wedding.

***

Stan backed the car out of the garage and Elsie,

shopping bags and all, clambered in. They drove to Redditch and parked up. The supermarket wasn't too busy for a Wednesday morning. Certainly not as busy as Mr Tesco would want it to be, but it enabled Stan and Elsie to get round in under an hour. Not a personal best, but, with Elsie checking the E numbers and sell by dates, it wasn't to be sniffed at.

They avoided the self-service tills without so much as a word to each other. They'd had a very unfortunate experience trying to scan a trolley full of groceries earlier that year. That day Stan had forgotten his reading glasses and Elsie had insisted on trying to redeem some shopping vouchers (two of which were out of date). A heated debate followed with the young assistant whose job it was to help the old folks get through this self-service challenge unscathed. The duty manager was called and there was some unpleasantness near the Ugli fruit counter. Although they pretended not to be listening, two of Elsie's Women's Institute friends in the next but one aisle, must have overheard Stan's colourful vocabulary. Neither Stan nor Elsie have mentioned it since and certainly not attempted the self-service challenge again. At least Elsie did get all her vouchers honoured including the two from the previous month.

Stan hated shopping.

It had started to spot with rain as Stan wheeled his timber trolley up alongside his Volvo estate in the B&Q car park. Whilst attempting to strap the loft flooring onto his roof rack with a long length of cord he carried with him for such jobs, a strong gust caught one of the packs which started to lift, and if it hadn't been for a passer-by with a trolley full of late flowering perennials, Stan and his loft flooring would have taken off like a kite.

Eventually he got the six packs securely strapped to his roof rack despite Elsie, who sat in the passenger seat giving him advice through a half open window.

'Looks like you're going to be busy Stan, building an ark are we?' Dennis Jenkinson, gaffer at the Crown and Anchor laughed as he passed, casting his eyes towards the leaden skies.

'Nah, I'm taking this lot home to help shore up my escape tunnel,' answered Stan, without so much as a sideways glance.

Elsie glowered and shut the window.

By the time they got home it was coming down in bucketfuls. They unloaded the shopping as fast as they could through the front door and then Stan opened the garage doors and untied the flooring. With the movement of the load, the knots had tightened, but with great difficulty and a bit of effing and jeffing, Stan managed it. He thanked the Lord the flooring was in plastic wrapping, still mostly intact.

Bertie came through from the utility, saw the open garage doors, Stan wearing a coat and thought his luck was in. He stood in the doorway with his lead in his mouth. 'You've got no chance, pal. If you think you're going walkies in this lot you can forget it.' He raised his voice. 'If the good lady of the house can hear, it's time for a nice cup of tea and racing on the telly.'

Both meetings at Lingfield and Towcester were off. The rain, now coming in from the west, had already wreaked havoc on the horseracing, much to Elsie's delight. She had the morning paper. 'There's a film on Channel 5, it's got Steve McQueen and Dustin Whatsisname in it. It's the one where they're imprisoned on an island.'

'Papillon?'

'That's it.'

'We've seen it.' But Stan knew that wouldn't make any difference. If Steve McQueen was in it, Elsie would go through a pot of PG tips and a packet of chocolate digestive in a daze. It went through Stan's mind, *How many times has she watched Steve McQueen try and jump that soddin' barbed wire fence in The Great Escape? What if one day he gets over it?* His chin dropped. *Blimey, she'd need her Tena Lady that day!*

Stan fell asleep whilst Steve McQueen was building his raft...

***

A phone began bleeping on some distant planet.

'That was your phone.' Elsie shook Stan's arm and he awoke with a start, wiping away a stream of dribble connecting his chin to his shirt front.

Stan groped for his phone down the side of the chair and managed to put on his reading glasses whilst he opened a text. 'Shit! That was Frank Richards. I was supposed to meet him and Bodkin down at the Crown and Anchor half an hour ago.' He pulled on his shoes, still lying in the hallway where he left them two hours ago, grabbed his coat off the peg and made for the door.

'You're never going out in this weather, for heaven's sake,' snapped Elsie. 'You'll catch your death – and you've got that loft to finish.'

Stan muttered something through gritted teeth as he pulled on his coat and picked up a large green and white golf umbrella leaning in the corner of the hall. He sidestepped Bertie, who had again thought his luck was in, and disappeared through the door slamming it shut behind him.

The clocks didn't go back for a few weeks yet, but with the afternoon turning into evening, and the dark rain clouds overhead, it might just as well have been November. The street lamps and the lights from the shop windows shone that bit brighter in the gloom as Stan half walked and half ran across the Market Square. A gust of wind threatened to turn his green and white umbrella inside out, but he managed to cling onto it, turn and face the wind and got a good drenching for his trouble.

He stood for a moment dripping and panting in the doorway of the Crown and Anchor, closed up the umbrella, gave it a shake, and grabbed hold of the doorknob to let himself in.

At the sound of the opening door Frank turned around on his stool. Their eyes met.

'Sorry,' Stan mouthed silently. He removed his coat and hung it next to Frank's trench coat and parked his umbrella in the stand below. He looked around. It was quiet alright, even the jukebox was silent. Normally at this time, even on a Wednesday, there'd be a few thirsty souls having a quick one on their way home from work. Frank had obviously been in conversation with Gloria; other than that there were just three lads playing darts and old Walter and his dog over by the bay window.

No Bodkin, wonder where he is?

He walked over to Frank and put an arm around his shoulder. 'I said sorry I'm a bit late, Frank. I nodded off in front of the telly and...'

'You prat! Can't you ever keep your big mouth shut?' Stan froze. 'We have a brief but confidential telephone conversation about the possibility of getting The Bombastics back together and it seems half of Worcestershire knows about it.'

'Jeeez! I knew I'd mentioned it to somebody.' Stan gave his forehead a quick, sharp smack with the palm of his right hand. 'I had a few beers last night, must've loosened the old tongue. Sorry if I told someone I shouldn't have.'

'Someone? What's with the 'someone'? Even the bloody Dartboard Three over there, know about it.'

Stan looked over to the oche boys and a grimace contorted his face. 'Sorry Frank,' he mumbled.

'Sorry, sorry, sorry, it ain't good enough.' Frank was angry and stood almost nose to nose with Stan now. 'I've had confidential discussions with an important outfit about this gig, they're at a critical stage and I was sworn to secrecy. If they find out you've been blabbing off, it could blow the whole thing.'

Stan backed off and sat on the barstool next to Frank.

'It could affect other things too.' Frank also sat back down, a bit calmer now. 'I got a cruise liner gig and a sixties tour coming up. You know how these people work; they talk to each other. If it gets round that Frankie Atom's got a big trap, I could lose the bleedin' lot!'

Gloria had drawn Stan a pint of his usual and placed it on the beer tray in front of him. She decided to try and lighten the conversation. 'You don't remember putting 'Teenage Crush' on the jukebox then and strutting up and down with your air guitar?'

It was Frank's turn to grimace now. He put his head in his hands and groaned.

'Then you were holding court telling anybody who'd listen about appearing on Thank Your Lucky Stars and Top of the Pops. You even promised the Dither Sisters signed copies of 'Teenage Crush' when it was re-released and got to number one.'

Stan took an embarrassed gulp of his Anchor bitter and screwed his eyes up. He looked mortified.

Frank sat up straight. 'Number one? I hardly think so. I found a Frankie Atom and The Bombastics box set reduced from seventy-five pence to fifty pence at a car boot sale a few Sunday mornings ago. The Bombastics best years being sold for small change!' Then suddenly Frank started to laugh. He spluttered his words out. 'Signed copies? You're a clown, Stanley Ravenscroft. What d'yer think they're gonna do, re-release it on 45rpm with a paper sleeve? It's all iPods and Androids and downloads with the kids these days... Ooooh look, it's Stanley Ravenscroft, my grandma's favourite heartthrob. I'll get him to autograph my Android. Ha!'

'He might get asked for a selfie,' suggested Gloria.

'Selfie?' laughed Frank. 'If they can get all his chins in.'

'Just a minute, what's with the box set?' Stan was definitely pissed off. 'Sounds like a bit of Frankie Atom bullshit to me; the best we ever got was a Greatest Hits LP.'

'Okay, maybe I exaggerated a bit.' Frank shrugged and smiled at Gloria. 'That's Showbiz!'

Old Walter had put his hat and coat on and was pulling a reluctant Monty across the bar room. 'See thee Gloria.' He put his empty glass on the bar as he passed. Monty glanced nervously in the direction of the dartboard, then made a dash for the door.

'Cheerio, Walter – and you Monty.' Gloria smiled sweetly. 'See you tomorrow.'

Stan saw his opportunity to change the subject. 'Where's Bodkin? When I saw the time I thought you'd both be here waiting for me. It's not like him to be late.'

'He texted me while I was on the train.' Frank brought up a thread of messages on his phone and read them out loud. '"Sorry. Gonna be late, but just wait 'til you see who I'm bringing."

'I texted him back, "You've found Sugarlips?" He came straight back with a "No. Still haven't heard a thing."'

'Who the hell is Sugarlips?' asked Gloria.

'She was our sax player,' replied Stan. 'Her real name is Carol Meadowsweet, but the way she played sax, someone called her Sugarlips and it stuck.'

'Barry,' said Frank.

'Barry what?' said Stan.

'It was Barry that first called her Sugarlips,' added Frank. 'Gotta be honest, we completely lost touch with her so the problem is we can't find her now. We phoned her mum and she seems to have changed her mobile number, so we're waiting on her phoning home. Mom isn't too happy either, Shoogs hasn't phoned her for over three weeks.'

Stan continued. 'When the band broke up she started gigging around the jazz clubs in London. I heard she went over to Amsterdam and Paris. Someone even said she was working in Greenwich Village in New York, but that was probably only a rumour.'

Frank took up the story again. 'The last we heard she was living with some guy in London and had a little girl. Strange really, considering how close we all were, that our worlds just drifted apart like they did. Last time I saw her has to be thirty years ago. I was gigging in Finchley and I saw an ad on the entertainments page of *The Standard* for a jazz club called the Blue Onion. Can't remember the name of the resident band, but the flasher 'Guest Appearance of Miss Sugarlips' hit me right between the eyes. That night I was free and the club was only a short taxi ride away, so I went along. Carol was sensational. Like all of us she was a bit older, but unlike some of us,' he looked at Stan, 'she'd put on very little weight; she'd certainly kept her figure. I'll tell you this for nothing, she was still very sexy and her sax playing was out of this world. We spent a bit of time together, caught up on the gossip and had a few laughs about the old days. She seemed genuinely pleased to see me. However, I could tell something wasn't quite right; I couldn't put my finger on it, but we exchanged phone numbers and a week or so later, I tried to get in touch, but the number just rang out and never went to voicemail. She never phoned me.'

'Sounds like there's more to that particular lady's story,' said Gloria, raising an eyebrow. She gave up offering Frank a top up and put the remainder of the bottle on the counter by his almost empty glass. 'This'll save time, pay me when you're done.'

Bodkin's name lit up on Frank's phone as it vibrated on the bar where he'd placed it. The ringtone was very familiar. Frank's own guitar intro to 'Teenage Crush', a hit record over fifty years ago. Frank put it on speakerphone. 'Bods.'

'Frankie boy. Where are you?'

'I'm with Stan at the Crown and Anchor where we arranged to meet, remember?'

'Well, give it a couple of minutes and then go to the door and see what pulls into the square.'

'It's pissing down out there!'

'No it's not. It stopped about twenty minutes ago. See yer in a bit.'

There was a click as Bodkin rang off.

'Sounds like we need to move outside.' Frank nodded towards the door. 'Come with me.'

Stan followed Frank across the bar, taking their drinks with them. By this time young Matt, Gloria's part-time assistant, had taken up his duties behind the bar, so she followed. Frank opened the door. It was quite dark outside, but Bodkin was right, it had stopped raining, although it was still windy. The lights from the street lamps and windows danced and shimmered in the gusts on the wet Market Square cobblestones and the surrounding tarmac roadway. It was deserted, except for a couple of cars parked in the bays that ran alongside the Crown and Anchor. Iridescent puddles glistened in the parking spaces left vacant.

'Teenage Crush' rang out again. Frank answered.

'Are you there yet?' It was Bodkin back.

'Yes, we're here waiting. What's going on?'

'Look over the far side coming out of Sheep Street.'

They turned their gaze over to the distant corner of the square. A vehicle pulled out of Sheep Street. It wasn't possible to see much at first because of the dazzle of the headlights, but as it turned to follow the roadway, at the same time illuminating the darkness of the shadows cast by St. Bartholomew's church and its spire, they could see it was a Volkswagen camper van. As it neared they could pick out more detail. It had a white roof and window frames whilst the bottom half was a sort of muddy green, or was it blue? It had a split front windscreen, each half having its own wiper blade.

'Are you thinking what I'm thinking Stan?' gasped Frank.

'I think I am,' nodded Stan. 'Surely it can't be; the colour's all wrong, but it's bloody similar.'

By this time the Volkswagen had made its way around the square and had come to a halt in the end parking space next to the pub. The driver's door opened and Bodkin got out, grinning from ear to ear. 'Well, aren't you going to come and say hello to Jezza?'

Stan and Frank, still clutching their drinks, walked slowly over to Bodkin and the parked vehicle. Neither said anything whilst they took in the glistening, steaming motor in front of them.

'It is,' said Stan at last. 'Look at the number plate, GOE 305; I'll never forget that number.'

Frank turned to his old drummer. 'Fuck me gently Bodkin, where did you find her?'

There was an embarrassed cough, Gloria had followed them and was stood right behind them.

'I do beg your pardon Gloria, I didn't realise you were

there.' Frank touched her shoulder apologetically. He turned back. 'I don't remember Jezza being this mucky green colour, but everything seems to be in good nick for such an old girl.'

'Mucky green? I'll have you know that's not only chartreuse green, Frank Richards, that's metallic chartreuse green. She's had a re-spray and the guy who owned her has either repaired or replaced anything that looked dodgy. He's souped her up too, she goes like the clappers.'

Stan and Frank, with noses pressed up against the side windows, scanned the interior.

'It's all looks the same, even that old radio's glowing away there, but the upholstery's been changed,' said Stan.

Bodkin switched the engine off, slammed the driver's door shut and locked it. He then checked that the passenger door was locked. 'Come on, you two. It's a long story, let's go inside and have a drink and I'll tell you all about it. I'm parched.' Bodkin stopped in front of Frank. 'It's good to see you Frank, you old tosser, it must be eighteen months.'

'Old tosser yourself, Bodkin.' Frank gave Bodkin a man hug and they disappeared into the Crown and Anchor, arms around each other, followed by Stan and Gloria.

CHAPTER 4
'DRIVIN' IN MY CAR'

Madness

Bodkin wasn't really a petrol head, although he did enjoy driving and he had a thing about old cars, especially old foreign cars. So when Bernie, his near neighbour, asked if he'd like to join him on a long weekend at Santa Pod and take in the annual Volkswagen Bug Jam, he had no hesitation in saying yes.

The idea was they would travel down early on Saturday morning in Bernie's customised Beetle, camp over night and if the weather stayed fine, linger on into Sunday afternoon.

***

Bodkin had been in the same class as Stan at Tanners Green Secondary Modern Boys' School. Barry had been in the same year, but a grade higher. Bodkin first played drums in the Boy's Brigade and joined Stan and Barry in 1956 to form a skiffle group. They called themselves The Tanner Men, what might have been called a Lonnie Donegan tribute band a few decades later. There were five or six, sometimes seven, of them in the group. Then again, there might be only four; it all depended upon whose parents were prepared to put up with them practising their three-chord repertoire in the garage, or back garden if it was sunny. They got to play once a month at the Fordrough Youth Club, with an occasional gig at the school dance or the annual village fete. If everyone turned up they'd have four guitars, a tea chest bass which Stan played, washboard and thimbles (later on, a dilapidated old collection of bass drum, snare drum and cymbal which Bodkin had found at Treasure Trove, a local junk shop), and a mouth organ which little Jimmy Potter, who sat next to Bodkin at school, never really learned to play. They practised long and hard, but as Stan's dad once told them after listening to 'Freight Train' for the umpteenth time, 'That freight train, freight train that's going so fast. I think it went that fast you just missed it.'

Then, one Sunday morning, Bodkin heard Elvis sing 'Hound Dog' on Forces Requests, and decided rock 'n' roll was the future. He persuaded his dad to pay for proper drum lessons and sign as guarantor on a hire purchase agreement for a proper drum kit, complete with kettledrum, hi-hat, and two cymbals.

During the school holidays, Stan, Barry, and an older kid named Martin Spilsbury, who played guitar and sang, arrived on Bodkin's doorstep. They too were now hooked on rock 'n' roll and it didn't take long for them to talk Bodkin into joining their new combo, The Bombastics.

Bodkin wasn't his real name, it was Duncan Robert Adams.

In Eastbourne during the mid nineteen fifties a doctor,

named John Bodkin Adams was accused of bumping off a few of his elderly patients (a sort of role model for Harold Shipman). The notorious Bodkin Adams became headline news around the world, his picture on the front pages of every newspaper. The trial lasted months and questions were even asked in Parliament. Controversially, Doctor Bodkin Adams was found not guilty of murder, but guilty of fraud. Although initially struck off, he was eventually reinstated as a general practitioner; those of his patients who were still alive formed a queue to be treated by him once more.

Meanwhile back at Tanners Green Secondary Modern Boys' School, Duncan Robert Adams, was now nicknamed Bodkin by all his schoolmates. The more he protested, the more it stuck. Within a few months only Bodkin's teachers and his mum and dad still called him Duncan.

***

Over sixty years later, Bodkin was still tall and well packed; he'd put on a little timber, but he still looked fit. He was invariably dressed in jeans and T-shirt, Doc Martens, and a sleeveless body warmer, or if it got cold, a leather jacket and beanie hat. He'd lost most of his hair before he was thirty and in recent years, like so many twenty-first century baldies, had taken to completely shaving his head. More recently he had grown a moustache and goatee beard.

Bernie pulled up outside Bodkin's semi, right on time; 7 a.m. precisely.

Bodkin was waiting, watching from the front window. He kissed his partner Julie on the lips, picked up his tent roll and backpack from the hallway and let himself out of the front door.

'See ya Sunday.'

'Yes… and behave yourself.'

Bodkin placed the tent in the foot well of the back passenger seat and swung the backpack off his shoulder and squeezed it into the space left on the back seat of Bernie's Beetle. It shared the seat with Bernie's tent, sleeping bags and a battered old leather suitcase which Bodkin guessed was packed with Bernie's essentials.

Bernie was rightly proud of his 1964 Beetle. Bodkin knew he'd only paid four thousand for it, but had spent a small fortune on restoring and customising it. Even Bernie wasn't sure what he doled out, but he had it insured for eleven grand. As all custom car owners do, he'd given it a girly name. Brenda.

Brenda had been given a yellow ochre re-spray. She also had a lot of sparkling chrome. Bumpers, hubs, vents, wing mirrors, door handles, and twin exhaust tailpipes. She had smoked privacy windows and a sunroof, which Bernie had opened on this beautiful sunny Saturday. Inside she had smart red leather upholstery and a chromed up steering wheel and gear shift. Bernie had all the gadgets; a multi-stack CD player with four speakers, plus iPod and SatNav connections. No wonder Bernie couldn't remember how much she'd cost!

'I'm glad you brought your own tent,' grinned Bernie. 'I can imagine some of the comments from our lot if they saw me sharing a two man ridge tent with a dude who looked as though he was one of The Village People – sweetie!'

'Oooh, you are a one,' minced Bodkin in his best Dick Emery, as he belted himself into the passenger seat. Julie gave a wave from the doorway and Bodkin blew her a kiss as Bernie drew off.

Bernie was a regular at Bug Jam with the rest of his VW owners club, The Vee Dubble-yers. That morning they had all arranged to meet at the Hathaway Retail Park just off the A34 and travel down to Bedfordshire together, in a long line of Beetles, Sciroccos, Ragtops, Golf GTIs, and Devon campers. Some old, some new, many customised. There were even two Trekkas, and to Bodkin's surprise, some very rusty-looking camper vans. Bernie explained to Bodkin that owners would proudly boast of their rat look campers. There were even trophies and prizes over the coming weekend for the best rusty, ratted models, he explained.

As they gathered ready for the off, Bodkin could see many of them had black, red and gold Vee Dubble-yers T-shirts on. He also noticed a lot of them had little plastic 'VD' badges stuck to the inside of their windscreens. Bodkin smiled to himself – *VD? Surely they realised, they must do!*

They checked in, one at a time, at the Santa Pod gate and made their way to their designated camping area. The whole place was already buzzing with activity in the warm July sunshine. It looked as though many of the Bug Jammers were up and about. There was the smell of bacon frying, as late breakfasts were cooked on Primus stoves, coming from tents and campers as far as the eye could see. The bars and catering stalls were busy too, with the large hairy Bug Jammers carrying crates of beer back to their tents.

It was all very bright and colourful. Two enormous canvas Big Tops stood out beyond the cars and tents. Bernie pointed beyond them and slightly to the right, at a striking red and white striped structure, maybe half a mile away. 'It's the main stage for the live music, where we'll be head bangin' tonight, Bods.'

Over to the east Bodkin could see a fun fair. From the large illuminated wheel, spinning and turning above the other attractions, and the distant screaming and shouting, it was open for business. *So early in the day? I hope those bacon sandwiches have gone down.*

Under the guidance of Bernie, Bodkin spent the rest of the morning and afternoon discovering what Bug Jam was all about. There was stunt driving, bug racing and monster trucks crushing poor little Novas and Minis. There was power bike racing and motocross and drag racing, which was what had made Santa Pod famous. There was even human racing on cycles and other contraptions.

Some of the Vee Dubble-yers had their rusty VWs entered in the Best of Rat contests, but Bernie had other ideas; he wanted to take Brenda for a spin, with Bodkin riding shotgun. No doubt about it Bernie could handle that Beetle and Bodkin missed the chequered flag because his eyes were closed. Brenda finished up with some very impressive time trial certificates.

Afterwards they drank plenty of beer in the late afternoon sun and after Bodkin had treated himself to a Saturday night chicken vindaloo and chips, Bernie said he was glad he was on his own in his little two-man ridge tent and not sharing with Bodkin.

After dinner a large group of Vee Dubble-yers, carrying large crates of real ale, made their way across the campsite for the entertainment. Some made for the comedy stage and others went for the 'Queen' tribute band, but Bodkin and Bernie joined the main party heading for the main stage, for a night of rock 'n' roll. Headlining was one of Bodkin's favourite bands, 'We Three Kings'. They were his favourite band not least of all because the drummer, Milo Masterson, was one of his former pupils at Redditch College where Bodkin took an evening class.

Bodkin thought some of the support acts had struggled, particularly the ones early on, but as a pro maybe he was expecting too much. Anyway, the VW crowd enjoyed it all and despite the amount of alcohol being consumed, they were good-humoured and in very good voice.

Then on came 'We Three Kings' with a storming set that had the crowd going mental. At the end of the set they were screaming for more and the boys did two extended encores. Milo and his bandmates, guitarist Johnny King and bassman Brian Bates, certainly earned their corn as the star turn that night. The light show was pretty sensational too. Bodkin had never been a particular fan of pyrotechnics and lasers lighting up the sky. He couldn't help wondering if they should be directing lasers up into the night sky at all; after all they weren't that far from Luton Airport. Perish the thought they brought a Frankfurt bound Lufthansa down into rural Bedfordshire.

As the crowd broke up and made their way back to the scattered campsites, Bodkin got separated from Bernie and his crew. He needed a piss. He finished the beer he'd carried back with him and dumped the can in one of the black plastic rubbish bins dotted around and already spilling over with cans and fast food cartons. The urge was getting stronger. Rather disorientated, and more than a little drunk, he scanned the horizon for the toilet block.

It should be easy to spot in this moonlight… but I can't see the bleedin' thing!

He was now getting desperate. Then he saw Brenda up ahead! He dodged in between the parked VWs and tents and found himself close to his own tent. After carefully looking around to make sure he couldn't be seen, he decided to give the toilets a miss and empty his bladder behind the VW camper parked a couple of Beetles away from Brenda. Unfortunately, after the amount of beer he'd drunk, once he'd started, it just didn't seem like he was going to stop. Then he heard the sound of voices. A group of about half a dozen appeared to his right. He recognised some of them as Vee Dubble-yers.

Jeezus! They're getting closer, that soddin' moon's getting brighter and it feels like I got a gallon to go!

Watching them carefully he sidled around the back of the camper and behind the neighbouring Beetle, ducking slightly to keep out of view; not an easy procedure when your jet stream's in full flow! He was now bathed in golden moonlight and anyone sticking their head out to see where the hell the sound of Niagara Falls was coming from would have had a front row seat. He dodged back into the shadows which meant pissing all over Brenda.

'Sorry, Brenda luv, not a word to Bernie, this is our little secret, eh?' he mumbled to the little Beetle.

At last the flood abated and with a few last squirts and a deft flick of the wrist, he was home, almost dry, and safely zipped up. He stepped nonchalantly out of the shadows and one of the Vee Dubs spotted him.

'Oi, Bodkin, wotcha up to?' shouted the Vee Dubble-yer in the string vest. 'Nickin' hub caps by the light of the silvery moon?'

'Guilty as charged, m'lud,' retorted Bodkin. 'But the pickings are slim.'

'If you find a set of alloys for a 1984 Scirocco it's cash up front,' laughed his mate in the New York Yankees top. 'No questions asked.'

By this time he was amongst them; there were seven of them, but he'd met so many new people that day he had no chance of remembering names.

'Want a can?' String Vest pushed forward a dog-eared carton that looked to have once been a twelve pack.

Bodkin thrust his hand into the top of the torn carton, there were a few left; he grabbed one. 'Cheers.' He pulled the ring and held the can aloft.

'Cheers,' most of them responded, clanking their cans against his.

'Cheers,' they echoed.

There was some more light-hearted banter whilst they stood drinking, then it was time to turn in for the night.

Bodkin picked his way back to his tent, being very careful to concentrate on each step avoiding any wet grass, or tripping over a stray guy rope. He made it and sat for a minute or two, finishing his can.

The noise from the funfair was starting to die down now and there was a strange smell in the air, a mixture of burgers and cannabis. As talk and laughter started to cease, so the lights from tents and campers gradually started to disappear.

Bodkin unzipped the front of his ridge tent and clambered in on all fours. He searched round for his torch, couldn't find it, so felt his way onto the sleeping bag Julie had made for him out of an old Candlewick bedspread they'd rescued from the loft. The night was far too warm for him to get into it, so Bodkin stooped down in the dark and tipped himself over with a backwards half somersault. That's when he found the torch was underneath the blanket.

He lay awake for a long time on top of his candlewick. It wasn't from the pain of landing on the torch, which would leave a nice bruise in the morning; it was the warm muggy night and, wearing only boxers he tossed and turned until, after what seemed an eternity, he eventually fell asleep.

Bodkin dreamt that night.

He was driving Brenda. He was on his own and driving fast. Where to, he didn't seem to know, but there was some irresistible compulsion to get somewhere. Dawn was breaking as he thundered along a deserted dual carriageway that cut deeply through a patchwork of fields, hedgerows and thickets. To begin with, they were dark greens and dull golds, but as the rising sun spread morning over the landscape, they rapidly turned into vibrant, verdant greens, burnished golds and lemon yellows. Onwards he drove, up and over undulating countryside that stretched into the distance. The roadside signs with names of small towns and villages flew by; 'Welcome to Patcham', 'Drive carefully through Little Denstone' and 'You are now leaving Ashingworth'. It was like one of those low budget black and white rock 'n' roll films he used to love to watch at the local flea-pit all those years ago, when Elvis Presley or Little Richard or whoever it might be, travelled across small-town America on their way to stardom.

He slowed as the dual carriageway ended and quite suddenly the road became a winding, narrow country lane. Now there were people walking in the same direction, just a few at first, then the number grew and soon it seemed like dozens. God knows where they'd come from; he had to manoeuvre the car with great care around each bend on what had become little more than a twisting track. Because of the bumpy surface and the sheer volume of humanity, he had slowed to no more than five or six miles per hour. Eventually he abandoned Brenda and joined the others on foot. Mothers carrying babies, fathers with toddlers on their shoulders, groups of youngsters, young couples holding hands, middle aged couples arm in arm all making their way towards – towards what? Every face was smiling and gazing forward, some with hands shielding their eyes from the bright sunshine. No words were spoken, there was not a sound except for the swish of feet and legs pushing their way through what had now become long grass.

They made their way alongside a thick hedgerow which took them up the side of a hillock and around an outcrop of rocks. As they reached the top and began descending the other side, an enormous field opened before them. As he was swept along, Bodkin could see droves of people pouring into the field from other directions too. From over a ridge to the left of them, from out of a forest of sycamore and beech trees to the far right hand side of the field and straight ahead, yet more people, no more than silhouettes against the glint of a distant river caught in the morning sun.

As they crossed the field from their different directions the masses were congregating in front of a large red and white striped structure, which as Bodkin got closer he could see was a stage exactly like the one he'd been in front of that very evening. Although there were hundreds of people already there, Bodkin found himself at the front of the crowd looking up at a five-piece band. The front man was a tall blonde haired guitarist singing emotionally into a microphone, backed by guitar, bass, drums and a flamboyant black guy throwing his arms and body around over his keyboard, but it was like they were miming.

There was no sound whatsoever. Not from the band, not from the singer, not from the crowd.

Bodkin watched, transfixed, as the band members started to fade. There was a sort of silvery grey aura around each of them to begin with, but gradually their whole beings started to shimmer as they became translucent. Not just them but their instruments too; and what was that stencilled on the front of the bass drum? The Robbie Ro… too late, it was gone. As Bodkin half turned and took his eyes off the stage, the people around him too were shimmering and fading. The stage and its red and white striped awning started to change too and through the tremulous images Bodkin could see in the distance the bright blue early morning sky was now full of angry black clouds.

There was a crack of forked lightning in the distant blackness and then a loud clap of thunder rolled across the sky.

Bodkin awoke with a start.

Jeezus, my head – and my mouth tastes like a badger's bum.

Fingers of sunlight slanted through the tent flap that lay half-open. He flicked both flaps wide open, watching carefully to see if a badger had indeed crept into the tent to share his candlewick with him whilst he slept. He picked up a bottle of sparkling water he'd left just outside the flaps and drew long and deeply on it. It wasn't sparkling anymore and it was warm from the morning sun, but it got rid of the taste of badger bottom.

He remembered fragments of the dream but the images were fading fast.

That red and white stage, it's like the one last night. That five-piece band with the blonde singer. The Robbie something or other band and everything fading, there has to be an explanation. Brenda! I left her in some field. I hope I locked her.

Strange dream, but then dreams were.

***

'What on earth's up with you?' Bernie asked Bodkin over a bacon buttie and black coffee breakfast. 'It doesn't look as though you've had much sleep. Hey, you didn't pull did you? You crafty old sod, no wonder you sloped off before the rest of us.'

'You've got to be kidding, what sad old biddy is gonna want to shag a bald headed old tosser like me?'

Bernie half choked on his hot coffee. 'I'm sure that'll make Julie feel wonderful when I tell her.'

The look Bodkin gave him was enough, and Bernie smiled. 'Only kiddin', big man.'

Bernie and some of the other Vee Dubble-yers wanted to see the Sabbath Dragsters out on the main strip, but Bodkin didn't fancy it, preferring some time on his own to explore the parts of Bug Jam he'd not yet seen. They all arranged to meet back at the campsite to pack up and get ready to leave. Many of them had to work on Monday morning and there were bound to be delays getting out of Santa Pod and then across to the M1.

Bodkin went back to his tent and packed away his things, last of all striking his tent, rolling it up as tightly as possible around the tent poles and getting it into the ridiculously tiny canvas sleeve at the third attempt. *Never had this trouble putting a johnny on.*

He put the tent and his backpack onto Brenda's back seat, opening her up with the spare key he'd been given, then twice made sure she was locked securely; he remembered the dream.

He decided to have a wander around the far side of the site and soon found himself amongst the traders. Although it was primarily for enthusiasts buying and selling VW parts and bits, they had been joined by a number of other stallholders. Some selling music on CD and vinyl, even a few 78s, Bodkin noticed; 'Everything from Deanna Durbin to The Killers', a hand-painted banner proclaimed. There were DVDs and videos, mobile phone bits, T-shirts galore, also jeans, jackets, leather goods, footwear, and a mobile tattooist.

By late morning smells of every fast food you could think of wafted around the area. Burgers, hotdogs, kebabs, fish and chips, chicken portions, curries, pastas, and pasties. Bodkin spotted a Spanish stall selling tapas and paella. *International indeed.* Bodkin got himself a large bratwurst and a bottle of German lager and sat in the shade of the stallholders' awning to eat his lunch.

After he'd finished he moved away from the food arena and beyond the jumble sale of VW spares and car booters. The odd scraps of last night's dream kept coming back to him, the bass drum in particular. The Robbie Ro... *Robbie Royal, Robbie Rocket, Robbie Rockstar. What was that all about?*

Row upon row of motors now stretched in front of him. He passed Beetles, Sciroccos and Golfs in assorted colours; a lot were expensively customised, just as many were rusty and ratted. All of them seemed to be for sale. Most were locked and had phone numbers stuck inside the front windscreens. Some had prices.

Ahead of him lay dozens of VW camper vans.

He smiled to himself remembering how a VW camper had been important to The Bombastics and Bodkin Adams in particular.

***

When Martin Spilsbury had left The Bombastics it also depleted their transport. Martin had a beautiful old 50's Humber Snipe. It had large spacious seats and an enormous boot, or so it seemed to them in 1962 and they were able to get themselves and all their gear into it. Other bands they played with used to laugh and call them the Quality Street Gang when they drew up in this stylish, but ancient monster of a motor. It seemed old, even in the early 1960s.

With Martin quitting the band, not only did they lose the Snipe and travelling in luxury, it meant that Bodkin was the only driver. Barry held a motorbike licence, but that was not a lot of use when you were hauling sound equipment around; he was taking driving lessons, but had never spoken much about how he was progressing. Bodkin didn't have transport of his own, so he used to borrow his brother Wally's Ford Thames van. Wally didn't mind; the only problem was that Wally was a plasterer by trade; with little time to clean the back of the van out properly between Wally getting home and the band hitting the road. The Bombastics' equipment and The Bombastics themselves very often turned up at gigs with a coating of plaster dust over them. With Carol always being given the passenger seat, it was usually paper, rock, scissors, to decide who sat on the rear wheel arches and who had to slide around on the floor. Bodkin laughed to himself as he remembered they nicked some old blankets and cushions from the back room of a pub they played at, somewhere in Birmingham. Didn't bother him, he was the driver and had his own seat. It was Frank's dad that changed all that.

Bodkin recalled it was a bitterly cold Saturday morning in December 1962. The snow that had fallen during the week still covered the village roofs. Because it was so cold, much of it had turned to ice on the pavements and roads and in the fields and hedgerows beyond. The temperature couldn't seem to move above freezing point to create a thaw and, unbeknown to Britain, it wouldn't for months yet. The Bombastics' gear had been marooned in the village hall since they'd practised the week before, just prior to the snow arriving. They'd had that night's gig cancelled because of the weather, and similarly the village hall had had to cancel events, so the village hall committee had let them leave their speakers and amps and Bodkin's drums behind the curtains, up on the stage.

In the weeks before, Frank had settled into the band really well and his mom and dad were regulars when the gigs were local. It didn't take Jack Richards long to see the problems they had getting their equipment and themselves to the venues spick and span and on time. He turned up that Saturday morning at their weekly practice session and parked a brand new gold and white Volkswagen Devon Camper in the village hall car park. 'This should help solve your transport problems,' he'd said as he passed the ignition keys over to Bodkin. 'I just need you to fill in some of the details on this form so I can sort the insurance out, then you're ready to go.'

They stood staring through the village hall window, dumbstruck for a moment, but only for a moment. Out the door they rushed and descended en masse on this gorgeous gleaming VW beast.

'Bloody 'ell,' Bodkin gasped. 'This is unbelievable.' He clambered into the driver's seat.

Carol curled up on the front passenger seat and Frank slid open the side door and climbed in, followed by Barry and Stan.

'This is brilliant!' shouted Stan, bouncing up and down on one of the rear passenger seats. 'This is comfort, man. No sliding around on the floor of Wally's van, ending up looking like one of the bleedin' claymen out of Flash Gordon.'

'Bugger me, there's loads of room in here, we'll get everything in and there'll still be room to stretch some of our fans out horizontally,' winked Barry.

'There'll be none of that nonsense.' Carol turned to nail Barry with one of her looks. 'This is for getting to the gigs in comfort, so you keep yer hand on yer ha'penny!'

'Only kiddin',' grinned Barry. 'And by the way, for your information it's more like a half crown.'

Carol turned back and snorted, but said nothing.

'Blimey, Dad, it must have cost a fortune,' said Frankie to his father, who was peering in through the open doorway.

'Look on it as an investment,' smiled Jack. 'You can pay me back when you've had your first number one.'

Just under four years later, they presented him with a cheque. He never did cash it.

***

Bodkin now turned down the last walkway and as soon as he saw her, he knew.

A lot of the VW campers in this line had that rusty look, or ratted, as their proud owners called it, but there in the middle of this mass of turquoise, green, grey, gold and rusty bodywork stood a metallic green Devon, with split windscreen in chromed frames. The customised bumper and door handles, roof rack and VW logo were also highly chromed, but it was none of these expensive modifications that had really caught Bodkin's attention (he knew the colour and the chrome were completely wrong). No, it was the number plate. GOE 305

Bodkin hurried over to it. *Is it really you Jezza? Are you here to be sold? If you're for sale, baby, I'm buying you.*

Few of the motors on sale were attended and like the vast majority Jezza stood in line locked up and lonesome. What was different was the neatly printed card placed inside the windscreen

ROCHESTER CLASSICS

0121 466 9100

Most of the others had mobile numbers scrawled on bits of cardboard torn from Belgian lager six packs, or pizza boxes.

As it happened there was a guy on duty next door, guarding a ratted blue and white camper parked alongside. He had an unkempt grey beard and wore a well-worn leather cowboy hat; it made him look a little like something off a ZZ Top poster. Bodkin asked him if he'd seen Jezza's owner.

'No, I takes over from my brother 'bout an hour ago,' ZZ Top replied in a broad Gloucestershire accent. 'Twas all locked up when I arrived… 'tis a mean-looking beast, eh?'

Bodkin didn't answer him, but nodded his thanks as he took his mobile phone out of the hip pocket of his jeans and carefully poked the phone number off the card into it with his forefinger. He waited. 'Please leave a number and a short message and I'll call you back.'

'Shit!' cursed Bodkin, then realised he was being recorded. 'Ooops, sorry about that. Hello, I'm here at Santa Pod and might be interested in your Devon camper van GOE 305. Perhaps you could get back to me.' Bodkin then left his number.

You'd have thought they'd have left a mobile, they must be here

somewhere. Why a bloody landline, for fuck's sake?

Bodkin tried the number again before they left Santa Pod and another three times on the journey home. He tried it twice more that night, the second time whilst Julie was slipping into something more comfortable in the bathroom. As Bodkin was listening to the message again, telling him to leave his name and number, his jaw dropped. Julie came through the door wearing just three red hearts. Whenever Julie had complained that she had to lose weight, Bodkin always smiled and told her she was bonny. Well tonight 'bonny' definitely fell well short.

'I bought this at Jenny Robert's Ann Summers party, especially to welcome you back.' Then she caught sight of herself in the full-length wardrobe mirrors. She stood transfixed for a moment, then exploded with laughter and collapsed in a heap on the bed. 'It didn't look like this on Jenny's teenage daughter,' she managed to splutter from somewhere under the pillows.

Bodkin pulled the duvet back from under her, stretched across to turn off the bedside lamp and pulled Julie in alongside him. He slipped his arms around her waist, pulling her against him. He tried to put a thought from earlier that day right out of his shaven head. *What sad old biddy's gonna want to shag an old tosser like me?*

It was the next day, after leaving yet another voicemail, that found Bodkin sat contemplating over an Americano trying to recall the scraps of his dream that he still remembered.

That name on the bass drum. The Robbie Ro... Could it be Rochester of Rochester Classics? It'd be spooky if it was.

His mobile vibrated in his pocket. *At long last.* Then as he managed to wriggle it out of his tight jeans, he saw Stan Ravenscroft's name blinking on the screen. 'Hiya, Stan, how yer doing?'

'Hi, Bods.'

They exchanged pleasantries and a few insults and gave an update on each other's nearest and dearest.

'Listen Bodkin, I've had this call from Frank. Someone is talking to him about a Bombastics reunion. He wants us to meet up.'

Bodkin thought about telling Stan of his dream and finding a VW Devon camper that looked like it was Jezza. He thought better of it. Maybe save it for later when he'd found out for sure.

'When's he thinking of, and what about Sugarlips? Last time we spoke nobody had seen hide nor hair of her.'

'First of all, it's going to have to be September, Frank's on that Storming Sixties tour of Scandinavia in August and they're busy rehearsing at the moment.'

'Blimey he's on that? He must be raking it in.'

'Not what he said. A bit quiet on the gig front; says he only got this tour because one of the Shakin' Earthquakes has got to go in for a hip replacement. Anyway, at this stage he just wanted to know if you're up for it.'

'Yeah, you know me Stan, I'll give it a go. Haven't had the drums out for a month or two, but you can count me in.'

'Now on to Sugarlips. Because of this reunion malarkey, Frank's been in touch with her mom. Nothing yet, but we've got her on red alert to let me know. Look, Bodkin, Elsie's got the tea on, I'm gonna have to go. Frank's going to come here to Fordrough and we can meet at the Crown and Anchor. I'll be back to you soon as we can fix a day.'

'Cheers, Stan, love to Elsie, cheerio.'

'Tara-a-bit, Bodkin, love to Julie too.'

After another fruitless call, Bodkin decided to try and

find Rochester Classics on the internet, maybe meet him face to face. He Googled the name and up popped a screen full of Rochester Classics. He slid his finger down the screen. A travel agent in Woking, a golf driving range, a hair stylist. There, tucked in between an interior furnisher in Rochester, Kent and a bar and grill in Rochester, New York State, was Rochester Classics in Stechford, Birmingham.

A customised car specialist in Stechford, on the east side of Brum; it has to be the one. Look, the bloody phone number's wrong! It's 0121 465 9100, not 0121 466 9100, no wonder they didn't get back to me. So who's been getting my messages? The prats. Hey, it's only in Stechford, it'll take me three quarters of an hour at the most to get over there.

He fed the postcode into his satnav and backed his Volvo out of the drive.

CHAPTER 5
'THE STRANGER'

The Shadows

With Frank and Carol joining the band, Stan set about getting the fees up and true to his word, he spoke to the four agents who got them regular work; he got favourable responses from three of them, getting their fee up to the magic £20 mark. However, Goldstars, the agency that gave them most of their work, was having none of it. Benny Goldman said he wasn't too bothered about a female sax player, he wanted to hear the new front man; if he was good, then and only then, would The Bombastics get a bigger payday. He said he'd try and get along to the Cosmos show in Wolverhampton. It was one of his and he stressed to Stan they'd only get paid the fifteen quid that had been agreed.

They played their outstanding gigs without any

problems, in fact the audience reaction to the new line up was great, particularly the way the young girls started to crowd around the front of the stage where Frankie stood.

There'd been a slight panic when the boys realised they needed to get Frank out of his school trousers, and the Bombastic outfit that Martin left behind was far too big. However, with a bit more of Dad's Treble Chance jackpot, they managed to get him fixed up with a sequinned shirt and black slacks.

The downside for Stan was Benny Goldman. He never bothered to turn up to Wolverhampton and couldn't say when he'd get along to another of their gigs. He flatly refused to pay them any more money until he'd seen and heard them. 'You can take it or leave it Stanley. I've got bands queuing up for work. I'll get round to you when I can; until then it's fifteen pounds for Goldstars bookings.'

Meanwhile, Stan went about setting up a showcase, where he could invite agents from London and the Home Counties. The Bombastics were good mates with Johnny and the Heartbreakers, a group they'd played with a number of times. Their hometown was Bedford, an ideal location for what was wanted, so Stan phoned Bill Daniels, the Heartbreakers' manager, to see if he could come up with the right venue for The Bombastics.

There was no hesitation from Bill; it was his home turf and he immediately recommended Westhill Working Men's Club. The Bombastics had never played there, but according to Bill it was ideal for a number of reasons. It had a spacious function room with good acoustics, a proper stage with curtains and lighting, good comfortable dressing rooms and a great crowd; they always turned up in numbers, they loved their rock 'n' roll bands, they danced all night and they were never any trouble. Bill was able to give Stan the Westhill secretary's number there and then. When Stan studied the road map he could also see that it was only a few miles off the M1, travelling north or south. *Perfect!*

Stan spoke to the Westhill secretary and agreed a date with him, then suggested that if they could have the room for no charge the Westhill members could come into the concert for free. Stan's thinking was that if they had a jam-packed room full of atmosphere, these cockney agents were more likely to be impressed. The Westhill secretary was delighted to go along with him; a full house meant busy tills.

Stan had a word with Mr. Jones, the Fordrough village newsagent, to see if he could get him a copy of *The Stage*. After chatting with Stan, when old man Jones found out what it was for, he said he'd also get him an *Evening Standard* and any other regional newspapers from around London that he could get his hands on. Old man Jones came up trumps; *The Stage*, *The Evening Standard*, *The Croyden Echo*, *The Hertfordshire Herald* and a fistful of others from around the home counties.

Stan and his girlfriend Elsie spent hours poring over the small ads and entertainment pages, circling likely looking contacts and compiling a list which Elsie numbered thirty-four. Then Stan spent the next two evenings and most of the following Saturday making calls. It was a bit frustrating at times, with people unavailable or not returning calls, but he stuck at it and in the end spoke to twenty-seven of the thirty-four he had on his list. Quite a lot were London-based agents, but he ventured further afield with his phone calls, checking on Wally's road map to make sure they were within striking distance of Bedford. He was quite proud of his sales pitch; the more he made the better he got. He told them what a hotbed of talent Birmingham was, with a number of really top rock 'n' roll bands. He told them that The Bombastics were the pick of the bunch and he'd reserved a table for them at Westhill Rock 'n' Roll Club (well it sounded better than Working Men's Club). He promised he would send them invitations, with tickets and directions.

Each one was sent a personal invitation and two tickets; the cost of which was covered by some of the measly fifteen quid Benny Goldman had paid them for the Cosmos gig.

And so the night came round, it was the last Saturday of October; the last Saturday of the summer of 1962. The weather had been fine all week. It was starting to turn chilly, but a large silvery moon, one the country folk of Fordrough called a poacher's moon, lit their way and welcomed them to Bedford.

The Westhill members turned up in their droves which pleased Stan, but it was the agents he was hoping he'd get a good turn out from. He wasn't disappointed. Stan and Bodkin introduced themselves to as many as possible before the concert started to try and make them feel important; Barry was kept well clear of proceedings and Frank and Carol were told to keep him in the dressing room.

'Sit on him if necessary,' growled Bodkin.

'Come on Carol, you heard the man,' grinned Barry. 'Would you like me to lie down?'

Bodkin's look was enough.

In all eleven of them turned up, mostly from the capital, but there were agents from Oxford, Colchester, Reading and Brighton. Funds among The Bombastics were a bit low, but Frank's dad had told them to set up a deal with the club to give all the agents and their guests a complimentary drink (just the one, he'd emphasised), and he gave Frank a roll of fivers to cover it. Stan said he'd get a receipt.

There was also, as Bodkin was to describe him later, a snazzy-looking geezer in a grey mohair suit, who sat on a stool at the bar smoking Black Russian cigarettes and sipping Gordon's gin and tonic.

The concert couldn't have gone better; they'd worked hard rehearsing during the preceding weeks and the night was one of those magical nights when it all came together. They opened with Chuck Berry's 'Rock and Roll Music'. Frank's guitar playing and singing was just incredible and his harmonies with Barry were right on the money, even better than during the hours of rehearsals. Carol played some really raunchy sax breaks and looked quite delightful in a short white dress with matching ribbon in her hair. It was noticeable, whilst girls gathered around the stage in front of Frank, there was a bunch of teenage boys watching Carol very closely. With Bodkin, Stan, and Barry laying down an irresistible thumping beat, they stormed through the first set and had everybody up dancing. Certainly there was no time to sit down at Westhill Working Men's Club.

During the break, the snazzy-looking geezer in the grey mohair suit came knocking on the dressing room door. He introduced himself as Daniel Hoffmann and gave Stan a simple white business card with his name on it; there was also a Bayswater address and telephone number.

'People call me Danny,' he said. 'I've brought you in a few drinks, you must be gasping after that performance.' He'd been followed into the dressing room by one of the club's young barmen, carrying a tray with an assortment of soft drinks on it. Coke, 7Up, lemonade and orange, even a jug of lemon barley squash. He was right, they were parched, and the guys guzzled greedily.

'That was a great show boys... oh yes, and girl!' He gestured towards Carol with a warm smile. 'I'll be blunt, I like your style, I love your music and I wondered if you would maybe consider a change of management?'

'Change?' laughed Barry. 'We don't have a manager to begin with; we're the monkeys that work for peanuts.'

'That's not quite true,' broke in Stan, clearly pissed off.

'I handle the bookings and organise the diary. It was me who organised all this tonight.'

'And from the look of the way things have gone, a damned good job you've done too,' smiled Danny.

That made Stan feel a bit better, but not before he'd lanced Barry with glare.

'I'm not here to tread on anybody's toes but I think I could help you a lot. I'm well connected with the people who own dance halls and clubs in the South East. I'm quite well known to the media guys, you know, the press, radio and television. I've also had dealings with recording studios'

He took a Black Russian cigarette, tapping it on the box before putting it in his mouth. He quickly took it back out, holding it up between finger and thumb. 'Sorry, how thoughtless, you don't mind if I do, do you?'

'No, I'm just about to light up myself,' answered Barry, a cigarette already between his lips.

Danny smiled, flicked his gold lighter into life and leant forward to light up Barry's and then his own.

'I'm going to be straight with you right from the off. You need to know that I've had a chat with a few of the agents you invited here tonight. Most of them know me and they know I only deal in top quality merchandise. The fees I'd negotiate would be the very best and I'd guarantee value for money, but then you've shown them that with your show so far tonight.'

The atmosphere in the dressing room had changed, none of the usual banter. They were excited, for sure, but they were a bit shocked too; this manager thing was something they had to discuss amongst themselves, even Stan wasn't sure what to say. They glanced nervously at each other.

Danny Hoffmann saw this. 'Look we've broken the ice,

you've listened to what I wanted to say and I can assure you there's a lot more to talk about. There's plenty for you to think about and bounce off each other.' He looked at his wristwatch. 'Hey, you've got a show to finish. Go knock 'em dead, we'll have a scrum down later.' He turned tail, swept out of the room and took up his place back at the bar. A fresh G&T awaited and he lit up another Black Russian.

Their second half performance was even better, as The Bombastics rocked their way through a repertoire they'd worked so hard to piece together over the last few weeks. What really stunned them was the reaction from the gaggle of girls, fifteen, maybe sixteen years old, that had gathered in front of the stage and were staring doe-eyed at Frank. It was when he slowed things down to do his ballad segment they heard the screams for the first time.

He crooned the old Elvis classic 'I Want You, I Need You, I Love You'. There were a few stifled screams from two or three of the girls. Then when he launched into 'It's Only Make Believe', the roof came off! Seven, eight, maybe ten of the girls; and this time the screams weren't stifled.

Stan gave Bodkin a knowing nod and Barry turned towards the two of them, raising his eyebrows. Over at the bar, Danny Hoffmann smiled to himself and ordered another G&T.

They tried to wind up the night with a couple of rousing rockers, but Westhill wanted more. It took a couple of encores, before the crowd would let them close the show.

They collapsed, exhausted, in the dressing room chairs, but there was still a buzz none of them had experienced before.

'That was awesome,' said Carol.

'I'll say it was,' said Bodkin, sweating profusely, appearing from under a towel and with his shirt stuck to him. 'We certainly didn't do ourselves any harm tonight.'

'Those agents have to be impressed. Stan, get the diary out and put those fees up to fifty quid, immediately,' quipped Barry.

'Those girls, I – well you know – I felt a right lard-head out there.' Frank was genuinely embarrassed. 'That's the first time I've ever been screamed at.'

'And it won't be the last time,' came a voice from the doorway. Danny Hoffmann entered the room and sat down in the last remaining empty chair. 'Can I ask you what you expect to get paid on a gig like this?'

'Well this was free,' answered Stan. 'It was a one off, we wanted a packed house to create the right atmosphere and impress the agents who came.'

'Okay, I understand and it worked,' nodded Danny, 'but what would you charge on a normal night out?'

Stan was really out of his comfort zone here, in front of everybody and talking to a man who looked like a mean negotiator. 'Well, w-w-w-we'd normally get twenty-five guineas,' he stammered.

They'd never, ever, been paid twenty-five guineas; they'd never been paid twenty-five *quid!* The others looked at him, waiting for his nose to grow bigger.

Danny was silent for a time.

'Let me be bold and say you need me boys – and so does this charming young lady.' He smiled again at Carol. 'For twenty-five guineas I wouldn't cross the road, let alone put on the show you've just done.'

He pulled what looked like a diary from the inside pocket of his mohair suit.

'Barry was right, you're playing for peanuts and that's

not right.' He was scanning the pages of his diary. 'I've got a couple of days next week when I can come up to the Midlands. Would you like to talk?'

'I think we would,' answered Stan.

'Yes,' the others chimed in unison.

'What day are you thinking of?' asked Stan. 'Most of us work, so it may have to be in the evening.'

'That's okay.' Danny had a pen poised over his diary. 'Sooner the better, what about next Wednesday evening, is that okay?'

They looked at each other, nodding.

'No problem for me,' said Bodkin, putting both thumbs up.

'Looks like Wednesday, then, what about time and place?' said Stan.

'You're from somewhere south of Brum, is that right?' Danny wrote 'Bombastics' on Wednesday October 31st in his diary.

'More or less.' Stan nodded his head. 'Three of us live in a North Worcestershire village called Fordrough and the other two not far away in south Birmingham.'

Danny wrote 'Fordrough' underneath Bombastic in his diary. 'Okay, I'll find it. I'll book into a local hotel. You give me your number, Stan, and I'll call and let you know which hotel, the drinks will be on me. We should meet at 7 p.m.' Danny wrote Stan's number down and then shook his hand. 'Great show, I know we can go a long way together.' He smiled that smile again. He then shook hands with all the others, asking their names and thanking them too. He paused as he took Carol's hand. 'And may I ask your name, Miss Sultry Sax Player?' That smile again!

'Carol Meadowsweet,' she replied, looking down rather demurely and knowing her cheeks were reddening up.

'Sweet by name, sweet by nature.' Danny laughed gently.

Bodkin thought, *That could've sounded like some corny old chat-up line, but not the way snazzy boy said it.*

Danny turned in the doorway to face them all and with palms stretched towards them. 'See you all Wednesday, and don't sell your souls to the devil before I see you again.'

'You mean to any of the other agents here tonight?' Barry smirked.

Danny gave a broad smile and disappeared out of the door and down the corridor.

There were no other agents waiting to speak to them, of course. Daniel Hoffmann had exchanged business cards with every one of them.

'Do you think we can trust a geezer like that?' asked Bodkin, slightly miffed at the way he charmed Carol. 'He seems a bit of a smarmy bastard to me.'

'One thing's for certain, he seems to know his way around,' said Stan. 'Did you see the way they kept his G&Ts topped up? Nobody took his barstool either.'

'Bugger me, he'd charm the birds off the trees, if you ask me,' added Barry.

Breaking down the gear and loading it onto Wally's wagon, sparkly clean and free of plaster for the evening, didn't seem the chore it usually was. There was a lot of excited chatter on the way home. The junctions back up the M1 just flew by.

'Let's stop at the Blue Boar and have a cuppa,' said Frank as they passed the sign for the services. 'Take it out of the old man's bank roll, he won't know.'

Bodkin pulled into the services and they piled into the restaurant.

'Tea or coffee?' Stan asked everyone.

'And would Miss Sultry like a toasted teacake?' asked Barry with a twinkle in his eye.

Carol blushed as she shook her head. Bodkin just glared.

Danny Hoffman was the topic of conversation as they sat round the table with their drinks.

'I liked what he had to say,' said Carol. 'He just oozed confidence, maybe Barry's fifty pounds isn't so far-fetched after all.'

'Did you hear him say he'd had dealings with the recording studios?' added Frank. 'That's what we're all after, isn't it?'

'Let's wait and see what all the others have to say,' snapped Bodkin. 'We don't have to go with the first one to make an offer. There may be something better on the way.'

CHAPTER 6
'SIGNED, SEALED, DELIVERED'

Stevie Wonder

Danny had taken a room at The Shillingworth Spa and Hotel, a sprawling half-timbered pile that was formerly the estate of the Shillingworth family, until the Right Honourable Frederick Viscount Shillingworth picked the wrong numbers on the roulette wheel for the umpteenth time that night, and was forced to sell it to the Huyton Group. They transformed it into an eighty bedroom hotel, with a spa and a nine-hole golf course. It lay two miles off the main Birmingham Road, just north of Fordrough. Danny phoned Stan on Sunday afternoon and suggested they meet in the bar on Wednesday as arranged at 7 p.m. Stan got in touch with all the others, confirming the arrangements and adding, 'Blimey! You don't stop at the Shillingworth for thirty bob a night.'

***

Barry took his driving test on the Tuesday morning and passed first time. He hadn't told anyone about the test; they knew he was having lessons with a local driving school, but that was as far as it went. He didn't want any of them knowing what stage he was at, and certainly not that he was taking his test, he knew the piss taking that would go on if he failed. Even his mom and dad were kept in the dark. He turned up at Bodkin's, late on Wednesday afternoon, waving an official-looking slip of paper, striding up the front path and shouting, 'I passed, I passed – this here's my passport to the highways and byways!' Bodkin was taken aback.

Slapping the palm of his hand on the side of Wally's van which was parked in the driveway, Barry was full of it. 'C'mon drummer boy, let's rock 'n' roll baby.'

Bodkin stood frowning on his front doorstep, with his arms folded. 'Is this one of your stupid pranks?' he growled. 'You're not getting anywhere near that motor until I've seen that piece of paper you're holding.' As Barry got near, Bodkin snatched it, unfolded it, and cast his eyes over it. 'God help us, this is legit!'

'Told yer,' chirped Barry. 'Now give us those keys, Four-skins.'

'Whoa! Slow down, Harper.' Bodkin held a defiant finger in front of Barry. 'Let's see how you drive first, there's a lot of expensive equipment inside that motor, not to mention some very important people. I also need to check the insurance document and see if you're able to drive it. Be just our luck for you to go and wrap it round a tree and we ain't covered.' He went back inside the house for his wallet.

Despite Bodkin's hesitance to let Barry get behind the wheel, he realised that at last he would get a bit of help with the driving; he could certainly do with that. After hours behind his drums, he then spent more hours behind the wheel, not only picking them up and getting them to the gigs on time, but also dropping them off afterwards. It was often the wee small hours before he got into his bed.

He smiled at Barry, folded the insurance document back up and slipped it back inside his wallet. 'Seems like you're good to go, but…' he pointed a threatening finger which almost went up Barry's nose, 'let's take it easy to start with, right?' He pulled the keys from his trouser pocket, unlocked the driver's door and handed them to Barry. 'We've got plenty of time to get to Stan's and there's only him. Carol's dad wants to be there so he's giving her a lift and they're going to pick up Frank on the way, so relax.' There was no holding Barry, he grabbed the keys and clambered into the driver's seat.

If Bodkin was surprised, then Stan was flabbergasted when he saw Barry pull up outside his house with Bodkin in the passenger seat. 'Blimey, the chauffeur from hell! When did they let a nutter like you loose on the roads?'

'You cheeky bastard, I passed yesterday morning; first time as well, so up yours.' Barry thrust a middle finger skywards.

'I've seen how you ride that motorbike of yours, pal. I know of people hiding behind bus shelters and in shop doorways in case you passed by and offered them a pillion lift.' Stan balanced himself on a cushion on one of the wheel arches. Barry pushed the gear shift into first and promptly kangaroo hopped into the road.

Stan went sprawling across the empty van. 'Jeezus Christ, mind out! Just remember you got two future rock stars on board.'

'Don't you start all that crap too,' sighed Barry, looking

at Stan through the rear view mirror. 'I've just had Four-skins bending me ear. I've just gotta get used to this clutch.'

When they arrived, Carol, her dad Dennis, and Frank were sat in the lounge bar talking to Danny, who was smoking his customary Black Russian. A glass of gin and tonic stood on the table next to him alongside a sheet of A4, turned upside down. Carol held a glass of orange, Frank and Dennis were drinking coffees.

Danny jumped to his feet to shake hands with them. He remembered each of their names. That impressed Stan. *Hmmm, not bad. He's only spoken briefly to Bods and Barry.*

Danny called the waiter over and they each ordered a drink. Stan and Bodkin ordered beers and Barry, with his sensible head on, ordered a coffee. They drew chairs up a little closer to the table and settled down. Danny began. 'Right everyone, I have to say I really liked what I saw and heard last weekend, so I'll ask you again. I'd very much like to become your manager.'

'Well you were the only one who was impressed,' said Stan. 'None of the other agents or club owners has been in touch, not a soddin' dicky bird.'

Danny smiled. 'Oh, they were impressed alright. I spoke to every one of them at some length. I told them all I'd be in touch just as soon as we'd sorted a few things out.'

'You mean you took over our bleedin' showcase? Our contacts – geezers Stan had invited personally?' Bodkin was not happy.

Danny held his hands up in mock surrender. 'Take it easy big man! I told you the other night, you're working for peanuts and you are certainly not monkeys. I know many of these guys and, forgive me for saying this, but you're just kids with a lot to learn and they'll take advantage of you.' There were some furtive glances around the table, but nobody said anything and they all saw Dennis Meadowsweet gently nodding his head in agreement.

'I intend to get you work at the right money, but at the same time we need to get you known outside Birmingham and the 'geezers' of whom you speak, tend not to pay unknown bands the top rates. We also need to hound the recording companies. If we can get you a recording contract and into the hit parade, the lolly gets really interesting.' Danny was in full flow. He picked up the A4 sheet and waved it in front of them. 'Going back to your showcase, you did yourself no harm at all, I've had all of those agents and club owners make contact; every single one. They're typed out on this sheet. I've also taken the liberty of pencilling in some dates.'

He saw panic on Stan's face.

'Don't worry, they're all quite flexible at this stage, and I have also sounded them out on fees. If you decide I'm your man, I'll get a very fair rate from them. If you don't want to go with me, I shall hand over all the contact names, proposed dates and possible fees and you can deal with it yourselves. The hard work all done for you.'

Stan had been quiet, particularly after Bodkin's little showcase outburst. 'Danny, I like the sound of this but what do you get out of it?'

'Twenty per cent,' Danny replied without hesitation.

'TWENTY PER CENT!' wailed Bodkin. 'There'll be sod all left for us!'

Danny smiled. 'Listen Bodkin, this is a gamble for me, there's going to be some personal outlay getting the whole thing up and running, but as I said, I really thought you were very good and I'm prepared to back you. When you're rich and famous, it'll mean I've made a few shillings too.'

'Will this twenty per cent be net or gross?' asked Dennis.

Danny could see Carol and the boys looked confused, so he explained. 'Your dad's asked a fair question, Carol. He knows it would be unfair of me to take my cut off the gross figure, before all expenses are deducted; things like petrol and accommodation. Almost unscrupulous, you could say, but you'll see when you read the contract that my twenty per cent comes off the net figure. I intend to take it monthly, after all expenses have been paid.'

Dennis clasped his hands together and smiled. 'That's very fair.' That made the boys feel a bit more assured.

Danny changed tack. 'First we have to get you known, get The Bombastics brand out there, then we can start to get you into some of the top venues that pay the top prices.'

'So what have you got in mind for us?' said Bodkin. 'A Royal Variety Performance at the London Palladium?'

Danny laughed. 'All in good time, eh? There's a few other places around the UK we hit before that. You'll be doing some miles, but as you turn full time professional you'll get better and better.'

'Full time?' asked Bodkin. 'What sort of money are we talking about here?'

Danny stopped and looked at each one of them in turn. 'For many reasons, you have to turn fully professional as soon as possible. This will be reflected in your earnings.'

'You say you're being paid twenty-five guineas a gig,' said Danny. 'Well I'm going to start you off at £25 a week each and I'll be looking to have you working four maybe five nights a week.'

'Twenty-five quid EACH!' Barry nearly choked on his coffee. 'Fuck me, where do we sign?'

'Barry!' scolded Carol. 'Do you have to use that language?' Barry looked sheepish and mumbled an apology.

'I do have a contract for us all to sign,' continued Danny. 'But first I feel we need to go through a few things, so that we all have a clear understanding. To begin with, as you would expect, you work exclusively for me. If any impresario or promoter, no matter how high-falutin' they may sound, any radio or television station, newspaper or magazine, you name it, wants to hire, record, write or photograph The Bombastics, they come through me, Daniel Hoffman. That means you can concentrate on what you're good at… making music.'

Carol and the boys listened intently.

'Before I start talking to any record companies, there's a number of things I want you to consider. First, I want you to start writing your own songs. I think that's going to be very important. There's one hell of a vibe coming out of Liverpool and Manchester at the moment. Bands like The Beatles have just had their first hit, wrote it themselves and they say there's a lot more to come.'

Bodkin broke in. 'Martin left us to go over to one of the night clubs in Hamburg, the Beatles were in the same city at another club. I think it was The Star Club or something like that. When he came back home a few weeks ago, he was telling me how good they were, played all the rock 'n' roll stuff that we do and write a few of their own things too. Martin said their manager had landed them a recording contract with Parlophone.'

'I think you'll find their manager got them an audition; it was the Beatles who landed themselves a recording contract, playing their own songs, so I believe.'

'Their first single's in the top twenty, 'Love Me Do',' Frank added. 'Simple little tune, nothing that we couldn't manage. Maybe they'll go on to do better, who knows?'

Barry's eyes lit up. 'Maybe we should go to Germany, play at one of those night clubs, plenty of work, young Fräuleins aplenty, it sounds like it could be...'

Bodkin stopped him. 'No way, Jose! Martin was telling me the club they work at is a shithole. They have to play for eight hours every night with only three breaks, they only get Mondays off and five of them have to doss down in one pokey little room to try and get some kip. It's right next door to the gents bog and stinks. To crown it all the money's crap and they have to buy their own food too!'

Danny took control again. 'Despite all those wonderful amenities Bodkin has highlighted, I do not want you going to Germany. You need to be here in the UK where it's all happening. The record companies are looking for groups who can bring along new material, so if you write your own stuff, it'll give you the edge, so to speak.'

'I've been writing a few things; have done for a couple of years,' Frank said, rather quietly. The others looked at him, surprised. 'I haven't shown them to any of you yet,' continued Frank, slightly uncomfortably. 'I wasn't sure about them, whether you'd think they were rubbish and that I was a bit of a prat with big ideas.'

'Bugger me, cocky little Frank Richards becomes the shrinking violet, who'd have guessed it?' laughed Barry.

'Frank you must let us hear this stuff, it could be very important.' Danny sat up and spread his arms dramatically. 'This could be a seminal moment in the history of The Bombastics. It might just be the start of something.'

Danny drained his G&T, looked around, and signalled the waiter, who was collecting glasses in the foyer. 'I also want to look at your image. We need to make you stand out from the crowd. You're pretty tight musically, but what you need is some onstage pizzazz.'

Danny ordered another gin and tonic. 'Anyone want a

top up?' No one did.

He reached into a briefcase beside him and pulled out a catalogue. 'I was at the New York Rockefeller Club in Manhattan last Easter. They had this band, a bit more doo-wop than you chaps. They were pretty sensational, but not just their music; they looked a million dollars, as the New Yorkers might say.

'By pure chance I happened to be sitting on the next table to their manager; sitting back to back, so to speak. I told him how fabulous I thought they looked and sounded and how I just loved their suits. During the break he went backstage and when he returned he gave me this catalogue. He told me to keep it, said he'd got plenty of copies, so I folded it and stuck it in my inside pocket. Never for a minute thought I'd use it; just shows you, eh? I want you to look through it, but particularly at the suits on page thirty-four. I've put a business card marker in it.'

He handed the catalogue to Stan, who opened it at the bookmark, his eyes widening as he studied the full-colour double-page in front of him. 'Wow, these look pretty smoky.' Bodkin and Frank squeezed along the settee to look over his shoulder.

'Those are s-s-s-some s-s-s-suits,' whistled Frank.

'S-s-s-sure are,' imitated Bodkin.

'Zoot suits,' confirmed Dennis, who'd come to stand behind them. 'Many of the American jazz bands used to wear them in the forties and fifties. Tell you what, you'd look the business dressed in those.'

Danny pulled a folder out of his briefcase. 'Their manager also gave me a photograph of The Broadways, that's the name of his band, take a look.'

The Broadways were a five-piece band, black guys, all dressed in white zoot suits except the one sat at the piano who wore azure blue. The white suits were in posed positions, playing guitar, sax, bass, and drums. They wore blue open-neck deep-collar shirts and white Cuban heeled boots. The guy sat at the piano with his fingers stretched over the keys had a smile that stretched the length of the Mason-Dixon Line. He wore a gold lamé shirt, the collar spilling over the lapels of his jacket. His Cubans were matching gold lamé. All of them had greased hair that glistened in the studio lights. They looked magnificent.

The photograph was handed around to nods of approval.

Barry was beaming. 'Bugger me, we ought to change our name to The Fanny Magnets dressed like that.' Carol tossed her head back and tutted, the others just ignored him.

'They look fantastic, we'd certainly stand out at the Phantom Coach in those outfits,' said Stan.

'There's a few bob's worth there, Danny,' said Bodkin.

'Don't worry about the cost, we're image building here,' said Danny. 'And what's the Phantom Coach?'

'It's a local pub we play at regularly,' answered Stan.

'I'm sure it's been very important to you, but we're definitely aiming higher than a local pub.' Danny picked up the fresh drink the waiter had put on the table in front of him. 'I really do believe the sky's the limit if you listen to me. Skol!' He raised the glass towards them.

'What about me?" asked Carol. 'I can't really wear one of those zoot suits, can I?'

'You certainly cannot,' smiled Danny. 'Turn to page seventeen in that catalogue.' He nodded towards where it now lay on the table. Stan picked it up and thumbed through the pages, opening it at page seventeen and laying it across Carol's lap. She took a sharp intake of breath.

The brunette model, posed holding a microphone

stand, was dressed in a long, flowing red dress. It had a full-length slit up the side revealing her leg to just above the knee and a matching red, sling-back stiletto on her foot. The bodice was low-cut, supported by the scantiest of halter neck straps that seemed barely able to hold everything together up top. She also wore long, elbow length red gloves.

'Dressed like that Carol, half the audience may not even notice the boy's zoot suits,' added Danny, still smiling.

Carol turned the colour of the dress on page seventeen, went all bashful and avoided making eye contact with her dad. 'I can't wear gloves like that AND play the saxophone.'

'Who's looking at the soddin' gloves?' leered Barry. Bodkin's gimlet eye nailed him, causing Barry to quickly change tack. 'I like the frock, it's tighter than Bodkin's wallet.'

They all laughed, even Bodkin.

'There's another change I'd like to suggest, it requires some serious thought.' Danny's perma- smile had been replaced by a more serious face. 'I would like you to change your name.'

They looked stunned.

'We've been The Bombastics since school,' pleaded Stan.

'Yeah, everybody knows us as The Bombastics,' added Bodkin.

'Just a minute.' Danny raised a forefinger. 'I'm only suggesting a minor change; I'd like you to become Frankie Atom and The Bombastics.'

Stan, Bodkin Barry and Carol sat there, taking that thought in.

Frank looked very uncomfortable; to him the following

ten seconds of silence seemed like ten minutes.

At last Danny continued. 'Since Bedford, I've given this a lot of thought. You have a very talented young man out front there, and from what I saw, the young girls think so too.' Then he spread his hands. 'Don't get me wrong, you're all very important to the band, indispensable I'd say, but I think Frank, or rather Frankie, has that extra something that will help sell records once we get you signed up.'

Frank looked even more uncomfortable. 'Look lads, I...'

Stan interrupted him. 'Let's spare your blushes Frank, it makes sense. Danny's right. I mentioned something very similar to Bodkin only last week.'

Bodkin nodded. 'We need to play to our strengths if we're going to break through. As long as you don't get any more cash than the rest of us, I'm okay with it.'

They all turned to Barry. He shrugged and smirked. 'Narrrr! It's me who pulls all the birds, it should be Barry Harper and The Bombastics?'

Carol whacked him round the back of the head with the rolled up catalogue she was now holding. 'I don't think Danny was talking about grabbing grannies. I think it's a great idea. Cliff Richard and The Shadows, Buddy Holly and The Crickets, Johnny Kidd and The Pirates – Frankie Atom and The Bombastics – it works!'

Danny's smile had returned. He reached back into his brief case and pulled out two contracts, three pages in each set stapled together. He handed them to Stan. 'Read this through; I've given you two copies, so get some advice if you will. It's a first draft and we can change anything you're not happy with. Look through the catalogue too, see if there's anything you prefer. Those were just my suggestions, but in the end it's down to you guys. Also you really need to give some serious thought to writing some of your own stuff. Develop and nurture what Frank... sorry, Frankie, may have started.'

'Going full-time professional needs some serious thought; Barry, Bodkin and me all have jobs,' added Stan. 'Mind you, if you get the amount of work you say you will, it seems like we need to make those decisions sooner rather than later.'

'That makes sense. Let's put a date on our next meeting.' Danny nodded as he took his diary from his inside pocket and flicked through the pages. 'Let's make it November 11th Poppy Day and Bombastics Day. As you know, I've got you back at Westhill for their Sunday Special, so it's ideal; we all get there two hours early and it'll give us a chance to dot the 'I's and cross the 'T's'

They all agreed.

They met on November 11th, turns out Westhill couldn't wait to get them back; it was a sell-out. Stan was slightly peeved they'd phoned Danny rather than him, but he let it pass.

The contract presented no problems and they'd all signed it, with Jack Richards and Dennis Meadowsweet signing on behalf of their kids, Frank and Carol, who were only sixteen. The zoot suits were ordered. Bright yellow for Stan, powder blue for Barry, luminous green for Bodkin, shocking pink for Frankie, and that long red dress for Carol.

They all agreed to go full-time as soon as Danny had the work coming in.

When the suits arrived from the States, Danny arranged a publicity photo shoot at Coventry Cathedral just before the snows came.

Frankie Atom and The Bombastics were on their way.

CHAPTER 7
'MY HEART BELONGS TO DADDY'

Marilyn Monroe

Carol Meadowsweet was a daddy's girl. A very musical daddy's girl.

Daddy Meadowsweet was Dennis; he played clarinet in the Ronnie Hayworth Big Band. He also played clarinet and saxophone, when he could, in a traditional jazz band along with his pal, Richie Davison who played trombone in the Big Band. They called themselves the Goodtime Footwarmers. His jazz band took mainly local bookings, playing in clubs around Birmingham and the Black Country, they tended to play more for love than money. With the Big Band, Dennis and Richie could be away on tour, sometimes for three or four weeks at a time, often backing the big US stars of the day, over here on a European tour, or promoting their latest record releases.

Young Carol idolised Dennis and wanted to be just like her daddy.

Although he never let it show, Dennis had been disappointed that Carol's big brother Michael, showed absolutely no talent or inclination to play music, so when six-year-old Carol first picked up her daddy's clarinet and actually got a sound out of it he was delighted. To nurture that early promise he bought her a recorder, an instrument much more suited to the tiny fingers of a child of such tender years than his clarinet. By the time she was nine, she had mastered both soprano and baritone recorders. During the last year of her junior school days, the curriculum included music and when recorders were handed out to the class she was so far ahead of the other ten-year-olds, that teacher got her to help some of her classmates to master their technique.

During the summer of 1957, Dennis bought a Charlie Parker LP home and played it ceaselessly. Early in the morning and late at night, the strains of 'Ornithology' or 'Now's the Time' drifted through the Meadowsweet household. Many a late summer evening, the sound of Dennis's clarinet intertwined with The Yardbird's mellow saxophone floated gently from their open French windows. There was often a not-quite-so-mellow accompaniment from a recorder wafting down from an upstairs bedroom window too.

***

Carol's mother, Mary, was shopping in Birmingham in late September of that year, when she passed George Clays in Broad Street. Clays sold musical instruments of every kind; pianos, woodwind, percussion, brass and string. They were also in the vanguard for the growing demand for electric guitars and amplifiers.

Mary spotted a neatly hand written card cellotaped to the shop door window. After reading it and smiling to herself, she entered the shop and spoke at some length to the grey-haired assistant that approached her. He took her through to their storage area, lifted a black leather case down from one of the shelves, undid the catch and lifted the lid. Her eyes lit up. After chatting for a while, they shook hands and he filled out a sales docket whilst Mary Meadowsweet wrote out a cheque. They exchanged paperwork, shook hands once again and she left the shop much in the way as she had entered, smiling to herself. The assistant removed the card from the window.

***

After breakfast on Christmas morning the Meadowsweets unwrapped their presents. Dennis had bought his wife the most beautiful angora stole that she'd been hinting about since August. Michael had every thirteen-year-old schoolboy's dream; a number 4 size Meccano set, and young Carol got Sooty and Sweep hand puppets, complete with xylophone which they (and probably Carol too) could fight over.

Dennis was quite surprised when Mary went out to the kitchen and returned with a box so large she had to use both arms to carry it. It was beautifully wrapped in Christmas paper, printed with little smiley snowmen, and a red ribbon tied in a large bow. On the tag was written 'To Dennis from Mary, Michael and Carol XXX'

Dennis untied the ribbon, carefully removed the wrapping paper, and lifted the lid of the black case inside. The present would both surprise and delight him. It would also completely change the life of the eleven-year-old girl kneeling on the carpet beside him.

Lying on the blue silk lining of the case, was a second hand Selmer tenor saxophone.

***

Dennis was not a musical snob, he just loved music – all types; modern jazz as much as traditional jazz, blues as much as swing and his collection of Classical records was inherited from his father's collection of 78s on Shellac. His cosmopolitan taste clearly rubbed off onto his little girl. During the school holidays Daddy sneaked her into a few of his jazz nights. Sitting in a noisy cellar breathing in the fug of cigarette smoke (and God knows what else), surrounded by weekend Bohemians brimming over with alcohol wasn't perhaps, the best thing for a girl barely in her teens and when Mommy had to wash her dresses reeking of the previous night's tobacco, Mary eventually put her foot down; firmly.

In a few years time Dennis and his daughter would both be totally sold on a new sound coming out of America. Rock 'n' roll.

Carol passed her eleven plus and went to grammar school. Her prodigious talents were soon recognised by her music teacher, Mrs Fanshawe.

Lois Fanshawe had mustered together a half-decent school band, mainly made up of woodwind and brass (definitely no guitars), played by willing youngsters and a few stalwart teachers. Over the years, some talented kids had passed through the ranks of the Lordsfield Grammar School Band to leave, five years later, as reasonably accomplished musicians. Carol joined as an accomplished eleven-year-old and left a very talented sixteen-year-old.

Although Carol played clarinet in the school band, at home she had taken to playing Dad's 1957 Christmas saxophone. Rock 'n' roll was sweeping the nation and all the kids were heavily into the American and British stars of the day. Carol was no different, she loved rock 'n' roll, but she wasn't going gooey-eyed about the singers such as Cliff Richard and Billy Fury like her classmates; she was listening to the different styles and taking in the instrumentation. Some of the tenor sax solos she copied became note perfect and at the same time, listening to her dad's jazz records, she soon started to develop her own style and technique. It got to the point where Carol was playing Daddy's saxophone more than Daddy. Dennis didn't mind; to listen to a fifteen-going-on-sixteen-year-old play a raunchy, sensual sax break was bordering on surreal.

When Mom and Dad had front row seats at the 1961 annual school concert, Lois Fanshawe allowed Carol to put down her clarinet and pick up her saxophone. It was Carol's last year and Dennis felt a shiver of excitement go through him when Carol played her version of 'How High the Moon', which he recognised was inspired by Yardbird's arrangement. He had to gulp hard. Mary offered him one of her hankies which he pushed away, somewhat embarrassed.

Carol was leaving at the end of that school year and Lois Fanshawe was desperate for Carol to audition for The Birmingham Symphony Orchestra where she knew somebody and had 'had a word'. She took advantage of having the three of them together after the school concert; the stage was deserted, just the last few chairs being stacked away by school monitors. She commandeered the last three chairs and gathered everybody around her upright piano, inviting Mary Meadowsweet to take a seat on the stool and organising a pot of tea from the school canteen next door. Carol had orange squash.

'I know you're a professional musician Mr Meadowsweet – may I call you Dennis?'

He nodded and sipped his lukewarm tea.

'Carol is such an exceptional talent and you'll know how important it is that she's put into the right hands and given the correct ongoing tuition and guidance, to play alongside fellow musicians of the very highest standard.'

Dennis opened his mouth to respond but she charged on; Lois Fanshawe was giving no quarter.

'I've had a word with Jeremy Roland at the Birmingham Symphony – did you know they took Martin Davies, our wonderful French horn student four years ago? Anyway Jeremy said if you telephone him, he'll arrange for you to take Carol down to the Town Hall for an audition. Let him hear her and at the same time let her see the wonderful facilities there. I've told him so much about you both. It really is a tremendous opportunity. I – I have his number here somewhere.' She balanced her cup and saucer on top of the piano and picked up her handbag to take a folded slip of paper from one of the side pockets.

'This is very kind of you to go to all this trouble, Mrs Fanshawe,' said Dennis. 'Mary and I know what a source of inspiration you've been to Carol.' He thought to himself at the same time, *Sorry, Mrs F, you're too late. Carol's got her heart set on jazz, blues and rock 'n' roll and I don't think you or Jeremy Roland will change that.*

'Oh do call me Lois, please,' Mrs Fanshawe pleaded. 'I'm sure her musical preferences are natural enough, when one knows her father is such a gifted jazz musician, but I'm also sure you'll agree that at Carol's tender years it is essential to expand her horizons. We must gently blow that spark within her until it glows brightly and bursts into life.' She thrust her head back, closed her eyes and clasped her hands in front of her still holding the slip of paper. 'Let her light shine upon the world.'

Dennis shot an awkward glance at Mary, who was biting her lip. Carol just gaped.

Lois Fanshawe opened her eyes, leant toward Dennis and pressed the folded paper into his hand. Dennis promised to make contact, looked at the folded note, folded it yet again, and slipped it into the ticket pocket inside his jacket. He knew Carol owed a lot to Mrs Fanshawe; she had given so much of her time, encouraging Carol with her beloved Classics and helping her read music. The last thing he wanted was to hurt her feelings, but Dennis knew he wouldn't be making that call. Carol's heart lay elsewhere.

***

Carol often went with her school friends on the short bus ride to the Thursday Rock 'n' Roll Nite at the Phantom Coach, an enormous pub on the main Birmingham Road. This impressive Art Deco building with its blue neon coach and horses sign was a familiar sight to travellers on the A45.

Thursday night rock 'n' roll at the Phantom Coach had become a firm favourite with teenagers around the area and the Lordsfield Grammar School Ladies were regulars. Carol's gang were attractive girls, especially blonde-haired, long-legged Carol herself, and the local lads would pester them to dance, but Carol was more interested in listening to the bands that gigged there. Some had sax players, but most didn't. Some had girl singers, but very few had girl instrumentalists and none had girl instrumentalists who'd just turned sixteen.

She remembered The Bombastics, they were one of the more popular local bands. They had plenty of energy onstage and liked to laugh and joke with the audience. She remembered they had a line up of two guitars, bass and drums and a couple of them sang. They had a good following, so it came as a bit of a surprise when their advert appeared in the *Birmingham Mail* for a guitarist/singer. It was her mom who spotted it. Mary knew Carol was straining at the leash to get into a band and was surprised when Carol initially dismissed it, saying they were looking for a guitarist/singer not a sax player, particularly a girl sax player who couldn't sing.

It was her dad who persuaded her to think again.

'The main aim is to let them hear you and listen to you play,' he told her. 'Maybe they don't realise they need a sax player until they hear the right sax player; and that's you.'

So he hatched a plan. He phoned the number in the ad and spoke to a chap named Stan Ravenscroft. 'Apparently he plays bass in The Bombastics,' Dennis told Carol. 'He told me that the vacancy had occurred because their lead guitarist and singer had joined another band who'd got a residency at a club over in Hamburg; sounds like he's left them in the lurch, plenty of work, but no front man. Anyway, I told him a little white lie, said my name was Dennis and arranged to be at Fordrough village hall next Saturday at four o'clock for an audition.'

'Little white lie?' screeched Carol. 'More like a soddin' great black one, with pink spots! What do I do when they work out, that instead of a guitar player named Dennis, they've got a sax player with tits who goes by the name of Carol, eh?'

'That's when you blow them away, sweetheart,' grinned Dennis. Then straightening his face, he said, 'And I don't think your mother would like to hear you talk like that, young lady.'

***

Carol's tummy was full of butterflies as they sat in Dennis's car in Fordrough, outside a pub called the Crown and Anchor, just round the corner from the village hall. They'd got there far too early and sat listening to the car radio. Dennis crossed over the square to the newsagent for a *Daily Sketch* and a packet of mints. They watched at least two hopefuls carrying guitars walking past the pub towards the auditions. At two minutes to four, Dennis opened the boot of his car and handed over their saxophone. He gave her a peck on the cheek and said, 'You're good Carol, go and show them how good.'

She took the saxophone case, gave her dad a nervous smile and set off. As she got to the village hall door, she bumped into a chap with greased back hair and long sideburns, dressed in a purple mohair suit and white winkle-pickers; he'd stood back clutching his guitar case against him to let her through. He'd wished her good luck. She thought that was nice.

It was Stan that greeted her; he had a bass guitar strapped over his shoulder. Stan introduced her to Barry, who played guitar. He was quite good looking and from the glint in his eye as he looked her up and down, she knew he was one she would have to keep an eye on. The drummer's name was Bodkin, he was both tall and broad-shouldered; he put down a teacup half-full of fizzy pop to shake hands with her and she was surprised at the gentle touch of such a big man. She recognised them all from the Phantom Coach.

She gingerly explained that her dad had arranged the audition and then opened her music case and took out a saxophone. They were clearly shocked that a girl sax player had turned up to audition for a singer/guitarist spot, but they seemed nice friendly kids and made her feel at home. She soon lost her nervousness as she played them a few bits and pieces that she thought would impress a rock 'n' roll band. She could tell from their body language that things were going well and she felt she was getting through to them. Bodkin led the way and soon all three were playing along with her.

Then this young guy, she guessed to be about her own age, came into the village hall. She was soon to find out his name was Frank. It turned out he'd already auditioned and had really wowed them. He picked up his guitar and started jamming with them. He was very good, not only on guitar, but on vocals too. She immediately felt really comfortable with him, her sax playing and his guitar playing seemed to go hand in glove; they followed each other so naturally and she could see that the others recognised that too.

Things happened pretty quickly after that. The Bombastic boys disappeared downstairs to discuss things, whilst they left her and Frank playing stuff on their own. They were not gone for long and when they came back upstairs they announced that they wanted both of them in the band. There were hugs and handshakes all round, lots of smiles and laughter. Stan said they didn't want to lose the bookings they'd got and stressed they needed to start rehearsing straight away; they agreed some dates. When she got back to the car her dad was really chuffed, so pleased for her.

The next few weeks were spent working very hard, putting together a decent playlist and polishing each number up until they were all happy with it. Dance hall promoters expected the bands that they booked to play right through to eleven, sometimes as late as midnight, with maybe just a half hour break; it was rare for them to ever have a support band. They soon realised that with a sax in the line up they could extend the length of the numbers, having a guitar break and then a sax break. Most of their stuff was twelve bar blues, so it was easy and it helped them fill out show time for the first few bookings, whilst they worked on extending their play list. Frank brought a load of new numbers to the band and Carol also added a few ideas that helped. Stan, Barry and Bodkin were good musicians, so the five of them blended together quickly. The audiences certainly seemed to enjoy what they were hearing.

The acid test came at the Nostradamus, where the owner was a Greek Cypriot name of Andros Popolopolous. He was a martinet who got angry at any shortcomings, real or imaginary. He was also renowned for reducing fees on the spot if he wasn't happy. He had a reputation amongst the bands that played his club, they nicknamed him Mr Obstropolopolous.

The Bombastics saw him standing in the wings listening to their new line up intently and watching the audience reaction. After the gig he came onstage, whilst they were breaking down, grinning and laughing and shaking hands with all of them. He gave Carol a kiss on both cheeks. He also made a fuss of Frank, and behind his back, Bodkin gave the others the thumbs up. They'd cracked it. After the show old Obstropolopolous counted out their cash with a smile, but never went as far as giving them a bonus. That was expecting a bit too much!

They got to know each other during those early months. Carol was a very pretty girl and as Barry said, 'Bugger me, she's got all the right bits and pieces and gives that horn a right good honk.' For which he got a dead arm off Bodkin.

'You big twerp!' squealed Barry. 'You could have ended my career with a single punch.'

Stan, Bodkin, and Frank became very protective of her, particularly Bodkin. During those early months, as their popularity grew, any leering loony was summarily dealt with. Not just the kids out front, but any randy club manager or lecherous stagehand who fancied his chances undressing her, had Bodkin and the rest of the boys to answer to. When they saw the size of Bodkin, that usually sorted any problem; the other boys were rarely needed.

Yes, Barry tried his luck a few times early on of course, but eventually it became mostly innuendo, taken as a bit of a joke by everyone and Carol certainly never felt threatened.

'It's just Bugger-Me-Barry being a bit of a prat,' Carol would say, dismissively. 'Nothing I can't handle.'

There were times when he overstepped the mark, like farting in the camper. The last time he did that – and it was the last time – they were driving back from Worcester in torrential rain when he let one go that nearly flattened everybody. Bodkin opened the driver's window to try and clear the air and only succeeded in giving one and all a good soaking.

Carol's first reaction was to clasp one of the scatter cushions over her face, then she decided to batter Barry with it, shouting, 'Barry you're a disgusting pig!'

Bodkin eyed him angrily through the driving mirror. 'Listen shitbrain, if you do that in the motor again I'll break your neck, have you no shame doing that in front of Carol?'

'I didn't realise it was her turn,' guffawed Barry, predictably.

With that, Bodkin pulled into the shelter of a petrol station and stopped the motor. He hauled Barry out by the lapels of his jacket, and out of Carol's earshot. 'The last time I heard that joke was in Junior School. Listen carefully bollock-brain, if you ever let one go like that in the van again, I'll take great pleasure in shoving your head right up your arse. Okay?'

Barry spluttered, 'O-O-Okay. Scout's honour, I promise to keep my bum shut.'

They continued up the A38 listening to the Teen and Twenty Disc Club.

Despite this minor altercation, everything was fine between Barry and Carol, in fact he made her laugh on numerous occasions. It was Barry who first gave Carol the name Sugarlips. She'd just finished a stunning extended sax break during their encore at The Hearsay Club in Swindon when Barry stepped forward and shouted into the mic, 'Ladies and gentlemen, boys and girls, let's hear it for Miss Sugarlips!' The crowd went wild. He didn't know where it came from, it was entirely impromptu, but they all loved it, including Carol, and it stuck.

***

Tragedy struck Carol's life just as The Bombastics were starting to enjoy success. It was the summer of 1966. They'd had a string of hit records and been booked on a package tour with American star Johnny 'Swivel-hips' Turner, The Jaguars, and The Four Coins. The tour had been on the road for three weeks and was reaching its conclusion. They'd played the Palace Theatre in Carlisle and made their way back to the hotel on the tour bus for some well-earned sleep, before continuing their journey the next day on up to Glasgow, Edinburgh, and a grand finale in Aberdeen. Johnny Turner guaranteed a good crowd with his enormous Trans-Atlantic hit 'South Street Twist' and with both The Jaguars and The Four Coins as well as themselves, riding high in the charts, all the theatres were sell-outs.

They all disembarked the char-a-banc in front of the hotel entrance and when Carol collected her key from reception, she was also given a note on a hotel compliments slip. Just three words were written on it. 'Ring home. Urgent.'

A sense of dreadful foreboding gripped her; she took a faltering step forward and put a hand on the reception desk to steady herself. Stan and Bodkin were with her and they both moved quickly to support her. She handed Bodkin the note and both he and Stan took a quick glance. They followed Carol as she headed towards the pay phone, in an alcove over on the far side of reception. She stopped suddenly, closing her eyes she sounded bewildered, barely mumbling that maybe it was better to use the phone in her room. Stan and Bodkin guided her to the lift. Not a word was said as the lift rose to the third floor and they walked the short distance to her room.

She dropped her handbag on the bedcover and balanced herself on the edge of the bed, dialled for an outside line and then her home number. What followed was the most excruciating few minutes either Stan or Bodkin had ever experienced. They were hearing one side of the conversation, but it soon became obvious that this was grave news. They could hear that Carol was talking to

Mary, her mom, and she began sobbing almost immediately. Holding the telephone receiver in her right hand, with her left hand she emptied her handbag onto the bedcover spilling the contents willy-nilly over both bed and floor. She grabbed at her handkerchief that had fallen out and began dabbing at her eyes and nose. Bodkin could see the handkerchief was inadequate and rushed into the bathroom to grab the nearest suitable thing, a fresh hand towel off the rack. He placed it beside Carol on the bed. She snatched it up and buried her face and the phone she was holding, into it.

She was inconsolable. The howling, sometimes muffled by the towel, sometimes not, was pitiful.

Stan and Bodkin feared the worst and they were right. Dennis Meadowsweet, Carol's daddy was dead. He'd been killed in a road traffic accident, north of Stoke-on-Trent, travelling home from a concert earlier that night. His good mate, Richie Davison, trombone player, had also died and two others were badly injured.

It was a nightmare of the worst proportions. Bodkin stayed with Carol to comfort her as best he could, making tea she didn't drink and listening to her crying and pleading for the father she loved so dearly.

Stan went back to the room he shared with Bodkin to try and think straight and work out what to do for the best. He took a bottle of beer out of the mini-fridge, flicked the top off and sat on the end of the bed, thinking. He was totally devastated for Carol and Mary, for Michael too. They'd all got to know Dennis very well, such a lovely man and a marvellous musician who had given Carol so much love and guidance. His thoughts cartwheeled. *Jesus Christ was she going to miss that man!* They were all going to miss him.

Even in a crisis, Stan was a pragmatic character. He realised they had three more concerts to do, certainly Carol wasn't going to make them and he guessed the rest of the boys, including himself, would find it very, very difficult to continue, impossible in fact.

Stan decided to phone the promoter that night and thought it better not to ring Danny initially. He would have to be told, but it was better now to talk directly to the man in charge of the tour, so he could deal with matters immediately. Stan had a phone number in his diary. He put his beer down, still untouched, took his diary out of his inside pocket and flattened the book open on the bed at the appropriate pages with the palm of his hand. He didn't have anybody's name, just 'Star Turn Promotions'. The number rang out for some time, but Stan hung on; he took a swig of his beer and waited. Eventually a voice croaked some sort of greeting. On the line was a very unhappy chappy, clearly not pleased to be woken in the early hours, but he was soon sympathetic when he was told the story. He fully understood that Carol had to get home to her family and that it would be very difficult for The Bombastics to continue on the tour.

He'd phone Stan back before the char-a-banc left the next morning, just before lunchtime. It turned out Dave Johnson, the name behind last night's voice was Mr Star Turns himself, and he did a sterling job. Not only did he find a band to fill in for The Bombastics; The Thistledowns, a Scottish group very popular north of the border, he booked tickets for Carol and the boys, plus their instruments, home to Birmingham, first class, on the 11:35 that morning. He also arranged with the hotel to call two taxis to Carlisle station.

The Jaguars and the Four Coins were devastated when they heard the news. All of them had got to know each other well on this tour and it was clear their sorrow was genuine. Johnny Turner hadn't stopped overnight, but had travelled ahead the night before. When he heard, he telephoned the hotel and spoke to Stan – Carol was in too much of a state to speak to him. He too, was genuinely upset by the news and passed on his condolences.

It took Carol a long time to get over the death of her daddy. The tears and anguish during those sleepless hours in the immediate aftermath of her loss, turned to an aching and longing for the man who had been her inspiration all of her young life. There was one morsel of consolation she managed to wring out of her grief, and that was that Dad had enjoyed the success his daughter was having with The Bombastics. She knew he was very proud of their TV appearances on Ready, Steady, Go and Thank Your Lucky Stars, and of the hit records they'd once dreamed about. She remembered with her dad listening to Charlie Parker and Boots Randolph, and those early rock 'n' roll records, in what seemed only yesterday. She played Yardbird's records a lot in those sorrowful days. That helped her a lot.

Her mother and big brother handled their loss differently. They missed him, of course they did, but both threw themselves into work. Mary had worked part time at Lewis's, a department store in the city. She took on more and more extra hours, doing late night opening and covering for colleagues. When she was at home she was constantly on the go; when she wasn't moving furniture from one side of the room to the other, she was moving it back again. Michael, like his mom, buried himself in his work at the solicitors he'd worked at since leaving school. The senior partners saw he was working long hours and two or three of them warned him to slow down but he took no heed. It affected things between him and his long time girlfriend and eventually their relationship broke down.

***

The Bombastics also had a problem. They were booked in for a very lucrative summer season in Torquay and the boys realised that Carol was not yet ready to be Sugarlips again. They knew that the sax sound was a vital part of The Bombastics success. They'd all worked hard to get where they were and they knew that just a few months out of the public eye could prove terminal. As Danny reminded them; the show must go on. They needed a stand-in whilst Sugarlips got over her loss.

Micky Drury played sax in The Cherokees, a semi-pro band from Coventry they'd played with a few of times over the years. He was an unskilled worker, but a very skilled sax player. They had no direct contact number for Micky and despite what Barry suggested, it would be very difficult to, 'Bugger me, just phone their manager and ask for the bleedin' thing!'

Stan discovered The Cherokees were playing at the Phantom Coach that Thursday. He knew the layout of the place very well of course, having played there so many times. His idea was to keep well clear of the main entrance and the back doors where the bands unloaded their gear and slip in unnoticed through the side door that the staff used. He thought it might be a good idea to disguise himself a bit, so he nicked his dad's reading glasses for the night, borrowed Bodkin's leather bomber jacket, turned the collar up and greased his hair flat, adding a side parting.

Problem was the glasses put his vision out of focus and after he'd tripped over the steps, nearly breaking his nose against the staff entrance door, he took giant, uncoordinated steps like he was walking on the moon. Once inside, he stood for a moment getting his bearings whilst The Cherokees pounded out 'Shakin' All Over'. He then loped his way across the dance floor in the direction of the bar and deftly (he thought), sidestepped a group of girls dancing in a circle. His foot tangled in the clutch of handbags they were dancing around and as he toppled over, he grabbed out to save himself. She was a big girl. Not so much in height as width, but even she couldn't save him and they both hit the floor with an almighty thump and were left 'Sprawling All Over'.

The language certainly wasn't ladylike as she attempted to pull down her skirt and haul herself up at the same time;

but for the out of focus glasses, he would have had a panoramic view of the promised land.

He got up himself, garbled an apology and blundered on. As he stumbled into the bar, Stan peered over the top of his dad's glasses. He could see that things were busy and he made his way to the far end, quietly congratulating himself that no one had recognised him.

'Alright Stan, what'cher doing here tonight?'

Stan peered again into the dimness behind the bar and recognised Tommy Watson, who had taken up his usual position at the end of the bar overseeing his staff.

Tommy Watson was the Phantom Coach's manager, with whom Stan had a lot of dealings.

'You weren't supposed to recognise me, Tommy,' Stan mouthed almost silently.

'Well I wouldn't have done if it hadn't been for Bodkin's jacket,' replied Tommy. 'What's with the glasses and the George Formby haircut?'

'Okay, okay, you win.' Stan took the glasses off and shoved them into his side pocket. 'I just didn't want to be recognised.'

'Haaaa! Frightened of being carried off and molested by teenage girls with no morals?'

'Can you do me a favour, Tommy? Let me have the use of your back office for five minutes, will yer?'

'Sure, no problem Stan.' Tommy looked puzzled.

'When the Cherokees have their break, can you nip into the dressing room and tell Micky Drury there's a phone call for him in your office. Don't say a word about me.'

'Again, no problem. I can do that for you, Stan.' Tommy still looked puzzled as he lifted the bar hatch to let Stan through, but at no point did he ask Stan what it was all about.

Micky Drury came into the office clutching a bottle of beer and looking very apprehensive; there was a look of sheer relief when he saw Stan.

'I know you haven't got a lot of time before you're back on, so I'll come straight to the point, Micky,' opened Stan. 'You know we're without Carol for a bit, after her dad got killed...'

'Oh, that was such terrible news,' broke in Micky. 'Poor Shoogs.'

'Well we have a busy schedule coming up, including a ten week summer season in Torquay. The sound of Carol's wailing sax is such an integral part of our sound that we really need a stand-in.' Stan took a deep breath. 'We'd like you to be that stand-in.'

Before Micky could answer Stan handed him an envelope. Micky opened it, took out the folded letter inside and took a few minutes to read it. A smile gradually broke across his face.

Micky Drury tended to drift from one day-job to the next, so he jumped at the chance of playing professionally. As he put it so succinctly, 'A hundred quid a week, a summer season in a three star hotel, ten weeks or more away from the bleedin' missus. Where do I sign?'

Stan had to put Mick right. There was no three star hotel, it was a self-catering cottage that the theatre leased and he would have to take his turn to cook and to contribute to the groceries; also when Carol returned there'd be no more Bombastic work for him, he was on his own.

Micky thrust out a hand. 'When do I start?'

Stan shook his hand. 'Rehearsals tomorrow, there's no time to lose.'

The rest of The Cherokees were not at all happy.

'Probably hopping mad, but they'll just have to put on

a brave face and bury the hatchet when we get Shoogs back,' joked Barry, pretending to hop around the campfire hollering like a demented Red Indian. Bodkin gripped the back of his neck and squeezed hard until he promised to shut up.

***

Carol became Sugarlips again that autumn. After the summer season finished, The Bombastics had got studio time booked for recording. Their record company had extended their contract and they were working on a second album. They'd all kept in touch with her and visited her on their days off; particularly Bodkin, who would drive up from Torquay and back every Thursday when there was no matinee. He always took her flowers and very often they were tulips or roses, always from the big Esso garage on his way through Worcester. As the weeks passed and Carol began to recover she started to see the funny side of it, dutifully placing them in vases around the house, when mother came home she would move them. Even through her grief she could see Bodkin had one enormous crush on her. The rest of the boys spotted it too; they called Bodkin her guardian angel, but never let it go too far. Even Barry could see how delicate the road to recovery was.

They were delighted when Carol announced that she intended to travel down to London to record with them.

The Bombastics were back together again and more success beckoned. It would remain that way for a few more years yet, a few more years before disillusionment set in – and another tragedy struck.

CHAPTER 8
'THE JOKER'

The Steve Miller Band

Bodkin and Barry didn't know much about each other in their early months at Tanners Green Secondary Modern Boys'. Although they were in the same year, Barry was in a grade higher than Bodkin and Stan. Bodkin was aware of this kid who always seemed to be acting like a bit of a prat in the playground. He was a make-believe Teddy Boy, had his school trousers tapered to drainpipes and always wore fluorescent socks. He was even more aware of him when Barry joined the Fordrough Boy's Brigade; it was then he realised he was a lot of a prat.

Barry's dad, Paddy Harper had served in the Irish Guards and seen action in North Africa, Italy and Normandy. He was invalided out of the army after being wounded in Belgium, following the D-Day landings. Post-war Britain was a struggle for Paddy and despairing of his son's childish behaviour, he'd insisted Barry went along to Thursday evening Boy's Brigade meetings and 'learned some feckin' discipline'.

Bodkin was into his drumming and an active member of the Brigade's band. Barry, when he bothered to attend weekly meetings, was more interested in messing about and disrupting activities, much to the chagrin of an already harassed captain and his adjutant.

It was Brylcreem that brought them together for the first time.

During his short time as a reluctant member of the Boy's Brigade, Barry signed up for Lieutenant 'Porky' Smethurst's life-saving detachment. Bodkin had also signed up. So off this party of would-be life savers would go, with their trunks and pyjamas rolled up in towels and tucked under their arms, to catch the four o'clock Midland Red bus every Thursday afternoon. It was just a fifteen minute ride to the public baths in Redditch; there was a free red plastic bus token that got them there and back. Most of the boys had volunteered because it meant half an hour off school. That was certainly the appeal as far as Barry was concerned.

After six Tuesdays' training, every boy was able to plunge into the pool, swim a length of the baths in their pyjamas and dive to the bottom of the deep end to recover a house brick covered in rubber. The final part of the course, before they received their certificate and life-saver's badge, was to grab some unfortunate volunteer round the upper torso (instructed by Porky Smethurst to splash about as frantically as possible in the five-foot depth to impersonate a drowning man), and frog kick them both back to the side of the pool, without either of them drowning.

Afterwards, showered, towelled dry, and dressed, it was

preening time in front of the two available mirrors. Most of this life-savers detachment were young adolescents who'd recently swapped their neatly parted, short back and sides, for Pompadours like James Dean or Tony Curtis with a duck's arse at the back. It was the order of the day for all would-be Teddy Boys. One or two had even managed to cultivate something resembling sideburns.

However, it took time in front of the mirror with a comb and a palmful of Brylcreem to achieve the right results.

The black, white and red Brylcreem machine hung on the wall to one side of the mirrors. The square-chinned matinee idol embodied on the front of the dispenser smiled his greasy smile. He reminded Barry of Dan Dare, pilot of the future without his space helmet. A generation of Eagle reading boys would probably have agreed.

Bodkin and Barry found themselves at the back of the queue. Each boy slipped a large brown penny into the slot, held one hand under the nozzle and slowly pushed the slider home with the other, to squirt out a white greasy palmful. There were various theories amongst the boys as to how the maximum amount of Brylcreem could be extracted. Slide it in fast, slide it in slow, bang it in hard or treat it gently.

Only Barry knew the real answer.

Eventually Bodkin was next in line, but as he went to put his penny in the slot, Barry caught hold of his arm. Bodkin looked around; there was nobody else about, Barry was last in the queue. Barry winked surreptitiously, knowingly tapped his temple with his forefinger, then touched his lips in a 'sssh' gesture. Bodkin stood aside and watched as Barry wiped the nozzle of the dispenser with the end of his towel; he then took a deep breath stooped low and clamped his mouth around the underside of the nozzle. Bodkin then watched Barry take an almighty suck, his eyelids flickering with the effort. When he ran out of puff he stopped and stood up, his cheeks full.

He grabbed Bodkin's right hand, held it palm upwards and squirted a whole handful of the white stuff from between his lips; he then spat the remainder into his own hands. They both laughed heartily as they rubbed far too much Brylcreem into their hair.

'When did you learn that trick?' Bodkin was still chuckling.

Barry took a few minutes to answer as he was swilling his mouth out under the tap in one of the washbasins. 'A few weeks ago, when we first started coming here. Gotta be careful though, need to keep a watch out for old Adolf Hitler, the attendant. He nearly copped me last week, but I kept my mouth shut – ha ha!'

'I must have a tanner's worth of the stuff plastered on my head,' exclaimed Bodkin, carefully teasing his quiff with a blue plastic comb.

'Bugger me, and the rest!' laughed Barry, turning the back of his head to face Bodkin. 'Here, make sure me DA's straight, will yer?'

Sharing a gobful of Brylcreem was only the beginning for Barry and Bodkin; within a few weeks thanks to Mr Bell's Music Workshop and Lonnie Donegan, their lives would become inextricably linked.

***

The music teacher at Tanner's Green Secondary Modern was Mr Bell, or Ding Dong as they called him. He gave up his spare time for an hour and a half every Tuesday and bravely allowed his class of fourteen to bring along an assortment of instruments. As first years most of them brought recorders, but gradually one or two progressed to clarinets and cornets; there was even an old silver trumpet which looked like it belonged in an antique shop.

However, it was the second year of music workshop that turned out to be the year of the guitar. Battered old acoustics to begin with, but within twelve months, a few of the boys brought along electric guitars and tiny amps. By the end of year two, the class had risen to twenty. Barry and Stan chose to be guitarists after hearing Lonnie Donegan on the Six Five Special TV show and Barry, in particular (when he concentrated), showed real promise. Bodkin was the one exception to all the would-be music makers; he wanted to play drums properly. His drumming in the Boy's Brigade had given him the bug, and although he wasn't allowed to bring his Boy's Brigade drum home, he did sneak out a pair of drum sticks and Ding Dong Bell allowed him to beat out his rhythms at music workshop on a pair of tambourines. He also discovered desk tops gave super reverberation.

A few of the boys decided to start a skiffle group. Barry was the most accomplished guitarist and Stan's dad helped him make a tea chest bass which he could plonk away on (he also found he could pick out a simple bass-line on his guitar). Bodkin kept a beat going with his tambourines and a washboard he'd been given. They soon learned a set of popular skiffle numbers of the day.

Then the sound of rock 'n' roll started to come out of the radio; Luxembourg became essential listening to teenagers. The Fiesta cafe in the village became the Fiesta coffee bar and installed a jukebox, which had American singers like Elvis Presley and Johnny Ray on it. Stan and Barry could be found at the Fiesta coffee bar most nights drinking frothy coffee and putting as many American rock 'n' roll records on the jukebox as they could afford.

Then one night at the village hall, on Fordrough youth club night, this Teddy Boy came along and played them some rock 'n' roll, live. There was just him and his big acoustic guitar. He had neither microphone nor amplifier, but for an hour he belted out all the rock 'n' roll songs they knew and some they didn't. All the kids loved it.

After he'd finished Stan and Barry had a chat with him. His name was Martin Spilsbury and, despite him being six years older than them, they hit it off. He let Barry have a go on his guitar and when he played and sang 'Heartbreak Hotel', Martin was impressed. It was Stan who asked him if he was interested in forming a proper group with them. Martin said a proper group needed a bass player and a drummer, not to mention amps and mics. Now it was Stan's turn to borrow Martin's guitar and as he picked out a bassline on the first and second strings he could see Martin nodding approval. They then told him about Bodkin playing drums in their skiffle group and how he'd just bought a new drum kit on hire purchase. They added that Bodkin was now taking proper drum lessons; expensive too, but paid for by his mom and dad.

Martin was interested and suggested they all meet up next day at The Fiesta and discuss things.

A week later The Bombastics held their first rehearsal. Three weeks, and many hours of practice later, they made their debut at the Fordrough Youth Club's Saturday Night Hop. They shared the bill with Mrs Morris, who brought her gramophone and record collection; mainly Guy Mitchell, Perry Como, Frankie Vaughan, and Connie Francis. Mrs Morris also had a thing about Tommy Steele.

Later that summer they finished second in the Birmingham Parks 'Beat Group' competition. They'd won their heat at Ward End Park two weeks before and took a lot of fans from Fordrough along to Cannon Hill Park for the final, expecting to win. However, a group from north of the city calling themselves Johnny and the Avengers won. The Bombastics were disappointed but finishing second did them no harm. Their picture appeared in the *Birmingham Mail* and they used that, and the small write-up they got, to get themselves more bookings.

THE MAN WHO STOLE ROCK 'N' ROLL

***

As well as playing guitar, singing and having some very unsavoury habits, Barry Harper wrote one of The Bombastics biggest hits. The others often referred to their chief prankster as Bugger-Me-Barry. He was also the band's official sex maniac. He was the 'Anytime, Anyplace, Anywhere' man long before Martini's ad men coined the phrase.

One of his favourite tricks in the early days when he found a local groupie who wanted a private rock 'n' roll session was to hang one of those 'Do Not Disturb' signs he nicked from a hotel, around the door handle of the van. This served to really piss off the rest of the band when it came to trying to load the gear into the van, so they could go home.

When their opportunity for retribution came, it was sweet.

As the hits records started, so the demand for The Bombastics came from all corners of the UK and Europe, particularly Scandinavia. The VW camper van had served its purpose and was kept under wraps for local gigs and practice sessions; now it was taxis and hotels.

Opportunity came calling for Barry at The Don Hotel in Aberdeen. Barry had pulled with Angelfingers, a couple of voluptuous mini-skirted singers who'd opened the show that night. He bundled them into a taxi and back to the hotel, managing to sneak them passed the night porter who was busy struggling with a crossword behind the reception desk, into the lift and up to his room on the first floor. He then hung the 'Do Not Disturb' sign on the doorknob.

Bodkin, who was sharing room 101 with Barry, had heard him chatting the two girls up and decided he was having none of it. He gathered together Stan, Frank and Sugarlips in the dressing room and told them his plan. They all followed Barry back to the hotel in a second taxi, about half an hour later.

Bodkin took the 'MAKE UP MY BED' sign from Stan's room next door, crept along the corridor and switched the signs. There was a good deal of sniggering; quite loud too, but as there was plenty of noise coming from the other side of the door they figured they wouldn't be heard.

Sugarlips was watching from along the corridor and when Stan gave her the thumbs up she dialled hotel reception from the internal phone by the lifts.

'I've just returned from The Princes Theatre after giving my all to the good people of Aberdeen.' She was using her very best damsel-in-distress voice. 'I'm totally spent and very tired. I return to my room to find that the bed hasn't been made up and there are no clean towels.' It was 12:30 in the morning and there was only the night porter on duty.

The poor old feller, who was later identified as one Sid McGarry, was very apologetic. 'I am so sorry, lassie, may I take your room number and we'll sort out the wee problem right away.'

'Room 101.' Sugarlips replied.

There was a pause, whilst McGarry checked the hotel register. 'There seems to be a wee error, so there does. I have a Mr Adams and a Mr Harper sharing this room.'

Sugarlips' tone changed. 'I can assure you Mr Night Porter, I am in room 101, on my own, very tired and wanting to get to bed. Furthermore I'm not responsible for silly errors made by your receptionist when we checked in.'

Sid spluttered, 'Aye, enough said, lassie, I'll be right along.'

He could have had a heart attack racing up the stairs to the first floor, getting the service trolley with clean towels, sheets and pillowcases out of the storeroom, and wheeling it along to room 101. Stan and Frank were in room 103 with Bodkin and Sugarlips next door in room 105. Both doors were ever so slightly ajar as Sid wheeled on by.

'It's just a shame there's nobody with a cine camera to record this,' said Stan, trying hard to stifle another snigger.

Breathless, Sid McGarry knocked on room 101, pushed his hotel master key into the lock and in one arthritic move barged the door open and backed in, pulling the trolley with him.

When he turned, he would later tell his wife, Mary hen, that he couldn't imagine how three people could be joined together in so many places at once.

Mary hen gave him a faraway look and continued her knitting.

Barry managed to get all the profanities he knew; and he knew plenty, into one sentence of joined up bawling. The girls screamed, grabbing at sheets and counterpanes trying to cover themselves up. One darted for the bathroom.

Sid choked out a sort of apology, did a quick reverse, and made off back down the corridor at great haste. A set of sheets he'd loaded onto the trolley slipped off and tangled around one of the rear wheels, sending the trolley into a side spin and tipping the whole caboodle over, scattering clean laundry, packets of sugar, coffee and little tablets of soap all over the hotel Wilton.

Barry never used the 'Do Not Disturb' manoeuvre again.

***

Then there was the incident in a bitterly cold Rochdale. They'd played The Imperial in the Lancashire mill town and had a really good night. Barry had done his usual trick of picking out a likely looking girl in the front row of the audience and making eye contact. This night he came up trumps. She was a stunning twenty-something, with dark backcombed hair, lightly hair-sprayed into a beehive. She wore a tight white dress that looked like it had been painted on. As The Bombastics' set neared the end he mouthed to her to come backstage after the show and slipped one of the security guys a ten shilling note to get her through the door at the side of the stage.

It turned out she was in her mid-thirties, married, and her husband was out of town on business. After a bit of snogging and heavy petting in the dressing room she suggested, rather than come back to The Bombastics' hotel, that Barry went back in her car and stayed the night at her place. Barry couldn't believe his luck. When they left by the stage door, she told him to wait right there on the pavement and she'd get the car from the car park across the road and pick him up. She was gone just a few minutes and returned in a magnificent white and chrome Mercedes.

Rather than go back to the hotel to change Barry stayed in full stage regalia; his powder blue zoot suit and white Cubans.

They travelled at some speed out of town for about four miles, turning down a country lane, eventually pulling into the driveway of an impressive yellow stone and cherry wood bungalow. The garden that Barry could see in the Merc's headlights looked picturesque, almost magical, with trees and bushes white with frost stretching as far as he could see.

Inside, the bungalow was tastefully and expensively decorated and Barbara, as she'd introduced herself on the drive home, poured him a scotch and Coke from a well-stocked bar, then left him for a moment to peel off her little white dress and get into something loose, low-cut and flouncy. She also let her hair down to tumble over her shoulders. Barry nearly choked on his drink when he saw her sweep into the room. It looked like there would be no holds barred that night... and so it was to prove.

Next morning at the hotel, Stan and Bodkin sat near

the breakfast room window that overlooked the town square. It looked bitterly cold out there, windscreens of parked cars iced over, early morning workers wrapped up in scarves and gloves; in fact there were one or two snowflakes falling. In front of them was the town centre bus terminus. One bus followed another, pulling in and disgorging morning passengers.

Frank joined them at the breakfast table, soon to be followed by Sugarlips. It wasn't long before the conversation turned to Barry. He was due to double up in a room with Stan.

'His bed hasn't been slept in; he hasn't been in the room all night.'

Bodkin remembered. 'Last I saw of him he was all over that girl he brought backstage, the one with the dark hair wearing a skin tight white dress. He was right down her throat at one point.'

Frank put down his coffee. 'I heard him arranging to be picked up at the stage door.'

'Going back to her place,' continued Stan. 'You can imagine what he's been doing all night...'

Sugarlips broke in. 'Spare me the details boys.' She busied herself pouring orange juice.

Stan was about to take a bite of toast when he suddenly dropped it back onto his plate. He half stood up and shot out an arm, his forefinger pointing through the window towards the bus shelter.

'Just look over there.' He was grinning from ear to ear. They all turned to look out of the window and across the square.

A number 27 bus had pulled into the terminus. Workers were pouring off it, their breath billowing on the cold morning air. Everyone wrapped in overcoats, many with their collars turned up, the menfolk in caps and the womenfolk in hats and scarves. All, that is, except one. There in the middle was Barry in his light, powder blue Bombastics polyester zoot suit, shocking pink shirt and white Cuban heeled boots. He too had his collar turned up and he was blowing into his cupped hands in an effort to keep warm. What the Rochdale workers made of him as he crossed the square and up the steps into the hotel, God only knew.

It appears Barbara got an early morning phone call from her husband.

'Jesus Christ!' she screamed as she shot out of bed and stepped into her knickers. 'Mick's meeting's been cancelled; he's on his way home and has stopped at a garage in Heywood to get petrol.'

'Who's Mick and where's Heywood?' Barry, cigarette dangling from his lips, was about to light up.

'He's my husband and it's less than half an hour away and don't you dare think about lighting that fuckin' thing!'

'Bugger me.'

Barbara was dressed, had the bed stripped, down the stairs and into the Hoovermatic before Barry had his Cubans on.

She checked round the house for unfinished drinks and nub ends. The Scandinavian rug was straightened, cushions plumped up and placed back on the sofa. She double checked the bathroom, gave the toilet an extra flush and then unceremoniously bundled Barry into her car, without so much as a cup of tea and drove out of the gate and down the lane, to the junction with the Oldham Road.

'Get out here, the bus stop's over the road.' She leant across him and opened the passenger door.

'You can't just dump me here, it's bleedin' freezing,' Barry pleaded, his hands gripped tightly together almost in prayer.

'OUT!' she shouted and grabbed a handful of coppers and silver from the ashtray next to the glove box in between them. 'Here's some change for the bus, catch the number 27; it'll take you right into town.'

Barry half waved goodbye, but Barbara totally ignored him, did a three-point turn and sped off back up the lane, leaving Barry to wait over half an hour on a cold and frosty morning for a very embarrassing twenty-five minute journey, during which he managed to avoid making eye contact with anybody.

CHAPTER 9
'WAYWARD WIND'

Frank Ifield

A Thursday night gig was not to be sniffed at, particularly at the Phantom Coach which The Bombastics considered home turf. Bodkin's brother Wally had come along that night, mainly to see if he could pull, but because of the atrocious weather, attendance was less than half the normal turn out and pickings were slim, so he didn't. As it was Barry's turn behind the wheel, Bodkin and Stan decided to get a lift back to Fordrough with Wally, leaving Barry with just Frank and Sugarlips to take home.

Waiting until they were alone, Bodkin cornered Barry in the car park, both ankle deep in freshly fallen snow, and grabbed him by the top toggle of his duffle coat. 'If you so much as try and lay a finger on Carol, I'll pull your bleedin' ears off,' he growled.

Now Barry was not foolish and he was not about to give a man, far too tall and far too broad for his own good, any of his smart remarks; not when he was being pulled in that close he could still smell the liver and onions Bodkin had eaten for tea.

'Trust me, Bodkin, Shoogs will be delivered home safe and sound and untouched by human hand.' Barry looked up at Bodkin, the malfunctioning blue neon of the Phantom Coach sign flickering on his face making him look even more fierce. 'Can you, Stan and Wally give us a push out of this snow and onto the road?'

Sugarlips was the last one Barry dropped off that night; he saw a glimpse of her thigh as she slid off the passenger seat, then remembered Bodkin's warning. As he pulled out of her road for the eight miles he had to drive home, he reached underneath the dashboard and flicked the radio on. The familiar green glow lit the cab and as always it was tuned in to Radio Luxembourg. Roy Orbison was warbling 'Only the Lonely'. The reception wasn't good, it never was on 208 Luxembourg, but this was more crackly than normal.

It's probably all to do with this bloody weather, thought Barry.

It had snowed in early December, deep and crisp and because of drifting, not very even. Snow like he'd never seen before. Over a foot of the stuff round by them and then it had drifted in the gale force winds, causing chaos all over the country. Local councils weren't ready for it; they'd managed to keep the main roads open, but some of the side roads were still blocked weeks later.

It was now the beginning of February and snow still covered hedges and trees, meadows and hillsides as far as the eye could see.

If only it'd get above freezing for a few days and start to thaw some of the damned stuff. Barry kept a firm grip on the steering wheel. The road had been gritted, but it was starting to freeze over and there was quite a strong wind still blowing snow off the fields.

Having only passed his driving test a few weeks ago, he took it very steadily, one of the few sensible things Barry managed to achieve. Being one of the drivers meant picking up and dropping off the rest of the band and that inevitably meant some untreated side roads were going to be encountered.

God help us if it snows again, falling on top of this lot, we'll all be right in it. The snow AND the shit. He smiled grimly to himself.

That's when the first flakes started to drift down out of the heavy sky. There was no moonlight and not a single star twinkled, so Barry guessed there might be a lot of snow up there in those clouds.

He made his way carefully along the main road until he came to an intersection, where he would turn left into Drovers Lane and pick his way across country and back to Fordrough. This road had been okay for most of the last few weeks, the farmers tending to keep it clear using their tractors, but visibility was definitely getting worse. The flakes were coming down faster and they were big ones too. Turning left into Drovers meant there was now quite a strong side wind blowing from his right. He was beginning to feel quite claustrophobic. Were things conspiring against him? The flakes fell faster and the wind picked up to gale force.

'Shit, shit, shit, shit, I can't see a bloody thing!' Barry shouted at the VW, he was starting to panic. 'I'm gonna have to stop.' He was now doing no more than ten miles an hour and the windscreen wipers were hardly coping.

If I remember rightly, there's a small lay-by not far along here, he thought to himself.

***

He remembered rightly of course, he knew perfectly well there was a lay-by not far along there. He'd been parked in it last month with Jenny Bosworth spread-eagled across the back seat, trying to get her underwear off. That was the first time he'd been trusted to do the driving on his own and a week or so before the snows came. Jenny was one of The Bombastics camp followers and she'd treated Barry to her favours a number of times before.

'Yer wastin' yer time, and anyway it's too flippin' cold for that sort of nonsense in the back of a van.' Barry took no notice. 'What sort of girl do you think I am, any road?' Fighting desperately to keep his left hand from up her skirt, his right hand from undoing the buttons of her blouse, and his tongue from down the back of her throat, all at the same time.

'I know exactly what sort of girl you are, sweetheart,' he'd leered, trying to grab another handful. 'Remember?'

She'd given him a sharp smack across the cheek which had made him sit bolt upright. 'You don't get it do you?' She poked him angrily in the chest. 'It's not just the cold, you dimwit, Aunt Flo's come visiting.'

Barry had looked at her blankly to begin with, then the penny dropped. 'Bleedin' hell,' he groaned.

With that he started the engine and headed back to Fordrough.

***

He continued his conversation with the VW. 'It must be just about here – no, not yet – bugger this snow!' he cursed through gritted teeth. The road and hedgerows were almost a complete whiteout, especially through windscreens that were hardly kept clear by the wipers. Snow had already built up quite a ridge covering the grass verge and he only had this to keep him from going down the ditch on his offside, or careering over the white line, which he knew was buried somewhere out there in the middle of the road.

Then, through the flakes, he spotted the litter bin that hung from a post at the back of the lay-by. Instinctively he jerked the steering wheel left, and praying he wouldn't hit either the litter bin or one of the trees that lined Drovers Lane, he skidded the camper to a halt. He checked in the wing mirrors, as best he could, to see if he was all tucked in. He didn't want another car, or worse still, some lorry crumpling up his back end, especially with him in it.

He was well inside the lay-by and although it was difficult to see through the offside wing mirror, there'd been no crunch so he hadn't hit the litter bin. He blew a sigh of relief, turned off the engine, closed his eyes and flopped himself back in his seat.

Radio reception was poor but he heard someone say the midnight news would follow Frank Ifield. Soon Frank was yodelling his latest chart smash 'Wayward Wind' from the radio, as a strong gust of wind shook the camper.

Barry opened his eyes with a start. *Thanks Frank, your timing's immaculate, pal!*

Barry knew he'd just have to sit this one out. He had the heater blowing some warmth into the cab and the radio for company. He never gave any thought that he might flatten the battery.

If he had, that thought wouldn't have mattered anyway.

Radio Luxemburg was still fading in and out, so Barry leaned forward to see if he could improve reception. He gently tweaked the tuner knob edging the needle each side of Luxemburg 208, but Barry Aldis either crackled or faded completely. He scanned the dial. *No point in trying Moscow or Budapest, they probably won't have heard of Elvis Presley, never mind Frank Ifield!* Then he spotted Hilversum. *The Dutch like British pop music… I read that somewhere in a magazine.* He twirled the knob sending the needle across the dial. *Hilversum, here we come.* There was Frank still singing about that Wayward Wind.

Strange! That's some kind of coincidence, Frank Ifield singing Wayward Wind on two stations at the same time!

The green light of the radio that had been gently glowing and winking started to turn white, bright white. There was a sudden brilliant flash.

'Bugger me!' he screamed, half blinded by the incandescent glow, as he flung himself horizontally across the passenger seat.

The next words he uttered would be twenty years later.

CHAPTER 10
'WE GOTTA GET OUT OF THIS PLACE'

The Animals

'And here on Wonderful Radio One is The Jam's chart topping 'Beat Surrender'', a voice blared out from the radio tucked underneath the dashboard.

Barry turned his head sharply. *Wonderful Radio One? And what the hell is The Jam?*

That wasn't Barry Aldis either. It was somebody calling himself Mike Read.

The bright white light coming from the radio dial was gone; it glowed the familiar green, but that wasn't the light that Barry was concerned about.

Daylight was streaming through the windows.

It wasn't snowing and night had turned into day. He could see through the windows that he was no longer in a lay-by and there were no snow covered trees or fields and no snowdrifts. Instead the VW was parked in a narrow street with Victorian red brick buildings towering up either side three stories high, four in places, as his eyes followed the curvature of the road until it disappeared out of sight two hundred yards, maybe two hundred and fifty yards, ahead of him. On the other side of the street, immediately opposite, two yellow parallel lines were painted in the gutters. These ran for fifty yards either way, and then there were cars parked nose to tail inside bays painted in white lines on the tarmac.

Bugger me, where IS this?

Next to every parked car, a grey pole rose out of the pavement; on the top of each pole was some sort of triangular box. Barry guessed these were the parking meters that he knew had started to appear in London. He'd read it in some newspaper and heard it on the news, that they intended to roll these parking meters out into cities like Birmingham and Manchester, but these were the first he'd ever seen.

He groped around for the driver's door handle, opened the door, and slid out of the driver's seat. He walked over the road to the nearest meter and peered through the little glass window; just as he did there was a whirr from behind the glass panel, then a tiny yellow flag clicked across the screen. It made him jump and he gulped nervously.

The first car parked in front of him on this narrow street was a low-slung sports model with a maroon, metallic paint job. He didn't have a clue what it was, until he spotted the manufacturer's name and logo on the radiator grill as he crossed the road. Audi Quattro. It looked new and very expensive. It also looked high-performance. Parked in front of it was a silver four-door saloon. He could see the badge on this one too. It had

Saab Turbo across the front grill. On the windscreen in large white letters were the names 'JEZ' and 'LIZZIE' in large white letters. Barry had heard of Saab, they made cars in Sweden. He guessed 'JEZ' and 'LIZZIE' must own it.

Barry crossed back over to his side of the road and gave closer inspection to a dark blue saloon parked quite tightly up against the rear end of his VW Camper. On the radiator grill he could see a circular red, white and blue badge and written across it the word Datsun. Was that the make of the car? He'd never heard of it.

Barry was totally confused. *Where the hell is this place? A street I don't recognise, full of cars with designs, body shapes and colours the like of which I've never seen before. This cannot be happening!* He'd always considered himself a pretty laid back character, but this was bizarre and it unnerved him.

He turned his eyes to the building he was parked outside. There was a green roller shutter door, above which was a black plastic canopy with the word 'Pandora's' written in gold. There was a matching gold fringe running around the bottom edge; in places it was either hanging loose or missing. The whole thing looked shabby and rather the worse for wear. To the left there was an alleyway, and a few yards up it were steps, with a hand rail leading to a metal door also painted green. It was slightly ajar, so from the angle Barry was at, he was able to pick out a sign saying 'Artists only'.

How could I be in a snowdrift in a country lane in the middle of the night one minute and the next be in, well here, wherever it is and whatever time it is? Is this some kind of dream? Bugger me! He punched his forehead with the heel of his palm.

An icy cold wind blowing down the street was a sharp reminder that this wasn't a dream. He pulled the hood of his camel coloured duffel coat up over his head, as he tried to collect his thoughts.

From out of the green side door next to the loading

bay came a guy, mid thirties, maybe older. Barry thought he was dressed rather strangely. He wore a dark grey padded waterproof jacket zipped up to the neck, around which he'd wound a grey knitted scarf. As he turned sideways-on to descend the steps, Barry could see his hair was long, with a mullet style at the back. At first Barry thought it was a trick of the light, but yes, he definitely had blonde streaks in it.

What sort of bloke puts blonde streaks in his hair?

Despite there being no sun, he wore black sunglasses. His blue jeans looked faded and had rips in the knees; they were tucked into black ankle length leather boots with deeply serrated soles. When he saw Barry standing alongside the camper with the driver's door open, his face turned to a scowl and he shouted loudly, his breath clearly visible on the cold air, 'Oi… whatcha doing in our van?'

Barry was nonplussed. 'Your van? What are you talking about, this is our van?'

By this time, Sunglasses was right in his face and looking very angry. 'Trying to nick it were you? How the fuck did you get into it anyhow?'

Now a second figure emerged through the green door. He looked younger than Sunglasses and a lot shorter. He was dressed all in denim and his hair was long, too. It was jet black and was cut jaggedly around his forehead and cheeks, emphasising what a pasty face he had. He paused to light the cigarette he had dangling from his lips. As he turned, he saw the ruction developing between Sunglasses and Barry and used both arms to vault over the handrail straight onto the pavement. He appeared to land awkwardly, but then Barry could see as he steadied himself, that on his left boot, protruding from the bottom of his jeans, he wore a leg iron. He hobbled across the pavement half hopping, half limping to stand alongside Sunglasses. Barry couldn't help but think of Chester, Matt

Dillon's sidekick in Gunsmoke. The two of them crowded Barry, pushing him back against the driver's open door, both getting very aggressive.

Barry was a lover not a fighter; he was also a quick thinker, and dangled his bunch of keys in front of them. 'Here are the ignition keys, and look, my house key is on the same key ring. So you reckon I'm trying to nick my own camper? Well not exactly mine, the camper belongs to The Bombastics.'

'Bombastics? Who the hell are The Bombastics?' sneered Chester. 'And that could be any old set of keys.' He turned to Sunglasses. 'Let's see if they work, Billy. Get him to start the motor, but let me get in the passenger seat first, just in case he tries to do a runner.' He limped his way around the camper van and climbed onto the passenger seat.

Close up, Barry could now see that Chester's jet black hair was out of a bottle and that he had tattoos on his throat, neck and the backs of his hands. Incredibly, to Barry, he wore black mascara around his eyes, and was that face powder he was wearing? He also had a silver ring in one of his ears and a matching one through the side of his nose.

Barry had met his first ever Goth.

As Barry sat in the driver's seat, he could feel himself shaking. *What if the key doesn't fit, so many strange things are happening!* It took him three attempts to slide the key into the ignition. *Bugger me, this is barmy,* he thought. *Get a grip; you're making yourself LOOK like a thief.* He pressed the starter button and fired up the engine.

'That don't prove nothing,' growled Chester. As he tried to grab the keys Barry was too quick for him, pulled them out of the ignition and gripping them tightly, slipped his fist into the side pocket of his duffle coat, as he slid back off the seat and onto the pavement.

Billy Sunglasses grabbed hold of the top toggle of Barry's duffle coat and screwed his grip to pull him close in face to face. It hurt, it was certainly tight and just a twist away from strangulation, Barry thought.

A gleaming silver saloon glided to a halt next to them. Barry spotted the familiar Jaguar mascot on the bonnet, but it was no Jag design he'd ever seen before. The window of the driver's door was already down and the suntanned face of a blue-eyed, handsome, thirty-something looked out on the confrontation. 'What's going on here, then?' From the tone of his question he clearly knew these two.

'This finger 'ere's trying to nick our motor.' Billy Sunglasses' grip loosened.

'I've tried to explain that this is our van,' protested Barry. 'I've even showed them I've got the keys to it. Look!' Barry pulled his fist out of his pocket and shook the keys defiantly.

'Jez, hang on there a minute; don't let Billy do anything stupid and we'll sort this out.' Blue-eyed handsome man checked his rear view mirror and pulled the convertible back into the centre of the street, parking it in the first space available, a hundred and fifty yards away on the opposite side. Barry watched him put money in the meter and walk back. He was dressed in a loose-fitting white linen suit. Like Billy, he had long hair in a bouffant style with a mullet and blonde streaks. As he approached, he was knotting a black woollen scarf around his neck. He crossed the road and Barry could see the hint of a friendly smile breaking around his lips; something of a relief after the bellicose attitude of his mates.

He offered a hand to Barry. 'Hello, Robbie Rochester. It appears we have a bit of a disagreement here.'

Barry took his hand. 'I'm Barry... Barry Harper.'

Normally a confident character, Barry looked lost and

unsure. 'Look, something really weird is going on here. I'm travelling back from a gig around midnight, get caught in a snowstorm, pull into a lay-by to wait for it to ease up and the next moment I'm sitting here.' He looked around almost helplessly. 'I ain't got a clue where I am, and to top it all I'm being accused of stealing my own van by Laurel and Hardy here.'

Robbie Rochester was silent for a moment, fixing Barry straight with his blue eyes. Barry could have found this intimidating, but there was something calm and reassuring about his manner and the way he spoke, unlike the others who'd undoubtedly been one step away from redesigning his face.

Robbie Rochester clapped his hands together and blew into them. 'We can't stand out here in this temperature arguing the toss. Let's go inside, it seems we need to talk.' Robbie ushered Barry up the steps and through the green door. The others trooped in behind them.

Inside, it was quite dark; there was concealed lighting, by which Barry could see they were backstage in some club or theatre, maybe a restaurant. They entered a small vestibule which led to two small dressing rooms. Robbie walked on, pushing through black tab curtains and into the wings of a small stage, from where Barry could see a dance floor surrounded by tables and chairs, some free standing, some fixed in alcoves. This was a club. At the far end of the room was a bar where a young guy was clinking glasses and bottles onto shelves. Either side of the stage Marshall amps were stacked; hanging from the ceiling directly in front of them was a lighting rig which was all in darkness. As his eyes became accustomed to the darkness, Barry made out a drum kit, keyboards, guitars on stands and three microphones, each on a stand. They descended four steps at one end of the stage, walked across the dance floor and took seats around one of the tables, dimly lit by the concealed lighting coming from the bar.

Barry still felt very disorientated and, yes, a bit frightened; he hoped it didn't show. His mind wandered, when would the others realise he'd gone – his mom would be the first to miss him, she didn't normally stay up waiting for him, but he knew she was nervous about him being a tenderfoot when it came to driving in snow and ice and she'd be all ears awaiting his arrival home – she'd be bound to call the police when he didn't arrive home, but how the hell would they find him? He looked at the faces around the table. He didn't like Billy and his little mate Jez, and had Robbie Rochester lured him into some sort of trap in this club?

Robbie untwirled his scarf and tossed it onto one of the chairs. 'Sit down,' he said. 'Take your coat off if you want.' Barry kept his hands in his duffle coat pockets and sat down.

'Would you like a cup of something? You can have something stronger if you like.' Robbie nodded his head towards the bar. 'You know you don't look well.' Then before Barry could answer, 'Jez, see if you can rustle up some drinks, maybe a pot of tea or some coffees.' Jez, got back up, hobbled around the bar and said something to the young barman; they both disappeared through the door at the far end of the bar.

Robbie turned to Barry. 'I was intrigued to hear you say you'd been gigging. Was that in a band?'

'Yes, I play guitar in The Bombastics,' said Barry. '...Look, what is this place?'

'You mean you're in a band and you don't know Pandora's?' It seemed Billy was still determined to take no prisoners. 'All the bands know Pandora's, including the crap ones.'

Robbie gestured for Billy to shut up, which is what Billy did, but not before adding, 'Any road up, I ain't never heard of no Bombastics, neither.'

Jez returned with four cups without saucers on a tray, half a bottle of milk and a bag of sugar with a teaspoon standing up in it. He put them all down on the table.

'Coffee, thanks Jez, that'll do nicely; I see we've spared no expense on getting out the best bone china tea service,' said Robbie and plucked out the teaspoon. 'Do you take milk and sugar, Barry?'

'Look, I'm not really sure I want one,' answered Barry.

'You're looking a bit washed out,' said Robbie. 'Probably do you good.'

'Okay, just a drop of milk and two sugars.'

Robbie poured milk in all four cups and added sugar. 'If you were in a heavy snow storm last night, you must have travelled some distance. It's been bloody cold round here, but there's been no snow.'

'Nearest was up in Yorkshire,' interrupted Jez. 'I listened out for this morning's weather forecast 'cos we're up that way on Saturday night, just outside Sheffield.'

Barry closed his eyes, almost as if he was in pain and slowly shook his head from side to side, 'No, this was south of Birmingham, near Redditch.' He could feel panic rising; he stopped and waited for a few seconds to regain control, then continued. 'There's something seriously wrong here — is this Birmingham? I honestly have never heard of Pandora's. I'm not even sure I know what day it is?'

'Ha! We catch you trying to nick our motor and now you're saying you can't remember anything?' sneered Billy. 'Oldest trick in the book, pal. How come you don't know it's Birmingham? If it's your van like you claim, you must've driven here, right?'

Barry banged his fist on the table in frustration spilling tea out of the cups. 'That's just it, I told you, I *didn't* drive here. I was sitting in a bloody lay-by in the middle of the night, not an hour ago!'

Robbie put a hand on Barry's arm to calm him. 'Yes, it is Birmingham; we're right in the city centre, Pandora's is in the Gas Street basin. There's music here most nights, but it's the weekends that pull the crowds. A few of us have played here regularly for the last few years and the owner, Tony Mendoza, lets us practice for free as long as we help young Micky tidy up the...' he trailed off. 'Are you feeling okay?'

Even in the dimly lit club, Barry looked ghastly.

Robbie moved Barry's cup to save further spillage. 'Maybe you had a bang on the head in that storm of yours and lost track of time.'

Barry blew out loudly, vibrating his lips and ran his hands through his hair. 'No, there was nothing like that. I parked the van up without any trouble, no bumps or anything like that.'

He looked into the distance between Robbie and Billy, clearly trying to concentrate. 'I remember trying to get a decent signal on the wireless, reception on Luxembourg was even worse than normal, so I'm twiddling the knob trying to find another station. Then all of a sudden there's a flash of white light; blinding it was. Next thing some bloke on the wireless is spouting on about Wonderful Radio One and playing something called Jam. Daylight's streaming through the window and the snow's gone.' He stretched his fingers over his eyes and garbled through hands. 'God, I didn't realise how implausible that was going to sound until I actually said it.' He lowered his head almost to the table.

Robbie's eyes narrowed. 'You say Radio One and The Jam like you don't know of them.'

Barry lifted his head, he looked confused. 'No, should I?'

Robbie flopped back in his chair. 'Radio One's only the

biggest national radio station and The Jam are only the biggest band of the eighties and now Paul Weller has announced they're disbanding and he's moving on. And you say you've never heard of them!'

Barry sat bolt upright. 'What did you say?'

'What, about Paul Weller disbanding the Jam?' asked Robbie.

'No not that bit.' Barry took a deep breath. 'You said the eighties. What do you mean by the eighties? The date? The *nineteen* eighties?'

Now it was Robbie's turn to look confused. 'Yes, what else would...?'

Barry held a hand up to silence Robbie. 'What date is it today?' There was a distinct crack in his voice as he asked the question.

Robbie looked at Billy, then at Jez for confirmation. 'It's February the eighth today, isn't it?'

Billy and Jez both nodded.

'Yes, but, *but what year?*' pleaded Barry, almost shouting.

'1983, of course,' answered Robbie.

Barry slumped forward over the table on his elbows. Even in this light they could see that any colour he'd had, had completely drained away. He stared ahead of him, and the look in his eyes was one of terror. His mind was whirling; voices drifted in and out of his head, but they were faint and seemed far away.

Robbie moved to the chair next to him. 'Barry, are you okay?'

'Barry, what's wrong?'

'Talk to us Barry.'

'BARRY!'

'He's in some sort of fuckin' trance.' Was this concern from Billy?

'He's taken something, popped a pill or been on the weed?' sneered Jez.

'Look Jez, you're not helping, maybe best you go and finish setting up. The boys are gonna be here anytime soon.' Robbie waved an arm towards the stage.

Jez shrugged, rose from his chair and departed. 'Only saying what I thought, why else would he come out with a load of bollocks like that?'

Robbie waved a hand up and down in front of Barry's eyes.

Nothing; not a blink, not a twitch.

'I don't like this at all.' Robbie gave Billy an anxious look.

'Barry. Barry, listen to me. Barry try a sip of your coffee.' Robbie pushed the coffee mug back in front of him. There was still no response. 'It's like he's comatose, and look at his eyes he's just staring; he looks terrified, this can't be right.'

'Maybe Jez was right,' said Billy. 'Maybe he has taken something.'

'I think we better call an ambulance,' said Robbie, again moving the coffee out of harm's way.

'It was you saying 1983 that spooked him?' said Billy shuffling in his chair. 'What I'd like to know is why is he dressed like my old dad? I mean, who wears a duffle coat these days, and what about all that Brylcreem in his hair?'

Robbie stood up and put his hands on his hips. 'You're right and how come a kid of his age – what is he? Eighteen? Nineteen? Who claims he plays guitar in a band, has never heard of the Jam and calls the radio a wireless?'

Barry's catatonic state was at odds with the maelstrom

going on inside his head – the broken, flickering neon sign of the Phantom Coach – Bodkin, ankle deep in snow, threatening to pull his ears off – Sugarlips' thigh as she slipped out of the camper. A kaleidoscope of images raced through his head – a starless, moonless night – swirling snow blowing against the windscreen – the green glow of the wireless – Frank Ifield yodelling – Luxembourg, Droitwich, Hilversum – a dazzling, blinding white light – 1983 – 1983 – *1983* –

'*1983!*' screamed Barry, thumping the table hard with both fists and spilling coffee out of the cups again and this time nearly knocking the milk bottle over.

Robbie, who had started to move away from the table to make that call, quickly turned back. 'Barry, can you hear me?' Robbie bent over him clasping his shoulders.

'1983,' he repeated, but this time it was more of a sob.

Barry's eyes started to focus on the lighting around the bar, then his gaze darted from table to coffee cup and finally met Billy's stare. He became aware of Robbie's grip and half turned.

'Blimey, you had us a bit worried there, welcome back to planet Earth?' said Robbie.

'You said 1983?' Barry's voice was no more than a rasping croak.

'Yes, 1983,' answered Robbie. 'Why do you ask?'

'See I told you – 1983,' Billy whispered loudly out of the side of his mouth.

Robbie put a finger to his lips to silence Billy.

Barry drew his right knee up underneath his chin and hugged it against him, locking the heel of his shoe on the front of the chair. He stared ahead; his eyes were wild, his words slow and quiet, but precise. 'We'd done Thursday night at the Phantom Coach. We were surprised they hadn't cancelled the gig because of the snow. There was a poor crowd, but it was a shitty night. We'd gone down really well, the new line up was getting better and better. It's one of the few mid-week gigs around is the Phantom Coach. Afterwards it was my turn to drop everyone off.'

Barry paused, almost as if he was double checking himself.

'Like I told you, I was on my own and the snow got that heavy I had to pull into a lay-by. I was tuned into Luxembourg, reception was awful and I could hardly hear anything, but I remember they said it was just coming up to midnight and the news would follow Frank Ifield's latest smash hit. When the snow started it was Thursday February 7th 1963. By the time the news came on it was going to be Friday February 8th 1963.'

He repeated, '**NINETEEN SIXTY THREE.**' Not quietly this time.

There was silence.

Robbie sat down in the chair next to Barry. 'You're hallucinating, that was twenty years ago. There has to be some explanation.'

Robbie suddenly snapped his fingers. 'Barry, who's Prime Minister?'

'Harold McMillan,' he replied without hesitation.

Robbie looked at Billy, then back at Barry. 'Harold McMillan? We've had a few Prime Ministers since Harold McMillan. No, it's Margaret Thatcher.'

'Margaret? A woman Prime Minister?' Barry clutched his head with both hands in anguish and screeched, 'God, what is happening? How did I get here?'

Robbie pressed on. 'What do you know about the Falklands War?'

Barry shook his head clearly distressed. 'Nothing –

bugger me, nothing at all.'

'Have you heard Michael Jackson's album, *Thriller*? Did you know Italy beat West Germany to win the World Cup last year?'

Barry shook his head again, slumped forward on the table, amongst the puddles of cold coffee and let forth a pitiful whine.

Robbie was lost for words.

Billy had taken off his sunglasses and was chewing one of the stems thoughtfully. 'Have you got the log book for the camper, or your driving licence?'

'Yeah, of course, your driving licence!' Robbie sat up, slapping the table. 'Well done Billy.'

Barry shifted in his chair, whilst he untoggled the front of his duffle coat and fumbled about inside the breast pocket of his jacket. He brought out a brown leather wallet and pulled the contents out onto the table. From amongst a small wad of bank notes and other pieces of paper, Barry picked out a small red book with a crown and the words 'Driving Licence' printed in black on the front cover. He opened the little book up and smoothed it out flat on the table in front of him. After taking a glance at the details printed on the open pages, he slid it in front of Robbie.

Robbie studied it. His eyes grew larger as his mouth slowly opened to a gape.

'C'mon, what's it say, then?' Billy didn't try to hide his impatience.

Robbie picked the little book up and read, 'Barry Patrick Harper. Date of birth 24th July 1944. Hereby licensed to drive a motor vehicle from 31st October 1962 until 30th October 1965 inclusive. God help us, what you've been telling us is true.' Robbie's words faltered slightly. 'Somehow you're twenty... you're twenty years ahead of your own time!' He shook his head in disbelief.

Billy only seemed to have half taken this bombshell in. 'I remember these when I was a kid.' Billy had picked up the wad of notes and fanned a dozen or more green one pound notes and a couple of blue five pound notes on the table. 'My old man's still got some of these in a sideboard drawer. I mean just what the fuck is going on here, time travel or what?'

'As I live and breathe, it's Doctor soddin' Who. Ask him where he's parked the TARDIS.' Jez was stood behind them. Robbie wasn't quite sure how long he'd been there, but he'd obviously heard enough.

Billy pointed a finger at Jez. 'Stop taking the piss, you little gothic twat, we've got a problem here.'

'Be still my flippant tongue,' laughed Jez. 'I just came to tell Robbie the boys have arrived; they're in the car park.'

Robbie turned to Barry. 'I don't really know what's happened here, there's a lot for *us* to take in, so God knows how you must be feeling. We need time to think this through.'

There came the sound of voices from backstage. Barry stared at four silhouetted figures pushing their way through the long black tab curtains and onto the stage. Robbie turned quickly to glance at the stage; when he turned back Barry was still staring straight ahead.

'Barry you're going to have to give me an hour or two, I got things I must attend to; they're very important to me and the rest of the boys.'

'Look, there has to be an answer to this, you don't just get propelled twenty years into the future. Think about the VW Camper, could that be the connection? You say it's your bandwagon and I certainly know it's ours. I can't believe I'm saying this, but maybe it's the link between two worlds?'

Barry didn't react; his eyes were empty.

'Look, this is my band that have just arrived, and there's stuff I have to go through with them.' Robbie put his hand on Barry's arm. 'Relax, if that's possible, I'm only a few yards away and Billy's right here to look after you. I need Jez to do some sound balance; you're a musician, you'll know, I have to get everything right.'

Robbie started to walk towards the stage, then stopped and turned. 'I know it's easy for me to say; you're the one who's in the wrong place at the wrong time, but you must try and keep calm. Remember, if there was a way in, there has to be a way out.'

Barry swayed back in his chair, he still looked like shit.

Robbie confided in Jez as they moved away; nodding towards the stage. 'Keep this to ourselves for now, I'll tell this lot Barry's some long lost cousin.'

CHAPTER 11
'LISTEN TO THE MUSIC'

The Doobie Brothers

There was a lot of laughter onstage as the four members of Robbie's band took their places.

'What's amusing you lot?' questioned Robbie, as he mounted the steps and up onto the stage in two bounds.

Twitch, the tall blonde lead guitarist, so called because of his curious contortions when he broke into a solo, was pulling the strap of a shiny pink Fender Stratocaster over his shoulder. 'Lenny was saying to steer well clear of O'Leary's Cafe for a week or two, especially his Paddyburgers.'

Lenny, the bass player and drummer Titch were still chuckling and through the black tab curtains, Robbie could hear his keyboard player Chaz chortling too.

'Sorry, you've lost me,' said Robbie. 'O'Leary's Paddyburgers, what's so funny?'

'Haven't you heard about Shergar?' replied Twitch. 'Been nicked from his stables over in Ireland.'

'What, Shergar the racehorse? The Derby winner?'

'The very one. The bloke on the radio reckons it could be the work of the IRA.' Twitch was plugged in and shaping chords.

Lenny cut in. 'You know Tich's penchant for O'Leary's grub; whenever we're coming home from gigs anywhere Sutton Coldfield he just has to divert and pull over; he just can't help himself.'

'Maybe it's 'cos it's the only bleedin' place open at that time of night!' shouted Titch from behind his drums.

'I've never been sure what he puts in those burgers,' continued Lenny. 'With his Irish pals, we could end up eating a Shergarburger instead of a Beefburger.'

Cue more chuckles and Chaz's grinning black face appearing through the tabs. 'You're a sick man Lenny Croft.'

'Not a chance, that'll never happen in England, it's the Frenchies that eat horses,' said Robbie, ignoring their twisted humour and picking up his guitar.

'Frogs and snails too!' Titch shouted again, pulling a gurney.

Robbie didn't have time for this. 'C'mon now, let's get going with this run through, I got some urgent business to attend to after this.'

Chaz was now at his keyboards, unravelling leads and connecting up into the mixer, Lenny had his bass already connected and was tuning up loudly. Titch the diminutive drummer was diddling, paradiddling and crashing cymbals.

Robbie plugged his Fender into one of the Marshall

stacks. There were a few minutes of tuning up, snatches of riffs on guitar and bass, some boogie-woogie piano and then rinky-dink organ and more paradiddles from Titch as they all settled down.

'Okay.' Robbie held both arms aloft. 'Let's get this balance right… Jez are you ready?' Jez was sat behind the sound control unit placed on a table over to the left of the stage. He raised a hand to acknowledge he was.

'Let's run through 'Warwickshire Girls' to warm up, then we must concentrate on the new stuff for Friday.' Robbie turned to his drummer and counted him in. 'One, two, three, four…'

A loud, driving rock sound filled Pandora's. There was a catchy keyboard riff before the vocal came in and as the song progressed, the same keyboard riff became even more catchy as it was repeated and repeated throughout the number. The lyric took a well-worn path; the tale of a man who travelled the world, saw many sights, loved many girls and probably sailed the seven seas, but whose heart would always belong to Warwickshire and the girls that lived there.

Robbie's singing had a rough edge to it, but it was powerful and very tuneful. By the time they'd half played it, stopped and half played it again, then got right the way through it, Jez had got the balance right. From behind the main mixer, he put both thumbs up to Robbie.

'You can't believe it, can you? That's still in the charts, that is,' said Billy. Barry jumped; he'd almost forgotten Billy was still next to him. 'Dropped a few places last Sunday, but it's had a bleedin' good run. Should've been a number one; would've been too if it wasn't for that 'Down Under' crap. Aussie tosspots!'

Barry had hardly heard 'Warwickshire Girls'. Part of him was far away from Pandora's.

He turned towards Billy to try and refocus and his attention was caught by his wallet and the contents spread across the table in front of him. There was his cash that Billy had left fanned out next to the wallet; his driving licence still lying open in front of where Robbie had been sitting. However, it was Danny Hoffman's business card that caught his attention, poking out amongst a number of oddments; a couple of petrol receipts, a copy of the VW insurance and scraps of paper with telephone numbers hastily scribbled down in hotel rooms. He stretched across and picked it up. Yes, there it was, Danny's phone number. *Why didn't I think of that before?*

'Is there a phone here?'

'Yeah, of course there is.' Billy rocked back on the rear legs of his chair and jerked his thumb towards the door behind the bar. 'It's in there, go through to the office.'

Barry left his chair and was round the bar and through the door in seconds. He'd grunted something about using the phone to the young barman, who was on his knees filling up the bottom shelves with bottles. He'd given Barry a cursory glance, pointed towards an open doorway and carried on with his stacking.

Why Billy followed Barry, he wasn't sure. Maybe he'd thought Barry was going to run off. *What if he does? So what? Just a problem we don't need out of the way. There again, he does still have the keys to the camper; don't want him taking that for a test drive.*

He found Barry leaning forward, arms locked straight at the elbows with the heels of both palms on the edge of a desk and still holding the business card between finger and thumb of his right hand. He was staring down at a cream coloured telephone with a look of utter puzzlement on his face.

'What's up?' Billy stood in the doorway and Barry slowly turned his face towards him.

'There's no letters, there's no dial, it's just buttons with numbers on them.'

'What do you mean, no letters?'

Barry held the business card towards Billy. 'I was going to phone our manager, Danny; but how can I with just these numbers?'

Billy took the card and immediately saw the problem. 'Daniel Hoffman. Telephone BAYswater 7351.'

'Blimey, we went all numbers years ago.'

Barry closed his eyes to try and clear his mind. He wasn't going to panic; he'd done that once and had no desire for a repeat performance. His head was spinning with self-pity and fear but he had to control it.

Get a grip, Barry Harper. Surely Robbie was right, if there was a way into this strange time warp, then there had to be a way back. Maybe it is the camper, maybe it's the wireless; could it be something to do with that Hilversum station? I need to get back inside that van, that's where the answer lies, that's how I arrived here. But what will I be looking for? Some kind of doorway with a sign saying '1963 – Step right this way'? – Hardly!

Billy might be the problem when it comes to rooting around in the VW. I still don't think Billy trusts me, I certainly don't trust Billy. I need to keep control, wait for Robbie. Now I do trust Robbie? Well I hope so!

Keep calm Barry Harper, and like I said… GET A GRIP!

Billy watched him open his eyes, stand up straight and throw back his shoulders. He then patted both side pockets of his duffle coat with open palms and sighed, 'I must have left my fags in the VW. You don't have a spare smoke do you, Billy?'

'Yeah, but I warn you now, Robbie doesn't like anyone smoking in his vicinity, he reckons it messes with his vocal chord.'

Billy took a packet of Gold Leaf out of his jacket pocket and tossed them over to Barry. Barry's face was a picture of surprise as he caught the packet. 'What are these?'

'Fags. That's what you asked for wasn't it?'

Barry had never seen Gold Leaf before and when he flipped open the lid he knew he'd never smoked tipped cigarettes before. He knew of cork-tipped of course, actually tried them, but never filter-tipped. He didn't say anything, took one, and drew in deeply after Billy had given him a light from a green, plastic lighter. He exhaled. It wasn't half bad.

'Let's go and listen to some of the music.' He strode past Billy, chin out, and led them both back to the table next to the dance floor. Billy eyed him suspiciously.

The band seemed to be polishing up three numbers. To Barry's Bombastic ear, it all sounded pretty good, but he could see Robbie wasn't entirely happy and they went back and forth over parts of each one until he was satisfied.

Barry was enthralled and it helped him put his worries to one side for the time being. What struck Barry was the overall sound. It was different to anything he'd heard before and the difference was definitely the sounds coming from the keyboard player. Here was a guy, Chaz Packer, who was quite flamboyant, throwing his head back and forth and waving his arms around as he stroked the keyboards to produce these harmonics, even though this was no more than a practice session.

'Those keyboard sounds are great, I've not heard anything like that, your guy seems to be playing two keyboards at the same time.' Barry was far more composed now.

'That's the synthesiser, pal,' said Billy, keeping a deadpan face. He'd also lit up a cigarette.

Barry didn't have a clue what a synthesiser was and he

guessed Billy knew that too.

Billy blew out a cloud of smoke; it was blue in the half-light of the club as it drifted up into the blackness of the ceiling space. 'Robbie's always banging on about them sounding too electric, like Depeche Mode, but that's crap, they sound nothing like 'em.'

Billy knew that Barry wouldn't have a clue who Depeche Mode were either, but he carried on regardless. 'Too much of a perfectionist is Robbie, never satisfied, going over the same old things, time and time again. After a bit it starts to get on yer tits.' Billy flicked ash from his cigarette into the ashtray. 'There was no need for all this lot today, dragging the boys in to go over the numbers yet again when they were perfect last week. It's us, too – me and Jez. I was on a promise with one of the waitresses from here, been working on her for weeks; wouldn't have had a problem there, I can tell yer. Now I'm stuck here babysitting you whilst Mr Fussy goes through his repertoire yet again.'

Robbie was stood right behind him. It hadn't registered with Billy that Robbie had finished singing and left the stage. He'd left Jez and the band starting to pack their gear away.

Robbie coughed and began. 'If Mr Fussy gets things wrong next Monday and as a consequence, 'Warwickshire Girls' makes me a one hit wonder, we won't have need for an underused and overpaid roadie, will we Billy?' Robbie waved a hand in the air to waft away Billy's cigarette smoke. 'And how many times have I told you about smoking those bloody things when I'm around?'

After Billy's warning, Barry was pleased he'd finished his and already stubbed it out in the ashtray.

Robbie turned to Barry. 'How're you feeling now? You seemed to be listening quite intently to what we were playing. Did it help take your mind off things?'

Careful not to let the temperature rise again, Barry checked and took a deep breath. 'It's still very difficult, I thought I was going off my head at first, but I've given it some thought, I have to stay strong and just hope you are right; if there was a way into 1983 there has to be a way back out. It's no good getting myself into a state, I have to try and keep cool and try to trace things back. I liked your music,' he continued. 'I did listen to a lot of what you played and yes, it helped. Loved it in fact. It's a different sound to the one we make, but the style's aren't a million miles apart. What was that Danny and the Juniors sang? 'Rock 'n' Roll Is Here To Stay'.

'What's that, one of your nineteen-fifty-frozen-to-death songs?' scoffed Billy, still smarting after his dressing down.

'Make yourself useful Billy, help Jez get the gear packed away.' Robbie took a chair opposite Barry. 'Monday's important for us, we need to show Chekka that first record wasn't a fluke. I think I've written two or three songs that should please them, anyway.'

'What's Chekka?'

'It's our record label; you've not heard of them?'

Barry shook his head. 'No, look, sorry Robbie, it seems to have all been about me. Billy told me a bit about you; that you've got a record that's still in the hit parade.'

'Hit parade? Blimey, that's what my mom calls the charts.' Robbie couldn't help but smile. 'Sorry, no offence. Yes, 'Warwickshire Girls' was a surprise hit really. It'd been released for over a month and nothing was happening, then John Peel started playing it every night on his radio show and it just took off. Now comes the challenge of the follow up. Problem was, the record company weren't sure about the other songs I'd recorded at the same session as 'Warwickshire Girls'; said they were more suitable for the album we're doing. They wanted some new stuff by next Monday which gave me less than three weeks. It's been a heavy time, especially with all the extra engagements coming in because of the hit, but I think we've done it.' Then looking over towards Billy he said, 'Though there are those amongst us who don't fully appreciate that.

'The boys prefer 'Bar Room Brawl', but I reckon 'Broken Hearted Nobody' will be our follow up. It was actually on the original demo tape that I sent out to everybody last year, but I rewrote part of it and we've slowed it down a bit, made it a bit more plaintive. I think it's the best thing I've written and with a bit of luck the Chekka boys will like the new version.'

"Broken Hearted Nobody', that's the slower one, right? The one you kept going over. Great hook line, very commercial, I'd say. 'Bar Room Brawl', that's the rocker. You could see the boys liked that one, they really tore into it.' Barry paused for a second. 'I said boys, I don't even know the name of your band.'

'The Robbie Rochester Band. When I got some interest in my songs, I put the band together from guys on the circuit, guys I'd been hanging out with and we went down to Chekka records and cut some tracks. Never gave much thought to a band name, Chekka said they wanted my name on the label, so we kept it simple, hence The Robbie Rochester Band.'

Robbie looked across at the guys packing away onstage. 'Twitch and Titch were with me in a previous band. Lenny was playing bass with the Ramrods for years.' Then laughing, he said, 'He may even have been around in your time. I found Chaz playing keyboards in a soul band; he came down to the audition at Chekka and just sort of stayed.'

'Billy and Jez were with me in the original band too. Despite his grumpy demeanour, Billy's actually reliable and very loyal. Jez is brilliant with the mixer.'

Robbie broke off and shouted across to Jez, 'Have you got any of those demo tapes we did?'

'Somewhere here!' Jez shouted back. 'I'll bring one over.'

Robbie's voice quietened. 'You said you'd given some thought to how you got here?'

'Even more to how I can get back,' said Barry ruefully. 'Like I said, I thought about your idea of getting back the way I got in. It has to be something to do with the camper, or more probably that wireless. I was trying to find a decent reception on the dial between Luxembourg and Hilversum and that's where that blinding white light came from and everything went bananas.'

'Sorry, you've lost me. I understand wireless, another of me mum's favourites, but Luxembourg and Hilversum?' That smile was playing on Robbie's lips again.

'They're two of the stations worldwide you can pick up on the dial, along with others like Warsaw and Brussels and Moscow; you must have seen them on the wireless in the VW, have a look! Luxembourg is the only place you can pick up non-stop pop.'

Robbie shrugged and shook his head. 'Yeah, I've seen them on the dial, but the camper is Billy's territory and he never tunes in to them, it's all Radio One, Capital and other local stuff, which, incidentally are all non-stop pop.'

Jez appeared at the table. 'Here you are Robbie, one of the cassettes you wanted.' He slid the little tape along the table to Robbie, who in turn slid it across to Barry.

Barry picked it up and studied it with wonder. 'It's a little reel of tape.'

Jez grinned. 'I guessed you wouldn't have seen anything like that before, it'd all be reel to reel in your time. Anyway I've got something here to help.' Jez brought his left hand from behind his back and produced a small grey and silver box, with wires hanging from it. 'You'll be able to listen to your little reel of tape on this; it's called a Sony Walkman.'

Robbie took the Walkman from Jez, untangled the straps and wires, then took the cassette tape back from Barry. He clicked a button on the side of the little machine and a flap on the front of it popped open. He pushed the cassette into the aperture and shut the flap with his thumb.

Barry was fascinated.

Robbie picked up a tiny set of earplugs on one end of a long black lead coming from the Walkman and handed them to Barry. 'Stick those in your ears.'

Very tentatively Barry pushed them in and when Robbie clicked another button Barry visibly jumped, startled at the sound so loud and very clear. Once he was over the shock he recognised the song as 'Warwickshire Girls'.

Robbie mimed for him to watch whilst he manipulated the controls. Slowly and deliberately he pressed stop – then play – then fast forward – then fast backwards – volume up (Barry cringed) and finally, volume down.

He pushed the Walkman over the table to Barry who gingerly picked it up. Carefully at first, he pressed the buttons, stop, play, eject – the flap popped open! He looked helplessly at Robbie, who leant across the table and snapped the lid shut again. Fast forward, fast backwards, soon Barry was like an eight-year-old at Christmas. He ejected the tape, pushed it back in and snapped it shut like Robbie had showed him. He pressed play and nodded his head to the music in his ears.

'Okay?' Robbie mouthed, putting two thumbs up.

'YEAH, THIS IS BRILLIANT!' shouted Barry, far too loud, the music pounding in his ears.

Robbie smiled at Jez.

They left him to it and made his way over to the boys in the band, who were now on the point of leaving. He called Twitch over to the front of the stage.

'It sounded good to me, we're gonna knock 'em out on Monday.' Robbie's voice darkened as he half whispered. 'Keep Packer off the white stuff, if he cocks up in that recording studio, his Yamaha and the shiny chrome stand he puts it on will enter a dark place he'd never have believed they'd fit into.'

'C'mon Robbie, it's not all down to me. You're there too!' complained Twitch.

'You tell him, Twitchy boy,' Titch the diminutive drummer boy cackled from the back of the stage.

'How's yer long lost cousin, Robbie?' Titch continued. 'Still lost in space?'

'What d'yer mean by that?' Robbie glowered, but not at Titch. That was aimed at Jez and his big mouth. Jez was shuffling back and forth, busy coiling up leads and plugs and pretending he didn't hear the conversation going on less than five yards away.

Robbie returned to Twitch. 'See you tomorrow. We need an early start on Monday, so no partying after the Sheffield gig; we need to get back pronto and get some rest on Sunday. I reckon we should meet up at Corley services for 7:30 a.m. in case there's hold ups on the M1, you know what it can be like on a Monday morning.'

CHAPTER 12
'NEW KID IN TOWN'

The Eagles

Barry switched the Walkman off, took the earplugs out, stood up and shouted across to the stage. 'Do you want some help with that lot?'

Robbie was sliding amps, drums and guitar cases to the back of the stage, Billy and Jez were starting to hump some of the larger pieces out the back and into the car park.

'Always do with a lift!' shouted Billy, one of the long black side tab curtains sliding off the speaker he was carrying as he passed through it.

Barry saw this as an opportunity to open up the camper and see if The Bombastics' gear was still in the back of it. *That'll blow away any doubts that even Robbie might be having.*

Barry slipped the Walkman, tape and all, into his duffle coat pocket and crossed over the dance floor to lend a hand. He picked up the snare drum case, tucked two collapsed mic stands under his other arm and grabbed the handle of the case holding the cymbals.

The VW stood exactly how he'd left it. Jez waddled ahead of him lugging a heavy Marshall amp in each hand.

Bugger me, he may have a dodgy pin, but he's a strong little sod.

Jez put them down on the pavement whilst Billy slid open the side door. Barry put the snare drum down by the amps and peered over Billy's shoulder. He was aghast to see it was empty, save for a blue metal toolbox and a set of jump leads which weren't his anyway. He also saw to his horror that the back seats had been ripped out.

'Jeezus where's all our gear gone?' he uttered, clearly distressed; he tottered forward and put his free hand on the camper's bodywork to steady himself.

By this time Robbie had joined them. 'Don't freak out, it doesn't mean you've lost it all. There's a lot of weird things going on; I don't have an explanation, but maybe your stuff just didn't pass through time with you.'

But for the moment Barry couldn't think of anything that made sense, all he pictured was those expensive VOX amps and guitars, Sugarlips' sax and Bodkin's drums dumped in the lay-by in a swirling snow storm getting buried deeper and deeper, or worse still, scattered along a time-tunnel like from a lorry gradually shedding its load along some cosmic carriageway.

'I need to look in the front,' gasped Barry, pushing past the others and making for the driver's door.

Jez and Billy both looked at Robbie. 'Leave him,' he said, catching Billy by the shoulder as he moved forward to grab Barry.

Barry took the keys out of his pocket, had the driver's

door unlocked and was inside in a jiffy. He took a deep breath. The radio with its familiar half-moon dial was still there. Barry blew out a long sigh of relief.

By this time Jez and Billy were at the passenger door and Robbie was at the open driver's door. Barry slipped the key into the ignition and switched it on. He then turned one of the black knobs on the radio. It clicked, lit up green and the sound of the Carpenters singing 'Yesterday Once More' filled the cab. Another sigh of relief. 'Thank God for that, it's still working okay.'

'Course it's bleedin' well working, it's been looked after, pal,' snapped Jez, jabbing a finger towards the radio. 'That wireless, as you called it, is a collector's item.'

Barry started to twist the tuning knob, cutting Karen Carpenter off just as she got to the part where they're breaking her heart. A succession of stations came and went. Pop music, classical music, English chatter, foreign chatter. He turned the knob slowly and deliberately, not rushing in case he missed that vital hot spot.

Robbie could see the expectation in Barry's eyes. 'You're searching for your escape hatch, aren't you?'

Barry didn't answer, but by the disappointment appearing on his face it was evident.

Robbie continued. 'It may be more than just a frequency on a radio dial. It could be the time of day or night. It could be weather systems, it could be the influence of the moon or the sun. It could be a combination of any of them.'

Barry didn't answer.

'Maybe you gotta turn round three times, scratch yer arse and shout Abracadabra.' Jez remained straight-faced as he put a cigarette between his lips and lit up.

Barry didn't answer.

'You two, go and get the rest of the gear loaded and get that bloody thing away from me.' Robbie grimaced and waved a hand in front of him to blow away the trails of smoke being drawn across the cab and over to his side.

Barry had now twisted the needle right across to the other side of the dial. He tutted his exasperation, twisting the knob back and forth over the Hilversum station, but this time not so slowly or deliberately.

'Barry, this just isn't working, for whatever reason. Let's go and find something to eat, you must be starving, I know I am.' Robbie gave Barry a friendly slap on the shoulder with the back of his hand and stepped back from the VW. 'We'll go in my car, let's leave the boys to load up.'

Barry hadn't given food a thought. The fact was, it was hours since he'd eaten. Mom always fussed over him eating properly; this time she'd almost stood over him whilst he ate the shepherd's pie she'd cooked specially so he'd have something hot inside him before driving all those miles in the snow and ice. *Thank God you did, Mom; that was at least four hours before the Phantom Coach gig.*

Then he thought again. 'Bugger me, the last time I ate was over twenty years ago,' he chuckled to Robbie, in spite of himself.

Robbie understood the humour and chuckled too.

Robbie shouted some instructions to Billy about making sure young Micky locked up; he was struggling down the steps with another speaker. His reply was inaudible, which, from the look on his face, was a good job. Robbie then ushered Barry up the street and over the road to where he'd parked his Jag. As they stood by his car he read Barry's thoughts.

'Don't worry we're not taking that escape hatch of yours away, Billy's bringing the VW round to my place tonight. When it's loaded up with all our gear, my garage is the safest place.'

Barry half turned to look at the camper one more time, shrugged, and opened the passenger door to get in. He was impressed with the Jag's soft leather upholstery as he settled into his seat.

'Clunk Click every trip,' said Robbie, hooking the seat belt with his thumb, extending it in front of him and clicking the tongue into the buckle. 'You need to put your seat belt on. It's the law.'

Barry twisted to his left found the seat belt tongue on his side, pulled the belt around him and fastened it into the buckle.

'It's a new law, you can't get away with it now,' said Robbie, starting the engine. 'Mind you, I've been wearing mine for years.'

They drove to the top of the street and turned left at the T junction onto a main road that Barry recognised. 'This is Broad Street, right?'

'This is Broad Street, that's correct.'

'Bugger me, it's changed — well some of it has, anyway. I recognise those shops and that pub over there, The Westward Ho!' Barry pointed to his right. 'There's the Royal Orthopaedic Hospital. I visited my old man when he was in there having his leg done; an old war wound from the D-Day landings. He never talks much about the war, but Mom said he was never the same after he came home and I know he was very bitter about the way he was treated after fighting for his country.'

The lights ahead turned red and they pulled to a halt. Robbie said nothing and there was an awkward pause. As they moved off once again Barry broke the silence. He gestured with his thumb through the passenger window. 'This furniture shop Lee Longlands was here, but other buildings have changed completely.'

'There's plans to change even more,' said Robbie. 'They're building a massive indoor arena behind the library and the Hall of Memory. It'll have all the big shows and sporting events, probably rock concerts as well. All part of a plan to create a pedestrianised square, apparently.'

By this time they'd reached Five Ways and Robbie swung left, down what was to Barry, a new dual carriageway. They sped through two or three sets of green traffic lights and then slowed down and moved into the far right hand filter lane where there was a red.

'The Bristol Road! We use this road a lot to get to bookings north of Birmingham. On our way up through Selly Oak and Northfield, are we?' asked Barry.

'Not as far as that.' Robbie negotiated the lights which had turned green, waited his chance and did a sharp U-turn across Bristol Road into the car park of McDonalds. 'Don't expect you've seen one of these places before, eh?'

Barry shook his head. He took in the brightly lit red and yellow frontage and the Golden Arches, all very unfamiliar to him. 'This was the Bristol cinema last time I passed this way. Bugger me, it can't be that long ago I saw Elvis in King Creole!'

'We'll you won't find him in McDonalds, but there's a guy works down the chip shop swears he's Elvis.' Barry looked blank.

Robbie smirked to himself. *How's a kid from 1963 going to understand that? Best not try and explain that one.*

Robbie led him to a table in the window. 'Be easier if you leave this to me; you take a pew.' With that he made his way to the counter.

Barry untoggled his duffle coat, slid it off and lay it over the empty chair next to him. He looked around at the plastic and Formica tables and chairs. The only other people this side of the counter were a young couple with a toddler in a high chair; there appeared to be more food on the floor than in his mouth.

Well out of range, over here, fortunately.

Five minutes later Robbie returned to Barry with a strange assortment of polystyrene cartons on a tray. Robbie pointed to each in turn. 'There's a Big Mac in that one, French fries in that one and coffee in the cup with the lid on it – be careful you don't scald yourself on that!'

Barry lifted the carton lid and took out the Big Mac. 'It's a beef burger. The square meal in a round bun!' He took a big bite.

'I think you'll find that was Wimpy, not McDonalds, but you've got the right idea.'

'What did you call these? French fries? They're just thin chips.' Barry picked up three or four and pushed them into his mouth, then carried on the conversation with his mouthful. 'They're alright, though.'

'You're catching on.'

McDonalds might have been a new experience, but Barry was hungry and he soon wolfed down what was in front of him without another word. Robbie took his a bit more steadily.

Both fully fed, they had chance to linger over the coffees, which were still very hot.

Robbie, watching Barry very closely, began, 'I know not finding the right frequency on the radio pissed you off and I'm sorry I was rather busy, but we can concentrate fully now on what the hell has happened. Maybe it was a combination of things at the same time that brought you here. Three o'clock in the afternoon is a lot different to midnight and even though you could see neither, the sun and the moon have entirely different influences, not to mention the weather... Snowing quite heavily, you say?'

Barry swilled the coffee round his cup. 'More like a bloody blizzard.'

'Then there are the planets; what are we in, Aquarius?' said Robbie. 'When the moon is in the seventh house and Jupiter aligns with Mars...'

Barry cut across Robbie before he burst into song. 'If you're meaning Horoscopes, I don't believe in all that mumbo jumbo.'

'I wouldn't rule anything out at this stage. Another thing to consider is location. You say you were south of Birmingham, somewhere near Redditch, yeah?'

'Yes. In a lay-by in Drovers Lane.'

'Well, it's something to think about, put a few of those things together and Hey Presto! Back to the Swinging Sixties you go.' Robbie made jazz hands and rolled his eyes.

'Why do you say *swinging* sixties?' asked Barry.

Robbie slapped his forehead. 'Sorry, I'm being dim. You came here from February 1963; all the fun hadn't really started then, had it? Man, are you in for a surprise when you get back home, Beatles, Stones, Flower Power, Woodstock, the summer of love, sex and drugs and rock 'n' roll. 1963? You don't realise what's about to hit you!'

'You said Beatles, you mean the group from Liverpool?'

'Only the biggest band on the planet.' Robbie was in full flow now. 'Believe me, you've got a lot ahead of you. Sixties music, sixties fashion, sixties culture; President Kennedy, Bobby Kennedy and Martin Luther King all assassinated in the States.'

It was all too much for Barry to take in at once.

'In 1969 the Yanks had men land on the moon,' continued Robbie.

Barry looked astonished. 'Bugger me, that sounds as

likely as Britain having a woman Prime Minister; what was her name again?'

'Maggie Thatcher, but that wasn't during the sixties, that was much more recent; just over three years ago, in fact.'

'When did these come in?' Barry had taken the Walkman out of the pocket of his coat on the chair next to him and put it on the table between them.

'Cassette tapes have been around since the middle sixties. Walkmans came on the market during the seventies, but even they're on their way out, we'll soon have something they call the Compact Disc.' Robbie spread the fingers and thumbs of both hands to form a sort of circle. 'About this size they are, and they hold over 20 songs.'

'What, both sides?'

'No, the ones I've seen only have one side.' Robbie looked at his watch. 'Hey, we better get moving or Billy's going to be there before us. We can talk more on the way.'

They grabbed their things.

Robbie pulled left out of the car park and turned towards the city centre. 'We're heading for my place in Solihull, but I'll take you the scenic route and let you see how Brum's changed. To be honest, I can't remember when the Queensway, the Aston Expressway and Spaghetti Junction were finished. Maybe you'll recognise them.' Robbie flicked his right indicator and steered his Jag into the centre lanes that led down and underneath the traffic island they'd been approaching. 'Here's the Queensway, duck your head and tuck your elbows in.'

Birmingham was busy at this time of day and the light was just beginning to fade. Robbie turned on his headlights, and with the rest of the early evening traffic in those two lanes, passed under the city centre.

'Bugger me, all these tunnels weren't here, that's for sure.' Barry was wide-eyed. 'I remember seeing plans in the newspapers for a big motorway junction and people saying it looked like a giant bowl of spaghetti, but it certainly wasn't built, well not that I remember anyhow.'

'That's coming up in a few miles. This is the link road to it.'

Now the road changed from a two lane underpass to the wide, seven-lane Aston Expressway. Robbie pressed his left foot down, gently increasing the speed. 'Gotta be a bit careful along here, they reckon there's speed cameras on these gantries.' He took his left hand off the steering wheel and pointed across Barry and through the passenger window. 'Look, over there. Villa Park!'

Barry pressed his nose against the passenger window. 'Bugger me, they've made a few changes to that; it looks a lot bigger, certainly a lot higher.'

'Probably because of the World Cup, if I remember right.'

'Oh yeah! I forgot we've got the World Cup in three years time.'

'Sorry, Barry, we *had* the World Cup – seventeen years ago and you won't know this, of course, but we won it.'

'Won it! You're jokin'!'

'No, really. We beat West Germany 4-2. I was only a kid, still at school. We watched all the matches on television in black and white. There was one hell of a rumpus when we beat Argentina in the quarter finals and the referee sent the Argentine captain off. Can't remember what his name was, but he wasn't happy!'

'Did we have to play Brazil?'

'No, they got knocked out early on. We played Portugal in the semi finals. If I remember we beat them 2-1. I do remember Bobby Charlton scored a screamer from 25 yards.'

'How many goals did Jimmy Greaves get? Quite a few, I'll bet.'

'None, he got injured in one of the early matches and couldn't get his place back. Geoff Hurst scored a hat-trick against the Germans in the final.'

'Geoff Hurst? Who's he when he's at home?'

'West Ham striker. Played alongside Bobby Moore and Martin Peters; they were West Ham too!'

'Striker? What's a striker?'

Robbie threw Barry a quick glance. 'Are you serious? – Yes, maybe you are. A striker is the man who gets your goals. A centre forward, or an inside forward like your man Jimmy Greaves.'

'Anyway, it was a long time ago,' said Robbie. 'Look, cast your eyes ahead and behold Spaghetti Junction.'

The light was still good enough for Barry to see the full vista of the Gravelly Hill Interchange.

'That's a big bugger and no mistake,' gasped Barry. 'I hope you know which road to take. Glad I'm not driving.'

Robbie knew, of course, and they travelled South down the M6, winding their way through Chelmsley Wood to Solihull. They talked of many things; Vietnam, JFK, Beatlemania, Elvis, Bob Dylan, Jimmy Hendrix, John Lennon…

…and inevitably, Mark Chapman.

CHAPTER 13
'SEVEN DAYS IS TOO LONG'

Chuck Wood

Barry just couldn't get to sleep. His brain was in overdrive. *What had my mom and dad done when I didn't arrive home? Was the Hilversum frequency on the wireless the doorway back home? Was Robbie right about all that moon and stars nonsense? And, oh my God, what had happened to all The Bombastics' gear? Sugarlips would never forgive me if I'd lost her dad's sax!*

Then a thought suddenly exploded in his head. The house was silent, the room was pitch black. He sat upright in bed, his heart pounding; he almost shrieked out.

HE WAS LESS THAN FIVE MILES AWAY FROM HIS HOME IN FORDROUGH!

His mom and dad, they'd be sixty-odd now, were they

still alive? He shuddered at the thought. His dad had struggled to get around twenty years ago, so how was he coping now? Bitter at the hand that life and country had dealt him? His mom, who'd spoiled him something rotten – 'you little tripehound' – that's what she called him when she was summoned to see his teacher, or an angry neighbour came calling.

How would Fordrough look now, twenty years on? The village where he'd grown up? The old school? The new school they'd started building...

His mind whirled.

The Bombastics, Stan, Bodkin, Sugarlips and Frankie? Were they still together? Had they been successful? Had they had hit records? Well with England winning the World Cup and a woman Prime Minister, it seemed like anything could have happened!

Should he go to Fordrough, just to have a look? What if he bumped into somebody he knew? Would they recognise him?

MY GOD! WHAT IF I BUMPED INTO MYSELF?

He threw himself over, buried his face in the pillow and screamed long and hard.

***

Robbie had given him the spare room to sleep in. They'd talked far into the night about his predicament, he and Robbie and Janice. Janice was Robbie's very attractive girlfriend. She had long blonde hair, long tanned legs, large hazel eyes and her plump, full lips were painted bright red. She lived with Robbie; they weren't married. Barry's mom wouldn't approve of that.

When Billy had dropped the camper off at Robbie's home, Barry had made another futile attempt to find the time portal or doorway or tunnel or whatever it was, by twisting the radio tuner back and forth over Luxembourg and Hilversum; even Droitwich, Moscow and Budapest. All to no avail.

It was Janice who persuaded Barry to let it rest and to go inside where it was warmer, she'd make them all a nightcap and they could discuss things. Despite himself, Barry didn't mind his arm being twisted by a lady who looked like Janice. He'd never been one to resist the turn of a shapely ankle, or in Janice's case, thigh. It did go through Barry's mind that he was having carnal thoughts about a girl who was probably about ten years old in his world. He told himself to behave.

Janice had mixed them all whiskey and Cokes. Barry wasn't a big drinker; he'd had the occasional pint of beer with Stan and Bodkin, but wasn't that keen. He'd drunk the odd whiskey and he'd had a bad experience on barley wine after a groupie in a short skirt and killer heels got him back to her place after a concert in Manchester. It turns out her parents were on holiday in France. Her mother was partial to a barley wine. They'd raided her stock that night and Barry suffered big time the next day, and some of the day after, if he remembered correctly.

He'd never tasted whiskey and Coke together, so he sipped the first one tentatively.

The three of them sat round the glowing, imitation log fire and talked long of Barry's experience the previous evening, to see what he could remember, maybe discover some vital fragment he'd missed.

'It would be a lot simpler if, like Alice in Wonderland, there was a white rabbit,' said Janice. 'All we'd need to do is find the rabbit hole.'

Barry, on his third whiskey and Coke burst into a fit if the giggles.

'Actually Barry, that may not be as daft as it sounds,' Robbie explained. 'Maybe it's the lay-by that's the key to this.

I'm not suggesting there's going to be a white rabbit checking his watch, but somewhere in that lay-by there could be a portal that could take you back to your own time.'

'We can go back to Drovers Lane and have a search round,' suggested Barry. 'What about next Thursday? That would be exactly a week on; I can try finding the same frequency on the dial on the stroke of midnight.'

'Maybe better to go before that, in the daylight; midnight's going to be a bit dark to try and find anything,' interrupted Robbie, taking a newspaper from the magazine rack next to the fire. 'I like the idea of exactly one week on, the movements of both the sun and moon are going to be much the same – and look,' he tossed a folded-back copy of one of the Sunday papers from the previous weekend onto the coffee table in front of them. 'According to their stargazer, we'll still be under the influence of Capricorn. So the stars and planets will be on our side too.'

'I told you I don't dig that jumbo mumbo,' slurped Barry, taking another mouthful of his whiskey and Coke. He drained his glass. 'I really love your souped-up Cokes.' He held up his empty glass towards Janice.

'Let's have a time out and give rabbit holes a rest, for now,' suggested Robbie, and he got up to put on some music. 'Here's a Birmingham band who've hit the big time in the eighties. Duran Duran. They used to play regularly at the Rum Runner, just down the road from Pandora's.'

Barry listened to 'Rio'.

'Big hit for them at the end of last year; just before Warwickshire Girls broke for us.'

'Did they influence your style?' asked Barry.

'Not at all,' said Robbie, stiffening slightly. 'Don't get me wrong they're a great band, but it was punk that did it for me. I was just a kid in my first band playing what was called glam rock, doing covers of all the big hits of the day like so many other bands.'

He could see Barry was struggling with these concepts.

'Let me explain the difference between glam rock and punk. We glam rockers covered ourselves in glitter and make-up; it was all very pretentious and more about image and gender bending.'

'Gender-bending?' frowned Barry.

'Gender-bending was boys dressed to look a bit like girls,' said Robbie. 'Lipstick, eye make-up; mother's not sure if their sons were boys or girls.'

'You're kidding.' Barry was wide-eyed. 'Didn't you get booed off stage?'

'No, the kids loved it; they were part of it,' laughed Robbie. Then his smile disappeared. 'To be honest, banging out inane ditties like 'Telegram Sam' and 'Blockbuster' started to become very tiresome. It was the same old, same old. Then came the shot in the arm we all needed. Punk music exploded onto the scene. Just listen to this.'

He carefully placed the needle head on track one of the new album he'd put on his stereo. They waited just a few seconds and in came the Stranglers with 'No More Heroes'.

Barry immediately put his glass on the table and was up on his feet playing air-guitar. 'Now you're talkin' Robbie!' he shouted above Hugh Cornwell's vocal. 'This is more like rock 'n' roll.'

'All of a sudden music was back in the hands of the kids,' nodded Robbie. 'Stuff coming out of the States from bands like The New York Dolls and The Ramones, influencing young bands over here. Punk spawned a thousand bands; we had the Sex Pistols, The Clash and the Buzzcocks and this lot, The Stranglers. You're right, it was probably very similar to the way the early rock 'n' rollers changed the face of music in your teenage years, back in the fifties.'

'Absho-lutely,' slobbered Barry. 'I'll drink to that.' He picked up his empty glass.

'I think coffees might be a good idea,' suggested Janice, as she took his glass and disappeared into the kitchen.

Robbie took the hint and turned the volume down. 'Here's something that'll interest you,' said Robbie, sliding out a glossy magazine from between the larger books on the bookcase next to his stereo. 'It's what we were talking about earlier on.'

Barry took it from him. On the front cover was a full colour picture of Bobby Moore being held shoulder high, holding the Jules Rimet trophy in his left hand and below the banner headline; 'WORLD CHAMPIONS'.

'I don't recognise those two holding Bobby Moore up,' said Barry.

'That's become a very famous picture; that one's Ray Wilson.' Robbie pointed at them in turn. 'And that's Geoff Hurst, he scored the hat-trick, remember?'

Janice brought through a tray with three mugs of coffee on it.

Barry opened the rather dog-eared front cover and started to thumb through the pages.

'That was my pride and joy when I was at school,' smiled Robbie. 'Me and Tommy Holden, who sat next to me, were going to get the autograph of every player.'

'And did you?' asked Barry, sipping his coffee. 'I can see this one's been signed, look, best wishes Gordon Banks.'

'Yeah, I got that one when Stoke came down the Villa,' nodded Robbie. 'Got the three West Ham lads too, the same way. You'll find Roger Hunt, Jackie Charlton and George Cohen in there, but the rest escaped me. Couldn't get anywhere near the Manchester United team and gradually enthusiasm petered out, like these things do and the magazine got put to one side.'

Then Robbie began to chuckle. 'I did better than Tommy, mind. I remember we had a major row one day, that almost led to a punch up. All the class were gathered round baying for blood. He'd got a few of the shadow squad autographs: Jimmy Greaves, Terry Paine and Ron Flowers and tried to say they were equivalent to my West Ham autographs. This was serious stuff for two thirteen-year-olds. Fortunately, Mr Millward came into the classroom, realised what was going on, and confiscated both books until the end of term. I remember thinking when Villa played Everton, I missed out on Alan Ball because he took my book away.'

Robbie was still chuckling as he switched the Stranglers for the Police on his turntable. They played a few more tracks whilst Barry thumbed back and forth through the World Champions book. 'Come on then, time we turned in,' said Robbie, putting his coffee cup back on the tray.

Robbie showed him to the spare room where Janice had laid a clean towel. She'd also borrowed a fresh T-shirt, socks and boxers from Robbie's drawer. It was the next morning when Barry worked out what boxers were and how much men's underwear had changed in twenty years.

Barry took the book to bed with him in the hope that it would help him drop off, but it proved to be a difficult night for sleeping.

***

The next few days Barry spent with Robbie and his band. He went with them to the recording session at Chekka Records and a couple of gigs, one at the Tower Ballroom in Sheffield and another at the Hippodrome in Wakefield.

The recording session went well, up to a point and Robbie was right, the revamped 'Broken Hearted Nobody' sounded really good. Chekka's A&R man, Jacques Halliday was with them most of the day; he'd brought with him two demo records which he wanted them to record. Robbie wasn't happy; they reluctantly learned them both and recorded them along with 'Broken Hearted Nobody' and 'Bar Room Brawl'. There wasn't time to record the other songs they'd been working so hard on. It had been a long day; they'd got to the studio at ten o'clock that morning and now here it was approaching eleven in the evening, and they had a two hour drive home on a bitterly cold night.

Before they left London Jacques told them he wanted a complete album from them by summer. He was happy with the day's work and felt there were two singles they could release to promote it, but he wanted at least five more new songs.

Over a coffee at Newport Pagnell Services on the M1 Robbie confided in Barry. 'To be honest I find writing songs bloody hard work. I once read how Paul McCartney took just a few minutes to scribble 'Scrambled Eggs' on the back of a fag packet and the next thing 'Yesterday' becomes a monster. Don't know how he does it; takes me forever and as Billy and Jez will testify, I can get a bit grumpy with them, perhaps with Janice too for that matter.'

Next morning, Robbie knocked on the spare room door with a complete change of clothes for Barry; jeans, T-shirt and a black knitted sweater. Barry was about the same size as Robbie, maybe not quite as broad across the shoulders, but the fresh clothes would do just fine, if a little bit loose. Anyway, it was still right in the middle of a cold spell, so Barry was always in his duffle coat. Robbie also gave him a toothbrush, shaving gear and deodorant. He'd never seen an aerosol before. Aftershave was as close to perfume as Barry had come in the early sixties, but now here was this stuff in a can. 'Adonis antiperspirant', it said on the label. He pressed the red plastic button on the top and it sprayed a sort of minty-smelling mist all over him.

Nice smell, but let's see if it stops me sweating like they say. The word 'antiperspirant' on the side of the can made him chuckle to himself when he remembered the Mum Rollette joke they used onstage, after Sugarlips produced one of those roll-on antiperspirants out of her handbag before a Bombastics' gig. Stan picked it up in the dressing room and read the instructions on the side of the stick, 'Twist, and push up bottom'. They'd all laughed at that, including Shoogs.

***

As suggested they decided to find Drovers Lane in the daylight, just to make sure. It was still there, they could see that from Robbie's A-Z road map, but was the lay-by still there? They didn't want to be going round in circles in the dark looking for it. As they had the Wakefield gig on Wednesday they decided to do their dummy run on Tuesday morning.

After getting back from London in the early hours, the Tuesday morning start became a Tuesday afternoon start. Robbie and Janice sat in the front seats of the Jag, with Barry in the back. Janice had Robbie's A-Z road map in her lap with an old brown envelope book-marking the page where Drovers Lane could be found. However, they'd agreed to go along with Barry's suggestion; he thought it would be a good idea to start at the Phantom Coach and follow the route he'd taken that night, just in case anything sparked a memory and gave them a clue as to what might have happened. It never dawned on Barry that it would take them to both Frankie's house and Carol's house. As it turned out, it never mattered.

Robbie thought he knew the location Barry described on the A45, but said he had no recollection of a pub called the Phantom Coach. They searched around, but to no avail. They pulled in behind a red Post Office van parked in a service road and waited for the postman to return from the office block he was delivering mail to.

He laughed. 'Phantom Coach? You gotta be kidding, that was pulled down years ago. There's one of them Travel Express hotels there now.'

They decided to push on.

Robbie studied his A-Z map now open on Janice's lap. 'If we take a left here – look,' he ran his finger across the page. 'We can join the main Warwick to Stratford road, then if we travel sort of north east for a few miles there's Drovers Lane, a left hand turn.'

Barry felt guilty leaning over the front seats to look at the map. He couldn't stop himself studying Janice's long, long legs. He'd never seen such a short skirt. He sat back in his seat and contented himself with looking for clues through the window whilst he cooled down.

Half an hour or so later and they were approaching Drovers Lane.

Barry stared out of the window clearly bewildered. 'None of these houses were here, it's all built up now. Just exactly how many houses have they put up? It was all fields last time I came this way – last Thursday!'

'Yeah, you can see it's all quite new, but not *that* new. I bet they're about ten years old,' said Robbie, putting his foot down as they crossed over of the Worcestershire county boundary. Eventually they saw the 'Fordrough 5m' sign, pointing across the road from the hedgerow. As they turned left, the Drovers Lane black and white street sign, partly obscured by overhanging bushes, confirmed they had reached their destination.

'Bugger me, this has changed too, those warehouse units weren't there, it looks like it's some kind of factory centre. God, what if they've taken out the lay-by?' There was real concern in Barry's voice.

He needn't have worried, within a hundred yards or so, the lay-by appeared on their left. It now had a kerbed border and tarmac had been laid. There was a blue sign with a large white P on it and the litter bin was still there, maybe not the original one, but as Barry said, 'I could hardly see beyond the windscreen wipers, never mind studying bloody litter bins.'

Robbie parked his Jaguar in the lay-by and they sat there in profound silence for a minute or two, maybe longer.

Then Barry said, 'Do you mind if I get out for a fag and just take stock?'

Janice half turned in her seat and from the expression on her face seemed as though she was about to question Barry's move, but Robbie put a hand on Janice's shoulder and stopped her. 'Go ahead Barry,' he said. 'Take as long as you want, we understand it's important to you. Look for anything that might be connected with last week's strange happenings, and do your coat up, it's freezing out there.'

'And don't go chasing rabbits,' added Janice.

Barry gently slammed the door shut behind him and walked a dozen or so paces beyond the litter bin. He took a cigarette from the packet of Gold Leaf that Billy had given him, poked it between his lips, scratched a Swan Vesta into life along the side of the box and lit-up. He flicked the match away, sucked in on his cigarette, inhaling deeply and blew a long trail of smoke into the cold afternoon air.

His eyes scanned the hedgerows and the spinney that separated the lay-by from the field beyond and the rear end of two of the industrial warehouses beyond that. His eyes fixed for a moment on the trunk of the large oak tree that stood not ten feet away. *I don't remember any of this. Come on Harper, you didn't really expect to find The Bombastics' gear piled high against that tree, did you?*

If there are two worlds, twenty years apart, that have collided and somehow I've got dragged through from one world into another, what are the chances that 1963 is going to hang on for a week and wait for me to get back? Surely it will have gone spinning on into eternity without me?

He shuddered and took another deep drag from his cigarette.

Bugger me, what if there are hundreds of worlds spinning around and bumping into each other? What if I jump through the wrong time portal and completely miss my world? I could end up a medieval lute player with a band of wandering minstrels, or playing one of those weird synthesiser things in the next century.

He finished his cigarette and flicked it down the storm drain that sat beneath the litter bin. *Down in one!* He smiled, but there was no amusement in his eyes.

By this time both Robbie and Janice had got out of the car and were peering back at Barry round the boles of two trees in a dense thicket at the other end of the lay-by. Robbie was about to call out, 'There's no doorway here, no flight of stairs, no escalator, or rabbit hole.' Then he thought better of it. 'Nothing here, Barry!' he cried.

They all clambered back into the Jag and Robbie delayed starting the engine, looking at Barry through his rear view. 'You know we're less than five miles from your village.'

'Yes, I do – and yes, I've thought about going back there, if that's what you're going to ask.'

'Let's have another look.' Robbie slid his forefinger across the map. 'We could go that way through Fordrough, pick up the motorway the other side for a couple of junctions, and we'd be back on the Solihull road, no problem.'

'It may help you Barry, be kind of cathartic,' added Janice. 'Home is where the heart is and all that.'

'What if I see people I know? What if I see Mom and Dad?' Barry's eyes widened. 'What if I see me?'

'Then you'll know one thing for sure Barry – you got back!' said Robbie. 'We needn't stop, we'll just drive through, let you see how it's changed in twenty years. I used to read a lot of sci-fi when I was a kid, you know, Ray Bradbury and Arthur C. Clarke stuff. The one thing time travellers don't do is alter the past; it can have an immense effect on the future, even catastrophic. I suppose the reverse is also true; mess about with the future at your peril.' He looked at his watch. 'Hey! The light will be starting to fade soon, so if you want to do it we need to get going.'

Barry leant forward, elbows on knees, gripping his hands together and staring at the dashboard of the Jaguar. After ten seconds or so, he sat back and sighed. 'Go on then.' He deftly buckled his seat belt like he'd been doing it all his life.

Robbie pushed the Jag into first, crept forward, checked his wing mirror and pulled out into Drovers Lane.

Barry saw the familiar church spire before he saw the village sign, 'Welcome To Fordrough'. The same old cottages still stood on either side of East Orchard Farm, as they followed a goods lorry and two cars towards the centre of the village. As they came to the T junction Barry could see that Market Square had changed quite a bit. The village hall was still there, as was the Crown and Anchor pub, and he suspected quite a few of the shops around the southern side were the original buildings, just different businesses to the ones he remembered. It was the north and east sides that had been completely rebuilt. There was a small shopping precinct with a dozen or so brightly coloured shop fronts. He could see a butchers', a shoe shop, a book-makers and a hairdressers on the side facing him, but it was the Co-operative supermarket, with its expansive glass frontage and car park that really took his eye. This had been built on the site of the old factory centre which had been home to two or three thriving industries in his youth, a needle maker, a bicycle shop and repair centre, where Barry used to have a Saturday job, and a cattle feed merchant. It also looked as though the butcher's slaughterhouse had gone. The centre of Market Square looked much the same as it used to be, although he did notice there was now an ornate wooden notice board and what looked like a local map standing in the centre. A lot of it seemed to have been sectioned off, with white lines for car parking. As they got closer he could see it wasn't a notice board at all, it showed 'Pay and Display' charges, and there was also a ticket machine.

I wonder if they still have the Wednesday and Saturday markets. Probably not.

'I'm going round the Market Square and heading out towards the motorway,' said Robbie.

'That's the main route out of here, Sheep Street,' replied Barry, pointing. 'Most of the housing lies to the North West, or used to.'

As Robbie waited at the traffic lights on the main Birmingham Road, an old gent in a trilby and carrying a walking stick, crossed in front of his Jag and into the Market Square.

'Bugger me, that's Ding Dong Bell our old music teacher.' Barry sounded quite excited. 'Mr Bell was the one who got us all playing music. He was nearly sixty when he held the music workshops so he must be knocking on eighty now. I wonder if he'd remember me?'

Barry had the rear offside window down in a trice.

Robbie went to stop him. 'Better not let him...' He was too late.

'Mr Bell!' he shouted. 'How are you, sir?'

The old man stopped in his tracks and turned to face the Jag. They saw him squint to focus on Barry. His look of curiosity changed to one of astonishment and he staggered back slightly, steadying himself with his cane. Astonishment now became horror and he twisted arthritically to hurry away into the crowd of Co-op shoppers, turning just once, to look back to at the Jaguar, before disappearing through the supermarket doors.

There was silence in the car as they waited for the lights to change.

Then Barry spoke. 'Perhaps it wasn't such a good idea shouting at old Ding Dong, he could've had a heart attack. I suppose it was a shock for him, seeing me look the same twenty years later, as when I left school three years ago.'

'It looked like he'd seen a ghost,' said Janice.

Robbie watched Barry through the driving mirror, but never said a word.

The lights changed and Robbie followed the road ahead and exited Market Square via Sheep Street. Barry was right, most of the housing did lie to the north of the village, but there was a lot more now than he'd known. A sprawling housing estate dominated what used to be Beecher's Farm and, next to it, the old Fordrough Primary School.

'They used to say that this was all green belt, couldn't be built on.' Barry lay sprawled across the back seat to get a better view. 'So what happened, knocking down our old school and building a massive estate on old farmer Beecher's land?'

'Take a look over here, Barry.' Janice was pointing across Robbie to an ultra-modern glass and bricks building. She read the black and gold sign to the side of the main gateway, 'Fordrough First & Middle Schools.'

'Bugger me, I knew it was being planned. I suppose that's to fit in all the new families that must live on that estate, back there.' Barry squirmed lengthways back across the seat to look through the onside window. 'It's a much bigger village today than the one I left just last week, I can tell you.'

About a mile further on, with the modern housing left behind and now only sporadic cottages dotted along each side of the road, they passed beneath a bridge.

'That'll be the motorway,' said Robbie. 'Right at the next island and junction two will be just half a mile.

***

That night, Barry had just the one whiskey and Coke and went to bed early. Robbie and Janice stayed up for a while, chatting.

'That incident with Barry's old teacher worries me,' said Robbie. 'You said something that may just be true. You said he looked like he'd seen a ghost.'

'Yes, I remember,' Janice replied. 'The poor old fellow looked terrified.'

'What if he thought he was seeing a ghost,' continued Robbie. 'What if Barry never made it back twenty years ago? What if the village declared him missing presumed dead?'

'Good God!' exclaimed Janice, putting her hand to her mouth. 'I never thought of that. No wonder Ding Dong cleared off in the way he did.'

'Maybe nothing in it, so best not say anything, eh?' said Robbie. He put his arm around Janice and gently kissed her.

***

The two gigs had gone well for The Robbie Rochester

Band. They pulled good crowds in at both, no mean feat at Wakefield considering it was a cold Wednesday night in February. For Barry, visiting these two Yorkshire towns was further evidence of how much their world had moved on. There was so much more traffic in 1983 and it moved so much faster too!

Travelling up to Sheffield on a Friday afternoon, they got stuck in a long tail back. It reminded him of the times as a young lad he sat in the back of his dad's car on the way to Devon. They always got stuck on the A38, nose to tail through Bristol and Taunton and other towns he'd now forgotten. 'Are we there yet?' he'd keep asking. It was always hot and dusty and seemed to go on for hours. He remembered how the stifling heat in the car on the journey down to Devon always seemed to change, just in time to keep them in their caravan playing cards or Monopoly, whilst the rain battered the roof and windows.

But this was *three* lanes of traffic stuck nose to tail on the M1. They'd sit there stationary for fifteen or twenty minutes, then all of a sudden all three lanes would take off, sometimes reaching eighty miles an hour, only to grind to a halt again a few miles further up the motorway.

The Wakefield theatre was right in town next door to the Gaumont cinema. The film showing was *ET: The Extra Terrestrial*. Titch explained, 'It's about an alien kid who gets stranded on Earth when the mother ship takes off without him. A gang of American kids befriend him and help him get back home. It's been a smash hit, this must be the second time it's done the rounds.'

Immediately, Jez started limping around the dressing room pointing his forefinger at Barry. 'Phone home.' He repeated, 'Phone home.' This time shaking his finger aggressively.

Barry looked nonplussed.

'He's takin' the piss, Barry,' said Lenny. 'Take no

notice, tell him he's the one that looks like a freakin' alien.'

It was during the gig, in the same dressing room that Barry experienced his first trip. The mirror in the dressing room was discoloured and mottled where the silvering was damaged. When Barry came in through the door after watching from the wings, he noticed Billy had taken it down from the wall and placed it on the table in the middle of the room. He'd emptied a sachet of white powder onto the surface of the mirror and was chopping and sifting it with the edge of a plastic Access card and separating it into lines.

'That's heroin, right?' questioned Barry.

'Right. It's always part of the rider when we come to Wakefield,' grinned Billy. 'The management here can be very generous. Do you do Smack, Barry?'

'Never. A few of the London bands are doing LSD, but we've never touched it. Some prat in one of the local bands suggested we try crushing aspirin into Coca-Cola to keep us going on a long gig, but it never worked for me.'

'Wanna give it a snort?' Billy offered him a cut off straw.

'No thanks.'

'You're as bad as Robbie and Lenny, they won't touch it neither, nor Jez, not when he's working.'

The door burst open and the boys in the band entered the dressing room, laughing, shouting, rubbing their sweaty bodies with towels and gulping water out of plastic bottles.

Chaz was the first one to spot their little treat. 'Hey Billy boy, hand me my nose flute,' he joked. There was a minor scramble to be first when Twitch and Titch spotted the white lines.

Barry watched the four of them (Billy too) put a finger on one nostril and snort the powder up through the other.

When Robbie, and then Jez, followed them into the room and saw what they were doing, Barry expected him to explode, but he just shook his head and mumbled, 'Just remember, Smackheads, we gotta second half to do yet.'

'Smackheads? Dickheads more like,' added Jez.

He moved over to the other side of the dressing room and helped himself and Robbie to coffee. He looked over to Lenny and Barry. 'Either of you want one? It's better than what they've got, trust me.'

When the boys had finished their break and gone back onstage, three of them pretty high, Billy and Barry were left alone again. Billy was scraping together the residue of white powder left on the surface of the mirror and added to it the last shakings from the polythene bag it had come in. He scraped together a weedy thin line, maybe only half the length of the ones Chaz and the others had snorted.

A stupid smile played on Billy's lips as he offered Barry the straw he'd been using. 'Last chance, Barry. Maybe it'll take you back to the sixties.'

Was he serious? Hard to say if he's taking the piss when you can't look him in the eye 'cos of those sunglasses.

'Go on!' Again Billy offered the straw.

Barry stood silent for a moment. *Bugger it, why not?* He took the straw.

Copying what he'd seen the others do, Barry pressed the forefinger of his left hand hard against his left nostril, closing it completely. With his right hand, he pushed the end of the half straw into his right nostril, either forgetting or ignoring that Billy had stuck the very same straw stuck up his own nose not twenty minutes before; he directed the other end to the white line. Counting in his head, *One, two, three*, he sniffed deeply, moving the straw along the line until it was all gone.

He half expected it to bring on a fit of sneezing, but it

didn't. He half expected to see fire breathing dragons clawing their way up the walls, but he didn't. In fact, to begin with, nothing happened.

Then slowly he felt this wave of euphoria build within him, filling him with warmth.

He'd been aware of the posters and photographs around the walls, of artists that had appeared here in Wakefield. Some were new, most were old and faded, held up with rusty drawing pins or cellotape now turned brown. All had autographs and scrawled messages from distant, mostly forgotten, performers; many of whom were now treading the boards somewhere beyond the pearly gates.

The colours of the posters grew brighter. The smiles on those faces began to glow. The messages danced and throbbed before his eyes.

'Though we're apart you're in my heart,' one said. 'All the luck in the world,' said another.

Barry was ecstatic, he hugged Billy. He pirouetted around the room stopping in front of a poster of a smiling Dickie Valentine. He fell to one knee and burst into an Al Jolson rendition of 'Christmas Alphabet', singing to Dickie, just to Dickie. He wanted to break down the dressing room door and go out onstage with Robbie, his best friend ever and sing with him. Dance with him. He would have too if Billy hadn't locked the door.

Robbie gave Billy a severe bollocking when he'd finished the show and saw the state of Barry. 'Don't you think he's got enough problems without an idiot like you giving him a quick trip around eternity?'

It was a long drive home for Barry, sweating and anxious on the back seat of Robbie's Jag. He began to feel quite sick and suffered sharp stomach cramps. Just north of Nottingham Robbie had to stop the car for Barry to vomit. Robbie lectured him on the remainder of the journey and Barry swore he'd never do drugs again.

He never kept his promise.

CHAPTER 14
'LIKE I'VE NEVER BEEN GONE'

Billy Fury

They left Robbie's home in Solihull at about 10 p.m. Robbie's Jag leading the way, with Janice alongside him and Barry in the back. Billy followed in the VW, from which they'd removed all the gear, leaving it in Robbie's garage. Billy had said, if Barry was somehow going to be abducted by aliens the camper may go with him and they didn't want to lose all the sound and lighting equipment too.

Robbie told Billy not to be such a prat, but nevertheless thought it might be prudent to leave the gear at his place. They'd arranged to meet Jez at the Little Chef on the Stratford Road. Billy had thought if they were going to lose the camper he'd need a lift home, but he never mentioned it.

Jez was alone waiting in the car park, Jez and Lizzie on the screen of his silver Saab. Barry would never meet Lizzie. They all went inside the restaurant and ordered tea for three and coffee for Janice and Jez.

'Don't you fancy a quick trip around Fordrough on the way to Drovers Lane; it's not out of our way?' Billy asked Barry.

Before he could respond Robbie broke in. 'Let's stick to the plan, lads. We may only get one chance at this so there's no point in adding unnecessary risks.' He never mentioned their visit two days before, nor did he mention Fordrough's new school, the Co-op supermarket or Ding Dong Bell. Barry and Janice said nothing.

Robbie paid the bill and they set off again, the Jaguar leading the way, then the VW followed by the Saab as they made their way cross country, eventually turning into Drovers Lane and the lay-by.

It was a cold night and as Barry got out of the Jag, he could see his breath on the night air in the yellow glow of three sets of headlights. The temperature had plummeted over the last couple of hours and frost had formed on the trunks, bare branches and twigs of trees and bushes and on the wooden fencing and evergreen hedges that enclosed the parking area. It lit up in the headlights like thousands of sparkling diamonds. There had been cloud cover all day; the snow that had been forecast never happened, but the dark, moonless and starless night sky still looked full of it. He lit a cigarette.

'Twenty minutes to lift off, eh?' Billy had joined Barry. 'Seems odd we're here trying to send you back twenty years to a place that's not fifteen minutes down the road, don't it?'

'You're like a dog with a bone,' came Robbie's voice, as

he walked round from the driver's side. 'Forget about Fordrough, let's concentrate on the job in hand. Barry, whereabouts did you park that night; we may as well try and get the position as near accurate as we can?'

'Bugger me, there was a blizzard blowing, I could hardly see through the windscreen.' Barry hesitated. 'I know I was very close to that litter bin when I pulled in, I thought I was going to demolish it.'

Robbie looked back at the bin. 'Okay, probably not the same one and maybe not in the same place, but we'll give it a go.' He called over to Jez, who was leaning against the open door of his Saab. 'You pull up here in front of me and Billy, you reverse back a bit as near to the bin as you can.'

They went about their manoeuvres and once repositioned, all of them switched their headlights off. It was now eerily dark. It would have been eerily black if not for the interior light of the Jaguar that Janice had switched on.

They all clustered around the open door of the VW camper as Barry slid into the driver's seat. Jez hugged himself to keep warm, Billy stamped his feet, cupped his hands and blew into them, Robbie put his arm around Janice, who was wrapped snugly in scarf and gloves, and squeezed her towards him. It was bloody cold. Barry pulled his set of keys out of the pocket of his duffle coat, picked out the ignition key and slipped it into the keyhole on the dashboard. Then his hand went towards the knob to turn the radio on.

'Not yet!' shouted Robbie, looking at his wristwatch. 'There's still two minutes to go.'

'Do you think I should start the engine?'

'Was the engine running when it all happened?' asked Robbie.

'No.'

'Then leave it, let's concentrate on the radio.'

Janice recapped. 'We got the same night, the same time and the same star sign. Just needs you to find the right frequency on that radio. It's just a pity it's not snowing.'

Then in the best Captain Kirk voice he could muster, Jez added, 'Get ready to beam me up Scotty.'

Robbie would have rebuked him for being childish, but at that moment starting the countdown was far more important. 'Sixty seconds, fifty-nine, fifty-eight…'

They all took a step back as Barry took hold of the door through the open window and slammed it shut.

'Forty-seven, forty-six, forty-five…' Robbie continued.

Barry leant forward to switch the radio on and it fizzed into life, giving off its familiar green glow. When he looked back through the driver's window, snowflakes were drifting down from above, settling on the hair and shoulders of the four outside.

'Thirty-three, thirty-two, thirty-one…'

A wind had picked up as Barry looked through the split windscreen of the VW and into the distance. Though it was dark he could see the snow falling steadily and being blown sideways in flurries.

'Twenty-five, twenty-four, twenty-three…'

Barry lodged his left elbow on the front corner of the passenger seat and took the radio's tuner knob between forefinger and thumb of his right hand.

'Sixteen, fifteen, fourteen…'

He guided the needle on the dial slowly and deliberately across Moscow, Droitwich, Budapest, and Lyons. There were snatches of classical, jazz and pop music plus the gabble of foreign voices as he went.

'Eight, seven, six…'

Barry slowly centred it on Hilversum. Nothing happened. He very gently twisted the knob between finger and thumb back and forth over Hilversum.

'Three, two, one...'

The green light turned white. A whooshing sound filled the camper. The last sound he heard from 1983 was Billy (he guessed) shouting, 'Fuckin' hell, get back, get back, the things going to explode!'

There was no explosion, but just as before the light grew into a bright, brilliant white. This time, however, he could feel forces pulling him in two directions, as if one force wanted to keep him and the other was determined to pull him through. What felt like a giant hand tightened around his rib cage squeezing him sideways and upwards, whilst another squashed his pelvis and thighs deeper and down.

Bugger me, I can't breathe, I'm – I'm – I'm being ripped in half. Aaaargh!

Then suddenly he was released and the sound of 'Wayward Wind' filled the cab.

Barry's mind quickly focussed to recognise Frank Ifield yodelling from the wireless underneath the dashboard. The dial was green and winking gently at him. He looked through the window. It was barely snowing, just a few flakes blowing almost horizontally in strong winds that were shaking the Volkswagen. No Robbie, no Janice, no Billy nor Jez.

The record finished and Barry Aldis (yes, it was definitely Barry Aldis) announced the midnight news headlines for Friday February 8th.

He listened transfixed, as a woman's voice with a slight Irish lilt told Radio Luxembourg listeners that John F. Kennedy, the US President, had made it illegal for US citizens to travel to Cuba – that following the death of

Hugh Gaitskill, Harold Wilson, George Brown and Jim Callaghan will vie to become leader of the Labour Party – Liverpool sensations, The Beatles, were booked to record their debut album later that week at Abbey Road studios under the guidance of experienced Parlophone record producer George Martin – Finally, the weather. A lot of the country was still locked in a deep freeze, with many minor roads still blocked and the coming weekend's sporting calendar likely to be wiped out yet again.

The music continued with Barry Aldis spinning Cliff Richard's 'Bachelor Boy'.

Barry collapsed forward over the steering wheel and shouted to the VW camper, 'Yes, yes, YEEESSSS!'

He then threw himself back in his seat, spread his hands over his face and cried like a child. Through the tears and snot he blubbered to himself and the camper, 'It worked, I'm back, I'm home!'

Then realisation slowly crept over him. The tears stopped as he stared through his fingers at the beige vinyl fabric of the VW roof liner. His hands slowly slid down his face and dropped into his lap. He reasoned with himself. *Okay I've been in 1983 for a week, exactly a week, almost to the second. That's how we planned it.*

He pulled a packet of Gold Leaf and a box of Swan Vesta out of his left hand pocket, poked a cigarette in his mouth and lit up. He drew in fiercely.

So how come Frank Ifield's still singing Wayward Wind at exactly the same time and how come the midnight news headlines are for Friday February 8th?

The penny dropped. *I'm back in exactly the same spot at exactly the same time as I left. The week I've just spent in 1983 has vanished. No Robbie Rochester, no Billy, no Jez. It's just as though it never happened.*

It was a dream, of course it was. They say dreams only last for seconds, don't they? That's the only explanation there could be. Some sort of weird dream and like all dreams it'll fade pretty quickly.

He opened the window to flick his cigarette butt away. He watched it spark through the air and quickly sizzle out as it hit the snow bank on the edge of the lay-by.

That's when his thought of it all being a dream also sizzled out. Cigarettes. Gold Leaf; they were Billy's. If he needed any further proof he suddenly remembered something else. Indisputable proof of his time travel. Barry slid his hand into the right hand pocket of his duffle coat. He pulled out the grey, metal Walkman, complete with leads and ear plugs.

'Bugger Me.' He breathed in deeply, then blew out loudly through his teeth puffing his cheeks right out. He pushed one of the ear plugs into his right ear, twisted the Walkman around until he found the 'Play' button and pressed it. He listened to a few seconds of 'Warwickshire Girls', switched it off and lay it carefully down on the passenger seat next to the carton of Gold Leaf.

He switched on the interior light and turned sharply in his seat. He peered into the half light at the back of the camper. Yes, there were the VOX amps and guitar cases, there was Shoog's saxophone and all the seating was back, behind which he could see the top of Bodkin's drums, exactly as they'd been stacked back at the Phantom Coach. All the gear was safe, thank God.

Looking out again through the open window, he noticed the strong cross wind had blown a lot of the newly fallen snow off the road and it had drifted high against the hedgerow down the left hand side of Drovers Lane. He guessed there must be a similar drift blown from the field up against the hedgerow on the opposite side of the lane, but it was a sturdy and dense evergreen and had sheltered most of the road surface, exposing Tarmac where the council, or maybe the farmers, had ploughed previous snowfalls away.

It was hardly snowing now, though the wind wasn't giving up and Barry thought he might as well give it a go and drive the five miles or so, back into Fordrough. Some of it may have to be in the middle of the road, some perhaps right over on the wrong side, but if he took it steadily, there seemed to be nothing in the way of other traffic about. In places, where the wind had disturbed the last snow fall, he could see the road had been gritted; that'd help.

One thing that did occur to him was that when he got home, his mom and dad might still be waiting up and worried about him. Hey, not half as worried as they would have been if I'd gone missing for a week and left the camper in a lay-by.

He shut his window, pressed the starter button and fired up the engine. It started first time, *Why shouldn't it? You only turned it off five minutes ago!*

He drove home without incident. He met a couple of cars coming the other way, but they too were taking it very steadily.

Nearly all the way home, his head was full of 1983. *It happened, it really did, but how can I tell anyone, who would believe me? I can hear Bodkin now, asking me if I could help find the fairies at the bottom of his garden. Even Jez and Billy had continued to take the piss – and they knew!*

He realised how lucky he was to have bumped into Robbie, what a decent bloke he'd turned out to be. Maybe one day he'd get the chance to pay him back.

Just think, he'd be about ten years old at the moment. Wonder if he lives in Solihull yet? Janice too, she was nice. Then he remembered those long legs that went right up to her bottom and he reached over for a cigarette, trying to ignore movement in the trouser department. *Bugger me, she's also out there somewhere, aged about eight.*

He turned the volume on the wireless up.

'Here's the one from Billy Fury,' said Barry Aldis. '"Like I've Never Been Gone".'

Barry laughed loudly. 'You got that one right, Mr Aldis!'

By the time he got home and pulled onto his drive he'd made his mind up that he wouldn't say a word to anyone yet. Not to his mom and dad, nor to any of the band. He needed some time. That way, there wouldn't be any awkward questions to answer; after all he was only a bit late and they would have expected that with the state of the roads. He made sure the Gold Leaf and the Walkman were well hidden. He put them in his trouser pockets under his duffle coat.

As soon as they heard him the porch light went on and two figures appeared at the door. Mom had her dressing gown and slippers on. The look of concern on her face that only mothers get, had changed to a look of relief. Dad was still in cardigan, shirt and trousers hovering in the background. He had the evening paper in his hand.

'We've been very worried about you, our Barry.' Mom stepped onto the front garden path, 'They shouldn't put on you like this, making you drive in this weather. You've only been driving a few weeks, it's not right.'

'Would you come back inside, Martha? Sure, you'll be catching your death.' Dad shook the paper at her.

'Or slip over and break your flippin' leg,' added Barry. 'It's like an ice rink out here!'

Barry locked up the camper and they all went inside. Mom soon had the kettle boiling and whilst she was making the tea, Barry made the excuse of taking his duffle coat upstairs. He threw it on the bed and then took the Walkman and cigarettes out of his pockets and shoved them under a pillow. He then returned downstairs and they settled around the kitchen table. The stove door was open and although the fire inside was burning down, it still kept the kitchen cosy and warm, a lot different to outside. Barry sipped from a vast mug of hot tea as he told them all about his problems, the sudden blizzard, the lay-by and the difficult drive home. Well, not all.

Exhausted from his twenty year hop and the strain of concentrating whilst carefully guiding the VW along wintery country lanes, he flopped onto his bed, slipping his hand under the pillow just to reassure himself that the Walkman and the packet of Gold Leaf were still there and well hidden (not that he was expecting Mommy or Daddy to come in and give him a goodnight kiss), better safe than sorry. He quickly fell asleep.

In the hours just before light, as dreamers do, he joined R.E.M. for a strange and troubled reunion.

He was back at his old school, not the modern new building he'd seen in 1983 Fordrough, but the red brick village school he'd grown up in as an infant and junior, then finally as a senior.

Mr Bell was taking music lessons. Around him other pupils were playing instruments of all kinds. Woodwind, brass, strings and timpani. The racket being created was deafening. Barry was playing his Harmony guitar, but the noise he was making, like the other would-be musicians, was truly awful. Ding Dong was shouting and pointing at him from across the room. He was clearly very angry.

Then a guitar player at the front of the class turned; it was Robbie, he looked angry too. He had Janice next to him, she was sobbing uncontrollably. Billy and Jez appeared on the far side of the classroom; they were both snarling and pointing towards him. There was a girl next to Jez and she was dressed as a Goth too; white face, straggly black hair, thick black mascara, silver rings through her ears, nose and eyebrows. Was this Lizzie?

He looked back at Mr Bell. Ding Dong had been joined by Twitch and Titch, Chaz and Lenny. They were chanting and pointing at him too, like some angry football crowd. What they were chanting he couldn't hear above the tuneless cacophony filling the room.

Barry threw his guitar down, he had to get away from them. He started to push his way over to the door. As he pushed through the lines of pupils, they turned into angry white-faced Goths too. Black lipstick, black tresses, black tattoos – black – black – black!

Barry seemed to be making no progress, the door seemed farther away.

To his left, Robbie, now guitarless, and Janice were picking their way across the room and would surely cut him off before he could escape.

Why were they all so livid?

He must get to that door. He strained every muscle, every sinew, but he seemed to be getting nowhere. Billy and Jez were now close behind, Robbie and Janice too, had closed in on him from his left. The bedlam in that room reached a crescendo. The last thing he saw were Janice's eyes. Tear-stained, smudged eyeshadow and mascara! But it was her look of pure hatred burning into him.

He woke up with a jolt, soaked in sweat, his heart thumping.

Barry lay there wondering from where the hell a dream like that came. *It'll go as quick as it came*. It never did; that look in Janice's eyes would stay with him.

It would be many years before he told someone about 1983 and the Robbie Rochester Band.

CHAPTER 15
'18 WITH A BULLET'

Pete Wingfield

1963 was to be a groundbreaker for Frankie Atom and The Bombastics.

Danny started work on filling the diary. The Bombastics had gigs dotted throughout the tail end of 1962 and the early weeks of 1963, which in many ways was a blessing. The main one being the dreadful winter that hit the UK early in 1963. The work Stan had already booked in was mostly local work and they only lost two gigs to the weather, because the promoter cancelled, not The Bombastics. They could all see the bookings coming in from Danny. He would phone Stan every evening and confirm dates and venues. The odd booking appeared in February and March, but April, May and June were getting busier by the day.

'It's getting bleedin' chocker,' Bodkin told Stan when Danny had phoned with a couple more gigs, one in the home counties and the other in South Wales. 'I think we ought to make that decision about going full-time. There are more midweek dates coming in than I thought there'd be and even with Barry sharing the driving, I'm knackered at work. I sat down for a minute and fell asleep in one of the arm chairs we'd just unloaded. Out the game for nearly an hour I was. Fortunately it was over the lunch hour so nobody took much notice.'

Bodkin worked at Spencer & Taylor's, a furniture and fancy goods warehouse in Birmingham, picking orders, loading the vans for delivery and occasionally driving the 'cock-up' van (as it was known to the despatch department). This was a spare vehicle, often used for late emergency deliveries, to placate customers screaming blue murder down the blower because S&T had missed their delivery or sent out the wrong stuff. One afternoon he'd been given a very late 'cock-up' delivery in Coventry. Old Jock Johnstone, his manager, told him to bring the van back next morning to save him coming all the way back into Birmingham. Unbeknown to old Jock, The Bombastics had a gig at the Co-op Hall in Nuneaton only a few miles away. The 'cock-up' delivery was a Silver Cross perambulator, meaning there was still plenty of room on board. So Bodkin went home and loaded up The Bombastics' gear. He collected three of the others, who were more surprised at seeing a Spencer & Taylor van pull up outside their homes, than they were that he was over an hour early.

The pram was a surprise present for a wife bringing a brand new baby home the next day and the idea was to call by on the doting husband in Coventry, on the way to the gig in Nuneaton. It would save Bodkin a lot of time to-ing and fro-ing and it would be S&T who paid for the fuel. Perfect; except that Barry still hadn't got home from work when they called. They waited – and waited – and waited. When Barry finally arrived, it was too late to do the delivery, they had to go straight to Nuneaton.

'Well I didn't know, did I? Bugger me, I'm not psychic, am I?'

Next morning Bodkin called by just as the Coventry customer was opening, but the balloon had gone up the previous evening when the pram didn't arrive, as promised.

Bodkin got hauled up before Mr Tristan Taylor, but wasn't too bothered one way or the other; he felt more guilty that old Jock had been court-marshalled alongside him. To make matters worse, he gave the excuse that the engine kept cutting out, so he'd limped home too late to telephone anybody. What Bodkin didn't know was Mr Tristan's daughter, Miss Marjoram Taylor, had been with her friends to the Nuneaton gig to see The Bombastics and told Daddy how surprised she was to see a Spencer & Taylor van in the Co-op car park.

***

Frankie Atom and The Bombastics parleyed in the all-night Sunset Café on the Wolverhampton-Stafford road on Wednesday April 3rd, in the wee small hours on their way back from Stoke on Trent. Things were sorted and decisions made before they'd even finished their teas and coffees, or Stan his bottle of Coke.

Barry worked in an architect's practice. He was a junior and bored out of his skull filing, running errands and sticking envelopes through the franking machine; Mom and Dad weren't at all happy about it, but Barry wasn't going to miss this chance.

Stan worked at the Austin in Longbridge making cars, pay was good and he and girlfriend Elsie were saving hard to get married. Initially, she was not happy about Stan giving up a steady job at the Austin, but £25 a week was enough to convince her. Mom was totally behind her little boy despite Dad being very worried about Stan giving up his apprenticeship.

Frankie hadn't bothered to try and get a job. When he wasn't playing his guitar onstage, he was playing his guitar at home and working hard on his song-writing.

Sugarlips had enrolled at college for a design course, which she said she could take or leave, depending on the gigs.

Bodkin also got a bit of gip from his parents, but took no notice; he said he didn't see himself getting a gold watch for distinguished service at Spencer & Taylor's.

So at 12:57 a.m. at the Sunset Café, they became full-time musicians.

Stan phoned Danny to tell him the next morning. Stan, Bodkin and Barry all handed in their notice at the end of that week.

***

They worked hard over the next few months, with Danny keeping his word and bringing them in regular work, rarely less than three and sometimes four, bookings a week. They got better and better, both musically and with their stage presence. They gradually built up a reputation as one of the best live acts on the scene. The Marquee in London, the Twisted Wheel in Manchester, the Cedar Club in Birmingham, and good old Eel Pie Island on the Thames. They were blazing a trail.

Barry never got round to telling them about his Volkswagen experience. Nearly six months had passed and 1983 was still vivid in his brain, but he said nothing. Oh, he meant to; he had every intention of getting everyone together and just telling them, but he always found an excuse not to.

Meanwhile Frank (a.k.a. Frankie Atom) was developing his song writing skills. 'Teenage Crush', his first effort, was already in The Bombastics repertoire. Right from the first time he played it to them, they'd loved it. Stan reckoned it would be a hit record if they could just land a recording contract. Frank wasn't quite sure to begin with, but after they'd all worked on the arrangement and then he'd heard the evocative sax solo Sugarlips had woven behind Frank's lyric of unrequited teenage love, he was hooked.

Frank had actually written 'Teenage Crush' when he was a fourteen-year-old schoolboy. His best mate, Dougie Short, had fallen madly in love with Miss Prince and art lessons just couldn't come around quick enough for him. Oh, to catch a glimpse of his lissom miss as she rode her bicycle through the school gates, the breeze fluttering her blonde hair or maybe gently lifting the hem of her summer dress. As any schoolboy will tell, it's what wet dreams are made of. Alas, Dougie was never to become the teacher's pet and the Teddy Bears', 'Born Too Late' inspired Frank to write his own version of his best mate's teenage heartbreak.

Frank was helped with his song writing by the Grundig reel-to-reel tape recorder he was given for Christmas. With the addition of a thirty-foot extension cord, his dad's garage became his recording studio.

He wrote more songs. He recorded them then changed the intros. Re-recorded them then altered some of the lyrics. Recorded them again speeded up, then tried them slowed down. Finally he was happy enough to play them to the other Bombastics from his Grundig, whilst sitting on the back seat of the VW travelling to a gig in Chelmsford.

'They're really good, Frankie boy,' said Bodkin, drumming his fingers on the steering wheel. 'Let's hear that jive one again, it's very catchy.'

'That'd be 'Jive Away the Tears',' replied Frank and slid the switch to spin the tape back. After a couple of stop-starts he caught the tail end of the previous song and started 'that jive one' over again.

Bodkin was right, it was catchy, with a repetitive hook line and everybody joined in, clapping and singing the bits they could remember. The VW camper rocked!

'See what I mean?' shouted Bodkin. 'It gets better and better, the more you hear it.'

'We could put that in the set,' said Carol. She looked at her wristwatch. 'We're going to be early getting there tonight. I say we go through it, see if we can come up with an arrangement; it's plain old rock 'n' roll, so we just throw everything at it.'

'Why wait until we get to Chelmsford,' said Barry, reaching into the back of the camper for his acoustic guitar. 'Let's get started on it straight away.'

***

The phone call from Danny that they'd all been waiting for came early one Tuesday morning in July. It was actually mid-morning, but when you've got home from a gig sometime after 2 a.m., you're still in bed and home alone, 10:30 a.m. *is* an early call.

The phone started ringing; it took Stan's sleepy head a little time for it to register.

He threw back the bedclothes and swung his legs out of bed. Still half asleep, he waddled across his bedroom, across the landing and into his mom and dad's room.

'Shit!' he cursed, as he caught his little toe on a caster wheel sticking out from under the corner of the bed. He hopped across to the telephone extension, which stood on the bedside table. He picked up the receiver in one hand, his throbbing toe in the other and croaked, 'Hello.'

'Stanley, it's Danny, I've got some news you'll want to hear.'

'Go on.' Stan was sat on the edge of the bed grimacing, his left leg crossed over his right, rubbing his toe.

'I've arranged for a chap called Martin Wainwright to come and listen to you at your Watford gig on Thursday.'

'Who's Martin Wainwright when he's at home?'

'He's an A&R man for Eternal records.'

'What's an A&R man?'

'Artist and Repertoire man; he's Eternal Records' talent scout, if you like Eternal and if he likes you enough, you get a recording contract.'

Now Stan was wide awake, any pain in his little toe forgotten.

'Blimey, Danny, what do we do, what do we say to him?'

'You just play your music like Frankie Atom and The Bombastics normally do; I'll do the talking.'

'You're going to be there, then?' Stan sounded relieved.

'I most certainly am. Danny Hoffman has had to be at his very best to make this happen and I want to be there with you when we close it out.'

'Thanks Danny, you're a star.'

'Just doing my job,' he laughed. 'Stan, I'll leave you to tell the others and make sure you've got Frankie's songs knocked into shape, it will be very important. I've told him you write a lot of your own stuff.'

'Don't worry about that, we've worked hard on them.'

'I shall speak to you before then no doubt, but I'll see you at The Red Pepper Club in Watford on Thursday. Cheerio.'

'See you Danny, Tarra-a-bit.'

***

Danny was still a bit of a man of mystery to his young charges. He made his money in the floor covering trade, or to be more precise, he made an awful lot of money in the floor covering trade. He'd inherited his father's carpet shop in St. Albans.

Benjamin Hoffman had built a busy and very profitable business, mainly selling carpet squares and rolls of linoleum to the local population, as fifties Britain slowly recovered from post world war depression. At last, people had got a bit of cash to spend on luxuries like television sets, washing machines and carpets.

Danny came into the business in the late fifties. After leaving university, he'd spent two years with his father's twin brother, Abraham. Uncle Abe was also in the floor covering trade but in 1951 had sold up, uprooted his family, and moved to Boston, Massachusetts where he opened a giant carpet and furniture outlet and over the next few years, had built it into a very successful business.

Benjamin was very keen that a young blood like Daniel learned all about new ideas and methods taking place in the industry over in the States and his brother's business gave Danny the ideal opportunity.

When Danny returned, he would change the direction of his father's business, and quite quickly too. Tufted broadloom carpet was bringing fitted carpet to the masses and to ensure they were getting their share, Hoffman and Son opened three more showrooms they'd named 'Carpet Matters', in Luton, Bedford and Cambridge.

However, Danny had learned from Uncle Abe that there was real money to be made supplying floor coverings into the commercial market. Public buildings, local government offices, shops, restaurants, pubs and clubs.

Danny set about getting to know the decision makers and making sure they were well looked after in return for their contracts, supplying and fitting flooring; something else he learned from Uncle Abe.

Over the next few years, he used only the best materials which he purchased at the best prices, personally negotiated with the manufacturers. He made it his policy to use only the most experienced floor-layers and he paid them just above the going rate; which meant he kept them. He made sure he rubbed shoulders with the people that mattered and cultivated good relations with people who were going to matter sometime in the future. As his reputation for quality and service grew, so did his business. There weren't many flooring contracts in the home counties that Danny Hoffman and Carpet Matters weren't involved in.

So it was through this unlikely connection that Daniel Hoffman met five young musicians from Birmingham. He had been to the Carpet Matters branch in Bedford and decided to call in at Westhill Working Men's Club, to check everything was satisfactory with the vinyl flooring, newly fitted in the snooker room, reception and enormous function suite.

Sitting in the lounge bar, enjoying a Black Russian cigarette and chatting over a Coke with the club steward, Danny spotted a large coloured poster behind the bar:

'The Sensational Bombastics   Saturday October 27th Admission Free'

'What's the idea of letting the punters in free, Bill?' asked Danny. 'Ain't going to make much money out of that.'

'It's their idea, The Bombastics.' Club steward Bill Gower raised his hands defensively. 'They're coming all the way down from Birmingham and not charging me anything. Apparently, they've invited club owners and agents from the Home Counties along. They're trying to break through in London and the South; they reckon that's what it takes to land a recording contract.'

'Hmmm, interesting,' said Danny thoughtfully. 'I bet I do business with quite a number of those club owners. Okay if I pop in to say hello?'

'Be my guest,' said Bill Gower.

So on Saturday October 27th 1962, Danny Hoffman and The Bombastics met.

***

The gig at The Red Pepper Club just could not have gone better. Danny brought Martin Wainwright into the dressing room before The Bombastics' set, whilst the support band were onstage. He came over as very warm and friendly, giving each of them a handshake and a smile as Danny introduced them.

'One of the things I'm looking forward to is hearing your own songs,' he enthused. 'Danny here, tells me you have a few up your sleeve.'

'We've got a couple in tonight's set,' said Frank. 'Plus I got three or four more finished that even these guys haven't heard yet.'

'Great stuff,' said Martin. 'I'll leave you to get on with it: go break a leg, as they say.'

Break a leg they did. The crowd were right up for it and Frankie and the rest were on top form. Before they started 'Teenage Crush' followed by 'Jive Away the Tears', much to the surprise of the others onstage, Stan stepped forward to Frank's mic and announced, 'Boys and girls, we'd like you to hear a couple of new numbers written especially for you tonight by our lead guitarist, Frankie Atom. We hope you enjoy them.' He winked at the others as he made his way back to his mark.

The Red Pepper crowd just wouldn't let them off. Three encores, and if it hadn't been for the stage manager Spotlight Cyril (Barry had nicknamed him), switching the stage lights off and the house lights on, it could have been more.

'We'll have the bleedin' rozzers 'ere if we don't empty this Club sharpish,' Cyril croaked at them, with a nub end in the corner of his mouth. 'Don't wanna lose our bleedin' licence, do we?' He then broke into a hacking cough.

Danny entered the dressing room, beaming. 'Well done boys, well done Carol. Martin Wainwright loved you, loved your songs too. That was a smart bit of work Stanley my boy, announcing the two songs; it concentrated his thoughts.'

'So where's he buggered off to?' Croaked Barry, puffing away at a fag stuck in the corner of his mouth. 'Where's our bleedin' recording contract?' He then mimicked Spotlight's hacking cough.

The others just had to laugh.

'You're jumping the gun, Barry.' Danny was rather taken aback, having not met Spotlight Cyril. 'There's a number of things got to happen before you replace Cliff Richard and the Shadows at number one in the hit parade.'

He sat down on one of the dressing room stools and reached into his inside pocket for his diary; he opened it up on his knee. 'You got a gig at Gino's in Enfield next Monday. Martin and I have arranged for you to have an audition at Eternal's studio next morning. He wants you to have more of your numbers ready, Frankie. He also wants you to work on a cover version of this.' He held up a 45rpm disc with a label and slipcover none of them recognised.

'It's a record that just entered the Billboard charts. It's called 'Little Bit Crazy' by The Delrays, a New Jersey band.'

'Bugger me, Spotlight,' said Bodkin slapping Barry on his back. 'Looks like Saturday morning's going to be spent rehearsing at the village hall.'

'Fortunate you're only in Leicester on Friday and Cheltenham on Saturday,' said Danny.

'What about my beauty sleep?' groaned Barry. 'I'm never gonna be the first nude centre-fold in 'Honey' if I get bags under my eyes.'

'Perish the thought.' Carol screwed her eyes up in disgust.

'Talking of beauty sleep,' said Danny. 'I'll book you into a hotel, save you driving all the way back home, just to turn around and go back again. You need to be at Eternal for ten o'clock.'

'There'll be no cigarettes and whiskey and wild, wild women, Barry,' continued Danny. 'You've all worked hard for this chance. Don't cock it up.'

'I'll take care of lover boy,' cut in Bodkin. 'Straight from the gig to the hotel, then it's coffee, and straight to bed.'

'What no foreplay?' pleaded Barry, throwing his hands up in mock shock. 'Not even a goodnight kiss?'

***

Danny booked them into a little family hotel in Enfield right across the road from Gino's. Next morning the journey to Islington was a very frustrating one because of the rush hour traffic.

'Imagine having to do this every morning just to earn a living,' groaned Bodkin as he pulled up yet again, behind a line of stationary traffic. 'I'd rather be in a rock 'n' roll band driving 200 miles through the night.'

'Me too,' chipped in Stan. 'As long as you don't wake us up 'til we're home.'

He got a Bodkin glare through the driving mirror.

When they arrived at Eternal Records, Danny was already there with Martin Wainwright who introduced them to Don Winston; he was to be their producer. They were also introduced to the recording engineer, Stevie Balshaw.

The morning went well. Martin Wainwright asked them what they'd managed with The Delrays' 'Little Bit Crazy'. They'd got it pretty well sorted, it was a simple enough twelve bar, and after a few minor changes by Don Winston, they made a decent job of it in only five takes.

'Okay,' said Don through the control desk mic. 'That was impressive, boys and girls. Now let's hear some of the material you've written, but just hang on whilst I come down there to join you.'

He came down from the mixing desk, pulled up a chair and joined The Bombastics on the studio floor. Frankie counted them in and off they went into 'Jive Away the Tears'. Martin was soon nodding and clapping along behind the control desk and when they finished Stevie Balshaw gave them a double thumbs up and a large grin from behind the sound proof screen. Danny sat next to Stevie, with his arms folded, wearing an enormous smile.

'That was something else, guys,' nodded Don, clapping his hands. 'You say you wrote that yourselves?'

'It was Frankie,' piped up Bodkin from behind his drums.

Barry added, 'He's got more if you want to hear them?'

'I surely do.' Don's eyes met Frank's. 'If they're as half decent as that one, we're on the right track, young man.' He shouted up to Stevie, 'Let's take that one again from the top, then we can listen to their others.'

A slightly tinny voice came back over the speaker. 'I've already canned it Don, just in case, thought we could save some time.'

'You heard him folks,' said Don, turning back to the band. 'Let's hear the next one.' Then he turned back to Steve, shouting, 'Get this on tape too, I'm coming back up.'

Any nerves at being in a recording studio for the first time, had now completely disappeared. The atmosphere in that one hundred and fifty square feet of north London, was electric.

'Teenage Crush' needed no run through, it had been part of their stage act for a few weeks now, so it was a highly polished little gem. When Don and Stevie heard the haunting sax, that was now such an important part of Frank's song about teenage angst, they were all blown away. There was some serious talking going on behind that screen, with Danny in full flow, but Don had made sure the internal mic was switched off, so Carol and the boys couldn't hear.

They did a couple of takes on one of Frankie's newer songs, 'Love You Honey', and at that point, Don called a halt to proceedings. 'Sorry guys, I got carried away,' he said. 'Martin reminded me, this is only an audition to see if you're right for Eternal Records.'

He came back down into the studio along with Danny, Martin and Stevie Balshaw.

'Look, guys, we have one of our weekly progress meetings here tomorrow morning with the directors, and I will ensure The Bombastics are definitely on the agenda. Any decision to give you a contract will be down to them, but they do listen to what I have to say and when they hear these tapes I think they'll be mighty impressed. You may know of our MD, Richard Arblaster. He was very popular in the early fifties; recorded under the name of Dickie Ambrose. 'Eternal Longing' was massive. It's where the name of the label came from.'

They all looked at each other blankly.

'You lot get your stuff loaded up and get on your way. The North Circular's going to be pretty busy in the next hour,' broke in Danny. 'Don and Martin have my number and they've promised to phone me tomorrow as soon as any decision has been made.'

Don shook hands with them all, saving a peck on the cheek for Sugarlips. Martin and Stevie joined in to help them with their gear and wish them au revoir.

***

It was arranged that Don would phone Danny as soon as he knew anything and then Danny would phone each of them with the news.

Just before noon the next day, Stan's mum answered her phone. Stan had heard it ringing and rushed through from the kitchen; when he saw her with the receiver to her ear he stopped motionless in the doorway. After the briefest of conversations, she handed the receiver to Stan, mouthing, 'D-a-n-n-y!'

Stan closed his eyes and crossed his fingers as he took the phone off his mother.

'You got yourselves a two year recording contract, Stanley my man.' Danny then had to wait whilst Stan did a giant hop, step and jump over the family dog. 'I've been back down to Islington and signed all the bits of paper. It's a two year deal and you're contracted to release eight singles and one LP during the two years, and there's a one year option if things go well. I've also negotiated a £500 advance which you'll pay back as the royalties start to build up, but don't concern yourselves with that, leave that to me.'

'Brilliant, Danny, soddin' brilliant! Thanks so much for everything you've done.' Stan sounded like he was on the brink of tears.

'It's you guys who've done it, Stan. I just pointed you in the right direction.' Stan could feel the glow of Danny's smile from eighty miles away. 'You better phone Carol and Barry now and I'll get onto Bodkin and Frank. I also need to talk to Frankie-boy about a publishing deal for his songs. Cheerio Stan and again, well done, mate.'

***

Eternal Records, Don Winston and Martin Wainwright in particular, decided to put out 'Teenage Crush' and the cover of 'Little Bit Crazy' as a double A-side, in mono. 'Teenage Crush' would go out exactly how they recorded it, first take and they had enough takes of 'Little Bit Crazy' to satisfy Don Winston.

For years after, Frankie would tell the story about one-take-Frankie comparing himself to Elvis, whose one take recordings were legendary at Sun Studio in Memphis.

Don told Danny that Eternal were very keen that 'Jive Away the Tears' would be the follow up, but he wanted the band back in the studios to make a few adjustments. He'd contact Danny again soon with free time slots.

On Monday September 2nd 1963, Eternal Records released the double header, 'Little Bit Crazy' / 'Teenage Crush'. Martin Wainwright had got promo copies in the hands of all the top radio and television shows, musical journalists and DJs, two weeks before the release date.

Danny did his bit too. Every club owner and pub landlord he had supplied flooring to had a promotional copy for their DJs and Juke Boxes. When he phoned for more copies he was told by Martin in no uncertain terms that punting out promotional copies was a definite no-no.

'Look Danny, leave this to me; you'll get us all in hot water.'

***

A major breakthrough came when Alan Freeman played

both sides in the new releases section of his Sunday record show, Pick of the Pops. Six days later this was followed by the disc being spun on Juke Box Jury, when David Jacobs chose to play 'Teenage Crush' instead of 'Little Bit Crazy'. The panel consisting of Petula Clark, Jean Metcalfe, Marty Wilde and Pete Murray all voted it a hit.

That meant Frankie Atom and The Bombastics had their record aired to over twenty-five million listeners on two prime time shows.

The Bombastics' concern had been Eternal releasing it as a double A-side. Their worry was it might split sales and they'd slip between two stools, but most of the shows did the same as David Jacobs and picked 'Teenage Crush'.

Word came through from Martin Wainwright that they would make their chart debut that week and they should listen to Pick of the Pops, which went out the next Sunday. So, on Sunday 15th September, they all gathered around a transistor radio in Frank's back garden. Frank's mom and dad and sister Suzie, and Stan's girlfriend Elsie joined them. It was a beautiful late summer afternoon as they listened to Alan Freeman's countdown.

There was a little squeal of delight from Carol as he reached number twenty and no mention of The Bombastics. 'We're in the top twenty, I can't believe it.'

'Unless that A&E bloke's got it wrong and we ain't in the charts at all,' grumbled Barry.

'It's A&R, you pillock, not A&E; which is where you'll end up if you don't button it,' growled Bodkin. 'Let's listen, eh?'

As Brian Poole and The Tremeloes' 'Twist and Shout' faded, Alan Freeman's voice came in. 'And making their chart debut at number eighteen are Frankie Atom and The Bombastics with 'Teenage Crush'.'

There was pandemonium as they all shouted and sang

the words they knew so well. There was much hand shaking and back slapping. Barry snogged Suzie, Stan hugged Elsie and everybody kissed Sugarlips, including Frank's dad, Jack. Doris, his mom appeared through one of the veranda windows with a tray full of glasses and a magnum of Moët & Chandon. She put the tray down on the garden table.

Jack picked up the bottle, twisted the cork and popped it skywards and into the herbaceous border; he then waited for Carol's sax to end the first chart airing of 'Teenage Crush' and signalled for them all to listen. 'I thought as this was to be a very special moment, we ought to mark it with something of a toast.' He charged each of the champagne flutes and waited for everybody to grab one. 'May Doris and I offer our heartiest congratulations to Frankie Atom – I still can't get used to that,' he laughed. 'To Frankie Atom and The Bombastics and their amazing success. May this be just the start of a glittering career in the rock 'n' roll business. Cheers!'

Everyone raised their glasses.

They didn't realise it at the time, but the next few days would be something of a welcome hiatus before the storm really broke.

That week they bought all the music papers, *New Musical Express*, *Melody Maker*, *Disc* and *Record Mirror* and spread them out in the dressing room of The Adelphi in West Bromwich. They opened them all to the pages where the charts were printed and just gawped starry-eyed.

Frankie was to recall many years later, when he did an interview for a local radio station, that seeing their very first record in the charts that week was probably the biggest thrill of his rock 'n' roll life.

It was Bodkin who first noticed that all the papers had them at number eighteen, except for the *Melody Maker* who had them entering the chart at number nineteen. He picked up the newspaper in his huge hands and ripped it in half, then he squared the halves together and ripped them in half again; finally, he effortlessly ripped the whole lot in half once more and handed the lot over to Barry. 'Here you are Barry, go and stick these in the bog, the toilet roll was running a bit low when I was in there, earlier.'

***

Barry walked round the Market Square in Fordrough with a folded copy of the *NME*, going up to acquaintances and complete strangers alike, asking, 'Excuse me, have you seen our hit record?' pointing at the charts. 'It's number eighteen in the Hit Parade, you know. Buy your copy at Perrins Electric Store over on Sheep Street whilst stocks last.'

Whether it was Barry's influence, nobody was really sure, but Perrins sold out before the weekend and had to wait until the following Monday for their next delivery.

***

Danny's phone never seemed to stop ringing during the last few weeks of 1963 and it was usually Martin. He lined up TV and radio appearances, interviews with newspapers and magazines. It seemed everybody wanted a piece of these hot shots from Birmingham.

Martin took on a booking from a friend of his for a nightclub in Soho and Danny had to put him straight; he told Martin, politely but firmly, that it was he, Danny Hoffman, who controlled the diary and any enquiries must go through him.

From number eighteen the record soared into the top five where it stayed for four weeks, peaking at three, held off the top spots by the combined efforts of The Crystals, Brian Poole and The Tremeloes and inevitably, The Beatles.

Thank Your Lucky Stars was their first TV appearance

and when they went across Birmingham to ABC Studios in Aston for the Sunday recording they were nervous. First they were relieved, then disappointed, to find they were going to mime to both 'Teenage Crush' and 'Little Bit Crazy'. They were a live group; lip-synching seemed strange.

Frank said, 'I haven't mimed since I was a twelve-year-old Elvis in front of the bedroom mirror.'

During a break Barry made a move on Spin-a-Disc girl Janice Nicholls, putting an arm around her and mimicking her Black Country catchphrase, 'Oi'd loike to give yow foive.' She was not happy. Fortunately, Bodkin was at hand and with the cameras down between shoots, he was able to frogmarch Barry back to the dressing room by the collar of his powder blue suit, whilst Stan reassured Janice that Barry was harmless and they were thinking of having him put down.

When Danny heard about the incident he explained to Barry behind closed doors, that with or without him The Bombastics' star was in the ascendancy. A contrite Barry promised to behave himself and was on his best behaviour when they met Sandie Shaw on the set of Ready, Steady, Go!

'The weekend starts here'. This went out live on a Friday night, but they still had to mime their hits. The kids in the studio were great dancers and stylish dressers, but apart from clapping they were strangely quiet; it was only after the show they found out the girls were under orders not to scream.

'Those poor girls,' said Barry in the dressing room. 'When they see me it must feel the same as having to wear a chastity belt.'

Straight after the show they performed live at the Lavender Tree in Kingston and then on to the Moon & Stars in Woking. Danny was pulling out all the stops for maximum exposure.

Next came a pre-recorded set for BBC Radio's Easybeat, which was broadcast the following Sunday morning. Because of the Musician's Union restrictions with needle-time, they were told that the four numbers they were booked to play must be live. The Bombastics didn't care, they loved playing live and when he interviewed them during the show it was pretty evident that host Brian Matthew loved them playing live too.

They also pre-recorded two Saturday Club programmes, the first of which was the week after The Beatles. Not that they were overawed by that; again, they were able to show what a quality band they were when it came to live music. Danny was very miffed when he found out The Beatles had been paid fifty guineas and he'd only been able to get thirty.

They lost count of the number of local TV and radio spots they did. Southern, Granada, Midlands, Scottish, and Frank's mom was thrilled to bits when they did a guest spot on Mike and Bernie Winter's Big Night Out.

After these airings Danny always seemed to have them playing at some nearby dance hall or nightclub, he never missed a trick. However, two things were now very different. Firstly, no longer were they were playing long hours; an hour at the most, with a local dance band or group supporting them. Secondly, a lot more girls were screaming and throwing flowers, teddy bears and cards onstage, usually with telephone numbers on them and usually directed at Frankie. No knickers yet, but that would soon happen.

There were countless interviews and photo shoots for the musical press, they even talked to the *Melody Maker*! Then there were the teenage magazines. Frankie was in demand. Photographed with his guitar, without his guitar, giving the boy next door smile, being the mean and moody bad boy, even at the wheel of Danny's Zephyr Zodiac; despite the fact that Frankie couldn't drive. All the soppy stuff that schoolgirls wanted to know; star sign, favourite colour, favourite food, favourite record and favourite film.

Also there was the re-recording of 'Jive Away the Tears'. This was recorded on 4-track along with four more Frank Richards (a.k.a. Frankie Atom) compositions during a three day stint in the middle of November. To be more precise, eight days before Lee Harvey Oswald appeared at the sixth floor window of The Texas School Book Depository and assassinated John F. Kennedy, President of the United States.

It made Barry shudder when he realised he'd known that was coming!

CHAPTER 16
'LET'S HAVE A PARTY'

Elvis Presley

In the end, Eternal Records changed the plan, or to be more exact, A&R man Martin Wainwright changed it for them. 'Teenage Crush' / 'Little Bit Crazy' stayed in the charts longer than expected. It dropped out of the top five, but then hung around the top twenty for several weeks. In the meantime Martin had listened to the other songs that Frankie Atom and The Bombastics had recorded and thought 'Love You Honey' should be the follow up.

'My thinking is that it's a great pop song and will sell shitloads anyway,' he reasoned. 'However, Don's new arrangement of 'Jive Away the Tears' is so catchy and bright we'll hold it back for a few months ready in time for the Christmas market, maybe even get you the Christmas number one.'

Don Winston had recorded bass, drums and guitar on one track, overlaid Frankie's vocals on track two with Barry's and Frankie's harmonies on track three. This allowed him to dub Sugarlips' sax onto track four, mixing it alongside Frankie's driving guitar. The result was breathtaking, they all loved it.

Another Frankie composition, 'One Hour's Sleep', again recorded on 4-track, would be released as their third single sometime during the summer. Sugarlips and the boys liked his thinking, they were more than happy with everything they'd recorded and trusted Martin Wainwright's judgement.

***

Danny was now filling every spare date months ahead. With a record in the charts he was now able to double the fees, although he was adamant they honour the £40 and £50 bookings he had agreed before 'Teenage Crush' and 'Little Bit Crazy' charted. He also doubled their pay. £50 a week made them feel like they were living the dream. Sometimes he got them two gigs on the same night. They'd do an hour at The Ritz in south Birmingham and then rush through the city to do an hour at The Plaza in north Birmingham, or its sister venue in Old Hill.

The strain of performing most nights, week after week, loading and unloading their amps and instruments, was starting to tell, particularly on Bodkin who still did most of the driving. A roadie from one of the support bands they'd gigged with had passed on a tip to help keep them awake. 'Amphetamines,' said big Pete, offering a handful of little white pills. 'Give you a lift. Work wonders for me with all the miles I have to drive this soddin' van.'

'We steer clear of shit like that,' said Stan. 'The only stimulant we take is Coca-Cola.'

The crunch came after a concert in Cardiff. Barry had suggested the dressing room elixir Coke was better when whiskey was added to it (although he never told them where he acquired the taste for that little combination). They'd all noticed he missed a simple count in to 'Johnny B. Goode', a number they'd done a thousand times. It was Stan that spotted the empty half bottle of Johnny Walker in the rubbish bin amongst the cola bottles, backstage in the dressing room.

'You're pissed, you little prat,' raged Bodkin. 'You know very well it's your turn to drive home tonight.' Barry staggered slightly as he ducked to avoid Bodkin's lunge.

'He can't drive in that state,' said Stan. 'You're gonna have to do it, Bods.'

Bodkin was white with rage. 'It can't go on like this, I drive all the way down here, I unload and load most of the gear, I sit behind those drums for over a hour and now, instead of relaxing in the back of the wagon with a bottle of beer, I've got to drive us home too. I could have got our Wally to do the driving and humping tonight, he's at a loose end at the moment; building trade's crap and there's very little work around.'

'Hey, maybe that's the answer,' said Frankie. 'Wally could be our road manager; do the driving and shift the gear in and out. We must be able to afford to pay him full time, with all the work we're doing.'

Bodkin, calmer now, sat down. Half a smile came to his lips. 'What a bostin' idea, I know he's sick to the back teeth of plastering. I'm sure he'd do it if the money's right.'

'We need to do this right, I'll phone Danny first thing, see what we can afford,' said Stan. Then he looked over to Barry, who had turned a strange grey colour. 'For being a complete prat Barry, you can start the loading on your own.'

'He can keep his hands off my stuff.' Bodkin raised his voice again. 'He's still pissed; I don't want none of my drums rolling down the stage door steps and across the friggin' car park.'

***

Danny thought Wally the road manager was a good idea, and suggested they offer him twenty-five pounds a week top line, but first see if he'd accept twenty.'

Bodkin was having none of that. 'He's our kid, I ain't having you pull a stunt like that. Give him the twenty-five, he'll do a good job.'

Stan and Bodkin met with Wally to ask him and he jumped at the chance. 'Twenty-five smackers, blimey! I'd have to plaster twenty-four hours a day to pick up that sort of money.' Then he stopped for a moment, taking in his new appointment. 'I ought to have some little business cards with my details on. Walter B. Adams, Frankie Atom and The Bombastics, road manager.'

Bodkin looked at Stan, but he didn't bat an eyelid. 'You can pay for them out of your first twenty-five,' he said.

Bodkin was right, Wally did a good job. As well as his driving duties he soon got the hang of setting up the gear, making sure the shirts and suits were clean and pressed and kept on hangers in the back of the VW. He added a clothes brush and a steam iron to the box with all the electrical bits and pieces in it and he kept the white Cubans clean and polished. To begin with Carol insisted on looking after her own stage wear, but it wasn't long before she trusted him to have her dress regularly dry cleaned. Wally also became pretty adept at helping Barry with the groupies, especially when he gave them one of his business cards.

When they were working more than three hours from home, or when Danny got them a string of gigs close together, which he was clever at doing, he'd book them into bed and breakfasts or theatrical boarding houses and very occasionally in the early days, hotels.

It was one such cluster of concerts in the North East, Gateshead, York and Hull that they were first introduced to marijuana. They'd seen Johnny Ace and the Detours rolling their own and when the conversation turned to uppers and downers the lads from Hull laughed when they discovered that the strongest thing they took was Coca-Cola. Barry and Bodkin were already smokers, so when Johnny Ace rolled them a joint to share, it didn't seem such a bad idea.

Of course they were aware of pot, a number of bands on the circuit used it, but they'd never bothered; this was the first time they'd even held a reefer. Barry lit up and inhaled, then passed it to Bodkin who did the same. After each of them had drawn on it a few times, the glow came over them. At this point, Stan and Frankie came in. Amidst the clouds of strange smelling smoke were two giggling Bombastics.

'Is that pot you're smoking?' Stan asked them.

'It most certainly is Stanley Ravenscroft Esquire,' chortled Bodkin. 'You should come and try some.' Barry carried on giggling.

To begin with Frankie and Sugarlips never got the pot habit, but over the next few months Barry, Bodkin and Stan became regular users. Wally was the official holder-of-the-pouch, his job was to keep the supply topped up. He kept it in a small leather purse which he hid in the back of one of the VOX amps, stuck to the inside with gaffer tape.

***

'Love You Honey' was released in March just as The Bombastics began a UK package tour with US heartthrob Deke Rivers. Also on the bill were The Satellites, The Boogie Boys and The Johnny Washington Seven. By the time they reached the fifth venue of their tour, which happened to be the Odeon in their home town

Birmingham, they were the *NME*'s and the *Melody Maker*'s hot tip to be back in the charts.

They always started the second half of the show with Deke Rivers topping the bill. The Odeon was sold out weeks in advance, the boxes and balconies packed with their fans and, of course, families and friends. The Boogie Boys had closed the first half with a rousing rendition of their hit record 'Commotion', which had the whole place jumping. Few fans left their seats for the twenty-minute break. The atmosphere was electric as anticipation for the return of Birmingham's own, reached fever pitch.

Behind the curtains, with The Bombastics wired up and ready to go, urgent discussions were taking place. Theatre manager Bert Sanderford, malt whiskey connoisseur with a face as red as a turkey-cock, Frankie, Stan and Denny, one of the Boogie Boys, were huddled together in centre stage. There was a lot of nodding of heads and smiling.

Frankie quietly passed the word to the others. 'Change in plan, we're starting the show with 'Love You Honey'.'

This brought raised eyebrows from Barry and Sugarlips and, 'What's goin' on here then?' from Bodkin, which Frankie chose to ignore. He winked and turned, ready to face his audience still the other side of the curtains. As he did, Boogie Boy Denny slipped through the curtains and stood in the spotlight; he raised both arms and slowly lowered them as the hubbub quietened.

He spoke clearly into the mic. 'Ladies and gentlemen, boys and girls, we are delighted to announce that Birmingham's very own Frankie Atom and The Bombastics have just entered the UK charts at number twelve with their new single 'Love You Honey'.' As he exited stage left, Frankie could be heard counting the song in, 'One, two, three, four!' and the curtains swept back as the zoot suits of many colours (and the long red dress) broke into their second chart hit. The place erupted.

The screaming reached eardrum-shattering decibel levels and there was panic amongst the front of house staff as they tried to stop teenage girls jumping up onto the stage, but fortunately their tight skirts and high heels were unsuitable for climbing and the stagehands kept the would-be assailants under control. When they'd finished their set and done their encore, the crowd were still shouting for more. From the wings, Deke Rivers graciously waved them back on to play one more number before he closed the show. If he'd had any worries about following The Bombastics he needn't have, the audience were well and truly warmed up and, backed by the Johnny Washington Seven, his string of hits went down a storm.

After the show Frankie's dad, Jack Richards, announced a 'bit of a party', at Ambleside, his Little Barnham home. A number of the family members and friends came by car and a few of the other band members either cadged a ride with Wally, driving Jezza who'd been especially brought out of storage for the night, or grabbed taxis.

It was certainly a night to remember. Looking back it would be easy to blame Jack and his well-stocked bar and he certainly did blame himself. Jack had spent a huge slice of his pools fortune making Ambleside his own personal Shangri La.

Little Barnham was not much more than a hamlet lying between Fordrough and the South Birmingham border. Jack's four bedroom bungalow stood with no more than a dozen houses and bungalows, mostly built in the thirties, along the only road that ran through the tiny village.

Those of the night's guests who hadn't been there before, would definitely admire the enormous veranda complete with indoor swimming pool, but Jack's pride and joy was his big boy's room. It housed a full sized snooker table, dart board and oche, the very latest state-of-the-art stereo system and a custom-made bar, with more spirits, vermouths, beers and mixers than you could shake a stick at. Focal point of this tacky bamboo and mirror construction was the line-up of upside-down spirit bottles, complete with optics.

Bodkin and Stan were just nineteen years old; Barry still two months away from nineteen. Sugarlips and Frankie were still seventeen. Apart from Barry, alcohol was something none of them really thought too much about. Bodkin and Stan would have the occasional beer and Frankie and Sugarlips only ever drank soft drinks. Barry's taste for whiskey and Coke could be a problem, but not as much of a problem as other stimulants he was starting to experiment with.

Frankie's mom, Doris, made platefuls of bacon sandwiches for everybody, with lashings of HP sauce, or tomato ketchup. Sister Suzie put six of her favourite 45s on the auto-change, and Bodkin and Barry started a game of snooker to the strains of 'Can't Buy Me Love'. They all joined in with John and Paul.

'It's their second number one over in the States,' drooled Elsie, draped around Stan's neck. 'When are you going to have hits in America? We could all go to New York and go up the Empire State Building.'

'Dunno, we haven't really had much time to think about it. Suppose it's up to Eternal,' replied Stan. 'If the Beatles can do it, why not us? Everything they've ever recorded seems to be in the Billboard Hot Hundred at the moment.'

'You need to tell Danny to get on the case, ask him what he's doing...'

At that point Jack came round with a tray full of drinks. 'As it's a special night, try one of these,' he said. 'Whiskey and Coke, the in-thing with all you kids apparently.' Stan took two, one each for himself and Elsie, Denny and Pete from the Boogie Boys helped themselves, so too did

Bodkin, Wally, Sugarlips and Barry. Jack returned to the bar and replenished the tray with more glassfuls of whiskey and Coke and shouldered his way through the lounge door where the rest of his guests were.

Just after one o'clock those sat in the lounge, drinking and talking, heard a car pull up in the drive and from the sound the gravel made as it skidded to a halt, it had been travelling at a fair old pace. Then came the sound of a blaring car horn.

Doris looked horrified. 'Jack – do something – for God's sake – they'll wake the neighbours!'

Jack leapt to his feet and swept back a curtain with one hand whilst carefully performing a juggling act with his glass of whiskey and Coke in the other.

At a crazy angle to other cars, parked either side of the front door, stood a Ford Anglia, its headlights blazing across the driveway, illuminating the next door neighbour's house and all the shrubs, bushes and hedges between. The passenger door was open and two figures, little more than silhouettes, were clambering out. The horn blared again.

Jack was apoplectic, but struggling to open the window to remonstrate, when the porch lights came on. Jack could now see it was a pale green Anglia, the model with the slanted-back rear window; he could also see a third figure getting out of the driver's door. *No doubt the damned fool who's woken up the whole bloody neighbourhood*, he thought. He then saw Bodkin, Barry and Denny appear to his left from the porch and crunch their way across the gravel towards the three newcomers. He put his glass down and rushed out of the lounge into the hall and out through the porch.

'Turn those blasted lights out!' he yelled as he ran across the drive. 'Who the hell are you, anyway?'

It was Denny who spoke. 'It's Brian and Jasper, two of the Johnny Washington Seven, and Gino their roadie.'

Gino took a step forward, a lock of his greased-back hair fell down across his forehead. 'Didn't want us at your little party, eh?' he snarled. 'Thought you'd give us a body swerve, which is not very friendly at all, is it?'

'Don't talk rubbish, Gino.' Barry sounded quite tough, maybe it was the marijuana, or maybe because Bodkin was standing next to him. 'Now do as Frankie's dad asked and switch those headlights off.'

'Who's a brave little boy, then?' scowled Gino. 'Careful, or daddy won't deliver your...'

Jasper pulled him back. 'Shut it, Gino. We come in peace remember?' He half turned to Brian. 'Do what the gentleman asks and turn those lights out.'

Jack was still seething, but thought it better any further discussions took place inside rather than in full view of the neighbour's bedroom windows. Once in the hallway, he turned to the three of them and Gino in particular. 'This get-together was to celebrate our Frank and his band back in their home town and back in the hit parade. It was spontaneous, on the spur of the moment and none of you were excluded.'

Gino, definitely calmer now, shrugged. 'Sorry, man, I thought that little toe-rag Barry might be backing out.'

'Backing out of what exactly?' Jack looked puzzled.

'I said shut it.' Jasper pushed Gino away and Brian ushered him into the snooker room leaving Jack unanswered. All three soon had drinks in their hands.

Wally was now head barman, recharging empty glasses. Whiskey and Cokes in the main, but also gin and tonics, vodkas or beers. Elsie preferred her Babychams and introduced them to Sugarlips. Frankie remained on Coke without whiskey and sister Suzie remained in charge of the music.

Jack should have read the early warning signs when he

had to get yet another bottle of Long John whiskey and a dozen Cokes out of his store cupboard. Drinks were flowing.

The first sign of trouble was when he heard splashing in the swimming pool and caught two of the Boogie Boys, Denny and Pete, skinny dipping and had to stop Suzie joining them. Already topless and about to slip out of her jeans he threw a very large towel at his daughter to help hide his embarrassment and her considerable charms, but all she could do was giggle.

'You could drown yourself the state you're in, you stupid girl!' ranted Jack.

'There's no way she would've drowned with those buoyancy aids!' shouted Denny from the safety of the water.

'Sorry, Mr Richards, we got carried away, we were playing a sort of strip-Jack-naked on the dartboard,' Pete drunkenly tried to explain. 'Then Denny hit the treble twenty, but his dart fell out. When Sue said his prick wasn't hard enough and didn't count, he only had his underpants left on, so he charged through into the veranda with his Y-fronts in his hand and dived into the pool.'

All three were very pissed and shaking with laughter. Jack decided to leave them to get dressed. It was then he noticed the end panel of the veranda glass frontage was open. The whole of this section slid back on aluminium tracks. This opened out onto a large patio area and made his indoor swimming pool virtually an outdoor swimming pool for when it was hot and sunny. However, this was March and the early hours of a chilly morning.

When he stepped into the doorway unnoticed, he saw Barry handing folded bank notes over to Gino. From where he was standing it was impossible to see how much, but it was a substantial wad, that's for sure. He then saw Barry rip open a little polythene bag, put something into his mouth and swill it down with his whiskey and Coke. Still unnoticed, he crept up behind Gino and Brian and made a grab for the two little polythene bags lying on the table in front of Barry. Completely caught on the hop, there was nothing any of them could do to stop him. As he opened his hand he could see there was still a small white sugar lump in the bag Barry had ripped open and two lumps in the unopened one.

'Drugs. So that's it.' Jack was furious. 'Barry Harper, you're a fool. Frankie told me some of you were doing marijuana, but what are these? Amfetamints, or whatever you call them?' Then looking at Gino and Brian he asked, 'And who are these, your suppliers?'

There was a moment's silence, broken by a scowl from Gino. 'Amfetamints? This is acid, you silly old fool.'

'Acid? What the hell is acid?' Jack looked confused.

'LSD,' sneered Gino. 'I serve it up on sugar lumps for my special customers.'

'How dare you use my house as a drug den,' fumed Jack. 'How dare you try and taint my Frankie and the rest of these kids with this filth.'

Barry, his eyelids half closed, totally ignored Jack as he gazed into the firmament with a stupid grin on his face. To him the stars were in full Cinemascope.

'Butt out, old timer,' snarled Gino. 'You'll get back to your whiskey if you know what's good for you.'

Jack's first instinct was to phone the police, then he thought of the trouble this would bring crashing down on his son – him too, for that matter. That's when he heard the scream.

Shit, what more could go wrong? he thought, racing through the veranda and snooker room, into the hall and through the front door.

The yellow light cast by the porch and the front room window with the curtains thrown back, illuminated a confrontation. Jasper had his arm around Sugarlips' throat, trying to open the door of the Anglia. Bodkin and Frankie were already in the driveway.

'Stay your distance, big man, or I'll wring her neck!' Jasper shouted at Bodkin. 'The snooty bitch hasn't been able to keep her hands off me all tour; so now's her chance.'

'He's a liar, I've hardly spoken to him – help me Bodkin – pleeeeease!'

'You hurt her and I'll rip yer cowin' face off.' Bodkin was trembling with rage as he edged closer. Sugarlips was crying uncontrollably, tears and mascara pouring down her cheeks.

'Let go of her now or you're a dead man, Jasper.' Bodkin shook a clenched fist in his direction. That's when he felt a sharp point in the side of his neck.

'I think it might be you who's a dead man, pal.' It was Gino, pressing the point of a flick knife into the side of Bodkin's neck. Bodkin couldn't turn to see Gino without pushing the knife tip further in, but he recognised his voice and the smell of the cheap aftershave that was always wafting about backstage when Gino was around. 'If Jasper wants to take the little tart for a drive, that's his business and nothing to do with you.'

Little tart! Bodkin went rigid with anger and as his neck muscles tightened he felt the point of the blade puncture his skin. He felt warm blood trickle down his neck, the sight of which made Sugarlips even more hysterical.

***

Completely unaware of the drama unfolding in the driveway, sister Suzie had dried herself off and put her bra and blouse back on. In the big boy's room the music had stopped, so she pulled the six 45s off the auto-change and put six more on. She'd bought the Shakin' Pyramids latest record and thought it would be fun to turn the volume right up. That's when the game changed completely.

'GONNA PARTY TONIGHT...'

To those in the driveway it was like a bomb going off.

'YOU'RE LOOKIN' MIGHTY SWEET...'

Just for a split second Gino lost concentration.

'THE MOON IS BRIGHT...'

Bodkin felt the pressure exerted on the tip of the knife slacken off.

'SO JUMP ALONG TO THE BEAT...'

With his considerable strength he sent his elbow deep into Gino's gut, completely knocking the wind out of him.

'KICK OFF YOUR SHOES...'

Just for good measure, as Gino sunk to his knees, Jack hit him over the head with the empty Long John bottle he'd left by the front door to put in the dustbin. Gino crashed full length.

'GET ON YOUR FEET, GET ON YOUR FEET...'

Doris ran into the snooker room to turn the music down. As she raced through the hall, Denny and Pete passed her and Stan and Elsie appeared out of Frankie's bedroom. When they saw Doris they both looked very sheepish and Elsie's hairdo looked more bed-head than beehive.

By the time Doris had pulled the plug on the Shakin' Pyramids, Bodkin was dragging Jasper across the drive by his hair whilst Frankie was comforting Sugarlips who, with her tear-smudged mascara, resembled a bedraggled Dusty Springfield. He had an arm around her shoulder as he led her back into the lounge. Most of the partygoers were in the driveway by now. Gino had started to come round and lifted himself onto one knee; Wally grabbed him and pulled him the rest of the way, twisting an arm behind his back. Jack opened the door of the Anglia and Wally threw him across the folded-back front passenger seat and he crumpled into the back seat foot-well, still groggy from the bottle across his head. Wally then put the backrest of the passenger seat up and looked round for Bodkin, who now had Jasper by the throat. Choking in Bodkin's fierce stranglehold, he was swung round the open door and shoved unceremoniously into the passenger seat, banging his head on the door frame as he went.

Jack furiously pointed a finger at Brian. 'Get these bastards away from here!' he shouted. 'If you're not off my drive in two minutes I'm calling the police.'

No need. As he said it a police patrol car pulled up the drive.

Jack had had no intention of calling the police and was horrified when he saw the Austin Westminster arrive. *At least they haven't got the blue lights flashing. God knows what the neighbours would think.*

Two police officers got out of the black patrol car and put on their hats as they walked towards the group of dishevelled-looking party animals, who were definitely not so full of high spirits as they'd been fifteen minutes ago. Plod Number One led the way, followed by Plod Number Two, who raised his eyebrows when he noticed the blood on the collar and shoulder of Bodkin's white T-shirt.

'Are you the owner of this house, sir?' said Plod Number One, directing his question at Jack.

'Yes, officer, I am.' Jack almost stood to attention.

'We've received a complaint from one of your neighbours about shouting and loud music coming from these premises,' Plod Number One continued. 'It looks as though there's been a bit of a problem here.' He was looking at Gino, collapsed on the back seat and Jasper, slumped in the front passenger seat of the Ford Anglia.

Brian climbed into the driver's seat and started the engine. Plod Number Two leapt across the gravel drive and stood in front of the car with the palm of his right hand outstretched. 'Switch off the engine sir, nobody's going anywhere until we have a few answers.'

'It was nothing officer, just a minor altercation,' pleaded Jack. 'I'll go round to see the Fosters first thing. We don't have a lot to do with them, but there's never been a problem.'

'That fool with the knife needs to be locked up!' shouted Doris, pointing angrily at the Anglia.

Plod Number One stiffened at the word 'knife'. He turned towards Doris. 'Knife, madam?'

Jack removed his spectacles with his left hand and pressed the palm of his right hand against his forehead. 'Doris!' He slowly slid it down his face, to shoot a look of disbelief at his wife.

'Him in the back of that car, the greasy one who looks like he collects fares whilst hanging on the back of dodgem cars.' Doris was still shouting angrily at the rear passenger window. 'Come out and face the music, you piece of garbage.'

'Steady on Mrs Richards.' Bodkin put an arm lightly around her shoulder. 'Perhaps you ought to come back inside, maybe have a drink, calm you down a bit.'

'It seems to me there's been a little too much drinking going on already,' said Plod Number One. He turned back to Jack. 'Where is the knife in question and was it used to injure the young man with blood on his neck and T-shirt?'

There seemed no point in trying to deny the obvious and Jack could feel the flick knife lying heavy in his trouser pocket. He'd picked it up off the drive after Bodkin had winded Gino and he'd finished the job with the whiskey bottle. He hoped neither of the two officers noticed the broken bottle. He'd just have to say it was accidentally dropped and smashed on the gravel. He put his specs back on and pulled the knife out of his pocket. 'I confiscated the knife,' said Jack. 'Young fella-me-lad was getting a bit frisky with it and I requested they leave.'

'Nobody's leaving just yet,' Plod Number Two reminded everybody. He was now looking carefully at Bodkin's neck. 'This injury looks more than a "bit frisky", it's quite a puncture you've got there, young man, and if I'm not mistaken it's very close to the jugular, or is it carotid? I can never remember.'

'Either one,' said Plod Number One. 'One slip and we could have been looking at a manslaughter charge, even murder. I need to start taking down some details, meanwhile I'm going to send for reinforcements.' First he took a notebook out of his breast pocket, then he shouted across to Plod Number Two, 'George, call the station, get them to send the paddy wagon.'

Plod Number Two (George), nodded and moved over to the patrol car.

By the time the Black Maria arrived, which it did accompanied by blue flashing lights and bells, the full story had been recorded in Plod Number One's notebook (apart from the parting of Gino's hair with the whiskey bottle). Assault with a deadly weapon was not what residents of Little Barnham did in the wee small hours. Plod Number One had arrested Gino and Jasper and he warned he may need Jack, Carol, Frank and Bodkin down at the station for more questioning and to make statements, but that could wait for now. Plod Number Two made it quite clear that nobody should be attempting to drive on account of the amount of alcohol that had been consumed. He also said he had a suspicion other substances may have been taken.

Neighbours, from both sides now, twitched curtains as the Johnny Washington two were being loaded into the back of the van. Apart from Frankie and Sugarlips, or Carol Meadowsweet as Plod Number One had written down, who had stayed in the lounge after giving her statement, everybody was now out in the front drive. All except one other, that is.

The partygoers and police had more or less finished their business and there was a bit of low-key conversation, as people spoke of calling taxis or perhaps arranging to bed down on sun beds in the veranda.

Suddenly the Shakin' Pyramids could be heard singing, not as loud as before, but just as clear. 'GONNA PARTY TONIGHT…' All eyes turned towards the front door. Out came dancing Barry Harper, with the same stupid grin on his face that he'd had when Jack left him just about an hour ago.

When he saw his audience, he first raised both arms aloft towards the stars, then bowed forward with an exaggerated flourish, swept his right arm across his body to touch his left foot, which was shoeless. Jack rushed forward to usher him back inside, but too late, Barry had seen the two uniformed policemen.

'Officer Dibble!' he cried to Plod Number One. 'Officer Dibble, would you like to take down my particulars?'

Plod Number One frowned. 'I think you had better calm down, sir.' But to everyone's horror, in a split second Barry had his arms wrapped around the policeman's neck and planted a big kiss on his cheek. Bodkin and Wally grabbed him by his shoulders and pulled him off, at the same time over-balancing and they all finished up sprawled on the gravel.

'Officer Dibble!' proclaimed Barry. 'I love you!'

There were some shocked faces, as well as some tittering going on in the ranks, which only served to antagonise Officer Dibble further. 'I should get dancing boy back under lock and key, before he joins the other two in the back of the paddy wagon.'

'The boy's had a drop too much to drink,' lied Jack. 'I'll get him inside right away.'

It was at that point that Barry stuffed a hand in his inside jacket pocket, and when he pulled it back out they all saw he had hold of two little polythene bags. A little white cube spilled out of one and disappeared amongst the grey and white pebbles on the drive. Oblivious to this Barry waved the other one containing two cubes in front of Officer Dibble's face. 'Come join me on a trip to the moon and stars on the back of a giant turtle...'

Plod Number Two stepped forward and grabbed Barry by the collar. 'The only trip you'll be making, Sonny Jim, is in the back of our fun bus.' With that, he read him his rights, arrested him, took the two cubes off him, and slipped them into one of his breast pockets. The officers in charge of the Black Maria opened the back doors so he could join Gino and Jasper.

Barry was to enjoy the next two nights in Steelhouse Lane nick; that was after he'd been charged, photographed and fingerprinted.

Fortunately next day was Sunday and the next stop on the tour was at Leicester on Tuesday so they had two days to get over hangovers and try and sort things out.

***

Danny had to be told and Stan made the call a few hours later when he finally surfaced, just before Sunday lunch. Danny drove up that afternoon, having arranged to meet with everyone at Jack's place, the scene of the crime. It would have been easy for Danny to lose his temper and rant and rave, but he needed to keep his cool as he organised damage limitation.

First of all he made copious notes, as he got all of them to go through the night's events. He explained he had spoken to his solicitor, Neil Tullow, and would brief him by telephone that afternoon so he could represent Barry next day.

His big worry was the bad press that he warned them was inevitable. He told them all not to speak to any of the press boys that this story would surely bring out of the woodwork. He made it quite clear to Jack and Doris, that his instructions also included them and to expect a posse of hacks to descend upon their house when the story broke.

He didn't want any of them at court except for Stan. The object of the exercise was to get Barry bail and if successful Stan would escort him straight out of court in Corporation Street, where Danny would be waiting in his new black Mercedes, to whisk him away before the press nailed him.

He would arrange that his solicitor would handle any statement to the press and they would just have to wait and see how the rest unfolded.

'What if they keep him locked up?' asked Sugarlips.

Danny stopped for a second, then he shrugged. 'You got no choice really, it'll be just the four of you.'

Stan blurted out. 'We can't do that, it'll screw the sound up and Barry's vocals are...'

Danny cut him short. 'No good worrying about something that hasn't happened yet, we need to cross that bridge when we get to it. Let's hope Judge Jefferies, the hanging judge, isn't in town.'

The three miscreants were hauled up in front of the court on Monday morning. Gino and Jasper were remanded in custody and thanks to Neil Tullow, Barry was given bail with a hearing scheduled for September 2nd.

Luck was on their side. Because the incidents had happened in the early hours of Sunday morning and with the court hearing so early on Monday morning, the news hadn't had time to break. The result was there were only the local reporters, who would normally cover the court proceedings, and probably just as important, Bombastic fans wouldn't have heard the news. So Corporation Street was deserted when Stan whisked Barry out of court, into the back of Danny's car and away without incident.

Inside court, the more serious charges of assault with a deadly weapon against Gino and assault against Jasper had tended to keep the limelight off Barry and his possession of drugs. Neil Tullow did a great job managing to keep suggestions of a wild party and flowing alcohol out of proceedings at this initial hearing.

CHAPTER 17
'HERE COME THE JUDGE'

Shorty Long

On Monday afternoon Danny went to see John Hinchcliffe (a.k.a. Johnny Washington) and made it crystal clear that if Gino and Jasper weren't thrown out, he would move heaven and earth to get the whole band replaced and off the tour. It was an easy decision for Johnny, the two of them were behind bars anyway, he wasn't going to cross swords with Danny Hoffman and he'd pick up another baritone sax easy enough. Until they got a replacement, they'd be the Johnny Washington Six. They'd also hump their own gear on and off the bus and save Gino's pay.

Danny had taken the precaution of booking all The Bombastics, including Wally, into a secluded hotel, tucked away in rural Leicestershire, that night. It took them out of the public eye; it was also close to Tuesday night's venue, the De Montfort Hall in Leicester.

Danny joined them that night for an alcohol-free dinner, even for himself. He realised they were still little more than kids and not used to alcohol, but he remained annoyed with Jack for letting the celebrations get out of hand. He was very angry about the knife attack on Bodkin and really upset about the assault on Carol; they all loved Sugarlips.

With dinner done Danny took advantage of having them all together to speak candidly to Barry. 'You've been a darned fool yet again Barry, but this time it's deep shit – er, excuse me Carol – possession of drugs is a serious offence. When your case comes up in September you could face a custodial sentence, or at the very least a severe fine. I haven't spoken to the others, but as far as I'm concerned I shall insist you're on your own paying that – maybe it will teach you a lesson.'

Barry was nodding his head, tears rolling down his cheeks.

'We have to take a long hard look at what's good for The Bombastics and your future with the band,' Danny continued. 'We all like you and you're an integral part of the band, but there are times like this when your bloody stupid antics tarnish the good reputation we've all worked so hard to build. When the nationals pick up this story, all hell will break loose. I'll be around to handle as much of it as I can but I can't be everywhere at once.'

'It won't happen again,' pleaded Barry. 'Why the hell did I get mixed up with Gino and his drugs? I'm a prat.' He never mentioned the pot they'd all been smoking (none of them mentioned the pot they'd all been smoking).

'You're a prat? You can say that again!' continued Danny. 'We've just got to hope the more serious charges against Gino and Jasper somehow take the attention off Barry Harper and his damned sugar cubes, but you being a

Bombastic is much more newsworthy, so don't hold your breath.'

He sat up straight and put both palms down firmly on the table in front of him. 'Look guys, it's not all bad news!' Danny's winning smile was back. 'Demand for you is amazing, with your growing reputation and records in the charts I could sell you twice a night, but rather than try and do that, I've doubled your fee. As before, there are gigs you will be committed to at your original fee and we must honour those.'

His smile got brighter. 'Starting immediately, I'm going to pay you £100 a week. I've arranged that the new amount is paid into your individual banks by Friday each week.'

'Hundred quid!' whooped Bodkin. 'I see one of those Pontiac GTOs sitting on my drive.' He flung his arm around Stan's neck and hugged him close. 'What's up Stanley, why the long face? You're a man of means now.'

'It's Elsie,' said Stan, almost choking as he wriggled free from Bodkin's arm lock. 'She keeps on about getting married; when she finds out I'm getting a ton a week...'

'I know a band that could play at your reception,' chuckled Carol. 'Mind you, we'd need a bass player to stand in.'

'No problem there,' chipped in Barry, now over his dressing down. 'You know the old adage – if you can piss you can play bass!'

There was a lot of laughter, even Stan joined in.

Eventually Danny continued. 'Eternal are over the moon and have given me a further advance which should help us develop things. It's got to be paid back, but with future royalties from the singles and the album your means should grow considerably.'

'You're all going to be worth a lot of money and I've been thinking, you should look at investing it; buying your own homes might be something to think about. I've arranged for a friend of mine, a financial advisor to make contact with each of you; his name is David Schneider. Take him seriously; the music industry is notoriously fickle and I feel you really should safeguard your futures for when all this is over.'

Danny took a folded document from his inside pocket and looked towards Frankie. 'I know you do all the song writing at the moment Frankie, but things have a habit of changing; maybe the others will be inspired to write a song or two. I've drawn up this contract that you should all sign. It's just for the song writing you understand, I wanted to keep it separate from any gig earnings or royalties. For convenience I've called the company, BombasticMusic.'

He spread the contract in front of Frank, smoothed it flat and offered him a pen.

'Don't you think we should get somebody to look at it before we sign?' asked Bodkin.

'Like who?' questioned Frank. 'If we can't trust Danny with this sort of thing by now, who can we trust?' He scribbled his signature at the bottom of the last page, then slid it on to Barry sitting next to him. Barry signed it without comment and passed it on to Bodkin, who studied it for a few seconds, shrugged, then signed it.

And so it went round the table, Carol, then Stan, then back to Danny. 'I'll let you have a copy of this Frank. Just remember, all of you; anything you write will belong to BombasticMusic and you'll get paid your share.'

***

The next day started well, but went downhill fast. Wally got them to the De Montfort Hall early, to try and avoid fans and reporters. This was partly successful; most of the national dailies had the story on the inside pages, the lurid front page headlines were to follow over the next few days. Two local papers had their people there, photographers too, but the Fleet Street boys had been caught on the hop and didn't make an appearance until late afternoon, with Carol and the lads safely inside.

Danny arrived a few hours before the concert and held court with all the press, in the foyer of the Hall. He kept it all as low key as he could, but with reports of knives and drugs and police arrests, the hacks smelt blood. They were not going to be fobbed off with Danny's account that The Bombastics were celebrating their return to the charts in their hometown of Birmingham and the party got a little boisterous. Nor did they believe that a minor scuffle with one of Johnny Washington's back room boys was soon sorted out. They also knew there were illegal substances found and that one of The Bombastics was involved.

When Johnny Washington's band turned up, two of the hacks managed to collar Brian and get his version of the weekend's events. With two of his pals sacked and currently under lock and key, Brian had evil on his mind. He described a wild party, fuelled with alcohol and drugs, music so loud that the neighbours were forced to call the police in the early hours. He told them of sex orgies, nude bathing and drunken fights with broken bottles and knives. He also named Barry Harper as the Bombastic who assaulted a police officer.

The telephone lines to Fleet Street were hot that night. That the concert was another fantastic success, with screaming fans demanding encores mattered not. The morning papers had a tale to tell.

Using the tour char-a-banc as a decoy, Danny and Wally managed to get them out of the goods entrance and into the VW camper van, with Barry ducking down low under a blanket in the back seat of Danny's black Mercedes.

When Danny saw the morning headlines he took the Lord's name in vain. The Bombastics had coast-to-coast coverage.

Every one of the papers gave graphic accounts of drink and drugs, nudity and sex. The Bombastics' name appeared large in all the exaggerated reports, along with photographs of the band. Distorted tales of the knife attack, with very little mention of Gino, and Jasper's attempt to kidnap Carol was covered in a few scant words that intimated she'd encouraged him. Unfortunately, Barry's drugs bust and his assault on police officers were printed large.

Trying to keep Barry and the rest of them out of the media spotlight had backfired, big time. After keeping them undercover for the Leicester gig, they were now due back on the tour bus, travelling round the South West and finishing up in the Home Counties. Danny was angry with himself. *I'm going to strangle that Brian when I get my hands on him, why did I ever mention Johnny Washington's back room boys?'*

One of Danny's many strengths was his ability to think clearly under pressure. By the time he had finished his second cup of coffee he was putting a plan into action. He phoned the editors of all the Dailies that had carried the banner headlines. If there was any reluctance to take his calls, when they knew it was The Bombastics' manager, Danny was put through immediately. He announced a press conference that morning at twelve noon sharp, at The Shillingworth Spa and Hotel. He'd already checked with The Shillingworth that the main Sir Oswald Suite was available and they were only too delighted to be at the centre of a national story

He then phoned Bodkin and Wally and told them to pick Stan and Sugarlips up and be at the hotel by 11 a.m. He told them he would organise Frankie and Barry; he would also speak to the tour promoter and tell him The Bombastics would get to Exeter Gaumont under their own steam for tonight's gig, then join the tour bus tomorrow. The promoter was okay with that, and even better, following the morning headlines, there had been a rush on tickets.

'You ain't gonna believe this Danny boy, since those newspaper stories the box office lines have been jammed.'

When he got to Barry's house, Danny could see there'd been a to-do. Barry had been caught red-handed about to flush his dad's copy of *The Daily Sketch* down the toilet. Paddy Harper knew that his son could be a 'fuckin' eejit' and he knew there'd been some sort of problem that weekend, even though Barry had managed to keep two nights in pokey and a court appearance away from his parents. There was no hiding anything now the whole story, including the Harper name, was on everybody's front page – and the balloon went up!

Danny did his best to explain to Barry's parents that much of the report was simply not true and he was picking their son up to speak to the press to try and put things right.

Danny ushered Barry to the front door. 'We'll sort this mess out, I promise.'

Martha wrung her hands and wailed, whilst Paddy cuffed him across the back of the head as he left with Danny. 'Yer still a fuckin' eejit, so yer are.'

At Frankie's there was a little knot of reporters outside the front gates. Jack came down to let Danny and Barry in, ignoring the questions being shouted at him through the railings. He couldn't stop apologising to Danny, who took no notice as he parked his car outside Jack's front door and got out.

'Get Frankie in the car,' said Danny, rather curtly. 'I'll deal with that lot.' He nodded towards the group of hacks and crunched his way back down the drive. He spoke through the gates to them and within minutes they had dispersed and gone.

He could see the surprise, not to mention relief, on Jack's face, and explained. 'I'm taking these two and meeting the rest of The Bombastics at The Shillingworth. We have a press conference to try and sort out this bullshit that's in all the morning papers. When I explained it to your little bunch of newshounds, they couldn't get over to the hotel quickly enough.'

Jack apologised four more times before Danny could get Frank into the car with Barry, through the gates and down the lane.

When Danny drew into the car park of The Shillingworth, Bodkin, Stan and Carol were sat waiting with Wally in Jezza.

'Follow me,' he barked, then turned, held his hands up and spoke in a quiet but determined voice, 'and let me do the talking.'

There were a couple of dozen reporters and photographers clustered in front of the top table, that the hotel had had set up in the Sir Oswald Suite. Danny gestured to the others to take seats placed behind the table. He waited for the hubbub to quieten and introduced himself speaking with an air of authority that hushed the press and made them listen. 'I want to correct a number of falsehoods contained in the morning editions of your newspapers; I am very disappointed that the story spun by Brian, from the Johnny Washington Seven, was not checked out before going to press, because it's utter tosh.'

He moved from behind the table, stepped forward and stood directly in front of them, so that most had to crane their necks to look up at him.

'The party has been a spontaneous idea to celebrate The Bombastics returning to the charts, whilst playing a concert in their home town. There was joy in the air and youthful exuberance spilled over. Yes, perhaps too much alcohol had been consumed, but the problems started when three of the Johnny Washington guys gate-crashed the party.

'The stories of drug taking are wildly exaggerated with only our Barry Harper involved and he has been charged, with his case due to come up in September. Frankie and Stan and Bodkin are totally innocent and poor Sugarlips was the victim not the perpetrator as will be proved beyond doubt when the case unfolds. The knife incident will also come before the courts and if you care to check this time, you'll find that two of the Johnny Washington boys are in custody to answer to that. More than that I cannot say because the matter is now *sub judice*, but take it from me you and your editors will be suitably embarrassed by the stories you printed today.'

'What about the skinny dipping?' snarled one hack from the second row.

'And the loud music, waking up the neighbourhood and making them call the cops,' came another voice from near the back.

'Yeah and the drunken sex orgy going on in the bedrooms,' shouted another. 'Were there Mars Bars involved?'

Danny waited just a second, until some of the laughter died down. 'Yes, there had been a bit of nude bathing in the householder's swimming pool. The energy of these youngsters, eh? Three of the guests, who'd had a wee drop too much, were involved, none of them Bombastics, I might add. As for a drunken sex orgy, I can absolutely assure you nothing like that took place.'

At this point, Stan poured himself a glass of water from the jug placed in front of them and managed to get almost as much on the green baize tablecloth as he did into the glass.

'As for loud music; you have to remember it was a party and it only became a problem when these gate-crashers arrived and the front door was open. I understand it was immediately turned down in deference to neighbours.'

There were lots of flash light bulbs going off and a lot more questions thrown at them, but with Danny fielding the awkward ones, they rode the punches and slowly and surely they seemed to get their message through. Exactly forty-eight minutes after arriving, Danny made their excuses and explained The Bombastics were due onstage in Exeter that night and they must depart.

The big concern was whether these headline stories had done any damage to their burgeoning image; the last thing they needed was a scandal like this, just as they began to establish themselves. Danny remembered the promoter's words about the sudden demand for tickets and that old adage about any publicity being good publicity came to mind. If ever there was an opportunity to find out if that was true, now was certainly the time.

He needn't have worried. All remaining tickets for the rest of the package tour were snapped up and the theatres in towns and cities like Truro, Plymouth, Bristol, Salisbury and Bournemouth were packed with adoring fans and screaming girls. The only hint of a problem was in Reading where a lonely protester paraded up and down the steps of the Princes Theatre waving a placard and chanting about the evils of sex and drugs and rock 'n' roll.

When the tour bus arrived at the front door instead of the stage door at the rear of the theatre, he was swept aside by a shrieking mob of teenage girls in short skirts and thigh boots. They may have bent his placard, but he went down with a smile on his face.

Danny was adept at finding ways of turning around adversity and somehow he managed to persuade the editor of the *News of the World* to change the planned sex, drugs and rock 'n' roll expose, to be published the following Sunday, into a world exclusive about The Bombastics' rise to stardom from a small Worcestershire village to national adoration. Danny encouraged the feature writer to talk about the temptations these young talented musicians were constantly under. If they had innocently succumbed, as Barry had, then the rest of the band would gather round and give support where needed. Danny gave the writer and his photographer complimentary tickets to the Bristol concert, invited them backstage after the show to meet Sugarlips and the boys, talk to them and take some photographs.

The photographer wanted some raunchy shots of Sugarlips holding her sax, but Danny reminded him of Carol's tender age and the starry-eyed and innocent feel of the article. The photographer accepted Danny's thinking on the matter, but nevertheless Bodkin kept him clearly in his sights. When all was done Danny, Bodkin and Sugarlips took the two of them to a nightclub.

They all bought the *News of the World* that weekend. The article was just what Danny had wanted and the pictures were very good too; the group shot of them ready to go onstage showed Carol's legs at their very best. The whole thing had been one thumping success and not for the first time, five Bombastics were all very impressed with their manager.

***

Sales of 'Love You Honey' exploded over the next few weeks. The more parents told their offspring how shocking and depraved these Bombastics were and they should spend their record money on wholesome artists like Cliff Richard and Frankie Vaughan, the more discs and concert tickets The Bombastics sold.

The package tour was an unqualified success and now

they were back to a diary full of one-night stands.

Like 'Teenage Crush' before it, 'Love You Honey' stayed in the top five for a lot longer than expected, before slowly dropping back out of the charts in the early summer. The third single, 'One Hour's Sleep', was released in July and with extensive coverage on radio and television it made its debut in the charts at number eight.

***

Its title about summed up Barry's sleep pattern in the days leading up to the court appearance. Whether he was at home in his own bed or out on the road in some hotel room, he was getting very little sleep. He would wake up with policemen and judges and worst of all, prison on his mind. There was one dream where he saw himself in a long line of prisoners trudging their way along endless corridors to slop out their nightly buckets. Other prisoners laughed and jeered from behind barred cells, as they splashed and sloshed their way. Amongst them were Gino and Jasper and the rest of the Johnny Washington Seven, still in their bright red trousers and waistcoats with the glittering JW7 on the left breast pocket, some waving fists or making obscene gestures through the open bars.

If Barry spent the night at home, he often woke at three or four in the morning, to find Janice's eyes glaring at him from the darkness. He'd find it impossible to get back to sleep again. He would get dressed, slip quietly out of his parent's home, get into the MGB Cabriolet he'd treated himself to, roll it silently down the gentle slope outside the house, start the engine when he was out of earshot and go for a drive. He'd make for a copse on the top of Cobley Hill where he could park up amongst the silver birches, light up a joint, and look down on the sleeping village. He kept his marijuana rolled up in an oily, torn off piece of towelling in the boot with the spare tyre and wheel-jack. He wouldn't have dared to smoke his pot anywhere near his father and none of them smoked near their manager.

If Barry was in a hotel room, quite often he would have female company. When he woke at the unearthly hour that was now becoming the norm, he would sit quietly on his side of the bed and light up. Most times, any company he had would sleep through his insomnia, but occasionally they would wake. He smiled to himself when he recalled the delightful young Miss Swansea, he didn't recall her real name, who woke to Barry's glowing reefer.

Realising he'd disturbed her, he gently whispered, 'Do you want one?'

In the darkness she raised herself onto one elbow and lashed out at him with a pillow. 'For God's sake, isn't twice enough?' With that she turned over and pulled the eiderdown over her head.

Eventually, Monday September 2nd came around and Barry arrived at court in a suit; even he wouldn't have been daft enough to appear in his powder blue zoot suit (although Danny, Stan and Bodkin did all phone him just to make sure he didn't even think about it). No, it was a sober charcoal grey Italian model, with collar and tie and gleaming black shoes. He met up with Danny's solicitor, Neil Tullow, and they went through every detail very carefully. Barry was to plead guilty and then shut up, leaving it to Neil to explain the extenuating circumstances.

As Barry said afterwards, 'I was shitting myself; I thought they were going to bang me up, for sure.' Only weeks before Gino had been found guilty of assault with a deadly weapon and supplying drugs. He got eighteen months. Jasper was given a six-month sentence, suspended for twelve months for attempted abduction.

To the relief of one and all, everything went to plan. The judge believed that this was a one-off as far as Barry was concerned. In his summing up, he said Barry had been very naive and become the victim of an unscrupulous dealer, but that with the help and support from his manager and the rest of his band he was worth giving a second chance. The assault on the police officer was considered horseplay and thrown out by the judge. In fact, there was laughter in court when Officer Dibble gave his evidence.

The jury were instructed to find him guilty of the possession of drugs. He was given a six-month sentence, suspended for two years and fined £150.

Barry's near miss taught him nothing. His drink and drug problems were to get worse and getting visas for foreign travel into countries like America and Japan would prove difficult.

***

Like the two Bombastic hits before it, 'One Hour's Sleep' stayed in the charts for a lot longer than expected. It peaked at number four, but was still in the top twenty in mid-November when Eternal Records' assault on the Christmas number one was planned to take place.

A&R man Martin Wainwright desperately wanted a Christmas number one and left nothing to chance as he forged his assault on the festive top spot. With a bit of help from Danny, he planned maximum coverage on all the important radio and TV shows. Then there was pirate radio; with unrestricted 'needle time' these non-stop music stations were now essential listening to the kids with their transistors.

A DJ named Emperor Roscoe on an old converted ferry named Radio Caroline and anchored off the seaside resort of Frinton-on-Sea was the first to play 'Jive Away the Tears'.

Danny didn't miss a trick. Killing two birds with one stone, he used a slice of the advertising budget of Carpet Matters in return for preferential and considerable airtime for Frankie Atom and The Bombastics records.

***

Martin Wainwright and Eternal Records got their number one when 'Jive Away the Tears' stormed to the top spot during the first week of December, but it was not to be a Christmas number one. The very next week a new release from the Beatles went straight to number one and stayed there for the rest of 1964. That record was 'I Feel Fine'.

'Have you seen this?' Carol came into the dressing room without a knock, choosing to ignore Barry peeing loudly into the toilet bowl with the cubicle door wide open. She laid a copy of the *NME* on the table. 'Look, the American charts, The Beatles have gone straight to number one over there too. Why don't we get in the Billboard charts too?'

'I've had a word with Danny, he says he's working on it,' said Stan. 'Something to do with Chekka and a problem they have with distribution over there, but he thinks they've found a solution. Anybody else heard anything?'

A high-pitched fart came from the direction of the cubicle then the sound of the toilet being flushed, followed by Barry zipping up his zoot suit pants and swilling his hands under the tap.

'Thank you Barry for your contribution,' said Bodkin. 'Talking out of your arse, as usual.'

CHAPTER 18
'ROUTE 66'

Nat King Cole

The pilot lowered the landing gear and the mechanical whirring sound was followed by the sudden thud which shook the Boeing 707 for an instant. Stan let out a gasp and clutched the seat in front of him. Bodkin leaned slightly forward with an evil grin on his face and spoke across Carol, who occupied the middle seat.

'Don't worry Stan, the captain decided against a vertical landing, so he's got the wheels out.'

'No, I-I-I was half asleep there,' stuttered Stan, trying to hide his embarrassment. 'It woke me up, made me jump, that's all.'

'Take no notice of him.' Carol put a sympathetic hand on Stan's knee. 'I don't like flying either, it's not natural; all this humanity cooped up in a giant cigar tube speeding through the atmosphere, far too fast, with only the clouds to act as a safety net.'

'Spare me the details, Shoogs.' Stan looked decidedly grey around the gills as he gently removed her hand. 'It's been a long flight. I've tried to read and I've tried to sleep, but failed on both counts.'

'Failed to sleep? That wasn't you snoring then?' continued Bodkin, still grinning. 'The air hostess came on the tannoy and apologised to the rest of the passengers for the sound of boiling mud and reassured them it wasn't anything to do with the in-flight meal they were preparing at the back of the plane.'

Stan eyed Bodkin. 'You're kiddin', right?'

'Take no notice Stan, he's trying to wind you up.' Carol leant back on her headrest, smiling.

Just then, the TWA purser passed down the centre aisle checking that seat belts were properly fastened. He stopped briefly at the seats opposite Bodkin where Frank and Danny sat. The front of Danny's double-breasted sports jacket had covered the buckle of his belt, but he opened up to reveal that he was safely tucked in.

'Hello again ladies and gentlemen, this is Captain Luke Kaminski.' A rather tinny, disembodied voice burst forth from speakers concealed along the length of the fuselage. 'We are starting our descent into John F. Kennedy Airport, New York. Our expected arrival time will be 10:20. It is sunny, but cold with a ground temperature around minus eight degrees. On behalf of myself and my crew, I'd like to thank you for flying TWA. Cabin crew, take your seats.'

As the 707 banked slightly and descended through some wispy cloud cover, through the window Carol and Bodkin could see vast areas of snow covered New York State. Stan refused to look.

***

The flight from Heathrow had been long and tedious, but largely uneventful. There had been a bit of a palaver getting their instruments on board in London. Sugarlips' sax and the boys' guitars hadn't been too much of a problem, but the drums and cymbals meant a lot of extra labelling and paperwork to process.

'Why don't we just hire a set when we get over there?' grumbled Stan. 'Leave this lot behind with the amps and speakers and stuff?'

'Hire a set?' Bodkin was clearly affronted. 'Those drums are an extension of my soul, without them there ain't no mojo!'

'Bodkin, what are you blathering on about?' butted in Danny. 'Let's get those little boxes ticked, signed off and get on this flight.'

They sat in the departure lounge for nearly an hour, smoking, sipping at coffee that had gone cold and discussing, yet again, the subject that for the last six weeks had refused to go away.

Barry Harper!

***

Danny had told them all that there was interest from American radio stations in 'Jive Away the Tears' and that he'd been in touch with an agent, Mo Williams, who worked out of Philadelphia. Between them, they had put together a three-week tour playing clubs and dance halls; sometimes they'd be on their own with a DJ, sometimes with a local band, there wasn't going to be a lot of money in it, but if they worked hard, talked to the radio DJs on their travels, they stood a real chance. The States was such a vast geographical challenge, but the 'British Invasion' was in full swing and if they could get their music on the airwaves they could break through.

It was after a gig in Chichester when Danny turned up unexpectedly. Immediately he came into the dressing room and slumped into one of the chairs – they knew all was not well. This just wasn't Danny's style.

'We can't get a work permit for Barry,' he said sullenly. 'My son Isaac spent nearly all day queuing down at the American Embassy last week. He eventually got all your others, but they refused to stamp Barry's, because of that drug conviction.'

There was complete silence in the room; Barry sat open-mouthed.

'I went straight down there myself and had to queue for over two hours to be met by this sour-faced uniform. I asked him if he knew your music, if he'd heard 'Jive Away the Tears'; I even showed him your *Record Mirror* front cover splash. He just said "No, sir," and shook his head.

'I tried to explain you were taking British music across the Atlantic for the pleasure of our American cousins. He looked again at Barry's application, then turned his expressionless gaze back to me and said, "Listen to me, sir, and listen carefully. We ain't gonna let no drug-addled Limey into the United States of America under any circumstances." With that he stamped 'entry refused' in red on the two forms, pushed one back across the desk to me and filed the other in the tray on his desk. "Thank you, sir, that'll be all and for the record I think we got enough music of our own back home."

'I tried another approach and got in touch with my Uncle Abe in Boston to see if there was any way round this problem, if we could somehow get a reputable sponsor for Barry. Uncle Abe and Cousin Max are very successful businessmen in Massachusetts and I thought they may be able to pull some strings and we could get Barry in under cover of darkness, as it were. Unfortunately, it was a non-starter.'

'So the American tour is off all because of Barry?' said Frank.

'No, it certainly is not, I've spoken at some length with Mo Williams; he's well connected over there and he's got you a stand-in. You pick him up in Chicago, work on the repertoire with him for a couple of days, and then you're off down Route 66. Mo's given him copies of all your hits, so he can practice.'

'Just a minute, you're handing out instructions as if I'm not here!' Barry had gone pale with shock. 'Are you kicking me out of The Bombastics?'

'I've never said that, but I'll tell you this Barry Harper, you've had enough warnings.' Danny sat up in his chair, wagging a finger at Barry. 'This is a three-week tour. I've had to pull in a few favours to make room in your schedule over here.' He pulled his diary from his inside pocket. 'You're going to have to miss that festival in Rotterdam and the Winter Party date in Stockholm, but there'll be other times. The Bombastics are *not* missing this American chance because of your stupid behaviour, Barry. As for your longer term future, you'll just have to stay home and cool your heels; see how they get on without you.'

There was silence again, but this time it was a skin-crawling embarrassed silence.

Finally, Frank spoke up. 'Danny, how do we know this stand-in is going to be up to it? I mean it isn't just playing guitar, if he doesn't learn Barry's harmonies, well, it'd be like Don without Phil.'

'We don't, we've just got to trust Mo. I'm coming over with you just to make sure everything runs smoothly. I've got us booked into hotels and motels all the way down Route 66 to Los Angeles. You guys are going to have to share a room; Carol will have her own, of course. Wally, we won't be needing you, Bodkin and I will share the driving and apart from the drums there'll be no gear to set

THE MAN WHO STOLE ROCK 'N' ROLL

up. Look on it as a three-week paid holiday.'

At this point, Barry grabbed his duffle coat off the peg where he'd changed and left the room without a word.

The next few weeks on the road were a bit difficult to begin with as they got used to the idea of a tour without Barry. It affected them on many different levels. Disappointment, concern, apprehension, and at the same time excitement and ambition. Gradually, The Bombastics' team spirit took over and when the jokes began, at Barry's expense, about the imaginary nameless stand-in everyone felt better.

He became known as the Space Cowboy.

Bodkin told Barry he'd be taking a copy of Bert Weedon's 'Play in a Day' so the Space Cowboy would soon be up to Barry's standard. Stan suggested that whilst they were over there, they could cut some tracks in Memphis with a genuine country rock artist like the Space Cowboy.

Frank said the Space Cowboy could stop in his old man's spare bedroom when he came back over with them. Nevertheless, inwardly, Barry was distraught. The last gig before they left for the States was at the West End Ballroom in Birmingham and immediately they finished, Barry disappeared. They all assumed, in true Harper style, he'd found a sleeping partner for the night. They should have spotted he'd left his powder blue zoot suit, but taken his guitar, which he normally left for Wally to load up with all the rest of the gear.

Unable to face the goodbyes and tormented by the uncertainty that lay ahead, he slipped out of the side door and into the first taxi on the rank in nearby Suffolk Street. He gave the driver directions to his mom and dad's house in Fordrough, slouched back on the seat and popped a couple of pills he kept in reserve in the zipped side pocket of his guitar case.

Birmingham town centre was still busy and the roads jammed because of long-term road works. Construction of the Bull Ring Centre and the inner ring road meant long lines of cars and buses waited at endless temporary traffic lights. By the time Barry's taxi was free and crawling down the Pershore Road towards Fordrough, the pills had him staring, eyes wide open at Janice, who was glaring with hate at him from the rear view mirror. It was a long journey home.

***

The 707 touched down smoothly and Sugarlips held Stan's hand; this time he didn't remove it, just closed his eyes and thought of Elsie.

They needed to get themselves, their hand luggage and olive-green Stan, across the ultra-modern Trans World Airlines Flight Centre to find the departure gate for the connecting flight to Chicago. They stood nonplussed, then from out of nowhere it seemed, Danny managed to rustle up a TWA porter with a trolley. He loaded up their bags and coats and guided them through the busy terminal. Skiers heading for the Rockies, golfers in baseball caps and loud checked trousers bound for Florida, a bunch of excited schoolgirls in an incongruous combination of warm winter coats, gloves, scarves and summer straw boaters with school badges; a mother hen with a fistful of boarding passes clucked over them. There were businessmen with attaché cases, reading reports, reading newspapers, reading departure details on the large double-screened monitor that stood high above the check-in desk and reminded Carol of a giant hair drier – and there were armed police; Frank could hardly take his eyes off their holstered guns.

Their porter stopped them at the end of a short queue leading to Gate 8; O'Hare Chicago, it said in lights on the display board above the desk. Danny pushed some folded dollars into the porter's hand, who smiled, saluted him and turned to pull his trolley away. Bodkin was panicking about his drums, but Danny assured him they would be on the flight along with their luggage and instruments, all transferred courtesy of TWA's baggage handlers.

As they crossed the tarmac to board their flight there was a mad scramble to put coats on. Captain Luke Kaminski was correct, it was sunny alright, but it was also bitterly cold.

Four hours later they had their luggage and instruments safely aboard a large trolley, had cleared customs, and were in O'Hare's car rental area at the InterStateCars desk. The others watched whilst Danny checked through a number of dockets the young lady, in the InterStateCars bright red and yellow tunic and pillbox hat, had put in front of him. They were both smiling as he took her pen and signed here and here, so everything seemed tickety-boo. She handed Danny a set of keys, pointed him in the direction of the exit door opposite, then turned her arm and jabbed her hand for him to be sure to turn left.

The late afternoon Chicago sun hung low on the western horizon as Danny led them to the rental car park, where most of the vehicles had been cleared of snow. There were cars on the far side still covered with snow, but all the cars around them were clear and ready to go. Danny checked the registration on his key fob and made for a long, sleek, gold Oldsmobile Vista Cruiser, with white roof and white-wall tyres, glinting in the setting sun.

'Jeezus, just look at the size of that thing,' gasped Bodkin, his breath billowing on the cold afternoon air. 'Are we doing our first concert in that thing?'

'Bugger me, as Barry would say,' laughed Carol. 'It's our hotel on wheels, right Danny? Tell us it's got separate en suite rooms in the back.'

'No, not quite Shoogs,' smiled Danny. 'Bodkin, I'll

drive to start with, I'm a bit more used to the American roads, but we got a lot of miles to cover over the next three weeks so you'll get more than your share; we can even let Stan get behind the wheel now he's passed his test. You have brought your driving licence with you, Stan?'

Stan nodded, he was still getting his land legs back.

'Let's get all the gear loaded up.' Danny walked to the back of the Olds where a large U-Haul trailer was attached. He lifted the back door of the station wagon and they put their cases and hand luggage inside, then he unlocked the trailer and they loaded up Bodkin's drums and cymbals, their guitars, and Carol's saxophone. Within a few minutes they were on the road out of O'Hare and headed for their hotel overlooking Lake Michigan.

The bright orange roof with the distinctive weather vane of the Howard Johnson hotel appeared to the left of the highway. The highway was completely clear of snow and had been salted, but Danny was taking it easy; it had been some years since he'd driven in the States and silly though he thought himself, he seemed compelled to keep checking in his rear view to make sure the trailer hadn't broken loose and been left in the middle of four busy lanes of rush hour traffic.

The parking lot had been swept, leaving a huge bank of snow between its far edge and the highway beyond. There were a dozen or so cars parked, only two of which were still covered with snow.

'Must have been a right heavy fall,' remarked Stan as they picked up their cases. 'It must be six inches deep on those cars.'

Reception was warm and not surprisingly, quiet. A middle-aged guy behind the desk in his turquoise Howard Johnson shirt and tie was busy talking with a newly arrived couple, maybe in their thirties, their dark blue and silver matching cases at their feet. Two youngsters, one little more than a toddler, had escaped for the moment and had their hands all over the glass front of the drinks and candy cabinet to the side of reception.

Over on the far side a young black guy, in a red and black check lumber-type jacket sat on his own, smoking a cheroot. An elderly couple had been sifting through a dispenser full of leaflets showing local attractions, but they disappeared through the main doors.

Danny and The Bombastics stood waiting.

The young black guy had been studying them: he pulled one last time on his cheroot, then crushed it in the large glass ashtray on the table in front of him. He blew smoke out, as he rose from his chair and walked across reception to the new arrivals.

'I'm lookin' to meet a Mr Daniel Hoffman and I was wonderin' if that gentleman might just be in your party?'

'He is,' said Frank, and he and Stan parted to let Danny through.

'How'd you do Mr Hoffman?' The young guy offered a hand.

Danny shook it. 'It's Danny, and I'm guessing Mo Williams sent you.'

'He most certainly did. Jerome Jones Junior, but people call me JoJo. I believe I'm to become a Bombastic for the next three weeks.'

'Then meet the gang.' Danny spread his arms to the others and then introduced them one at a time, pausing along the way whilst JoJo shook hands with each.

He gave them a simple 'Hi,' and a big smile. 'You're a real cool sax player,' he added to Carol's greeting. 'I've been listening to your records, learning your songs and I really dig the sounds you make, I understand why they call you Sugarlips.'

Carol felt herself reddening up, but was somewhat saved by the receptionist calling across to them, 'Welcome to Howard Johnsons, are you checking in?' The newly arrived couple were all done: father headed for the lift, carrying their cases, whilst mother rounded up the two kids.

As at InterStateCars everything went smoothly with the bookings; Carol had her own room, as did Danny, whilst the boys shared a family room. Danny turned from the desk and handed out the room keys.

He stopped at JoJo. 'I'm not sure what arrangements Mo Williams made for you JoJo, are you stopping here tonight?'

'No, not here in Chicago,' smiled JoJo. 'My place is but a short cab drive away. However, I'm here to guide you folks all the way down the Mother Road.'

'Mother Road?' quizzed Sugarlips.

'That's what some call Route 66,' replied JoJo. 'Others call it Maine Street, USA or The Will Rogers Highway. Take your pick.'

'I certainly hope you're eating with us tonight JoJo?' said Frank. 'We need to talk; there's a lot to do before our first gig in two night's time.'

'I'd love to.' JoJo caught Danny's arm. 'Danny, perhaps you've a mind to give me a copy of the clubs we'll be playing and the hotels we'll be stopping in over the next three weeks.'

'No problem.' Danny sounded rather puzzled. 'All booked and approved by Mo Williams.'

'Mo has a tendency to forget all about Jim Crow.'

'And who, may I ask, is Jim Crow?' asked Danny.

JoJo didn't answer him, but pointed though the glass frontage and into the car park beyond. 'Has that trailer you pulled up in got all your gear in it?'

'It has,' said Stan.

'Well you'd be advised to bring all that stuff inside overnight.' JoJo's voice dropped to a whisper. 'This part of Chicago has a busy night shift. Those guitars could be halfway to Pennsylvania by dawn.'

'Sod the guitars, what about my drums?' Bodkin strode towards the main doors.

'Stan, Frank, grab that trolley over there.' A smile broke on Danny's lips. 'I'll see if there's a room down here we can store them; we can't have Bodkin sharing his pull-out bed with a big bass drum!'

***

Dinner was a pleasant affair with The Bombastics getting to know JoJo. Seems he was born and raised in Little Rock, Arkansas, but his pa moved the family, JoJo, his ma, his two brothers and three sisters to the northern cities in search of work. His pa found work in Detroit, but hated the car factory so they moved on to Milwaukee before finally settling in Chicago, where his father got a job with the Chicago Parks District in the open air; a job he loved.

'I wanted to stay in the South with my guitar. I dreamed of fame and fortune just across the Arkansas-Tennessee State line,' said JoJo. 'Memphis – yessir – there was only one place to be, but what can a thirteen-year-old do when his ma and pa up sticks and move on out?'

'As it happens, things worked out,' he smiled. 'Nine years later, I'm part of Chicago's blues and rock 'n' roll scene, I do session work at Chess Records and I get to play with cats like you.'

'Chess?' Frank's eyes were on stalks. 'That's Chuck Berry, Muddy Waters and Bo Diddley... right?'

'Right,' beamed JoJo. 'Remember, I've been playing

your hits, listening and learning. Like a lot of you British bands, I think you've been heavily influenced by those guys.'

He flicked the ash from his cheroot into an ashtray and turned to Danny. 'Did you manage to put together that tour itinerary, Danny?'

Danny put his Black Russian down in the ashtray and used the back of his hand to smooth flat the foolscap sheet he took from his jacket pocket. 'Here you are, seventeen gigs between The House of Blue Light, here in Chicago and the Whiskey A Go Go in Los Angeles. I've handwritten the hotels and motels we're booked into along the way.'

JoJo took the paper and studied it. The others watched his eyes as he worked his way down the list.

'You look concerned JoJo,' said Danny. 'Is everything okay, there's nothing we should be worried about?'

'You folks will be just fine.' JoJo smiled but his eyes were expressionless. 'There are a few problems that I may have to face along the way and it's better you know about them before we set off.'

'I'm sure you heard of the troubles we've been having in some of our cities.' He held his hand up to prevent interruptions. 'This here's about white folks and black folks adaptin' to the new Civil Rights Act passed only last year. I mentioned Jim Crow earlier and it was pretty clear none of you guys knew what the hell I was talkin' about. The Jim Crow laws are about segregation; they've been around since slavery was abolished. Blacks couldn't mix with whites in schools, on buses, in theatres, restaurants, restrooms, even pumping gas or using the same water fountains. That is until now; the new Civil Rights Act means racial discrimination is against the law. However, sometimes these things move slowly whilst people get used to change, particularly in the South. I hear you guys will be sharing a room and that you'll want me to bed down with you. Now that's real friendly and it does my heart good to know you live your lives and play your music without prejudice, but I have to tell you that some of those hotels through Arkansas, Oklahoma and New Mexico may not let me share a hotel, never mind a room.'

'That's awful!' cried Sugarlips. 'They can't do that!'

'They can little lady, and they have done for the best part of a century now,' sighed JoJo. 'Like I said things are changing, there are good men, both black and white, fighting for the freedom of every man woman and child in this country of ours.'

'If anybody refuses you a room for the night, then none of us use the hotel and they lose the business,' said Bodkin.

'Whoa!' JoJo shook his finger and laughed. 'It ain't as simple as that out on rural Route 66. Sometimes there might not be another hotel or restaurant for many miles. Don't you folks worry, I have the solution.' He waved a green book he'd carried in his back pocket. 'This here's the Negro Travellers Green Book.' JoJo put it on the table and flicked through a few of the pages. 'This gives me a list of hotels, motels, restaurants, burger huts, drive-ins, even garages with restrooms, that will accommodate black people; I just need to plan ahead.'

'God forbid that it has come to that.' Stan slowly shook his head. 'What about audiences, are they likely to be prejudiced?'

'We'll be fine in cities like Chicago, Springfield, St Louis and Albuquerque,' said JoJo. 'It's the hick towns I'm not sure about, but rock 'n' roll has brought down a lot of barriers. Chuck Berry, Little Richard, Fats Domino, then Motown and Atlantic, they've all played a part; and God bless your Beatles and Rolling Stones, white boys who've pushed the boundaries still further.'

JoJo glanced at his watch. 'Hey, we've got a busy day tomorrow, I best call a cab. I'll be here fifteen after eight.'

His cab only took a few minutes to arrive and before he left, he warned them. 'You can see we had a whole mess of snow three nights ago and listening to the radio it seems like there could be another downfall of the white stuff sometime soon.'

***

Next morning after breakfast, they loaded their gear back into the trailer and with JoJo sharing the long front seat with Danny and Sugarlips he directed them to The House of Blue Light. He kept them away from the main highways and shopping areas, guiding them through run-down tenement blocks, shut down factories and slaughterhouses.

The club stood three blocks from bustling Maxwell Street Market, where JoJo told the others he'd started, busking on the street like so many others.

'The House', as JoJo referred to it, was actually a cellar club; above the doorway hung an unlit neon sign. Posters on the doors and surrounding walls told Chicago rock 'n' rollers which artists and bands were due to appear; Frankie Atom and The Bombastics posters were newly pasted each side of the doors; that familiar smiley group picture taken at Coventry Cathedral, with Barry beaming out over a cold Chicago morning.

Although there was snow on rooftops, walls and fire escapes, the streets were clear and Danny was able to park up right outside squeezing car and trailer in between a fire hydrant and a truck unloading greengrocery at the store next door. Whilst JoJo organised getting the front door open, the boys unloaded the trailer. The janitor, the only other person around, seemed to know JoJo quite well. He later explained that for three years he'd been part of the resident band at the club.

Inside the club was an oval dance floor surrounded by tables and chairs. There was a low stage on one side and what looked like a coffee bar on the opposite side. JoJo disappeared into the darkness at the back of the stage, but within seconds the stage was bathed in blue light.

'We can't work in that all day,' said JoJo, laughing and shaking his head. He raked the side of his hand over a bank of switches and yellow electric light lit up the club. JoJo switched off the blue lights.

There was a bit of nervous expectation from both JoJo and The Bombastics as they got together for the first time, but it all fell into place superbly as soon as they started. Frank suggested they jam a few old rock 'n' roll twelve bars to loosen up, and what better way to start than 'Johnny B. Goode'. Within minutes they could all see JoJo was a great guitarist and a damned fine singer.

On they went with 'Sweet Little Sixteen' and not only did he help drive a steady beat with his rhythm guitar, he added little embellishments that Chuck Berry would be proud of. Within a few hours they had put together a large part of their programme. Finally, Frank began the intro to 'Roll Over Beethoven' and JoJo followed his lead note for note. The two of them laughed together as they played; the other four were astonished.

'That was amazing,' said Danny, shaking his head in disbelief.

'We should keep that in the show,' suggested Bodkin.

'Who ever heard of that, a duo on guitar?' agreed Carol. 'It'll bring the house down.'

'We haven't got on to any Bombastic stuff yet,' said Stan. 'I'm sure there won't be a problem, but we ought to move on.'

Stan was right, there wasn't any problem. JoJo had learned them all and his harmonies with Frank were absolutely spot on. They ran through the five hits before their first day's rehearsal was over and the next morning they concentrated on polishing them all up. 'Teenage Crush', 'Little Bit Crazy', 'Love You Honey', 'One Hour's Sleep' and 'Jive Away the Tears; they were all in the bag.

They also got JoJo to try on Barry's powder blue zoot suit. There was good news and bad news. The suit fitted perfectly, maybe a little bit long in the leg perhaps, but JoJo hated it.

'I really can't wait to get out of Chicago trussed up in this; I'm just pleased none of my mates are here tomorrow night.'

Danny never came with them for the second day's rehearsals, he had a job to do; by the time he arrived at The House of Blue Light he'd fixed up live radio interviews on two of Chicago's biggest radio stations.

First that afternoon, they talked to Jim Stagg on his WCFL afternoon drive programme and early next morning to Clark Weber on his WLS morning show. Comparisons with The Beatles and The Dave Clark Five were inevitable, but they were able to promote both their Chicago gigs at The House of Blue Light and the following night at Papa Jones Place in Joliet. Both stations played 'Jive Away the Tears' and both DJs were interested in JoJo standing in for Barry who'd been left at home.

Danny had given them all strict instructions not to breathe a word about drugs and to say he'd been taken ill. Clark Weber questioned Stan a bit closer and when he was put on the spot, Stan trotted out some story about Barry breaking an ankle whilst skiing.

'What was all that cobblers about?' asked Bodkin. 'He's never been skiing in his life.'

'Men's downhill, ain't it?' retorted Stan. 'The amount of pills he's popping he's well down the slippery slope; that's close enough for me.'

***

The first gig was, well, strange. It wasn't full at The House and the kids seemed a bit cautious to begin with. The Bombastics did two forty-five minute spots, with a DJ who called himself Dancing Dave, supporting them. The first session started very slowly, with most of the kids looking at each other – boys looking at girls, and girls doing their best to ignore the boys, but by the time The Bombastics finished their first half set, the floor was half full.

'Strange indeed,' commented Stan during the DJ break. 'They're all kids, fifteen or sixteen by the look of 'em. Thank God they've livened up a bit.'

'I thought you guys knew,' said JoJo. 'Thursday night at The House is High School Hop time; they *are* fifteen and sixteen – they're all tenth grade, and the reason they've started to liven up is because they're getting stoned.'

'School kids on drugs?!' gasped Carol. 'Surely that can't be right.'

'Sure thing, the U S of A is going to the dogs,' growled JoJo, then his face broke into a grin. 'I was gone eighteen before I did dope!'

The second spot went really well. Those kids who weren't heavy petting were either dancing or clapping and jumping up and down. It also became pretty obvious where the drugs were coming from; Dancing Dave had more than records in his collection. Whether it was the kids getting into The Bombastics or the stimulants getting into the kids none of them were sure.

Back at the hotel, JoJo rolled some weed and offered it round and to everyone's astonishment Danny took a turn.

'That's not a Black Russian, Danny, that's cannabis!' said a stunned Bodkin. 'We've avoided having anything to do with that stuff whilst you were around.'

Danny laughed. 'I wasn't going to encourage you, was I? Especially after Barry's performance.' He then pulled a plastic pouch out of the inside pocket of his overcoat he'd hung over one of the empty chairs. 'Can't let JoJo supply all your needs.' He unrolled the pouch on the table and threw a packet of papers alongside. 'Help yourselves.'

Bodkin, Stan, Frank and Carol sat there agog.

'You never brought that lot through customs, surely?' said Frankie eventually.

'Not that stupid,' answered Danny, frowning. 'Let's say I was able to do a little shopping whilst you boys rehearsed.'

'This is Chicago, man!' whooped JoJo. 'Talking of which, there ain't no rush tomorrow with Joliet only 40 miles down the road, it won't take us an hour. Now I know you ain't tourists, but you is about to get your kicks on a damned important trip and I want to make sure you do the right thing.

'First of all we visit Big Al's Outdoor Shop and get y'all some proper hats and gloves; footwear if necessary. Don't worry Sugarlips, there's a ladies department. Then we gonna start out on Route 66 with breakfast at Lou Mitchell's Diner on Jackson. Uncle Lou's bin feedin' sixty-sixers since before Bo Diddley was a gunslinger.'

CHAPTER 19
'TRAVELLIN' BAND'

Creedence Clearwater Revival

They kitted themselves out with hats and gloves, and Danny and Bodkin each bought an impressive pair of calf length lace-up boots. Carol bought herself matching scarf and gloves and a fur-lined trapper hat that pulled down around her ears. When they saw it, Frank and Stan rushed back into the gents department to swap theirs over.

They arrived at Lou Mitchell's just after 10 a.m.

'Good morning folks, I'm Darlene and I'm your waitress this morning. I have to say you couldn't ride Route 66 without one of Lou Mitchell's warm breakfasts inside of y'all,' she laughed when JoJo explained his party hailed from England and were gigging all the way down to LA. 'I'm gonna recommend our omelettes done just how you want. Just take a look.'

She leaned over Danny and ran the top of her pen down the menu. 'While y'all decidin' I'm gonna bring fresh coffee over. Does anybody want juice?'

Within the hour, they were fed and ready for the day. They said their goodbyes to Darlene and walked back down the block, to where the Olds and trailer were parked.

'Things are changin' with all this interstate construction,' said JoJo, again sat on the front seat between Danny and Sugarlips. 'Sometimes we'll be on Route 66, sometimes on one of the new Interstate Highways, dependin' on how far they've built, you never can tell. Some folks say Route 66 will disappear, which is a shame, but you do have to understand the Mother Road is getting old, she's barely two lanes in some parts and these days folks are in a hurry and want to get there on time!'

'I ain't never been no further than Albuquerque in New Mexico, though I did do some work in California last year, but we flew into Los Angeles.'

They drove out through the city limits and into winter farmland. Acre upon acre of white fields stretched over the distant horizon. The heavy snow that had fallen in early February remained untouched for the most part. They could just make out farmsteads and barns dotted here and there.

'It's vast out here,' said Carol. 'Just look, those buildings look like toys; how much bigger are these fields than ours back home?'

'Them's the prairies, Sugarlips,' smiled JoJo. 'You should see them in spring; lush and green and splendid. They'll be with us for a few hundred miles yet.'

Danny switched on the radio and the car filled with the sound of Petula Clarke's 'Downtown'.

'Hey, you Brits have certainly taken over,' laughed JoJo.

They checked in at the Holiday Inn in Joliet and moved straight on to Papa Jones' Place that stood on the banks of the Des Plaines River. It was a big glass fronted building, overlooking the river which was partly frozen over. It was surrounded on three sides by shops and public buildings, one of which looked like City Hall; beyond that there were at least three church steeples poking into the cloudless sky.

Inside, the main function room was probably twice the size of the previous night. This time they would be supporting a Chicago band, The Loggerheads. The two girls looking after the box office told them they were a band that had enjoyed chart successes locally and were popular in this part of Illinois; they also told them to expect a big crowd.

At eight o'clock there were five or six hundred in the club, and there was still room for more. As the Bombastics' hour neared, there was no sign of The Loggerheads. Club manager and compère for the night, Bobby Baker, was seething and when they finally turned up only ten minutes before The Bombastics were due to go onstage, he waded into them about not showing respect for him or his guests from England, or Papa Jones' customers.

Danny too was angry, but he kept his mouth shut. He told Frank and JoJo afterwards how arrogant they'd appeared backstage in the large dressing room they'd all shared. All they wanted to talk about was The Loggerheads. The only interest they showed in The Bombastics was to ask Danny if they knew The Beatles. That did not go down very well with Danny and he told them so. He left them smoking pot and drinking whiskey, whilst he stood in the wings watching the show.

In complete contrast to the previous night everyone was up dancing from the start and a crowd of kids stood at the front of the stage clapping and singing along, even to songs they probably didn't know.

At the end of their session, after doing an encore, Bobby Baker came onstage. 'Boys and girls let's hear it for Frankie Atom and The Bombastics, all the way from England.'

The room was going wild; it looked like another encore was needed. The Loggerheads were in the wings, watching and waiting. JoJo moved over to Stan and Bodkin and with a quick sideways nod beckoned Frank and Carol across. 'Let's do that twin guitar version of 'Roll Over Beethoven'.'

'But we've only done it once before.' Frank looked anxious.

'Don't worry, it'll be perfect, you lead I'll follow.' JoJo smiled at the others. 'Okay, guys?' Bodkin put his thumbs up, Stan and Sugarlips both nodded.

They took their places and Frank counted himself and JoJo in. It brought the house down. The Loggerheads looked on from the side, open-mouthed.

'Follow THAT!' smirked Danny to himself and patted his boys on the back as they trooped off. 'Great – well done – fantastic!' He saved a kiss on the cheek for Sugarlips.

Then followed the commotion about Bodkin's drums.

Bobby Baker, still out onstage made the introduction. 'And now boys and girls, what you've all been waiting for, Chicago's own, LOGGERHEADS!'

They leapt onstage, frantically waving arms and guitars above them. As he passed Bodkin, their drummer brandished his drumsticks right under Bodkin's nose, shouting above the noise. 'Gonna have to use your drums, man!'

Bodkin tried to catch hold of him, but he was gone. Danny and Stan saw what was happening and grabbed hold of Bodkin. He was raging. 'What in hell's name is going on? Those are my drums. I'll break his bleedin' neck.

I'll rip his... '

'Let's stay calm, Bods.' Sugarlips stood face to face in front of the big man, put one hand on his shoulder and ran her other hand gently down his cheek. 'We can sort it out when they've finished; let's go to the dressing room and relax.' She took his hand and led him away.

'Wow! A spoonful of sugar calms the savage beast,' laughed Stan.

'Yep, it's a good job Carol was here,' added Frank. 'Can you imagine Bodkin rushing back on and dismembering a local hero in front of a live audience?'

The Loggerheads had a bad night. Whether it was following The Bombastics' rousing reception, their slipshod preparation, or the drink and drugs having an effect, was hard to tell; maybe a mixture of all. There was very little bonhomie in the dressing room afterwards, especially after Bodkin confronted their drummer. Fortunately, Shoogs had him calmed down by the time he told this particular Chicago drummer boy his fortune.

'If you *ever* get the chance to play my drums again, *DON'T!* Otherwise the only rhythm you'll be beating out will be on a hospital bedpan.'

Very few words were spoken between the two bands after that.

Whilst they'd been listening off stage to the Loggerheads, their lead guitarist making a complete hash of a solo, JoJo let them into a secret. It turned out he'd done some session work on one of their hits. 'They wouldn't know, they weren't there! It was added after they'd finished their recording session,' said JoJo. 'Hey, don't say a word you guys, their guitarist probably still thinks it's his riff on the record.'

***

Next morning they decided to split the driving. Bodkin

would start with JoJo riding shotgun and Sugarlips between them, which pleased Bodkin. It was still below freezing, but the roads were clear and had been salted. JoJo reckoned that in these conditions it would take them just under five hours to reach Springfield. Danny checked on his map and told Bodkin he would take over the driving at a town called Bloomington. Off they set.

'Just look at HIM!' exclaimed Sugarlips, pointing excitedly through the windscreen as they entered a small town name of Wilmington.

JoJo laughed loudly. 'That's one of the Muffler Men. They call that one the Gemini Giant.' The massive fibreglass spaceman stood maybe thirty feet high, holding a large rocket ship advertising a diner named The Launching Pad. Snow was still piled high on his helmet and on his outstretched arms holding the rocket, but the enterprising owner had somehow cleared it to show the name of his business. They were all glued to the window as they passed him by.

'You gonna meet plenty of those mothers on the Mother Road,' joked JoJo.

The journey was pretty uneventful and the covering of snow made one town look pretty much like another. They stopped in Pontiac to get petrol and when they reached Bloomington, they had lunch at one of the many diners before Danny took over behind the wheel.

'Before you pull away, Danny,' said Carol. 'Can Frank and I make a request?' Danny half turned to look at her. 'Can we make this car a smoke free zone? There's you with your Black Russian, there's JoJo with his cheroots, and there's Stan and Bodkin chain smoking those Marlboro thingies...'

'Yeah,' interrupted Frank. 'And we can't have the windows open because it's too bleedin' cold.'

'Okay, okay, that's fair enough,' agreed Danny. 'No more smoking in the car; from now on we have designated fag breaks.'

'*FAG BREAKS!*' JoJo's eyes widened and his mouth broke into a large, toothy smile. 'What do you mean?'

'Sorry, I mean cigarette breaks.' Danny hastily corrected himself. 'I completely forgot, fag has a completely different connotation over here.'

'Thought my luck had changed for a minute,' laughed JoJo, then his smile disappeared. 'And definitely no cannabis. If we get stopped for a traffic violation and the cops smell pot you may not be going back home for a long time.'

'Okay, all agreed?' Danny started the engine as he glanced around the car. They all nodded. As he pulled away he tweaked the dial to get a better reception on the radio.

'And here's your number one smash from the Righteous Brothers,' said the DJ, and on came 'You've Lost That Loving Feeling'.

'You can't turn on the radio without that song being played,' said JoJo. 'That won't be the last time you hear that, trust me.'

The Freedom Hall was situated in the old part of Springfield and was only a block away from their Springfield Park hotel. They left the car and trailer in the hotel parking lot and walked down to the venue to have a look round. There was nobody about, maybe not surprising, it was only just gone two o'clock. Frankie Atom and The Bombastics' posters were pasted to both sides of the large notice board that jutted out over the doorway, and also on the window of a shop that had closed down on the opposite side of the street. It was two doors down from the closed shop that Danny spotted the WGFB Radio signage.

'C'mon, let's see if we can hijack some free publicity whilst we're waiting.' He crossed the street, followed by the others. They entered through wood and glass doors with long, highly polished brass handles. In the lobby, a sign to WGFB directed them upstairs to the first floor. A middle-aged receptionist wearing her hair in a bun, peered at them over the spectacles she had perched on the end of her nose.

'Can I help you folks?'

'We're Frankie Atom and The Bombastics all the way from England. We're going to be the next big rock 'n' roll sensations here in the USA.' Danny was in full flow. 'Tonight we top the bill at The Freedom Hall over the way, and I thought perhaps your radio station would like an exclusive interview.'

'Well, sir, I think you may just have misjudged what we do here on WGFB.' She held his gaze with a stern glare. 'At the moment, Pastor Jeremiah McCann is discussing with our listeners how the love of Jesus can help family life here in Springfield.' For once Danny Hoffman was lost for words, and the sniggering going on behind him made it even more difficult.

Outside they really let rip, but Danny took it on the chin, joining in the laughter too.

'I should have seen that one coming.' JoJo was almost bent double. 'We got a lot of those Holy Joe radio stations round these here parts.'

The Freedom Hall was now open and they went inside to get used to their latest surroundings. Bodkin walked back to the car and brought the trailer down to unload ready for the gig.

Stage manager Brad Andersson and his sidekick Denny Watson showed them the ropes – literally! 'We can operate both the curtains and the lighting rig from here in the wings; show 'em Denny.' Denny flashed the lights; white to blue, to red, to green, to mix.

'So-phis-ti-cation,' purred Danny. 'I'll give you a copy of the lighting plan we use.'

Back stage was luxury indeed; three dressing rooms. 'Look at this lot, showers, flush toilets and lots of little light bulbs around the mirrors!' shouted Stan, excited. 'We've just gotta decide who shares with who.'

'I think I'll pass on that,' smiled Carol, pushing a door open with the end of her saxophone case. 'This one's single occupancy only.'

'Come on Stanley, you've pulled.' Bodkin put his arm around Stan and dragged him into the first dressing room. 'We've never taken our clothes off in a room on our own before.'

There was a good deal of cussing and laughing.

The gig went well – very well. The kids were magnificent, clapping and cheering and refusing to let them off. A crowd of twelfth-graders gathered in front of Frank swooning and screaming; at one point, two of them tried to get up onto the stage, but it proved too high and Brad was on hand to calm things down.

Frank and JoJo got back to dressing room three, took off their zoot suit jackets and hung them up. JoJo peeled off his sweat soaked shirt and wrapped a towel around him, whilst Frank levered the tops off two bottles of Coca-Cola. They both sat down exhausted. There was a kerfuffle in the corridor.

'You can't go down there.' It was Denny's voice.

Then a girl's voice. 'Don't be such a fuss-budget, Denny Watson, we just wanna say hello.'

'Yeah, Brad said it would be just fine,' came the voice of a second girl.

Denny's worried face appeared at the door. 'Excuse me boys, is it okay to say hi to a couple of fans? They won't stay long.'

'Sure,' smiled JoJo. 'Just bring them in.'

Two redheads pushed past Denny and made their way over to Frank. Both looked about sixteen or seventeen and both had their auburn hair pulled back into long ponytails. They just had to be sisters.

'Well hi, Frankie, I'm DeeDee and this is my twin sister Cindy. We just came to say how much we enjoyed the show.'

'That's great to hear, we know you like the Beatles over here in America. We're hoping you'll start to like The Bombastics in the same way.'

'Just listen to that accent, Cindy; isn't that the cutest thing you ever did hear?'

Both had stunning figures, although Cindy slightly hid her charms with a bright yellow trench coat, collar up, which almost reached down to her knee, whilst DeeDee wore a short candy-striped skirt and plain white blouse with a plunging neckline that left nothing to the imagination. They totally ignored JoJo.

Frank felt very uncomfortable. 'I don't seem to have a pen to give you my autograph; perhaps Denny has got one.' He half stood, but Denny had disappeared.

'It's not your autograph we want,' sighed DeeDee, untying her hair and shaking it loose. 'We share a room in the Halls of Residence just across the road and we figured out you may like to join us for a party.'

JoJo watched Frank struggling.

'Er, I... I can't... What I mean is... Oh dear...'

'Cindy has brought your invitation, haven't you Cindy?'

Without further ado, Cindy pulled the clip from her

hair so it fell loose round her shoulders and then with both hands opened up the front of her coat. She was wearing just a pale pink lacy bra and matching knickers that Frank could almost see through. Cindy proved to be even more voluptuous than her sister and Frank remembered thinking later, that for such a tiny bra to hold tits like that in place was a miracle of modern engineering.

Frank was lost for words.

'Come on you two, you'll get me in trouble.' It was Denny. 'Everybody's gone, except you two and I need to lock up.'

DeeDee looked round angrily and Cindy clutched her coat tightly to her.

'Hey girls, I got an idea.' It was JoJo; almost forgotten JoJo. 'We gotta shower and change; I know exactly where those Halls of Residence are. Why don't you give me the room number and I'll see Frankie gets over to you?'

Denny was doing his best to shuffle the two girls out of the room.

'23C!' shouted DeeDee over her shoulder. 'It's on the second floor – 23C!'

With that, they were gone and Frank looked at JoJo.

'Thanks,' he eventually said.

He never did go over to room 23C and JoJo never offered to show him the way.

***

They crossed the state line into Missouri and were completely blown away by the mighty Mississippi. Despite the temperatures, it hadn't frozen over and it meandered its way south to the Gulf of Mexico. They marvelled at the Gateway Arch which welcomed them to St. Louis; still officially under construction, but looking complete from where they stood. The observation decks were due to be opened to the public within the next eighteen months. Frank looked up at it, shielding his eyes as it glinted in the midday sun. 'I'd love to hitch a ride on one of those rail cars 600 feet in the air.'

Stan gulped loudly, turned away and made for the car.

Next day, they moved onto Republic, just south of Springfield, Missouri. This was the smallest gig yet in the smallest town yet, but the audience, perhaps 250 of them, went wild. There were kids, moms and dads and what looked like grandparents too. It all happened inside a restaurant that they later learned, was converted into a dance hall once a month, and then it was converted back to an eatery. Republic's big night out!

Next up, Joplin, on the way to which they had to stop off for a date with KXXD Radio.

'Not the God Squad this time then, Danny?' joked Sugarlips.

'I certainly hope not.' Danny sounded genuinely concerned. 'Mo Williams gave me the number; see if you can find it on the radio.'

'I was only pulling your leg, Danny.' Carol moved the dial. 'Still better check, we can't have you roasting in the fires of hell.'

She moved the dial slightly and picked up the tail end of KXXD's weather report. '...And a warning of a severe blizzard developing in Arizona and New Mexico.' Then the DJ introduced the throbbing sound of the Kinks' 'All Day and All of the Night'.

'Shit, man, that's right where we're headed.' JoJo's eyes widened.

'Chances are it'll blow itself out by the time we get there,' said Bodkin. JoJo never responded, but his look said it all.

It took them under two hours to arrive in Joplin, which meant they could relax and organise a few necessities. Danny took Frank and JoJo to KXXD, whilst Carol collected a suitcase full of their washing to take to the laundromat they'd seen on Maine Street.

'Leave this lot to me,' she said, and with a twinkle in her eye added, 'I don't want any of you getting your hands on my knickers.'

When they got there, they discovered Hank's Kleeners also did same-day dry cleaning. After chatting with Mrs Hank, they got a deal on four zoot suits and a long red dress and all back by 5:30 p.m.!

Turns out it wasn't Mrs Hank, there never had been one. Hank had gone to that great tumble drier in the sky ten years since and she, Alice Lafferty, and her husband Michael had bought the business. They also owned the diner two blocks down, so part of the deal was a table for six at six. Frankie Atom and The Bombastics were clean and fresh and well fed, come their eight o'clock appearance onstage at Bonnie & Clydes. They had a great night.

Next morning it was still freezing, but for the first time it was overcast, and without the bright sunshine they'd got so used to since they arrived in America it seemed that much colder. Route 66 to Tulsa stretched like a grey ribbon in front of them. Danny felt it best they fill up with fuel. The old man pumping gas also checked their oil.

'You folks goin' far?'

'Next stop Tulsa and then on to California and Los Angeles.' Danny explained they were from the UK and were touring right down Maine Street, USA (he remembered JoJo calling it that).

The old man gave Danny an odd look, then turned and disappeared into his garage. When he came out he was holding a gleaming shovel in each hand. 'Snow shovels;

eleven dollars the pair.'

Danny stood there thinking for a moment, then took more dollars out of his wallet. 'You got yourself a deal, here's the money for the gas and shovels and a little something for your kind help.'

'Thank you kindly, sir.' The old man smiled through nicotine teeth. 'I hope America likes yer music.'

***

They crossed through the bottom South East corner of Kansas and into Oklahoma. After passing through the small town of Baxter Springs, Danny became aware of a police car approaching in his rear view. Danny pulled to the right, thinking he wanted the passing lane, but about fifty yards behind them he hit his reds. Danny slowed, searching for the best place to pull over along a verge that was covered in frozen snow. As luck would have it a minor junction with a track leading to some hidden farmstead appeared, and he managed to manoeuvre the car and trailer just off the highway.

The whole interior of the Oldsmobile lit up, flashing bright red, as the State Trooper pulled in behind him. He didn't seem concerned that he was still on the highway, although in truth there were very few vehicles using it.

'Christ, what's wrong?' Danny said to the others as he watched the trooper climb out of his Galaxie. 'Has that bloody trailer come loose?'

The State Trooper put on his hat, nudged his sunglasses up the bridge of his nose and walked slowly up to the driver's door window which Danny had rolled down, running his eyes over the trailer and the occupants inside the Olds as he passed.

'No panic, sir,' he drawled. 'I noticed you had rental plates and you were hauling a trailer west. I was wonderin' where you were headed?'

Danny leant across Sugarlips, searched around under the dashboard and pulled out the foolscap with the tour schedule on it. He held the list up to the open window so both he and the trooper could see it. 'We're Frankie Atom and The Bombastics from England, playing rock 'n' roll for the good people of America. We make Tulsa tonight, then onto Oklahoma City, Amarillo, Santa F...'

'Can I stop you there, sir?' The trooper took off his sunglasses and putting his hand through the open window ran his finger to the bottom of Danny's list. 'They've reported blizzards blowing real hard west of Albuquerque, and fifteen inches of snow has already fallen on Flagstaff.'

'Are you saying we may have a problem?' Danny looked up at the Trooper.

'Well sir, if those blizzards move across the Great Plains, you most certainly could have. We had a case some time back, where the highway across the Painted Desert through Gallup, Winslow and on into Flagstaff, got blocked real bad. It all happened so suddenly and yet it took days for emergency services to dig out trucks, cars and station wagons like yours.'

'Better not mention the Donners, huh, officer?' grinned JoJo from along the front seat.

The Trooper, clearly surprised to hear an American accent, caught JoJo's eye. 'We sure don't; even more reason to play it safe though, folks. I've been to the United Kingdom a coupla times to visit my wife's folks, she's from Andover in Hamp-shire.' He was talking to Danny again. 'I loved your shires and your church steeples and your pubs on the village green, but believe me, sir, this ain't no English country lane. If you don't heed the snow warnings you could die out there!'

With that he stood up and put his sunglasses back on. 'Have a safe trip y'all, and good luck with the rest of your tour. I hope to see The Bombastics on the Billboard chart.'

He stooped and gave them a quick salute, then returned to his car. He followed them for a few miles and flashed them a goodbye as he pulled off the highway, at the small town of Quapaw.

The gig at the Welcome Light in Tulsa went as well as all their other gigs, but there was definitely an edge to the atmosphere in the dressing room and back at the hotel. Danny was worried about the weather ahead and that concern spread amongst the rest of them.

The four lads sat round their bedroom sharing a roll up. Bodkin lay flat on one of the beds, Stan perched on the end of it; the other two sat on the sofa bed, not yet pulled out.

'JoJo, what was all that stuff you and that copper were on about?' asked Stan. 'What was it? Darners or Dawners, or something?'

'Donners.' JoJo took the spliff from Frank and pulled on it. 'It all happened a long time ago up in the Sierra Nevada. Pioneers, eighty of them, crossing the Rockies for a new life in California; late nineteenth century if I remember my schooling. They got caught in winter storms and got themselves snowbound. Seems they ran outta food, some got sick and some just died of starvation. It was months before they was found and it appears those that was still alive had resorted to cannibalism.'

'You have to be kiddin'.' Stan choked on the spliff.

'No sir, that's a story that's been handed down through the generations. Only half of them made it to California.'

'Don't get telling Carol,' frowned Bodkin. 'It'll frighten her to death.'

'C'mon Bods.' Frank appeared through a plume of strange smelling smoke. 'She's a big girl. Anyway if you die on us first there'll be plenty of you to go round.'

They all enjoyed that one, including Bodkin.

***

They listened to the morning weather forecast on their hotel radios and gathered round the television in the lobby for news. It didn't add much to the storm's progress. Grainy TV pictures showed they were having a bad time in Arizona, but that was 800 miles away.

Danny checked with two travelling salesmen having breakfast in the restaurant. He reported back to the others. 'The fat guy with the droopy moustache is heading south to Dallas on the new interstate, the other guy has come in from the west, Amarillo way. Saw nothing of any trouble, but warned me it can happen quite quickly. Said to stick close to the truckers, they'll pick it up first, they're in touch with each other by CB, whatever that is.'

'Citizen Band Radio,' said JoJo. 'I gather you don't have it back home. Truck drivers use it all the time; talk to each other over short wave radio, about traffic hold ups and speed traps – and weather.'

'Never heard of it,' shrugged Danny. 'But it sounds like a good idea, sticking close by those truckers.'

***

It was quiet on the 66 that morning, but within two miles Bodkin slowed when he spotted the outline of a large truck way back in the distance. Gradually it closed on his tail; it was a red, white and blue Freightliner. Ten minutes later he pulled over, allowing it to speed past, then gradually accelerated until he was cruising at a steady sixty behind it. The trucker stopped at a Corn Dog coffee hut forty miles on, so The Bombastics did the same. When he started back up again they stuck close, but all in vain; within ten minutes he turned off down the same new interstate that droopy moustache had spoken of, signposted Fort Worth and Dallas.

'Shit, what if he's turned off because of blizzards?' Bodkin thumped the steering wheel with the palm of his hand.

'Too late to worry about that now,' said Danny. 'It was no good following him into Texas, anyhow we can only be an hour from Oklahoma City; we'll be just fine.'

Thursday 25th February in Oklahoma City would indeed be just fine, but Friday 26th would be one of those days when it seemed everything went wrong.

CHAPTER 20
'ROAD TO NOWHERE'

Talking Heads

Oklahoma City probably was 'oh so pretty' during the long hot summers, but now it was bitterly cold, mostly covered in frozen snow that refused to go away and that night's venue looked 'oh so pretty' dull. JoJo had worked this club before. It was an old warehouse of some sort; he reckoned it had been a furniture depository. It could have held a couple of thousand, but that night it looked a bit sparse, only a third full. They were out in the sticks away from the city and it was the coldest night yet, they told themselves. The DJ they shared the stage with told them it was a bigger crowd than normal, which cheered them up a bit, and those that had turned up gave them a great reception.

After Oklahoma City they'd allowed themselves plenty

of time to drive the 260 miles to Amarillo. They did their usual weather check on the TV in the breakfast room. The snow was definitely moving their way. Places like Denver, Albuquerque and Lubbock were reporting snowfalls.

'We'll be okay, there's plenty of hotels along the route.' Danny strode defiantly towards the parking lot, then stopped and turned in the doorway. 'Don't forget we got those shovels.'

'I'll remind you of that when you and Bodkin are digging us out of a drift,' quipped Frank.

They were west of Clinton, when they got the puncture. Changing the wheel was no easy task, with Route 66 as busy as they'd seen it for days. They cleared an area off road with the shovels and jacked the onside rear up. It was the last wheel nut that Danny couldn't budge. Bodkin stepped forward to give it a go, grabbed hold of the wrench with his right hand and pushed down hard. The wrench slipped off the wheel nut and Bodkin's hand smashed onto the concrete road surface. Bodkin roared in pain and clasped his crushed fingers under his left arm, dropping to his knees in anguish.

Danny used his foot to stamp down on the wrench and loosen the nut and with Stan's help, they got the spare tyre on. Meanwhile Carol did her best to tend to Bodkin's damaged hand; she managed to clean away bits of gravel with fresh snow and her handkerchief which she then wrapped carefully around his hand, to try and stop the bleeding on his knuckles, but just to touch his fingers made him flinch violently.

'I've broken the bloody things,' he cursed through clenched teeth. 'We got a one-handed drummer tonight.'

'Let's get along the road, see if we can find a doctor,' said Danny. 'We need to get this flat repaired too.'

The sky had darkened and it was starting to snow as

they came to a town named Clayton, it wasn't much of a town; a few streets of houses, a motel, a grocery store with a diner and a gas station and garage, outside which stood a thirty foot muffler man dressed in bright orange overalls and cap, holding a giant spanner across his arms; he was mostly covered in snow.

In contrast to his giant pal, the mechanic who'd been working under the hood of a beaten up Chevvy, wore grimy yellow overalls and had teeth to match. Squat and overweight, he seemed as wide as he was tall. He wore a dirty woollen trapper's helmet and had enormous greasy hands. Danny rolled the white walled flat towards him; Frank, Stan and JoJo shuffled into the workshop behind him out of the falling snow. A very large German Shepherd cross lay in the far corner, growling crossly. They were all relieved to see he was chained to a workbench.

'We ain't got no doctor,' the mechanic grunted, responding to Danny's question as he worked on the tyre. 'If we're sick, we drive into Elk.'

He carried on mending the puncture in silence, inflated it, bounced it up and down a couple of times, then let it drop at Danny's feet. 'D'yer want me to fit yer snow chains?'

'Chains?' puzzled Danny.

'Looks like yer'll need 'em.' He nodded towards the snow, now falling quite heavily, then turned to JoJo. 'I say, boy, go get your black ass out there – they'll be in the trunk.'

They were all stunned. Danny went to react, but JoJo took hold of his arm and put a finger to his lips, shaking his head gently. Frank almost snatched the keys off Danny, scowled at the mechanic and went out to find the chains. The dog jumped up and lunged forward, barking fiercely as he passed.

Carol had taken Bodkin into the store to try and find some painkillers. All they had was aspirin, which he swilled down with half a bottle of Mountain Dew. They'd worked out it was less than five miles into Elk City, but the snow was settling, and starting to come down even heavier. It was getting dark too; too early for dusk, so it was worrying to think how heavy the cloud cover up there was.

The newly reconstructed section of Interstate 40 ran parallel with Route 66 at this point and in the distance through the snow, about half a mile away, they could make out trucks moving very slowly. They too moved very slowly, but this was more to do with Danny taking it carefully; the sound of the chains clanking their regular beat on the compacting surface.

'Look, they've come to a halt!' Stan shouted, pointing towards the interstate; he was sat in the front alongside JoJo. Bodkin sat in the back, hunched forward, eyes closed with sweat trickling down his forehead. Carol had her arm gently linked through the arm of his damaged hand.

The line of stationary trucks disappeared into the snowy distance.

Progress was slow on the Mother Road, but at least they were moving. The first sight of problems was an abandoned car, pulled well over to the right and completely snowed under.

'What in hell's name happened to the driver?' asked Frank. 'There's nowhere to go, maybe we should look see if he's trapped inside.'

Danny pulled over and Frank got out. He picked his way over to the car and wiped his gloved hand across the driver's window. The snow fell away easily and Frank shielded his eyes to peer through the glass. There was nobody inside.

'He can't be hitchin' a ride in this stuff,' said Frank,

back in the station wagon. 'Apart from us, there's no one about.'

Within a few hundred yards the second part of Frank's statement proved wrong. They came up behind a line of stationary cars and trucks and after getting out to take a closer look, Stan, JoJo and Frank discovered it was a very long line. The drivers and passengers in the back three or four vehicles told them they'd been stuck there for nearly an hour. They feared the snow ploughs and snow blowers were going to be some time getting to them, probably concentrating on the interstate.

Danny switched the engine off and they waited, listening to the radio. 'This Diamond Ring' by Gary Lewis and the Playboys, The Beatles new release, 'Eight Days a Week', and a blast from the past, 'Claudette' by the Everly Brothers.

'A dollar to a dime 'You've Lost That Loving Feeling' comes on soon,' said JoJo.

Half an hour went by and the snow didn't ease up. 'We can kiss goodbye to any gig in Amarillo tonight,' said Danny. 'Can't even find a payphone to let them know, stuck here in the middle of nowhere.'

'And just who were you planning to play drums?' groaned Bodkin, taking more aspirin and Mountain Dew from Carol.

JoJo and Stan stood outside the Olds having a smoke when suddenly Danny started the engine. 'Enough of this, let's turn this rig around and get back to that motel. There's been nothing come the other way for ages, and night's falling.' By this time there were three cars queued behind them too. It was still snowing, as Stan and JoJo grabbed the shovels and did their best to clear an arc across the highway that would help Danny. Frank uncoupled the trailer and with Bodkin pushing hard with his backside they gave Danny some leverage as he gently revved the engine to pull the station wagon across the highway. After three or four manoeuvres back and forth to straighten it up, they were then able to spin the trailer around and reattach it. Slowly Danny accelerated and moved them gingerly into the deep virgin snow. The chains made it all work, everybody clambered back in and soon they were heading back to Clayton. The driver of the car immediately behind them, honked his horn and put his thumb up though the side window.

***

Danny and Frank went into Mitch & Joni's Motel reception. Danny rang the little brass bell that stood on the counter and Mitch came through from the back. Mitch turned out to be the mechanic who'd fixed their flat, now without his trapper's hat, but still in his greasy overalls.

'We'd like three rooms for the night,' said Danny.

'You ain't thinkin' of checkin' that nigger friend of yours into our motel are ya?' Mitch growled.

'He's a member of our band and we're guests in your country.'

'We don't allow no niggers in Clayton after sundown.'

Danny's eyes flashed angrily. 'What you're saying is against the law and you know it!'

Mitch moved forward, flicked open the register and sneered. 'Well looky here, it appears we're full and I guess if you call the cops, they'll be here in a couple of days, maybe longer.' He hadn't realised Joni had now appeared through the door behind him.

'How can you say you're full, there's not a single car outside any of the rooms?' pressed Frank.

Joni stepped forward and took hold of Mitch's arm. 'Can I have a word with you?' She led him out the back. They were out of sight, but not out of earshot; the walls of that office were thin.

'You're turning away three rooms? ARE YOU CRAZY?' Joni was shouting. 'Since they built that Goddamn interstate, our business has disappeared. We had no guests at all last week, and you're lucky to make a handful of bucks in that garage of yours, most of which you spend on beer. Now you go feed that dog of yours, who's howlin' for his dinner and leave the runnin' of this here motel to me!'

Joni came back into the office and smiled gently. 'Now, gentlemen, how many rooms was it you wanted, and will you be having breakfast with us?'

It turned out Mitch & Joni's Motel didn't have a family room that the four lads could share, the rooms they had were far too small; so Joni did them a deal on four rooms. Stan and Bodkin to share, Frank and JoJo to share, and single rooms for Carol and Danny.

***

Whilst Danny and Frank were organising accommodation, the others went to the store-cum-diner to organise dinner. Bodkin bought more aspirin and a bottle of Jim Beam. His hand wasn't quite as painful now, it was more of an ache, although it seemed to be throbbing up his arm as far as his elbow. More aspirin would be a good start, the whiskey would really help, but the undivided attention Carol was giving him was worth the pain.

Danny used the payphone in reception to make contact with Mo Williams and explained their predicament. Mo told Danny he wasn't surprised, he'd got a dozen or so other acts out on the road with similar problems. It appeared that even if they'd made some of the gigs, the club owners had cancelled because they were snowed in too. No punters, no show! He told Danny to keep in touch and to contact him collect-call if necessary.

As it turned out, they were marooned in Clayton for two more nights. There were no radios in the rooms, but reception had one, they had a radio in the Oldsmobile and there was a television in the diner. They were able to keep in touch with what was going on. There had been record falls in most parts of the USA and Canada, but, very surprisingly, heavy snowfalls as far south as Austin and Houston where Texas had suffered four consecutive days of blizzards.

Snow clearing concentrated on the interstates with snow blowers and snow ploughs working full time and after sitting tight that Friday and over the weekend, the first plough appeared mid-morning on the Monday.

They'd had plenty of time to think and talk. Stan phoned Elsie every day, he booked his toll calls collect-call and dreaded to think what Elsie's dad's phone bill would be when he got home. The store began running out of supplies, Danny ran out of Black Russians, JoJo ran out of cheroots and they all ran out of cannabis. Fortunately, there was plenty of Jim Beam and cigarettes with the taste of Marlboro Country.

JoJo had brought an acoustic guitar with him and he spent a lot of time with Frank teaching him how to pick, country style. No doubt about it, music and Jim Beam was the only way to relieve their boredom and most of that Saturday they spent in Stan and Bodkin's room, plucking and singing and steadily drinking the whiskey bottle dry; even Carol and Frank were developing the taste. Danny had returned to his room and Carol decided she'd go back to hers to try and get a bit of sleep. Bodkin said he thought that was a good idea, so Stan pulled the blind down for him and departed to phone Elsie. Frank and JoJo moved into their room with the guitar and what was left of the whiskey.

What happened next was a complete shock, maybe not to everyone!

JoJo was sat on Frank's bed, showing him a rather complicated guitar break; he was handing his guitar over to Frank for him to try it, when he suddenly said, 'That dressing room incident back in Springfield. Those redheaded twelfth-graders sure wanted to show you something and it sure wasn't their high school diploma! You seemed mighty reluctant.'

'I was just tired, it had been a long day.'

JoJo studied Frank long and hard. 'Hmmm, my guess is you're still a virgin Frankie, and this sure was your chance to graduate, if you get my meaning.'

Frank could feel himself reddening up and his thoughts were spinning, not sure whether it was the whiskey or JoJo unlocking some deeper truth. He reached out to take the guitar.

'Either that or you're in denial young Frankie, hiding feelings you just ain't come to terms with yet.' He held onto the guitar, not letting go and looking deeply into Frank's eyes. Frank felt a slight tremor go through him, but held JoJo's gaze.

JoJo released the guitar neck and ran his hand over Frank's shoulder, letting his fingers entwine in Frank's black curls. 'Relax, man. As they say, it takes one to know one.' With that he pulled Frank's head gently towards him and kissed his lips. There was no resistance from Frank, quite the opposite; he let the guitar slide onto the bed and took hold of JoJo kissing him more passionately.

It was this second kiss that Danny saw. Neither Frank nor JoJo had drawn the blind, and neither Frank nor JoJo had locked the door.

'What the hell are you two doing?' Danny burst into the room. Frank and JoJo sprung apart and the guitar slipped off the edge of the bed, banging onto the floor and sending a tuneless chord echoing around the room. 'All the problems we have and now I find I've got a couple of queers in the band.'

'It's not what it seems,' pleaded Frank. 'I got carried away with the moment, I'm no queer; perhaps the whiskey's gone to me head, I'm not used to it.' He screwed his eyes up and shook his head.

JoJo said nothing.

Danny was seething. 'It's not what it seems? So what in hell's name do two men rolling about on a bed kissing each other, mean exactly?'

He turned to JoJo. 'I don't know what happens here in America, but back home what I saw you doing is illegal. What's more, Frankie is not twenty-one years old, so you'd most likely be jailed for corrupting a minor.'

'Hold on, man. I ain't corrupted nobody. I was just showing my affection to a very talented boy; we was just kissing. Sure, there are laws against sodomy in this country, but they vary depending which state you're in; what we were doing was not sodomy.'

Danny could feel himself shouting now, something he rarely did. 'Maybe that's because I caught you...'

'Maybe, you all need to calm down.' Carol was stood in the doorway behind Danny. 'I think you may have forgotten how thin the walls are in this place.'

'Oh God.' Frank thrust his head into his hands and slewed sideways onto the pillow.

'Danny, it may have come as a shock to you, but I think the rest of us had known for some time that Frank was... well, shall I say, shy of girls?' Carol crossed the room and sat on the bed between Frank and JoJo; she pulled Frank up, put her arm around him and allowed him to cuddle up against her. 'We love you Frank, no matter what.'

'If this ever gets out, if the papers pick up on it, we're finished – The Bombastics are finished!' Danny was trying desperately to regain his composure. 'Can you imagine what your fans will say? Frankie Atom a poofter, Frankie Atom a faggot. Jesus Christ, this has to be handled so carefully.'

'Then let's talk it through with the others tonight over dinner,' suggested Carol. 'We certainly aren't in any rush to be elsewhere.'

***

Carol was right, neither Stan nor Bodkin were totally surprised about Frank. It was very difficult to begin with when Danny brought the subject up. Frank felt humiliated and sat there in silence nervously rearranging the food on his plate; JoJo pushed his plate aside and lit a cigarette. It was Carol who led the way and gradually the mood softened; the more they talked about it the more at ease they became with each other.

'Barry's been on about it for some time,' Bodkin told Frank. 'Onstage, you get the birds flocking; somehow he always seems to get the best ones backstage, but you're never interested – so him and our Wally fill their boots. I particularly remember that end of tour party at Valkyries in Gothenburg. I thought those two blondes were going to get into a fight over you, but you were more interested in the behind-closed-doors jam session going on with the two other bands.'

'Cilla,' said Stan. 'I remember one was called Cilla, 'cos Barry kept singing 'Anyone Who had a Heart' to her, but she was having none of it and completely ignored him; a bit like you ignored her, Frank.'

'It's not that I'm not interested in girls,' faltered Frank. 'I am; I enjoy their company. It's just this other sort of feeling I get inside me; I had it all through school – since my balls dropped, I suppose – pardon me, Shoogs. Things were different – I dunno – when I heard other kids talking at school, it just wasn't the same for me. I'm finding this very difficult...'

He looked across the table at JoJo. 'That's the first encounter I've had with a male, I swear and it'll be the last. Maybe it was a kind of infatuation, I do love JoJo's guitar playing; or, as I said to Danny and Carol, maybe the Jim Beam went to my head.'

'Maybe you pitch for both sides,' said JoJo, stubbing out his cigarette. 'Look guys, I've known about me since I was in eighth grade and I ain't frettin' about it. We have a sayin' over here; don't ask don't tell. You is what you is and that's a fact.' He took the Green Book from his jacket pocket and waved it in front of them. 'This here book's to help us niggers be treated like human beings in our own country, but there ain't no book for faggots, certainly no black faggots – or what was it you called us, Danny – poofters? Look, I'm real sorry I've caused young Frankie here such embarrassment, I guess we just got caught up in the moment. It won't happen again; at least not with me!'

For a minute, nobody said anything.

'Whatever it is, for the sake of Frankie Atom and The Bombastics, we are sworn to secrecy.' Danny took up the quarter bottle of Jim Beam and dribbled whiskey into each glass; Frank declined. 'This is our last drink for tonight. Frank, you take the spare bed in my room tonight. You'll be untouched by human hand! I can assure you of that. Tomorrow we need to make some decisions.'

***

Danny called them all together in his room on Sunday morning. They bought bottles of Coke, plastic tooth-mugs and packs of Marlborough with them. No whiskey.

'I've given our predicament some thought.' Danny lit a cigarette. 'We've lost the gigs in Amarillo, Santa Fe and

Albuquerque and the chances of us making Gallup, Winslow and Flagstaff look beyond hope. That leaves just Las Vegas, Barstow, San Bernadino and LA, but you've listened to the reports, parts of Arizona are still blocked.'

'So what do we do, it must be well over a thousand miles to LA?' Stan guessed.

'Well, like I said, I've thought about this and it seems we have a few choices. Even if they clear the route and we drive non-stop, we still might not make those dates. However if we back track to Oklahoma and the city airport, we could see if there's a flight down to California.'

He hesitated – nobody spoke.

'Or we could get a flight back to New York and go home?'

The room remained silent.

Danny continued. 'We've got to get back by the middle of next week. The new tour starts in ten days and I haven't booked hotels for the Scandinavian leg yet.' He looked at each of them. 'Look guys, after yesterday's incident things have changed. Frankie and JoJo have made being holed up here even more difficult. I know you're homesick Stan, and Bodkin you must be going through hell with that injury, so I've made the decision. We go back home.'

'I've checked and there's a hospital in Oklahoma where we can get Bodkin's hand seen to; the airport's open and there are regular flights to New York, as well as flights for JoJo back to Chicago. There's bound to be an InterStateCars rental desk.'

'All we gotta do now is wait for this road to be swept,' grumbled Bodkin, letting his swollen hand dangle limply between his legs.

'My guess is they'll have that interstate clear, so we just have to make it across to the intersection,' added Danny. 'If they haven't appeared by tomorrow, I say we go for it with the chains and shovels.'

Next day the ploughs appeared and by Monday lunchtime they were good to go. Danny made the difficult call to Mo Williams, but he fully understood. The gig at Barstow had been cancelled and he had bands who could cover Las Vegas, San Bernadino and LA. They agreed The Bombastics' next foray into America would be in the summertime.

Everything went well in Oklahoma City. The hospital x-rayed Bodkin's hand; only his little finger was broken, the rest were badly bruised. They gave him a local anaesthetic whilst they re-set it and put it in a cast that allowed him freedom with his thumb, middle and forefingers. They also gave him some painkillers and Danny paid with his American Express. Danny also used his American Express to get them flights to New York and JoJo on a flight back to Chicago. There was an InterStateCars rental desk and after a bit of quibbling, there was nothing more to pay.

'The terms of the agreement state that you would drop the vehicle and trailer off in Los Angeles, sir,' said the girl behind the desk, pointing at the paperwork with her ballpoint. 'So there will be a twenty dollar administration charge.'

Danny produced his best smile, something that had been missing for the last few hours. 'Young lady, we have enjoyed dealing with your company and I shall be writing to them to say so; I shall also tell them how I brought the car and trailer back eight days early, have paid for a puncture repair and left you two brand new shovels, ideal for clearing snow. I shall then add how we, that is, you and I, agreed that I would not charge you for these items and you would waive any administration charge.'

'Oh! Oh, I see.' She was clearly knocked out of her stride. 'I'm sure they'll be in touch if that isn't acceptable, sir.'

'I'm sure they will,' smiled Danny, putting the keys on the desk. 'Be sure to have a nice day.'

JoJo's flight was first out that evening. Danny had disappeared to make calls, buy a magazine or visit the restroom, nobody was sure. There were sincere man hugs all round and an embrace from Sugarlips.

'It's been fantastic working with you JoJo,' said Frank. 'I've learned so much in such a short time, it's just a pity we couldn't finish the job; I'm... I'm so sorry it has to end like this.'

'Don't be sorry, Frankie, just be true to yourself. Remember in this life, you're on your own until the end.'

'Hey man, that's a bit heavy.' Bodkin put his hand on JoJo's shoulder. 'Maybe the world's changing. Maybe attitudes will be different in years to come. We'll look after Frank, he's part of our family. You, JoJo – you just take care of yourself, okay?'

'You should come over to the UK and play some gigs with us.' Carol knew she was welling up. 'We can arrange that, can't we Stan?'

'I don't see why not,' replied Stan. 'Danny can get in touch with Mo Williams; see if we can sort some dates out.'

'Hey man, don't do that,' frowned JoJo. 'He'll want a cut.'

With that JoJo went back to the InterStateCars desk, took a business card out of the rack and borrowed the girl's pen. He then wrote his name and phone number on the reverse.

'Here you are, Stan,' laughed JoJo. 'Jerome Jones Junior, have guitar will travel.'

He caught hold of his guitar case and raised his hand. 'Bye ya'll, it's been a real pleasure.'

As he turned to walk towards the departure gate, he punched Bodkin playfully on his chest. 'Get well soon, big man, and let's hope 'Jive Away the Tears' hits Billboard this week and all this has been worth it.' He turned, waved once more and was gone. Danny never made the goodbyes. Frank watched JoJo disappear into the crowd of passengers boarding for Chicago.

The New York flight was delayed, the weather on the Eastern Seaboard had been just as bad apparently, and there were three and four hour waits for flights into most cities. It gave Stan a chance to sit in the bar and get a few drinks inside him. When they finally got off the ground, the plane was a turboprop which caused all Stan's Dutch courage to drain away, leaving him unable to resist looking through the window every ten minutes to see if the propellers were still attached to the wing.

Delays at JFK were even longer. They knew they had a six hour wait for the early morning flight anyway, but by the time they eventually took off they'd waited nearly ten. Stan wasn't allowed any more alcohol; with Danny in his own car and Bodkin unable to drive, it would be down to Stan to drive Jezza back to Fordrough from Heathrow. That was bad enough, but Bodkin saying 'Cheers Stanley,' every time he got a fresh drink didn't help one iota. They managed to get copies of both *Billboard* and *Cash Box* from the shop in the departure lounge, but they'd charted in neither. They went through them cover to cover and Frankie Atom and The Bombastics never got a mention; not a review, nothing about their early gigs in Chicago and Joplin, nothing in the 'Bubbling Under' chart. When they boarded the TWA Boeing 707, they dumped both magazines in the trash can.

***

Two days later Danny phoned Stan to check if everything was okay with Bodkin or would they need to get a stand-in for the upcoming tour.

'It just so happens we had a get together this morning at Frank's house,' said Stan. 'It was Barry's idea, I think he was feeling a bit left out. Anyway, Bodkin was okay, he was able to hold a drumstick in his right hand without any problem and as we won't be onstage for more than three quarters of an hour at a time, he reckons he'll be okay. Just to be on the safe side, I've been in touch with the Keynotes, the band opening up for us and their drummer is happy to be on stand-by.'

'And how about Frankie, how's he been, after everything that went on?'

'He's been very quiet, but there doesn't seem to have been any nuclear fallout. His guitar playing just gets better, which I think we can put down to JoJo's influence. Barry keeps harping on about his stand-in, the Space Cowboy as we nicknamed him, so we've all taken turns to wind him up. We've just told him that JoJo was an amazing guitarist and a knockout singer. Bodkin told him JoJo is trying to get a work permit to join us over here permanently, but we know that at some time soon we're going to have to sit Barry down and tell him what happened.'

'Leave that to me, Stan, but you're right, it must be soon.'

CHAPTER 21
'DON'T BELIEVE A WORD'

Thin Lizzie

With old Walter and Monty, his Yorkie, gone, Chopper, Curly and Pimples were the only others in the Crown and Anchor. Part-time barman Matt hurriedly slipped the book he was reading under the counter, as Gloria walked across to the bar to order fresh drinks. She helped Matt pour them and carried them over to the table next to the jukebox, a pint of bitter each for Stan and Bodkin and a glass of red wine for Frank, finishing off the bottle, and a glass of orange for herself.

She glanced over at the oche. *I left Matt alone with them in here for a little bit longer than I should have done. You never can tell what those clowns might do. Doesn't appear to be any harm done; anyway, we're here now if they give Matt any grief.*

She put her glass of orange juice on the table next to Stan and pulled up a chair. 'My mum loved 'Jive Away the Tears',' she said. 'It got you a gold record didn't it?'

Frank laughed. 'We loved your mum and a million other mums. It was quite a time, the Christmas of '64. Disappointing in many ways, mind you.' Frank suddenly went sombre. 'We just couldn't get it going in the States. The British Invasion was at its height and 'Jive' should have been a smash.'

'British Invasion? What was that?' asked Gloria.

'British acts storming the American charts,' said Frank. 'The Beatles, Rolling Stones, Wayne Fontana and The Mindbenders, Petula Clarke, even Herman's bloody Hermits. We're over there during America's coldest winter in recent memory, battling away in the snow and shit, trying to get airplay and there's these guys grabbing all the number ones.'

He stopped for a moment, deep in thought.

'Looking back, it affected us more than we thought, took us a bit of time to get over that,' he continued.

'The record buying public went off us for a bit after that,' added Stan. 'We thought we'd had our fifteen minutes of fame.'

'What he means is my next lot of songs were crap,' smiled Frank somewhat sardonically. 'We were contracted to Eternal to do an LP; and they wanted most of the tracks to be originals; at least three should be commercial enough for singles to help sell the LP.'

'What's an LP?' frowned Gloria.

'Tell her, old timer,' laughed Frank.

'It means Long Player,' explained Bodkin. 'It's what you call an album, nowadays; and by the way Frank, they weren't crap; we worked bloody hard on those songs, but kids are fickle, even sixties kids.'

'On reflection, it was definitely the pressure,' Frank continued. 'I wrote the early stuff in my own time, there weren't any deadlines. Then all of a sudden things change; now I've got to fill an LP, write six, maybe seven new songs, some of which must be chart toppers – and all in under a month.'

'You had more big hits though, didn't you?' Gloria asked.

'Eventually, but it was the next single release that was the problem,' said Bodkin.

'And the one after that.' Frank sipped thoughtfully at his wine. 'I never really liked 'Time and Again', I told Martin and Don it wasn't hit material, but they had it their own way.'

'It reached the top twenty!' said Stan.

'C'mon Stan, what was it, three weeks, peaking at number seventeen, was it?' Frank shook his head. 'Whatever it got to, it was a flop by our standards. Then 'Back in Your Arms' really bombed out. It never even made the Pick of the Pops top twenty and if it hadn't have been for the music press starting to produce top thirties, we wouldn't have charted at all.'

'Highest I saw it was number twenty-three in the *Record Mirror*,' added Stan. 'Shame really, I thought it was a pretty decent single, maybe a bit too much of a ballad.'

'I worked hard writing those songs in my studio.' Frank laughed as he explained to Gloria, 'I spent hours in our dad's garage with my guitar, putting stuff on the Grundig. I had about five songs finished and bits and pieces of another three or four others I was working on, but by now I was getting a severe case of the screaming ab-dabs.'

'Screaming ab-dabs?' Gloria looked puzzled.

'Self-doubt,' said Frank. 'I remember we booked Fordrough village hall two days before we were due down at Islington to record. We'd long since stopped using the hall for practice on a Saturday morning, but it just so happened the main hall was free for the day I wanted. I thought it might relax us all, make us more creative, back home in Fordrough where it all started.'

'It went very well, if I remember, Frank,' said Bodkin. 'We all had some input into the arrangements we wanted.'

'Trouble was The Beatles' amazing success,' Stan recalled. 'We tried so hard not to be influenced by what they were doing and be accused of copying them; trouble was they weren't only influencing music they were changing fashion too. Hair was getting longer, none of your greased back look anymore. Do you remember Danny doing his nut, because Barry and Bodkin combed their hair into Beatle mop-tops?'

'"You're not John, Paul, George and fuckin' Ringo," he said, "you're Frankie Atom and The Bombastics."' Frank laughed. 'Excuse my French Gloria, mind you, the only reason Bodkin started combing his hair forward was to hide his receding hairline.'

'It wasn't bleedin' funny at the time.' Bodkin stroked a hand over his shaven head. 'Bald drummers, bald guitarists, even bald singers, it's not a problem these days, but in 1965 you wore your hair round your shoulders, so for a twenty-year-old, going bald was a disaster. Then we played with an American band over in Amsterdam, can't remember what they were called; anyway, their drummer had the same alopecia problem, but he wore a bandana. I didn't fancy a headscarf, but Carol got me a denim cap; she said it looked fine, so that worked fine for me.'

'Lordy, Lordy, bless my soul, if Miss Sugarlips said it was fine, then Bodkin be a happy boy,' mocked Stan, fluttering his eyelashes.

'Do I detect romance was in the air?' asked Gloria. Bodkin picked up his beer and took a large guzzle.

'Best we don't go there,' said Frank, changing tack. 'We arrived at Eternal and were chuffed to find Don Winston and Stevie Balshaw were behind the glass again. The studio had been booked for three days and we could run late if we needed to. We were booked into a nearby hotel and there were plenty of pubs and restaurants in the area. We spent the first day putting down two songs, 'Stay Out Of My Life' and 'Black Sedan'. The second one, I remember vividly, had been inspired by Stan passing his driving test in his dad's black Ford Consul.'

'That's right,' said Stan. 'Do you remember it had a steering column gear change? I took us out for a spin to celebrate. Elsie, Barry, Frank and Frank's sister Suzie, who Barry was doing his damnedest to get off with.'

'That has to be same Elsie you're married to, Stan?' asked Gloria.

'Oh yes, the very same. Elsie Mine's-a-Babycham Ravenscroft,' nodded Stan.

Frank went on. 'I stayed behind that first evening with Don and Stevie, to work on 'Stay Out Of My Life'. I thought some honky-tonk type piano might sound right, so we tried it a number of ways on the 4-track and mixed it with what we'd already put down, until we got what we wanted. You can hear it and Black Sedan, on that first album. Neither even made it as a B-side.'

'Next day was interesting though, wasn't it lads?' Frank looked at Stan and Bodkin. 'Barry took us completely by surprise when he...'

'It's Barry I need to talk to you about,' interrupted Bodkin. 'I've heard something very concerning.'

They waited for Bodkin to continue.

'Look, best finish your story first, Frank,' said Bodkin,

realising his timing wasn't good. 'What about another round of drinks Gloria, before he continues?' He half stood, took a wad of notes out of his jeans and peeled off a twenty. 'Make mine a Coke, I've got to drive home.'

Gloria moved over to the bar and whilst Matt poured Stan's beer and Bodkin's Coke, she opened a fresh bottle of red for Frank. Again she glanced over to the oche to make sure the Dartboard Three were behaving themselves.

Bodkin came over to Gloria to pay with his twenty and then helped her carry the drinks back to the table. 'What about you, Gloria?'

'I'm okay this time, I've still got most of my orange juice left.'

Frank continued. 'We worked on another tune next morning, can't remember which one it was, probably 'Time and Again'. Anyway, Don decided we should have a bit of lunch at The White Horse over the road from the studio. An old Georgian coaching house with real ales, but more importantly, as far as Don was concerned, they did a mean sausage and tomato sandwich with Worcester sauce.

'Over lunch we talked about song writing. Not surprisingly the conversation turned to Lennon and McCartney. Don said he felt one the main reasons for The Beatles' amazing success was the competitive edge created by them writing separately, bringing their work into the studio, then letting the natural creativity of the two of them along with George and Ringo, and George Martin, develop the songs together. That's when he asked us if any other of The Bombastics wrote songs apart from me. Well you could have knocked me down with a feather when Barry said as calmly as you like, "I've written a couple of numbers."'

'Knocked us *all* down with a bleedin' feather,' added Stan.

Bodkin took it up. 'I told him to stop pissing around, we'd had enough of his practical jokes. In all the time we'd been together, from the Tanner Men Skiffle Group at school, to topping the UK charts, he'd never ever shown any inclination to write a song. Sugarlips went off on one too; told him to quit messing about and concentrate on the job in hand.

'Barry was grinning when he said, "Bugger me, what is it with you lot? I could have been hiding me light under a bushel." He then thumped his chest with his fist. "There could be a Bob Dylan in here bursting to get out. I'll play them to you when we get back in the studio."

'Then he suddenly put his half-finished glass of Coke down on the table, on top of his empty plate. "Tell you what," he said. "What about here and now? I'll just nip back over to Jezza and get my acoustic guitar. Got the keys, Wally?"

'With that, Wally threw him a bunch of keys and Barry disappeared out of the door leaving us all looking at each other stunned,' said Stan. 'I said to the others, "This is going to be interesting."'

Frank clasped his hand over his mouth to stifle a bray of laughter. 'Do you remember Don wearing his wise old head and saying, "Let's wait and see. I've been in this game a wee while, seen gifted artists disappear without trace; seen others with little or no talent become major stars. I've learned never to be surprised." Then he bit into his sandwich and squirted tomato sideways out of his mouth all down the front of Stevie Balshaw's clean white T-shirt. "Shit," he cursed. He grabbed at his paper napkin and only succeeded in knocking his beer all over the plate of egg and chips Wally was half way through. Did we laugh or what? In the end he did too.'

Stan picked up the story. 'Barry came back with his guitar and shuffled a few of us around to make space for himself. The bar was pretty full that lunchtime and although they were used to the odd familiar face popping in, with the Eternal recording studio just across the road, Stevie said it was unusual for anyone to bring their music into The White Horse. Everybody waited. Barry did a bit of minor tuning up, looked around at the lunchtime crowd, focused himself, he played the intro, that descending sequence of chords we now know so well, before he broke into song.'

Stan looked at Frank and Bodkin. 'It went something like this, you may know it Gloria. Da-da-da-dah, dum-de-dum, dah-da-da-dah.' He accompanied himself, strumming air guitar. Bodkin picked up the rhythm with his fingertips on the table and right on cue Frank sang.

'Your smile was so bewitching, it seemed like love-light in your eyes.

The words you spoke enraptured me, but your promises were lies.

You talked of love, you thrilled me so, I succumbed to your charms,

Beguiling kisses blinded me, as I held you in my arms

Shattered dreams and promises,
That's all I have, it's true,
Broken hearted memories,
And shattered dreams of you.

In bed I lie and cry alone, how could love be so cruel?
My hopes and plans just torn to shreds, you took me for a fool,
You're with another now I hear, your careless cheating way,
Will turn love's stupid game around and one day you will pay.

Shattered dreams and promises,

That's all you'll have, it's true,
Broken hearted memories,
Just shattered dreams of you.'

Gloria was thrilled and gave them a volley of rapid little claps. 'That was beautiful,' she giggled.

'The White Horse crowd thought so too,' said Stan. 'As Barry played the final chord, spontaneous cheers and applause broke out among the customers who had gathered round our table, some were on tiptoe and more were balanced precariously on the bench seat that ran along the back wall of the saloon bar.'

Frank added, 'We were stunned too. Me, Stan, Bodkin, Sugarlips, Wally, Don and Stevie – the lot of us; we all joined in with whoops and cheers. I remember Bodkin had joined in with Barry like he did just now, picking out the rhythm, rapping his fingers on the hollow panelling of the seating below where he was sat. When the hubbub subsided a bit, I said to Barry, "Where the fuck did that come from?" Then I had to apologise to Shoogs.'

'Sorry, Gloria, I need to apologise again.' Frank raised a hand. 'But we were so shocked that's exactly what I said.'

Gloria shrugged.

'Barry was grinning like that cat from Cheshire,' said Bodkin. 'He was going to play some more he'd written. That's when Don called a halt to it and said we needed to get back over to the studio and get the power switched on.'

***

Two days before his virtuoso performance in the White Horse, Barry had been deep in thought as he drove home from their village hall practice session when a tune popped into his head.

Dah da da dar dum, dah da da dah, dah da da dah dum, dah da da dah.

Then slowly some words came.

Broken hearted nobody, nothing now to you. Broken hearted nobody, Dah da da dah dum dum do.

He parked his car outside his house and sat for a minute or two in contemplation.

Robbie Rochester, of course! It's one of his songs off the Walkman. Why the hell has that suddenly come back to me?

He got out of his car, unlocked the boot and took out his acoustic guitar case and a little bundle wrapped in an oily rag. After slamming shut the boot, he let himself into the house.

'It's only me, Mom,' he called down the hallway as he ran up the stairs, two at a time.

'Want a cuppa?' she shouted back from the sitting room, where she was watching television.

'Nah, yer alright. I got something I need to get done.' With that he disappeared into his bedroom and shut the door. He took out his Harmony guitar and placed it carefully down on the bed. He put the little oily rag bundle on his dressing table. He carefully unfolded it and picked out the England's Glory matchbox. Inside was another tiny package, this time wrapped in polythene. He unrolled it and a number of little white pills spilled onto the dressing table. Without hesitation, he popped two of them into his mouth and swallowed hard. He scooped up the remaining pills, rolled them back into the polythene and returned them to the matchbox. He placed this on the oily towel, along with his weed and Rizla, which he folded and put into his empty guitar case. He wouldn't have dared smoke in the house, but the acid was undetectable.

He lay back on his bed, closed his eyes and waited for chemical nirvana.

Instead of nirvana, deceit came calling. A seed of an idea began to grow and germinate in his head. As the acid started to give him a warm, inner glow, so the idea grew and flourished. He opened his eyes and half sat up, resting on one elbow as he focussed on the top left hand drawer of his dressing table. He pulled himself closer to the edge of the bed, grabbed at the drawer handle and slid it open. Reaching inside, he pulled the grey metal Walkman out; the earplugs already plugged in, came out with it. Sitting down on the bed, he put the plugs in his ears and pressed the play button. The volume was high and made him flinch, but he soon turned it down. The tape was halfway through 'Bar Room Brawl'. He hadn't played the Walkman for months, but remembered 'Bar Room Brawl' was the third number on the little tape. He pressed 'Stop' and then rewound the tape back to the beginning. When he pressed 'Play', Robbie Rochester began singing 'Warwickshire Girls'. He pressed 'Fast Forward' and 'Stop' three or four times and eventually found 'Broken Hearted Nobody'. He picked up his guitar and plectrum, found the key and the chord sequence, nothing too difficult, just a twelve bar riff, but a really catchy tune. It was Robbie's original version, slower than the one he remembered they recorded at Chekka Records, but Barry preferred it. He needed to make some notes. He grabbed a pen from a jar on his dressing table and in his haste, he ripped July off The Bombastics' calendar pinned on his bedroom wall, to scribble down Robbie's lyrics and the chord changes. He then did the same with 'Bar Room Brawl' and a fourth number on the tape, 'Let's Run Away'. He noticed the tape was beginning to slur, sending Robbie's voice out of tune. He guessed that was the battery running down and when he slid open the battery compartment, four little batteries fell out. He'd never seen Duracell batteries before. He shuffled them around and carefully replaced them to try the Walkman once again. All he got was Robbie Rochester sounding like a Jacques Cousteau scuba diving commentary. He took the batteries from his bedside transistor, and although they were too small, by folding the gold foil from a couple of cigarette packets, he managed to bodge them into the compartment and he got a bit more life out of the Walkman.

That'll just have to do; I've more or less got what I wanted. Now, I just need to change a few things around, rewrite some of the lyrics, alter the intros a bit, – nobody's going to have a clue. Then he thought of Robbie Rochester and Janice's eyes. He shuddered slightly. *Well, not for a few years anyway.*

Being stoned seemed to inspire Barry, he worked quickly altering intros and middle eights, changing harmonies and, in some cases, rewriting the story lines. By the time he was done 'Broken Hearted Nobody' was 'Shattered Dreams and Promises', 'Bar Room Brawl' changed to 'Night Club Fight' and 'Let's Run Away' became 'Looking Back'.

***

Frank picked up the story again. 'We got back to the studio and sat round Barry, whilst he went through the song he'd played to us over at The White Horse, 'Shattered Dreams and Promises', said Frank. 'It didn't take us long to pick it up and Barry had already written down the lyrics on the back of an old Bombastic calendar.'

'You could tell it was an old calendar, Bodkin had hair,' laughed Stan.

Gloria looked at Bodkin.

'Back to my hairline again, are we?' said Bodkin. 'All I'll say is, back in the day the photographer wouldn't have needed a wide-angle lens to get Stan's belly in the picture.'

Frank ignored them. 'Barry insisted I took lead vocal, even though it was his song. He'd worked out some lovely harmonies and I have to say, it probably suited my voice better.'

'We put some blood, sweat, and tears into that session, I can tell you,' said Bodkin. 'Don got the basics down on two tracks, then we started to add Sugar's sax backing and the vocal harmonies. When Don and Stevie had finished mixing it, we knew we'd got something special. Don then got Sugarlips to play the middle eight and after Stevie mixed it behind my guitar solo, we all went up into the control box to listen to the playback. There were whoops of delight, it sounded just wonderful.'

'There was no need to do anything else to it. What we heard in the control box that afternoon is just how it sounded later that year, when it got to number one.' Stan was up from the table, slipping a pound coin into the jukebox and pressing a couple of orange backlit buttons. 'And exactly how it's going to sound in a few seconds, listen.'

The Rock-Ola whirred and glimmered. They waited while the wheel of 45s spun round and stopped. The arm lifted the record out of the rack, with just a glimpse of the familiar bright yellow Eternal label as it was placed on the turntable. Soon the Crown and Anchor was filled with 1965; the haunting sound of Sugarlips' sax intertwining with Frankie's cleverly distorted guitar intro, before Frankie and Barry began to sing a song that was to cause so much controversy eighteen years later.

"Shattered Dreams and Promises' was used to launch our first Long Player, 'Bombasticated'. Once the single took off, sales of the album followed,' said Stan. 'Barry had two other numbers, 'Night Club Fight' and 'Looking Back' which we put on the album, along with Frank's compositions and a few rockers from our stage show.'

'So Barry was writing some good stuff too?' questioned Gloria

'Not really.' Frank shook his head. 'We never got another thing out of him.'

'It's that we need to talk about,' said Bodkin.

CHAPTER 22
'WONDROUS STORIES'

Yes

Bodkin sat silent for a moment, gathering his thoughts. 'Look, what I'm about to tell you – well, you're really going to find this hard to believe; let me say, please don't interrupt, just hear me out before you make any judgements.'

Bodkin put his drink down and sat back in his chair. He told them about his weekend at Bug Jam. He told them about his strange dream and he told them how, whilst wandering around the VW traders at Santa Pod, he'd discovered Jezza.

'As you saw she'd been re-sprayed and tarted up with new chrome bumpers, mirrors, hub caps and all that stuff, but as soon as I saw that number plate GOE 305, there was no doubt,' said Bodkin. 'It was the Devon camper that Frank's dad had bought for us all those years ago. I had one thing on my mind; I just had to find out if I could afford to buy it.'

He explained how Jezza had been left locked and deserted, with just a name and telephone number printed on a card inside the front windscreen, and that because he was committed to a lift home with Bernie, he couldn't wait around for the owner to come back.

'It was the name on the card that started to ring a bell. Rochester Classics. I kept trying the number, but every time it just went to voicemail.'

'You remember the name Rochester, don't you?' he asked the others.

'Robbie Rochester, the plagiarism guy?' Stan said.

'Surely not the same one?' questioned Frank.

'After a number of frustrating phone calls, leaving messages and not getting a call back, I googled Rochester Classics and eventually found what I was looking for. It was a Birmingham address; a customised car business based in Stechford. I also found the number I'd been trying was a wrong'un, but instead of trying the number that came up on the web, I decided to drive over and find him.'

'Rochester Classics turned out to be two units knocked into one on an industrial estate, where these guys were souping up and customising old bangers. Ford Capris, Morris Minors, Austin Sevens, VW Beetles, you name it; there must have been ten cars in different stages of face lift, but there out on the front courtyard in her new chartreuse green and white livery was Jezza, exactly as I'd seen her at Santa Pod.'

'I asked one of the chaps working on a Capri, a guy in his late fifties, if I could speak to the gaffer, Mr Rochester.

He doesn't answer me, but turns and limps towards a metal staircase and shouts up the steps to the offices above, "ROBBIE, THERE'S A BLOKE HERE TO SEE YOU!"'

'Jeezus, you said Robbie!' gasped Stan. 'Robbie, Robbie Rochester, the guy Danny did for plagiarism?!'

'The very one,' said Bodkin.

'What the devil is plagiarism?' asked Gloria.

The Dartboard Three were preparing to leave and Gloria stood up to chirp a friendly, 'Goodnight lads.' As they passed by, Chopper and Curly gave her a grin and a thumbs up. Gloria got just a sullen look from Pimples and as they reached the doorway, they could all see he was the one with the crotch of his jeans hanging lowest. She shook her head ruefully and looked away; the pimples on his face were enough, she didn't want to see the ones on his backside.

'Plagiarism is when someone nicks one of your songs, tries to pretend they wrote it and gets royalties that should rightly be yours,' said Frank. 'We got caught up in a strange case long after the band had split. In the early eighties this outfit called The Robbie Rochester Band released an album off which they took a single they called 'Broken Hearted Nobody'.

'It was a late night jock on some local radio station that noticed the tune and some of the lyrics were very close to our 1965 hit, the one you've just heard, 'Shattered Dreams and Promises'. When we got hold of a copy of their album, we found 'Bar Room Brawl' and 'Let's Run Away' were also very similar to 'Night Club Fight' and 'Looking Back', both off our 'Bombasticated' album.'

'After The Bombastics broke up, Danny moved over to the States. He had an office in Manhattan and as well as representing some of the up and coming recording artists over there, he was also coining it in with a very successful publishing company he called Hoffman Melodies.'

'When he heard about the Rochester thing he went ape-shit and sued him,' added Stan.

Frank nodded. 'That's right, unbeknown to any of us, he'd bought the publishing rights to all our songs off BombasticMusic, he was the majority shareholder and once Hoffman Melodies got hold of them there was nothing we could do stop him. That means everything Frank and Barry had written, or will write, he gets eighty-five per cent and they're stuck with fifteen per cent which is what we all signed up for, remember that contract at the dinner table in Leicestershire? We'd sold ourselves down the river!'

'Bastard,' cursed Frank. 'He got us to sign that contract and said he'd handle everything, same as he had with all our bookings. Me and Shoogs were only kids; the others weren't much older and we all trusted him implicitly after the way he'd managed us for seven years. That shyster's the only bloody shareholder of Hoffman Melodies and now owns eighty-five per cent of everything I wrote because of that piece of paper I signed when I was sweet seventeen and never been pissed. That includes cover versions, compilation albums, television adverts – you name it.'

'A harsh lesson indeed; what about Barry?' asked Gloria. 'I suppose Danny hoodwinked him too?'

'He did,' replied Frank. 'Not that it worried Barry when Rochester was found guilty of milking his songs.'

'Why's that?' asked Gloria.

'He'd been dead nearly fourteen years,' answered Frank.

'Oh my God!' gasped Gloria, holding a hand to her mouth. 'I didn't realise that; what happened?'

'Drink and drugs, what else?' said Stan. 'He killed himself and his girlfriend when he drove his Jag into the Birmingham-Worcester canal. On their way home from a party, they were. He must have been completely stoned, he'd started injecting by then and they'd both been drinking heavily. Anyway, the police investigation said he took the canal bridge at Broad Heath too fast, hit a deer, smashed into the kerb where the road narrows; the car somersaulted over the bridge and landed upside down in twenty feet of muddy water. It was in the early hours, so nobody was around. They must have been knocked unconscious and drowned – there was no sign of a struggle inside the car. It was found by an early morning dog walker. When they fished the bodies out and did autopsies his veins were full of alcohol and acid, hers were too.'

'He'd been going downhill fast in the late sixties,' said Bodkin, sadly shaking his head. 'He won a lot of money, gambling on the 1966 World Cup. That's how he bought that bloody great place in Broad Heath, you know, the one that's now a care home; it lies on the left over the canal bridge halfway up Cobley Hill. He'd taken so much off the bookies, most of the Birmingham boys wouldn't take his bets. It all blew up with the one in the village, got really heavy.'

'Reg Mottershead,' said Stan. 'He was the bookie, him and his cousin Vince; they opened a betting shop in Bell Lane, other side of the square. Pair of nutters they were, the last thing you did was get into a dispute with them. Two of those lads who've just gone out, the ones who were playing darts, they're Vince's kids.'

'They're proper barmy, those two,' added Gloria. 'I was telling Frank about them earlier on.'

'Obviously in the genes,' said Bodkin. 'Anyway, they refused to pay out on his bet and it got really nasty. Barry had bet on Geoff Hurst getting a hat-trick in the final and they said it was a fix and he was getting nothing, not even his stake back.'

'How Geoff Hurst's hat-trick could be a fix, God knows,' interrupted Stan. 'Nevertheless, we couldn't believe the amount of luck he had with those World Cup bets and that Hurst bet took the biscuit. It's like he was getting divine inspiration.'

Bodkin went on. 'Barry was having none of it, no doubt he was high as a kite and he parked his car outside their shop during a busy Saturday's horse racing. He'd wired up his little Bayko amplifier, the one he'd had since the skiffle days, and then wedged it in the back passenger window. He wound the glass up tight to keep it in place and also get maximum volume when he let rip. He plugged in his microphone and blasted out to Mottershead's punters, plus anybody else within a square mile, not to place bets with Mottershead Bookies, they were bleedin' cheats. He told one and all that he had a legitimate winning betting slip with the official Mottershead time stamp on it and these thieving bastards were refusing to pay out. He managed to broadcast that message three times before Reg and Vince burst through the front door of their shop to shred him.

'Barry was all prepared, the car revved up and ready to scorch out of Bell Lane and off down Sheep Street. Reg managed to grasp the rear door handle, but got two broken fingers and gashed knees for his trouble as the car sped away. Barry's *coup de grâce* was throwing a generous handful of Xerox copies of his betting slip out of the front window, scattering them at the feet of Fordrough villagers. The leaflets told the story of the Mottersheads reneging on a bet and that punters should keep well clear of the place. It was a breezy day and people were picking them up the other side of Market Square two days later.

'Half an hour later, when things on the street had calmed down a bit and Reg had been carted off to A&E, Barry returned. He waited for the Sheep Street lights to turn green and drove round Market Square, blaring out his message at over a hundred decibels. Nobody could have missed it.'

'Blimey, what happened?' said Gloria. 'It all sounds pretty nasty to me.'

'The Mottersheads had to pay out,' said Stan. 'There was a lot of grumbling and unrest amongst their regulars and word soon spread around the village, and beyond. The view was if they didn't pay out on this one, then they could choose to cheat on anyone's bet. When punters stopped punting and the takings started going down they coughed up. They made a right song and dance about it; had to really, so everybody knew. Barry was still living at home, hadn't bought his mansion then. So they send a couple of their henchmen to his mom and dad's house. Poor old Paddy must have crapped himself when he saw those two monkeys walking up his drive. Anyway it all ended up with Barry receiving a cheque from Reg himself, out on the pavement in front of the shop. Local paper was there and they were 'persuaded' to have a front page report and pictures in the next edition. 'Record payout for World Cup punter' it read. Barry told us afterwards that whilst the flash bulbs were popping, Reg cooed gently down his ear that one dark night Barry was going to get his legs pulled off.'

'Over five hundred quid it cost them, that was a bloody fortune in 1966, said Bodkin. 'Still they were quick enough to take the bet, I expect they laughed all the way into their back pocket when they took Barry's money.'

***

It was the spring of 1966. A discarded newspaper lying in front of a dressing room mirror at the Coventry Belgrade started Barry thinking about the World Cup. It was two days old and forgotten by the cleaners. Barry checked the date at the top of the page; Saturday April

16th. It had been folded in half, back page out, probably by one of the artists in the Easter Eggstravaganza, which had finished at the weekend.

'World Cup Willies', ran the headline. On closer inspection it was an article about England's chances of winning that summer's World Cup, using Willie, England's little lion mascot, in a rather predictable play on words. It had Brazil as favourites, but with home advantage England should be a serious contender if they could overcome nerves brought on by the homeland's expectations. Below it was a grid of the draw for the group stages and who would be playing who.

I wonder what odds England are to win the Tournament? There could be some serious money to be won here. I need to sit down and think about all this.

Barry took a pen out of the little compartment in his guitar case where he kept spare strings and plectrums. He unfolded the newspaper and opened the inside back page to find an in-depth interview with Alf Ramsey. There was a large picture of the smiling, balding England manager. *Ideal, plenty of space to make a few notes. Now, let's try and remember all those things Robbie said and stuff I saw in that book of his.*

Barry concentrated hard, then, bit by bit started to scribble memories down on Alf's forehead. *Sorry Alf.*

England 4 West Germany 2 Geoff Hurst hat-trick.

One goal controversial Pic in Robbie's book.

Also a pic of Peters scoring one of them that's four.

England beat Portugal in semis, score ??? ... Bobby Charlton scores...

England beat Argentina in quarters, score??? ...

There was a picture in the book of Hurst after he scored against Argentina, was it the winner?

And Argentina captain sent off.

He flicked back to the back page to check the group stages and wrote down, on Alf's cheeks:

England v Uruguay & Mexico & France

West Germany v Argentina & Switzerland & Spain

Soviet Union v North Korea & Italy & Chile

Portugal v Brazil & Hungary & Bulgaria

To get to the quarter finals, semi-finals and final, these teams had to win matches. Bugger me, there is real money to be won...

His thoughts were broken by Carol and Frankie coming into the dressing room. The Bombastics had a concert to do, so Barry rolled up his newspaper notes and put them in his guitar case.

Next day the band were off and after getting home from the Coventry gig quite late, Barry had a lie-in. He actually awoke quite early, but lay in bed thinking about winning money – a lot of it! He wasn't sure what odds were being offered for the World Cup, he wasn't really a betting man, so he felt he'd try out Mottersheads in the village and see what they were offering. They were a rough bunch with a bad reputation, especially Vince the cousin, but they were bookies after all.

The girl behind the counter had to call on Reg Mottershead when Barry asked what odds they were offering for England to win the World Cup. Reg came through from the back room.

'Horses and dogs is our game, son, but I'll make a couple of calls see what's goin' on, right?' Barry nodded and Reg disappeared back into his office.

Ten minutes later he reappeared holding a scrap of paper. He peered at it through spectacles perched on the end of his nose. 'I'll give you 6/1.'

6/1? That's not very tasty, thought Barry. 'Is that the best you can do?'

'Take or leave it, son,' snapped Reg.

'What if I said England to win the World Cup and Geoff Hurst to score a hat-trick in the final?'

Reg burst into laughter banging the counter with his large right fist. 'What are you, some kind of fuckin' clairvoyant? And who the fuck is Geoff Hurst?'

'He's a West Ham player. He's a squad member.' *Shit! I shouldn't have mentioned Geoff Hurst, it's gonna arouse suspicion, that wasn't very smart!*

'How much you putting on, big spender? Sixpence? A shilling? Maybe even half-a-crown?' Reg was still guffawing.

'A fiver.'

'A FIVER! Listen sunshine, if you're so keen to donate five quid to the Mottershead foundation, who am I to turn you away? Make it a double. 6/1 on England and 14/1 on yer geezer Hurst and his hat-trick and I'll take yer bet.'

As he drove back home, with his betting slip in his pocket, Barry was annoyed with himself for going in at the deep end like that. *Word would get round, didn't these bookies talk to each other? Mottershead proved that by getting the 6/1 odds in the first place.*

There are plenty of smaller bets to be had that would go unnoticed. Knowing both England and West Germany are going to win their way to the final there is serious money to be made.

Barry put his plan together. He decided to leave the Geoff Hurst hat-trick alone – for now. Instead he drew up a plan of bets based on victories by England and West Germany up to the final, Portugal up to the semis and Argentina in their group matches. The Bombastics were travelling all around the UK playing gigs so he could visit bookmakers in many towns and cities incognito.

And so it was. Ipswich, Manchester, Newcastle, Frome, Swindon, Newport, Bridgend; he spread his bets far and wide. A lot of the bookies wouldn't take bets on single matches (some would of course), but they allowed him to double up and even treble up. He never bet more than a few pounds, at most five, and he kept his betting slips neatly in an old satchel with a notebook detailing where bets were placed, the amount of the stake and at what odds. He was ready to collect and reinvest any of his individual winnings if the losing bookie was game and if The Bombastics' engagements had him in the right place at the right time.

To begin with, the other members of the band never twigged Barry's trips to the bookies; after all, they weren't in each other's pockets all the time and they were used to Barry disappearing to share his love and understanding. It was only when Barry seemed to be spending rather more than they knew he was earning, that he had to confess he'd 'had a bit of luck with the odd flutter on the World Cup'. They left it at that; that is until an incident in Fordrough at Mottersheads.

His first tranche of bets was a total disaster when England only drew with Uruguay and a few days later, West Germany drew with Argentina. He was angry with himself for even touching that second one.

I knew they were both going to progress and a 0-0 draw was always on the cards. Idiot!

However, after that it was like giving strawberries to a donkey, as his Gran used to say. In fact, where he'd lost on those two early results, the bookies were even keener to take more money off him. That's when he started to up the ante and tempt them with the 4-2 score in the final, and much later into the tournament, the Hurst hat-trick.

He was right on another count too, bookies *did* talk to each other; some of the local bookies around the Midlands refused to take his bets for the semi-finals and final, but there were plenty around the UK that did. He nearly got a bit of a working over by a bookie in Islington, close to the recording studio, when he went to collect over £350 in winnings and asked what odds he could have for England to reach the final. This was before the last of the group stage matches had even finished.

'Honest Jack White', it said above the door. When he went inside early one morning, well before the horseracing had started, and handed over his betting slip the Moustache behind the counter turned and called through the door into the back office. 'Benny, you said to tell you when the punter with the World Cup bet came in.'

A stocky, middle-aged Cockney geezer with a broken nose appeared at the door. He looked at Barry, took the betting slip off Moustache and leaned over the counter, close enough to engulf Barry in a particularly pungent cloud of halitosis.

'Who's bin a very lucky boy then?' he sneered. 'Spoilt my week you 'ave, makes me wonder just 'ow you managed to pick those winners. With a bleedin' pin was it?'

'Just the luck of the draw, Honest Jack – er, sorry, Benny.' Barry was getting a bit warm under the collar. 'What if I reinvest my winnings? What odds will you give me for England to beat Argentina and Portugal and reach the final?'

Benny tucked the betting slip in the breast pocket of his checkered jacket, lifted a hatch in the counter and stepped through. He moved over to the front door and slid the top bolt. 'I don't know what your bleedin' game is and 'ow you expect me to give you odds on matches wot might not never be played.' He grabbed Barry by both lapels of his jacket and slid him along the wall, ripping down the double pages of the *Racing Life* that Moustache had spent half an hour pinning up.

'If I sees you in this 'ere vicinity ever again,' he shoved his face into Barry's, eye to eye, touching noses, 'I shall see to it you is buried, face down, up the road in 'ighgate cemetery, right next to Karl Marx. Alright, my son?'

Barry almost passed out with the stench of foul breath, but as Honest Jack let him go he had the presence of mind to snatch his betting slip out of Dishonest Benny's top pocket, dodge his flailing arm, get to the door and slide the bolt back. Benny lost his balance and stumbled against the wall, pulling down any remaining pages of *Racing Life*.

Barry opened the door and jumped out onto the pavement. He was relieved to see there were plenty of people about. 'Are you going to pay me winnings?' he shouted back through the open door, cupping his hands around his mouth. 'There's a cop shop over the road and I'm straight in there if you don't give me my cash. My bet was legit, and this slip proves it, so what's it to be, Honest Jack or Dishonest Benny?'

Benny stepped onto the pavement and stood motionless; he had a decision to make. He glanced at the police station, then back to the slip Barry was holding, then back to the cop shop. He turned to his cashier and, directing his eyes towards the safe, gave him a short sharp nod.

'Get Moustachio to come out here and do the swap!' shouted Barry. 'Cash for betting slip, no alternative.'

Within minutes the exchange was done. Honest Jack White had the betting slip and Barry had his cash, £376.17.5d. He was also rather impressed with the way he'd handled himself.

Barry was more careful when collecting other winnings at other shops. These were sizable chunks of cash he was claiming and there were risks involved. He soon had a system; never go into an empty betting shop, the other punters were the best protection he had. They were on his side. The bookie would always be the bad guy if he tried to double-cross a winning punter.

He collected most of his winnings without further trouble; there were a few moans and groans, but some bookmakers happily took his bets again, thinking his luck would run out and they'd get their money back. As the World Cup neared its end, so he picked out bookies who could be tempted to give him odds on the Hurst hat-trick. This is where the big money lay, particularly if he could double it up with the 4-2 result, the other goal from Martin Peters, or the 2-2 score after ninety minutes.'

He ended up winning nearly half a million from dozens of bookmakers throughout the UK. Apart from Honest Jack of Islington, he only had one other real problem and that was on his own doorstep in Fordrough. He should have known better than go to the Mottershead family bookmakers. They were crooks, and lunatics into the bargain. When he went to collect his winnings, he came face to face with Reg.

Remembering the problem he'd had with Honest Jack, Barry always made sure he didn't hand over successful betting slips before his cash was counted out. He took this precaution with Reg Mottershead.

'There's no way you're getting that cash until I'm in possession of that fuckin' slip,' scowled Big Reg. 'You must think me and our Vince came up with the fuckin' daisies.'

'There's nothing shady, Reg,' Barry tried to reason. 'You took the bet before the World Cup had even started. What reason could there be not to give me my winnings?'

Another voice came from the office doorway. 'I've got five 'undred fuckin' reasons.' It was Vince.

'So you're not going to honour my bet?'

'Got it in one, shitbrain,' growled Vince. 'Now do one and fuck off out of here.'

Barry decided on a strategic withdrawal.

'You haven't heard the last of me,' he uttered as he made for the door, waving his betting slip. 'There must be some Turf Accountants Association or something that won't like this one little bit.'

He left Reg and Vince laughing and slapping their sides.

Two weeks later Barry had his money. He decided not to chase any bookmaker's association, better to let the whole of Fordrough know the Mottersheads were dishonest gangsters. With a couple of LSD tablets inside him, a few dozen Xerox copies of his betting slip and a lot of decibels to spread the word, Barry pulled it off. Reg and Vince paid up. It was at this point the rest of the band realised the true extent of Barry's winnings.

***

'All that money was the beginning of the end for Barry,' said Stan. 'Within months he'd bought Broad Heath Hall, that damned great Victorian place halfway up Cobley Hill. What on earth would a single bloke want with a six bedroom mansion like that, we said at the time?'

'We named him Toad of Toad Hall,' said Frank. 'But as the months slipped by it got less and less funny. He had this bunch of cronies hanging around the place bingeing on alcohol, acid and weed, most of it paid for by him.'

'All of it, you mean,' said Bodkin. 'Then there were the women. A never ending stream of them, there were. He must have had his condoms delivered by Pickfords!'

'It was the acid and then cocaine that did it,' continued Stan. 'There were rumours, he'd started injecting by then; Barry and the rest of the acidheads called his library the shooting gallery. If truth be known, there wasn't much reading done in there! None of us were little innocents, by that time we were all doing a bit of pot, even Frank and Shoogs, but not on the scale of what was going on at Toad

Hall; with all that cash he'd won gambling, he was in another league; never mind the condoms, I think some of his suppliers were offering him quantity discounts on drugs too!'

'We all tried hard to stop him, but he'd got himself in so far he just couldn't find his way back,' said Frank. 'The self-destruct button was well and truly pressed and, looking back, there was no saving him from himself. He wasn't eating properly and with the drugs and the drink his guts were in a right mess.'

'You can say that again! That time at The Taboo in Birmingham,' added Stan, stony-faced, without any trace of humour. 'I had to shout to him not to turn his back on the audience. He must have followed through, he had a stain shaped like a map of Africa on the seat of his powder blue trousers. Shit! I can see it now.'

Gloria buried her face in the palms of her hands.

'I think we all knew our golden era was over. We'd lived the rock 'n' roll dream nearly seven years, longer than most, some would say. Now it was falling apart at the seams,' said Frank. 'Our hits had dried up and Eternal told us they wouldn't be taking up the twelve month option. Barry worried us; we felt he could go missing at any time, although to be fair to him, he never did. Danny had opened his office in Manhattan, so we hardly saw him. He left his dopey son Ike in charge over here. Then there was Sugarlips. She gave us a month's notice! Actually wrote a letter of resignation she did, like she was some personal assistant in a solicitor's office. She said she had no wish to be playing old Bombastic hits night after night, in dog-eared clubs where the punters stuck to the carpets. We also knew she had this urge to get involved in the jazz and blues scene.'

For a time the three guys sat there, lost in their own thoughts; Gloria remained silent.

'We've drifted a bit,' said Bodkin, putting his drink down on the table. 'Let's go back to Robbie Rochester in Stechford, it's important. He comes down from the upstairs office and introduces himself. Turns out to be one hell of a nice bloke. He was amiable, nicely spoken and clearly well-educated. I decided against asking him if he was the Robbie Rochester that The Bombastics tangled with thirty years ago; might not be the best of starts, I thought. I said I was interested in the Volkswagen camper outside and that I'd seen it at the Bug Jam at Santa Pod. I told him I recognised it from the number plate, GOE 305. In the sixties, I was the drummer in a band and this was the motor we travelled the countryside in. That's when his mood changed. The smile went from his face, his eyes narrowed. "Was this The Bombastics, by any chance?" he asked me, his friendly demeanour had disappeared. I answered yes, immediately. Although I recognised *his* name, he wouldn't have known me from Adam. So how the hell did he associate me with either the VW or The Bombastics?

'"Bombastards, more like." It was the guy with the limp, obviously listening in.

'"Keep out of this Jez," Rochester said, coldly. He looked back at me. "I think we'd better go upstairs to my office." He turned on his heel and I followed him up the metal staircase.

'His office was clean, bright and very tidy. It was also very colourful, with large framed pictures of vintage cars around the walls, each with vivid paintwork and sparkling chrome. I decided not ask him if they were cars he'd worked on, it was pretty obvious, and at that moment it seemed inappropriate. He sat down in a chair behind his desk and signalled me to sit down, gesturing towards a chair on my side of the desk. He just stared at me for a few seconds, his pale blue eyes, I have to say, were quite disturbing.

"'What's your game? Come to gloat after all these years? Haven't you lot and that Hoffman character, done me enough damage? My career, my credibility, my friends and even members of my family deserted me. Chekka ripped up my recording contract and I was demonised by both the music press and the gutter press."

"'Whoa! Hold on a minute," I protested. "I just came to buy a car. Look, I'm not going to pretend I didn't link your name with that plagiarism case, but you have to remember it was over fourteen years after The Bombastics had finished. I wasn't even in the country, I was working twenty-four seven in Puerto Banus when it all kicked off, it had nothing at all to do with me. I was trying to make a little tapas bar I'd bought work. Danny Hoffman owned the copyrights on all Frankie Richards' and Barry Harper's songs. We'd all signed some dodgy contract with him years before; he got most of the publishing royalties and they got a pittance. That's all I know, I was just the drummer."

"'Let me stop you there," he'd said as he held up a defiant forefinger. "Barry Harper never wrote any of the songs he'd claimed to. 'Shattered Dreams and Promises', 'Night Club Fight' and 'Looking Back', or whatever he changed the names to, were my songs, my tunes and mostly my lyrics."

"'But we recorded those songs nearly twenty years before your versions," I said. "How on earth could we have copied yours?"

"'Rochester looked me straight in the eye as he answered. "You clearly weren't around when this blew up?" he said.

"'No, I told you, I was in Spain."

"'Your Barry Harper travelled forward in time twenty years and landed smack in the middle of our 1983 rehearsals. He then listened to The Robbie Rochester Band polishing up new songs I'd just written; we even gave him a cassette tape copy of the bloody things and a Walkman to play them on."

'I told him I'd heard all those time travel stories, but they'd been thrown out by the judge,' continued Bodkin. 'I laughed at first and said something really stupid; I asked him if Barry had walked through a looking glass. To be fair, the guy kept his cool and told me all about the seven days Barry was with them and how they set up his return journey. When I'd had chance to listen to him, well, I have to say it started to make some sort of crazy sense.'

'It was a major part of his defence, Bodkin,' came in Frank. 'I was in court for most of the case and to begin with, a lot of time was spent convincing the presiding judge that there was a case of plagiarism to answer. I remember, he said Danny had to prove that Robbie Rochester had taken melodies belonging to Hoffman Music and used them in compositions he claimed to be his own. Both versions of all three songs were heard several times and experts from both sides gave their considered opinions. Well, it was pretty clear cut to anybody who could hold a three chord tune in their heads that they were the same songs, even some of the lyrics, particularly to 'Night Club Fight', were too close for comfort.

'However,' continued Frank. 'It was when Robbie Rochester told the judge that Barry Harper of The Bombastics had travelled forward twenty years to 1983, heard his songs and taken them back on cassette tape to 1963, and then had hits with them that there was pandemonium in court. It took the judge some minutes to restore order. Rochester stuck to his story, I remember he even had witnesses. They each told the same tale; how Barry arrived through some sort of wormhole in a VW camper van that Robbie Rochester and his band used to carry their equipment around in. He claimed it was the very same VW camper van that The Bombastics were using to transport their equipment, twenty years earlier.

'That's the one piece of evidence that did hold up in court. When the VW's log book was produced, it showed that Mr Jack Richards, my dad, was the original owner; it had then passed on to Bargain Motors of Evesham, then to a Mr Gerald Fitzroy and then finally on to Mr Robin Rochester. At this point, Robbie Rochester had tried to explain that it was the radio, still the same radio after all these years, that had created the time passage through which Barry had arrived and also returned.

'The chatter levels in court rose, some people were openly laughing, and again, it took the judge some time to restore order. He told the court that he found the whole story was far-fetched, absolutely ludicrous, and because the prime witness, Barry Harper, was dead, he dismissed Rochester's defence and gave his ruling. He found Robbie Rochester guilty of intentional plagiarism and ordered the court to reconvene seven days later, when he'd had time to consider and calculate costs and damages.'

'He was laughed out of court then, literally?' said Gloria.

Frank nodded.

Bodkin continued. 'You could see genuine pain in his eyes as he remembered the judge's ruling on damages all those years ago. Rochester told me, "A lot of it went over my head at the time, but I knew I was well and truly kippered. There were what they called mechanical royalties from Chekka for pressing the recordings, not just vinyl and cassette, but CDs which were new at the time. There were also performance royalties, as well as sheet music sales. Judge Daniels hit me with the lot. The single of 'Broken Hearted Nobody' had been on sale for over four months and sold over a million worldwide, it had been a number one in the UK, Australia, Japan, as well as selling well in many other European countries and we even got a Billboard 'Bubbling Under'. I thought we were off and running Stateside, but I didn't realise 'Broken Hearted

Nobody' was to become an elegy instead of a fanfare.'"

'I didn't like to ask him how much it cost him, but I didn't need to, he just went on and on about Judge Daniels,' explained Bodkin. 'He was very bitter. "Those bastard lawyers even calculated a huge royalty percentage on the album we released; it contained all three tracks and the Judge ruled it only sold because of the popularity of those three songs. Songs that I damned well wrote! The final bill completely wiped me out."

'It was then I heard footsteps on the stairs. Two figures appeared in the doorway, the little fellow with the limp, Jez, and a taller thin faced bloke with greased-back grey hair, sideburns and matching stubble around his chin. "Everything okay, Robbie?" he'd drawled.

"Yes, Billy," replied Robbie. "This is Bodkin, he was the drummer in The Bombastics."

'I said hello, but I could see hostility in his eyes. So it seemed could Rochester. "Bodkin says he knew nothing about Barry Harper's little trip to visit us and he was working in Spain when Hoffman filed the infringement suit." They still eyed me suspiciously.

"'Billy and Jez stood by me through those dark days," he said. "Nobody would touch Rochester, the musical pariah. I even had Jack Hartnell, the leading music critic of the time, name me Looney Tunes at an awards dinner. I wasn't there, I hasten to add, but the nickname stuck for a while."

'Here's a bloke, broken, battered, his career over and all I could think of was 'That's all folks!' How awful is that? I had a job holding it together, I can tell you.

"'Anyway, I re-mortgaged my house and had to use that bloody camper van for transport," he went on. "The only real assets I'd got left. It was no good moping and feeling sorry for myself, so I decided to try and build my hobby, my love of old cars, into a worthwhile business. These two guys helped me and we soon realised that there was a bigger demand for old motors than we'd ever dreamed and that it was also extremely profitable," he said. "To begin with it was all done in my garage and on my driveway, but Rochester Classics was gaining momentum. Billy and Jez handled the engine and bodywork reparations, and I did the re-sprays, interior designs and airbrush design work. Early growth was encouraging and as our reputation for top class work spread, so demand grew. We moved into this first unit just before the millennium and added the second unit when it became available a few years later."

"'You obviously did the work on the VW?' I said.

"'We certainly did, she was first,' he carried on. 'Like I said, GOE 305 was one of the few things we still had. She's been re-customised a few times since and we've had a few offers for her, but have never been tempted to let her go before now.'

"'She was the link with that wanker, Bugger-Me-Barry,' broke in Jez. 'If we were ever going to track down your thieving mate, it would be through the VW camper.'

'Robbie explained. 'Like I told you, he suddenly appeared out of nowhere in our camper and told us it was his. Well, the portal through which he claimed to have arrived, and the way we helped him get back, was something to do with the radio. The same radio that's still in it, we've never removed it. As I explained, back in '83 we decided to try and replicate the happenings at the time of his time of arrival.'

"'Midnight on a snowy February night in a lay-by just off the Birmingham Coventry highway,' recalled Billy.

"'Drovers Lane,' added Jez. 'I've never seen nothing like it. A load of bleedin' hocus-pocus is what I thought, then Bugger-Me-Barry twiddles the tuning knob and the next thing – woooosh – he's gone, but the bleedin' camper's still there!"

"'These two never really understood my faith in him. They thought he just wanted to steal our camper," said Robbie. "In the end they were right, he *was* just a thief, but they were my songs and it was my career, my tomorrows he stole, not my camper." The pain had returned to his eyes, but only momentarily. "When the litigation started, we tried hard to trace Barry, he was our only real hope; that's when we found he'd finished upside down in a canal with his girlfriend," explained Robbie. "So we tried to get back to 1963 by parking in the Drovers Lane lay-by at midnight and turning the tuner through the frequencies. All to no avail."

"'We tried that a few times," said Billy. "Frightened the livin' shit out of me, I can tell you. Imagine it going tits up and us finding ourselves lost in Jurassic Park. Don't bear thinking about!'"

Bodkin stopped for a moment to take a drink and gather his thoughts. 'My mind was churning over. This seemed so far-fetched and yet there was something believable about Robbie, especially with this totally unrehearsed support from Jez and Billy. Also, remember what Jez said, without any prompting from me, Bugger-Me-Barry. I repeat, Bugger-Me-Barry! How would he know that, unless he'd met him?'

A few customers were starting to drift into the Crown and Anchor now, but Gloria's young barman Matt, was coping adequately.

'I think I need another drink,' Stan said. 'From what I remember of the case, those two guys you speak about, Billy and Jez, must have been two of the witnesses he called in court.'

Gloria was up and across at the bar organising another round.

'Do I get the impression you believe this guy Robbie?' asked Frank.

'You need to meet him, judge for yourself,' replied Bodkin. 'It's such an incredible story.'

'Most people might call it a load of bollocks,' replied Frank.

'The Honourable Judge put it more succinctly, said it was far-fetched, didn't he?' added Stan.

The sound of 'Yakety Sax' came from Stan's pocket. He half stood up and shoved his hand deep into his jeans pocket, pulling out his iPhone. He extended his arm and squinted to read the screen. 'Shit, it's our Elsie,' he muttered.

'Well speak to her, it could be important,' said Gloria, putting drinks down on the table.

'Elsie, the love of my life, my reason for living, what can I do for you, my sweet?' Stan purred into his mobile, at the same time pulling a silly face for the benefit of his audience. It made Gloria giggle.

Elsie's immediate response brought a cringe from Stan, but then his face turned to an enormous smile as he punched the air. 'Wooohoooo! Thanks Else, that's fantastic, I'll tell the boys. Tarra-a-bit.' He blew a kiss down the phone and rang off.

'Sugarlips!' he roared, then realising how loud he was, he put a hand over his mouth. 'She's been in touch with her mom.' There was no hiding his excitement.

Frank and Bodkin were delighted, there was glass clinking and high fives all round.

'Wow, Miss Sugarlips is obviously quite an important lady!' Remarked Gloria.

'She certainly is,' said Stan. 'I'll pop round and see Mary tomorrow. She's got a mobile number and Carol knows one of us is going to phone her, so she won't be avoiding us.'

'Look, I need to get back, Julie'll be wondering where the hell I've got to,' butted in Bodkin, looking at his watch. 'Just let me finish with Robbie Rochester. I did a deal with Robbie for Jezza. We agreed four grand, which further illustrates the guy's honesty. I'd googled VW Devons of the same vintage in preparation for meeting him. They were easily fetching well over four big ones. Even the models not customised and chromed up were over three thousand quid. We shook on the deal and I arranged to go over with our Wally next day, to pay him and bring her back.

'And going back to your question Frank, about whether or not I believe him.' Bodkin hesitated. 'I ain't sure. Part of me thinks it's a load of bunkum, but having met and talked to the guy, I have to say he seems straight. His two blokes, they might appear a bit rough and ready, but they're pretty genuine too, and you can see there's a lot of mutual respect between the three of them.'

Again Bodkin hesitated. 'Something is wrong with this whole thing, but I don't know what.' He drained his glass, put it down on the table and got up. 'I must go. I told him I'd keep in touch. I didn't commit anybody to anything, but I thought you ought to meet him.' Frank and Stan looked at him rather pensively. 'I really think you should,' he repeated.

'We haven't talked about the reunion,' said Stan.

'Don't worry,' replied Frank. 'Now it looks like we're in touch with Carol, it makes sense for all of us to wait until we can all meet up. Sooner rather than later mind you, what I have to suggest won't wait for too long.'

'I'm intrigued,' smiled Bodkin. 'Phone me tomorrow when you've spoken with Mary.'

With that, he shook hands with Frank and Stan, gave

Gloria a peck on the cheek and disappeared through the door. Within a couple of minutes, they heard Jezza being fired up and driven away.

The pub had started to fill up now, so Gloria made her way back behind the bar to help Matt. Stan and Frank took their drinks and joined her, pulling up barstools the other side of the bar.

'What are you going to do, Frank?' asked Stan. 'Are you going back home tonight?'

'I'd planned to,' answered Frank. 'I'd like to come with you to see Mary tomorrow, so it doesn't make sense really, does it?'

'You can put your head down at our place,' suggested Stan. 'You might find yourself sharing a bed with Bertie though.'

'Bertie!' grinned Frank, raising his eyebrows.

'Don't worry, Bertie's our dog. He has this habit of jumping up on the bed at night.'

Frank laughed.

'Frank you can stop here if you want.' Gloria was laughing too.

'That's a very generous offer on our first date,' grinned Frank, now well into his second bottle of Shiraz. 'I hope you'll be gentle with me.'

'There'll be no monkey business, Frankie Atom.' Gloria saw him looking at her blouse with three buttons undone. 'We have four guest rooms which we hire out for bed and breakfast.'

They all chuckled.

'Since you're not on a promise you should come and stop with us, Frank,' insisted Stan. 'It's ages since you saw our Elsie.'

CHAPTER 23
'LIVING IN THE PAST'

Jethro Tull

Stan backed his Volvo out of the garage and left it in the drive with the engine ticking over. Frank stood in the front doorway, talking to Elsie with Bertie circling them, wagging his tail and sniffing at Frank's shoes, then his trousers, then his crotch.

'Stop that Bertie,' scolded Elsie, flicking the tea towel she was holding at the dog. 'He's always sniffing people's gentiles, it's so embarrassing.'

'Gen-i-tals,' Stan whispered out of the corner of his mouth, slightly embarrassed, as he pushed back past her to get his jacket.

Frank kissed Elsie goodbye, but he was still sniggering to himself as he got into the front of the car.

'Sorry Frank, she had a delicate upbringing did our Else.'

'Talking of genitals, it's a good job you lent me clean underpants and socks,' grinned Frank, waving a knotted Tesco bag in front of Stan. 'Not sure what Bertie would have made of these.'

They made their way over to leafy Shirley, in suburban south Birmingham. It had been some years since Stan had been to the Meadowsweet household, but he remembered directions without any problem. He and Frank were trying to work out how old Mary would be. They decided they weren't sure, but agreed she must be over ninety.

At that moment the smooth strains of sax came over the car radio. They glanced at each other.

Stan spoke first. 'I know it's Kenny G and not Sugarlips, but right on cue? Is that slightly spooky?'

Frank raised his eyebrows and nodded in agreement. 'You know, it's over fifty years since Dennis died, *fifty* bloody years. God, that was such an awful time.'

'You're right there, Shoogs never got over that. How does the old song go? "My heart belongs to Daddy". Bodkin tried his best, but that romance was doomed to failure.'

'There never was a romance, it was all in Bodkin's head. Poor Bods, he was bereft when Sugarlips told us she was leaving for London. I remember our resident diplomat, Barry, saying to him, "Looks like you gotta to keep bashing the four skins, drummer boy." Bodkin was seething, it's a bloody good job he didn't catch hold of him, he'd still be doing time.'

Frank paused. 'Makes you shudder when you realise how the years have passed. Anyway, let's change the subject – I wonder if brother Michael is still around?'

'We're about to find out.' Stan indicated to turn right

and slowed to a stop on the crown of the road, waited on a council waste truck to clear his way and swung into the drive of a large semi-detached, half-timbered house. Bright green ivy covered most of the front of both houses, but it had been neatly trimmed away from all the windows and the guttering. Somebody cared.

Frank rang the doorbell and they waited. They heard soft footsteps approach, the turning of a key in the lock, then the door swung open. They recognised Mary immediately and from the warm smile on her face she remembered them.

'Hello, boys,' she beamed. 'Stan and young Frankie! Do come in, please.' She stood to one side and with the wave of her arm, beckoned them on by. Both paused to kiss her gently on the cheek. Could it be she blushed slightly?

'Go straight down the hallway and left at the bottom. It's the kitchen, it's where I spend most of my time these days.' She followed them, passing large framed photographs of Dennis, holding his clarinet and Carol blowing her saxophone and Michael too, with his cap and gown; all of them smiling broadly, full of life.

'Get down, Pickles,' she shooed a large ginger cat down off one of the six kitchen chairs set around a large wooden table. 'Take a seat and I'll put the kettle on. Tea okay?'

'Yes, fine,' they chorused.

They watched her moving around the kitchen. She stood at about five foot in her slippers and grey leggings topped with a hand knitted yellow jumper. A tiny pair of peridot earrings with matching necklace and a pair of round gold-rimmed glasses glinted in the morning sun. They both saw how slim she was and not the slightest bit doddery, in fact she appeared very nimble, and if they were right about her age, she certainly didn't look it. She wore her grey, almost white hair up in a pleat, held together with a large tortoiseshell slide at the back. One thing there was no doubt about, she was Carol's mum.

Whilst waiting for the kettle to boil, she pulled a large biscuit barrel out of one of her cupboards; she took the lid off and placed it in front of Stan. The barrel was full to the gun-whales with Rich Tea, Lincolns, Jammy Dodgers, Chocolate Digestives, and Stan's absolute favourites, Bourbons. Either Mary had an enormous weakness for biscuits, or she had a huge circle of friends who nibbled whilst they nattered.

Stan watched the Bourbons getting larger and larger; they seemed to be saying, 'eat me, eat me.' He shifted uneasily in his chair, his saliva glands working overtime. He thought of his Fender bass strapped over his exceedingly large belly, and failed to notice Frank watching him and smirking.

Mary distracted him, as she poured the boiling water into a lilac and white tea pot and brought it to the table, putting it alongside matching cups and saucers, milk jug and sugar bowl. 'Milk and sugar, everyone?' she asked.

'Yes please, just one sugar,' replied Frank.

'I have two please Mrs M,' said Stan.

'Mary, please,' she smiled as she poured the teas, then she sat down and joined them. 'So how are you boys doing? It's a long time since you were teenage idols, eh? It was all happening then, wasn't it just?' She sipped at her tea.

'Well, Elsie and I have been married for nearly fifty years, golden wedding coming round in four years.' Stan raised his hands in mock horror, which made Mary smile. 'We had one of each, Steve our son is well into his forties now, married to Denise and has given us two grandkids, Stephie and Darren. Steve sells insurance. It's a bit of a black art to me, but you can see he's done very well. They moved to this four bedroom barn conversion near Kenilworth, a year or two ago; listed building it is, all timbers and reclaimed bricks. What they wanted with something that size is beyond me; their nearest neighbours are cows and horses, grazing in the fields beyond. Rosie was a bit of a late arrival; Elsie overdid the Babychams the night of our Silver Wedding.' Stan flickered his eyebrows and gave Mary a daft grin. 'Rosie's twenty now and a mature student at Dundee Uni, taking Economics.

'I drifted a bit after The Bombastics split. Played with a couple of other bands, but nothing ever came of them and I effectively hung my rock 'n' roll guitar up. That's when Elsie and I started a little flower shop in the village. It was hard work, but we did very well, not only bouquets, wreaths and potted plants, but Elsie got us selling cards and gifts. We sold it about ten years ago, and I have to say, I don't miss those early mornings driving to market. The new people have branched out a bit, bought the shop next door and started doing cakes, decorated to order. From what I hear it sounds as though they do very well indeed.' He took a mouthful of tea. 'I play guitar now and again, with a few old mates, nothing serious, just for fun really.'

He looked at Frank, who took his cue and sat upright in his chair. 'I got myself a little band together and went solo for a year or so, but the problem was with a lot of new material I'd written.' Frank stopped. 'Don't get me wrong, everybody said the songs were good, but I wasn't in any rush to record or publish them. I wasn't going to pour eighty-five per cent into Danny Hoffman's pockets.'

'Danny Hoffman? He was your manager, if I remember correctly,' said Mary.

'That's right. Danny Hoffman did a lot for us, no question, but the royalty thing was a complete and utter con trick; he did for us well and truly. Like the rest of the band, I'd signed this ridiculous publishing contract with BombasticMusic when I was seventeen and trusted Danny implicitly. Then when he started this Hoffman Melodies outfit in the States, he was able to sign over the rights to all our songs with BombasticMusic and there was nothing we could do about it. So he would be getting the lion's share of royalties on all those songs I wrote for The Bombastics. I remember, as if it were yesterday, speaking to him long distance, but he refused to renegotiate. I didn't want the same to happen with new songs I'd written, so I held back on them. It took a very expensive solicitor a couple of years to get me out of that lot. To this day, I only get a pittance for the old stuff, but at least any new songs I write are with a new publishing company and now I get a fair royalty. Trouble was, by the time all the litigation nonsense was over, Frankie Atom's star had faded. I never got another hit myself, but the songs I'd held back and others I'd written since, have been moderately successful for other people; I've been lucky in that they're still earning me a few shillings.'

'What about family, Frank?' Mary sipped her tea.

Frank put down his tea, sat back and blew out loudly between his lips. 'I was a late starter, Mary. Partly because of life on the road and partly because, well I guess you'll have heard, I was a mixed up kid. We had girls throwing themselves at us and I have to say I did go there on a number of occasions, but I had this attraction to boys as well. As a teenager in the early sixties all this was taboo; I'd have been called queer, poofter, or worse. So I suppressed it, hoping it would go away I suppose. Danny was adamant it shouldn't get out and destroy all the hard work we'd put in to make The Bombastics the success they were. The others, including Stan here and your Carol, closed ranks and protected me. It wasn't until the seventies, now on my own, when sexuality became a lot more relaxed that I felt at ease with my feelings. Having said that, it was somewhat ironic that my innermost yearnings were changing and I was no longer being aroused by men in the way I had been.'

'I hadn't heard that, Frankie, but thank you for being so

honest.'

'In 1981 I married Lisa; she worked at the publishing company who distributed my work. I'd known Lisa on and off for ten years or more and we just felt comfortable with each other. Unfortunately, our ship ran into stormy waters after exactly seven years. Yes, the seven-year itch and all that! It was nothing to do with my previous sexual preferences, it was more to do with my being away from home working so much. We decided upon a divorce, which proved costly and things between me and Lisa became fractious, especially where the children were concerned. Time, as they say, is a great healer and everything's a lot more amicable between us now. David and Joanna are grown up, started their own families and I see them both quite regularly. Lisa went through a very difficult time with her new partner Stefan, and it was me who helped her through it.' Frank lowered his voice to barely a whisper. 'She came home early one afternoon and found Stefan dressed in her silky nightwear, wearing her make-up and dancing around the kitchen to 'Heaven Must Be Missing an Angel'.'

'Oh dear.' Mary tried to look shocked, but couldn't help a smile. 'Did he get his marching orders?'

'Tout suite, Mary, with all his worldly goods in a suitcase and a couple of plastic bin liners.'

Mary put her cup and saucer on the table. 'And what about you Frank, is there anybody special in your life?'

'Not at the moment. There have been a few, all of them ladies I hasten to add; that bisexual stuff seems a long time ago now. On the occasions I do remember, I have to say it seems like another person – no, Mary, at the moment I'm old, free and single.'

Mary laughed politely; Stan raised his eyes to the heavens.

Frank continued. 'Anyway back to the music. Over the last couple of decades there's been a renaissance of the rock 'n' roll days. The old joke about nostalgia being a thing of the past is wide of the mark, 'cos it's lucrative. A lot of the sixties and seventies bands are in demand for the Silver Circuit. Mostly grandparents, they come along to sing and dance to the music they remember when they were courting. They're an appreciative crowd.'

'Is it for this silver circuit of which you talk, that you want my Carol's number?' asked Mary.

'Well, sort of,' said Frank. Stan could detect a change in Frank's tone; it definitely seemed a case of not wanting to say too much. He listened with interest. 'Stan knows I have suggested a reunion, but there's a bit more to it than that.' As Frank glanced at Stan there was a twinkle in his eye. 'I haven't told him the whole story and neither will I. Not yet anyway!'

Stan raised his eyebrows in mild amusement, but before he could say anything Frank added, 'After your performance in the bar of the Crown and Anchor the other night it's a good job I didn't.'

Stan looked suitably rebuked.

Mary clasped her hands together, rocking gently back and forth, chuckling to herself. 'Now, now, boys, you used to bicker like that when you were those star-struck kids just starting out.' She sat forward on her chair and reached for the teapot. 'Anybody for a top up? And you haven't even touched those biscuits!'

Stan didn't need asking again and pulled out two bourbons.

'We're very rude, Mary,' apologised Frank. 'It's been all about us. What about you; how have you been doing?'

'I'm very well, thank you, Frankie,' replied Mary, and her smile said she meant it. 'I get involved in a lot of local things, you know, Women's Institute, charity work, fundraising for the upkeep of St. Jude's, the local church, stuff like that. I used to go dancing once a week, but that's a bit beyond me now, so walking keeps me as active as I need to be at ninety-two.'

'Blimey,' said Stan. 'You're remarkably sprightly for a lady in her nineties, we'd never have guessed it.' He daren't look at Frank.

'I've got three grandchildren, and earlier this year our Michael's daughter Rebecca had Jake and made me a great-grandma for the second time.' Mary was clearly very proud.

'Forgive me, Mary, but was there anyone after you lost Dennis?' asked Stan a bit nervously.

'No, nobody,' she replied quite firmly. No sooner said, than she softened. 'There were gentleman callers, I did have one or two admirers.' Bashfully, she cast her eyes down at her hands holding her cup and saucer. *Was that another blush?* they both thought. 'No one was going to replace Dennis.'

There was a short pause, just the sound of Stan munching bourbons to break the silence.

'Put your teas down for a minute and follow me,' said Mary. She led them back through the hallway and into the room opposite. It was a beautifully laid out dining room, with a large oak dining table and chairs, which stood in front of a set of old fashioned French windows that almost covered the width of the far wall. Through the windows they could both see a carefully tended garden, but their eyes were quickly diverted away from the honeysuckle and clematis intertwining their ways up trellises and archways, when Mary switched on the interior lights of an impressive oak and glass display cabinet. On show inside were a number of lovingly framed photographs of Dennis. Some with a smiling Dennis on his own, others with the big band and still more of him playing with his jazz band. There was a particularly striking one of Dennis and Sugarlips, both smiling as they posed with their instruments, Sugarlips wearing her stunning red dress. Both Stan and Frank guessed it must have been taken just before Dennis died, but neither said anything. However pride of place went to Dennis's clarinet, immaculately polished and sparkling under the lighting.

It brought a lump to Stan's throat and Frank had to look away.

'Gosh, that's amazing, Mary,' choked Stan.

'I had that done for Mary Meadowsweet, only weeks after I lost Dennis and it's been there ever since.' Mary gave a wry smile. 'I suppose it could well have cooled the ardour of any gentlemen suitors.'

She led them back to the kitchen. 'Carol's a grandma, did you know?' said Mary, lifting the melancholy that was starting to descend. 'Dessie has a teenage son, Mikey, he was my first great grandchild.'

'I'd heard she had a daughter, but it's been a long, long time since any of us heard from her,' said Frank. 'She was playing at jazz clubs, living down in London when I last bumped into her, and that must be over thirty-odd years ago. We exchanged phone numbers, but she never kept in touch and the one she gave me was duff.'

'That's our Carol,' shrugged Mary. 'She's moved about a bit over the years. I've got postcards and little souvenirs from London, Amsterdam, Hamburg, Madrid and lots of other cities. 'Have a look at this.' She swung back one of the doors of a sideboard to reveal a poster pinned to the inside with drawing pins. 'The Blue Note, Greenwich Village, NYC', it read in dark blue letters on a pale background. There she was, Sugarlips, appearing with a band neither of them had heard of, but sounding very Gallic, Jacques Le Morceau Quintet.

'11th September 1980. Blimey, that's a few years ago!' exclaimed Stan.

'It's my birthday,' said Mary. 'I suppose that's why she sent it over to me. She was in Manhattan for months, right up until the NYPD found her visa had run out and immigration shipped her back. I'd seen very little of her in those days and I used to get really upset with her when her phone calls were so few and far between.

'Then one day I got this call from a hospital in Paris, the lady spoke in broken English, but I certainly understood it was about Carol, and that I was being transferred.' Mary's eyes were open wide as she told them. 'Oh my God, I was beside myself waiting to be put through to the ward. All I could think of was the night Dennis died in that road accident.'

'Then Carol's voice came on the other end. "Mom," she said, "I've just had a little girl. You're a grandma." Oh, how we cried, the two of us, hundreds of miles apart sobbing uncontrollably, unable to speak.'

You could see the emotion on Mary's face, even after all these years. She pushed her glasses back across the bridge of her nose with her forefinger, holding back a tear. 'This may surprise you,' Mary said, soberly. 'I never ever met the father. Henry was his name, he played trumpet in a jazz band, which is how they met. When they moved back over to London, Carol started to come and visit me, usually by train, bringing little Dessie with her, but never Henry. Always "too busy gigging", or "seeing to business".

'Then suddenly it was over, just as abruptly as I'd heard about it starting and the birth of the baby, they split. Just like that. He picked up his horn and went back across the channel. She said he couldn't settle in London and needed to get back to Paris. That was a bad time for Carol, she desperately missed her father and now here she was, an unmarried mother, deserted by her man, trying to raise a child by playing in jazz clubs until God knows what time in the morning. I found out some years later she got herself mixed up with one of the club owners. He was married, and infamously involved in drugs and prostitution. "You stupid, stupid girl," I told her. She swore to me that she was not involved in his supplying or pimping activities, but I just didn't know. My daughter was a distant stranger to me now. I begged her to bring Dessie and come back home, but she was having none of it. Fortunately for her, but not for Al Capone, he got busted, his club closed down and he's now enjoying an extended holiday in Wandsworth.

'Thank God, Dessie has grown up a beautiful young lady, well-educated too. She went to the LSE, got A-levels and ologies then got a job in telecommunications. I have to say I don't understand what she does, but I know she gets paid a lot of money and I know she met Tommy and set up home with him. He's a lovely chap, I've met him a few times.'

Mary got up from the table again and brought over a small black and gold photograph album.

'Dessie and Tom did this for me last Christmas.' She opened the cover to reveal the first page. Frank took a deep breath. Stan did the opposite and blew out through his teeth.

'That's S-S-Sugarlips – sorry, C-C-Carol, as I live and breathe,' stuttered Stan, struggling to catch his breath.

There was a little family group of Dessie, Tom, and young Mikey, who looked about fourteen. Mary slowly turned over the other dozen or so pages in the album. The likeness was astounding, Dessie was the same Carol that first walked into Fordrough village hall in 1963 and blew their socks off.

'Such happy family pics,' smiled Frank. 'I love this one. He stopped Mary from turning the page on a picture of mother and daughter.

'Uncanny,' said Stan, shaking his head. 'She's still playing her sax, I trust?'

'Oh yes, all the places I told you,' nodded Mary. 'I understand she's quite a star turn in the clubs, but like you boys, she's no youngster anymore, so she's definitely slowed down a bit.'

'My, my, how quickly the years have passed, eh?' said Frank.

'To realise how quickly the years pass, then you need look no further than the children,' sighed Mary. 'It doesn't seem five minutes since Dessie was in nappies, let alone young Mikey.'

'More tea boys?' Mary lifted the teapot.

'Not for me,' said Frank.

'Nor me,' said Stan. 'And certainly no more biscuits.'

'Mary,' said Frank. 'It's lovely to see you and talk about the old times, to remember Dennis and hear about Dessie and Mikey. We came here to get Carol's new mobile number, make contact with her and see if she'd like to be involved in our plans to get together.'

Mary got up again and moved over to the freezer to remove a single sheet of paper, held in place by a clarinet-shaped fridge magnet. She brought it back to the table and dropped it in front of Frank.

'I've written it down on my things-to-do pad,' she said. 'Phone her if you please, but you don't really need to.'

Frank looked up at her, clearly puzzled.

'You don't think she'll be interested?' asked Stan.

'That's not what I mean, boys,' said Mary. 'Carol is coming up here, from London this weekend. Dessie and Mikey will be with her. She's really looking forward to seeing you all again.'

'That's great news,' beamed Frank.

'We should do something special,' suggested Stan. 'Get everybody together and book a table somewhere. Chinese, Indian – there's that new Italian in Bromsgrove...'

'Whoa! Steady on Stanley,' said Frank. 'Let's think this one through, we've got some important things to talk about, I don't think we should be discussing them in a restaurant, in public.'

They bid Mary goodbye, each gave her a hug and kissed her on the cheek and promised they would see her soon.

***

It was Stan who came up with the plan. He called by at the Crown and Anchor with Bertie on his morning walk.

It was delivery day and the draymen, having dropped fresh barrels and loaded up the empties, were having a cup of tea over in the bay window. Dennis Jenkinson, the landlord, was finishing his morning chores. He'd shifted the new barrels of bitter, lager, cider and Guinness around his cellar and placed them to his liking. He'd cleaned the pipes ready for the new day and removed all the empty bottles for recycling. He was now humping plastic crates of mixers onto the bar, in readiness for topping up the shelves.

'Morning, Dennis,' chirped Stan. 'Is the gaffer about? I'd like a word.'

'Which one, my missus or Gloria?' replied Dennis, without so much as a sideways glance.

'I like a man who knows his station,' laughed Stan. 'Gloria. I have a proposition for her.'

Gloria's head popped up above the bar, where she'd been on her knees, filling the bottom shelf with tonic waters. 'You want to proposition me at this time in the morning? You rock gods are just insatiable!'

'What more could a man need; a good woman at home to do the cooking and ironing and a floozy at the pub who knows how to pull a good pint?' Stan plonked himself down on a barstool.

'Okay, big boy,' sighed Gloria. 'What can I do for you?'

'Gloria, we need a private room to discuss the things we talked about the other night. I wondered if we could have the back room for an hour or two?'

'Of course you can, but on one condition; after hearing some of your tales, you let me take the minutes. When are you thinking of?'

'Sugarlips is due up here Saturday morning and Frank and Bodkin are on stand-by, so if we said 7:30 p.m., is that okay?'

'It sure is; would you like me to do some food?'

'That would be fantastic, you're sure it's not too much trouble?'

'Not at all, Chef will be doing an evening menu from seven o'clock, so it's no trouble for him to cater for a few more and I'm on hand to help him. We have extra bar staff on Saturdays, so I can give Frankie Atom and The Bombastics my full attention. Why don't you invite wives and girlfriends along too. Make it a truly family affair?'

'What a terrific idea; as long as you can cope?' Stan pulled his barstool a little closer and in his best confidential voice whispered, 'There must be time for a swift pint, whilst we decide on the guest list and menu, eh Gloria?'

'Is a large bowl of lamb curry, with rice and naans okay?' Gloria unhooked one of the pint mugs hanging above the bar.

'Perfect. I'll try the Anchor bitter now Dennis has

finally cleaned the pipes and a packet of cheese and onion crisps for Bertie, please.'

'Cheeky bugger, I heard that.' Dennis appeared around the bar with a crate of bitter lemons.

CHAPTER 24
'BACK TOGETHER AGAIN'

Hall & Oates

Stan and Elsie were in the main bar when Carol and Dessie arrived. Carol wore a dark blue chiffon dress and a pale green short-sleeved jacket. She carried a large blue suede handbag that matched her suede court shoes. Her blonde hair was gathered quite elegantly to one side and from her ears sparkled small blue earrings.

Dessie wore tight – very tight – blue denim jeans, black ankle boots and a dark purple sleeveless top with a plunging neckline. Round her waist was draped a loose-fitting black leather belt. Her blonde hair tumbled around her shoulders, exactly the way her mom's had all those years ago.

Stan gave Carol the first of many hugs to come her

way, Elsie gave her the second. They were introduced to Dessie and just as Frank and Stan when they looked at her photograph, Elsie couldn't get over how much she looked like Carol.

'It's just like being transported back 50 years,' she gasped.

It was probably something Dessie had heard many times, but she smiled sweetly.

'Where's your little boy?' continued Elsie.

Dessie explained, 'Mikey decided to stop at home with his great grandma.'

Frank arrived next. He stopped a few feet away from Carol with a big, daft smile on his face.

'SHOOGS!' He flung his arms around her and hugged her close. 'You look absolutely amazing.' He gently pushed her back by her shoulders and kissed her on both cheeks.

'It's wonderful to see you all, it's been far too long.' Sugarlips seemed on the point of tears. 'I should have kept in...'

'Don't blame anyone, Carol, least of all yourself. We all lead busy lives and sometimes we just lose touch, that's life, as they say. Kismet's played us a kindly hand, 'cos here we all are back together again.' Frank still had hold of Sugarlips' hands, but let go of one to turn to Dessie. 'No need to ask who your mom is, you just have to be Dessie.'

'And you're Frankie,' said Dessie. 'I've heard you singing many times on my iPod.'

'On your iPod! Wow, there's me Frankie Atom, the internet sensation. Why thank you, kind Miss,' said Frank, giving Dessie a peck on the cheek. 'Now, how about a drink everybody?'

'Gloria has arranged a tab behind the bar,' said Stan. 'Just order from young Matt. As soon as Bodkin arrives we'll go through to the back room.'

They stood chatting whilst Frank organised the drinks.

'Bodkin's bringing an old friend with him,' Stan told Sugarlips. 'A friend you haven't seen for nearly fifty years.'

'It can't be Danny Hoffman, surely!' cried Sugarlips.

'No,' laughed Stan. 'I said friend, anyway the only friend he has now will be Lucifer, 'cos I doubt St. Peter would have let him through the pearly gates.'

'Oh my God, I didn't know,' gasped Carol.

'Here's Bodkin now,' said Frank, looking over Stan's shoulder. They all turned towards the door and saw Bodkin holding the door back for Julie.

When he saw Sugarlips, he too, paused momentarily, but not for him the big, daft smile. His was a look of self-doubt. It was Carol who took a step forward to him.

'Come here you great big, gorgeous bear of a man.' She wrapped her arms around his neck and planted a giant-sized kiss, right on his lips.

Both Stan and Frank immediately glanced at Julie, but there was not a hint of concern, just a smile of pleasure for Bodkin and Carol.

'Frank, you get the drinks for Bodkin and Julie,' said Stan. 'Me and Bodkin'll take Sugarlips out to meet our old friend. I presume you've brought her?' asked Stan, doing a steering wheel mime behind Sugarlips' back.

'Oh yes,' winked Bodkin. 'The lady is waiting, she's right outside.'

He took Sugarlips by the hand and ostentatiously led her through the door and outside to the parking bays. With an exaggerated wave of his arm, he announced, 'Carol, I give you Jezza.'

'Oh gosh!' Sugarlips put her hand to her mouth. 'Can it

really be? She looks so very different, but at the same time so familiar.'

'Oh, it's her alright,' said Bodkin. 'She's had a facelift and a fair bit of cash spent on souping her up, but look at the number plate, GOE 305. I've checked the log book, she's had three owners since we sold her, but the last one's had her since 1982. He's the one that's done all the work on her.'

Carol slid onto the passenger seat alongside Bodkin. Stan, Elsie and Dessie, who had followed them out, stood around the open door. 'This brings back some memories,' said Carol, leaning back in her seat and stretching her legs out as far as the seat well would allow. Then she went silent for a moment and sat forward staring at the radio. 'Is that the same radio?' The tone of her voice changed, as though she was probing. It was only very slight, but Bodkin noticed, Stan too.

'Yes it is, Shoogs, why do you ask?' As Bodkin looked at her he saw again the young woman he had fallen desperately in love with. He hoped and prayed he still wasn't, but only time would tell.

'Oh, nothing really,' Sugarlips replied. 'I-I-I just wondered if you can still get Luxembourg and some of those other weird stations on it.' She didn't sound convincing.

'Hey, c'mon everybody, let's get some food.' Stan sensed a tricky moment. 'We got some talking to do.'

Gloria had spent a good deal of time preparing the room, sliding all the tables together so they formed a big square in the middle of the room. She wanted them all to face each other, no matter where they sat. She had laid out placemats, cutlery and napkins. After consulting Stan and Frank she had also put place names, boy, girl, boy, girl, as best as she could. It didn't quite work out, so putting Dessie next to her mom was probably right.

After serving them to another round of drinks, Gloria brought in a giant terrine of curry, which they all agreed smelled wonderful. Stan suggested that Gloria join them and when she hesitated Frank insisted and pulled up a spare chair alongside his.

In between mouthfuls of curry, there was a lot of laughter and storytelling, as they reminded each other of the highs and lows of being a Bombastic. Even the hard times and the disappointments now took on a rosier blush, all these years later. Remembering some of the scrapes they got into inevitably got them onto Barry. Stan recalled Barry's 'Great Balls of Fire' incident in a south coast hotel, whilst The Bombastics were doing a summer season in Bournemouth.

'Although the shows were six nights a week, the theatre crowd, mainly holiday makers, liked the entertainment to finish early. We were usually done by ten o'clock and after we'd hung around to sell a few albums or sign a few autographs, maybe chat to any VIPs or special guests who'd been invited backstage, we'd often be back at the hotel before eleven.

'As the others will tell you, we used to take it in turns *not* to share with Barry, because of the company he'd bring back for late night entertainment, but there was only so much partying and shagging even Barry could accomplish in an eight week season.'

He apologised to Dessie, but she was giggling.

'Anyway, I was his roommate on this occasion and the old saying that the Devil finds work for idle hands was never truer. I remember the hotel bedrooms were large, plain, magnolia and boring. Even the curtains were plain beige. Each room had the same picture, that one of the 'Green Lady' that everybody seemed to own a print of at the time. Barry amused himself by taking ours down and balancing it on the sash window frame, so she looked out over the car park with her sickly, green face. Next to her he put a big notice saying 'DON'T EAT THE CHEF'S SPECIAL'. As our room overlooked reception, in full view of all newly arriving guests, Clive Blower (Barry had nicknamed him Blow-Job), the hotel manager, went ape-shit and made us take it down immediately.

'Unbeknown to me, Barry had a plan to get his own back. Following the Wednesday matinee, he and Wally, who for the eight-week run was stage managing rather than driving, sneaked paint and brushes through the rear entrance and up the back stairs. After the evening show they got back to the room, opened up a bottle of Jim Beam, probably popped a few pills, and set about their work.

'They pushed the two single beds, the side tables, chairs and the mini-fridge to one end of the room, then in thick lines of black emulsion they painted a musical staff up the wall. The five lines arched over the ceiling and down the wall on the other side. They had to pull one of the beds back and clamber onto it to reach the ceiling. They repeated this down the length of the room, moving the other bed, side tables, chairs and mini fridge up the other end of the bedroom as they worked their way across. They then painted an assortment of crotchets, minims and quavers the size of saucers along the length of the staff, even adding large treble clefs and bar lines.

'Barry then opened a tin of red gloss and with a smaller brush, painted the lyrics of 'Great Balls of Fire' underneath the staff. They carefully returned all the furniture and mini-fridge back to their exact positions, using the indentations in the beige carpet as their guide. Afterwards, Wally sneaked down the back stairs with the paint tins and brushes and dumped them in the hotel dustbins. Barry poured them each another glass of Tennessee's best and they lay back on the beds to admire their handiwork.

'They must have heard me arriving back and putting the key into the lock. Well, when I opened the door, I was dumbstruck and just stood staring at Jerry Lee Lewis's number one hit plastered all over the magnolia. Eventually I managed a couple of words, "You prat."

"'That's not the correct response, Stan,' grinned Barry over his tooth glass, still half full of whiskey. "Go directly to jail, do not pass Go, do not collect £200."

"'Jail? That's where you'll end up when old Blow-Job sees what you've done to his hotel room. You're both pissed."

"'He ain't seen nuthin' yet, but we'll soon put that right." Barry had the hotel phone in his hand. "Is that reception? This is Barry Harper in room 239. I want to complain in the strongest possible terms. We just cannot get to sleep for loud music. It's outrageous and you need to deal with it immediately." He put the phone down.

'Within five minutes, there was a knock on the door; it was Jenny Droopy-drawers, the deputy manageress. When the door was opened she blinked in disbelief. "What on earth?"

"'Another incorrect response," chortled Barry. "You're supposed to say, goodness, gracious, great balls of fire."

'Wally was in hysterics. I just sat on the bed shaking my head. Blow-Job went ape-shit again, Danny went ape-shit again. We got slung out of the hotel and ended up in theatrical digs. It cost a fortune to get the room redecorated, plus compensation for loss of business whilst that was done. We also got banned from the Nestledown Hotel Group.'

'Cheers Barry, thanks for the memories and the crappy digs.' Stan stood up and raised his glass. 'To absent friends.'

'Don't forget, Wally got sacked over the phone, by Danny.' Bodkin reminded them all. 'He had to go back to plastering on less than half the money. Just another one of

Barry's stupid stunts. 'Which brings me on to a more serious subject, before we get too pissed,' Bodkin continued. 'Carol, you won't know about this, but if it's true, something quite extraordinary has come to light in the last couple of weeks.'

The table was quiet as Bodkin began to tell Sugarlips and Dessie about Robbie Rochester. Sugarlips let him get into the story and as far as 1983 and the lay-by in Drovers Lane when she stopped him. 'Forgive me Bodkin, but I know a lot more than you think I do,' she began. 'In fact I know a lot more than most of you do.'

There was complete silence around the table, all eyes on Sugarlips.

'I need to take you back to one of the last gigs we did in Norwich, some club in the town centre. It was about two or three weeks before I left the band, in fact it was one of the reasons I decided to leave the band.' She looked across at Bodkin, and Julie sitting next to him. Her head was in turmoil. What she couldn't do was to reveal another of the reasons she decided to quit and move on.

Dear, dear Bodkin. I had loved him like a big brother, but for him it was different. He had long been my guardian angel, even the others in the band made jokes about how he watched over me. Woe betide any unfortunate teenager, fired up with testosterone, or some randy security guard who tried to access all areas with his Sugarlips.

Bodkin had always been the perfect gentleman. He never had, or did, lay a hand on me. It was when I announced to the band that I'd had enough, that I didn't want to be playing the same old string of hits for the rest of my life and wanted to try my luck playing jazz in the London clubs, that Bodkin became morose, hardly speaking to anyone.

Therefore, it came as a bit of a surprise, not to say relief, when he rang me and asked me if I'd like to go for a meal at the new Berni Inn that had opened nearby in Birmingham. I said I'd love to. The evening had gone really well, he'd been very attentive and thoughtful.

We'd talked about Danny moving over to the States and whether his son Ike was going to cope with getting us work. We discussed my decision to move to London and that's when I knew all was not well. Bodkin wanted me to stay in The Bombastics; he'd thought it all through. Maybe change our image, take a leaf out of Miles Davis's book, try a bit of jazz fusion; that should satisfy my penchant for jazz. I'd be an important part of the sound. He'd told me he felt I was taking a big chance going into the unknown. What if I couldn't find the work in London? It was then I told him I'd agreed a six-week guest spot at Ronnie Scott's.

He'd immediately got up, paid the bill and took my coat from the waiter. I had barely finished my coffee. There were big lumps of silence in the car as he drove me home. He smiled a little, but it was a distracted and troubled smile as he tussled with his anguish. He'd stopped the car around the corner from my mom's house. He'd taken my hand (for such a big hard hitting drummer, I was always surprised at how gentle his touch was), he turned halfway in his seat and looked into my eyes. That was when it all spilled out. He begged me not to go, he told me he loved me. Tears were welling in his eyes as he'd said I was the most important thing in his life and he didn't want to lose me. "We could get married, I'll look after you forever, Carol," he'd said.

I made up my mind there and then that I couldn't drag this out. I thought the world of Bodkin and I'd known that what he felt for me was more than brotherly love, of course I did; but marriage? NO!

I'd taken hold of his hand with both of mine and looked straight into his eyes, still brimming with tears. This had to be dealt with here and now. I told him he was very important to me, but I wasn't ready for marriage to him or anyone else. I said how much I'd loved the last few years working with the boys, but I was determined to give London and the jazz clubs a go. I gave him a hug, kissed him gently on the cheek. He'd started the car, driven round the corner and dropped me off outside my house. I smiled and waved him goodbye, but he never returned it.

There were still engagements to fulfil before I was due to depart, although Barry's death was to change that. Bodkin said little or nothing to me. It was a very difficult and very sad time.

None of this will ever be mentioned by me and certainly not tonight.

'Things were getting very awkward,' she carried on. 'The Bombastics' future was precarious to say the least. Danny seemed to be deserting us. Okay, he left his son in charge, but none of us was brimming over with confidence in that decision. Our recording contract was at an end and because I was getting no satisfaction from my music, you all knew I was on the brink of leaving which made things very difficult between us all. Then there was Barry's drink and drugs habits, they were just getting worse. His behaviour was appalling and we all knew he needed help.'

'The Norwich gig, which turned out to be our last, was one big bore. We'd lost our sparkle, churning out the same old songs seemed to be a drag. These were our hits, our lifeblood, but it was draining away and the audience must've been able see that. We'd got back to the hotel and most of you had gone straight to bed. There was just Barry, Brian and myself sitting in the cocktail bar. You remember Brian, the complete prick who took over from Wally?'

'Mother!' protested Dessie.

'Sorry, but that's how we felt about him. Anyway, Barry was having a row with the night porter, a squat, little guy with wavy hair and a big smile. Barry kept calling him Harry Secombe, and to be fair to him, despite both Barry and Brian giving him dog's abuse, he kept on smiling. Barry wanted to put a bottle of Bushmills on his room tab, despite not having his room card with him, so the night porter wanted him to either pay cash or use his Access card. Brian, who I know had been drinking in the dressing room whilst we were onstage, suddenly got up and teetered sideways, knocking over a plastic Mulberry bush, and gave the little feller a right mouthful. He stumbled over to the lift, managed to press the call button and almost fell into it when the doors opened. He didn't even say goodnight.

'In the end I got so angry with Barry I got my room card out and asked the night porter to put the whiskey on my room, telling Barry he must pay me back in the morning. Barry was delighted, I remember he had the seal off the bottle and the cork out before Harry Secombe had brought me the receipt to sign. He splashed far too much into my glass and even more into his glass and onto the table top, before offering a toast. "To Sugarlips, the saxiest sex player in Christendom – probably Norfolk too – or whatever this God forsaken place is called," he spluttered out, thrusting his glass aloft, causing half the contents to run down the inside of the sleeve of his jacket.

'I tugged at his other arm and plonked him back down onto the couch. He'd been popping pills onstage, we all knew that and this whiskey was only going to make things worse. "We need to get up to our rooms when we've finished these, Barry," I said, sipping my Bushmills; I didn't want him to think I was rushing him and risk starting another rant. Not that the night porter would be surprised, he'd seen and heard enough already.

'"You'll do fine in London, Shoogs. Bugger me, The Bombastics are finished, Barry Harper's finished, rock 'n' roll in the free world's finished." He came out with all that codswallop with a broad smile on his face, but I remember, there were tears in his eyes.

'"You'll be fine, Barry." I tried to say. We both knew how empty those words sounded.

'Then he really started to cry. He jerked forward, putting his elbows on his knees. Tears streamed down his cheeks, some of which must have fallen into his drink. I moved closer to him and put an arm round him. At any other time Barry would have tried to take advantage of the situation, but not this time. I'd literally given him a shoulder to cry on and another drink to cry into.

"'I've been a fool, let people down, I'm a thief.'"

"'What? Thief? You haven't been stealing drugs have you Barry? You can't steal drugs off the kind of people you've been dealing with, you'll end up...'"

"'No, no, not drugs.' He sat up straight, wiping his cheeks with the back of his hand. "Songs – I stole songs – songs that I told you all I'd written. 'Broken Hearted Nobody' and all the others."

"'Broken Hearted Nobody'? What do you mean?'"

"'Shattered Dreams and Promises'. It was 'Broken Hearted Nobody' when I stole it. I changed the words a bit so nobody'd recognise it, but bugger me, when it's released in thirteen years' time, the bloke who wrote it is gonna know it, that's certain and he doesn't deserve that, he trusted me and helped me. It's just not right."

"'Barry, what in hell's name are you talking about? It makes no sense at all.' I'd said. "You stole a song and changed the words and it won't be released for thirteen years? That's 1983 and you're talking about a hit we had in 1965!'"

'He then told me an incredible story of travelling through time in a snow storm, of meeting another band with an identical camper van. How he went to gigs and a recording session with them. The Robbie Rochester Band, they were called. They helped him get back to 1963.'

The others, sat round the table were speechless as Sugarlips continued.

'I told him he was pissed and talking gibberish and needed to get to bed. I pushed the cork back in the bottle of whiskey, still three quarters full, and manhandled him off his backside, as best I could. "I can prove it, I can prove it," he began shouting. The night porter came through from reception when he heard the racket.'

'"Can I be of any help?" he asked.'

'"It's all okay, Harry," Barry said. "This charming young lady is carrying me off to bed."'

'I shook my head and smiled at the night porter. "At least he's got his sense of humour back," I said. I tried to take the Bushmills off him as I pushed him through his bedroom door. He was having none of it and wrenched it out of my grasp as he fell into his room. I was really worried about him; God knows what cocktail of drugs he'd already taken that night and finishing off a bottle of Irish whiskey... well, he could kill himself!'

'As I lay in my bed that night, I remember thinking perhaps that's what he wants to do. Next morning he looked like shit, and waited until there was just the two of us left at the breakfast table; actually there was three, but you Stan had got up to get more tea. Barry was still high or drunk, no doubt about that and he started gabbling. "I can prove what I told you last night. Just come round to my house when we get home." I then put a finger to my lips as Stan turned to come back to the table. He shrugged and nodded an okay.'

'We managed to snatch a brief word to arrange a meeting and the following night I drove round to Toad Hall. It was a sprawling mansion of a place he'd bought with all that money he'd won,' she explained to Dessie, Julie and Gloria, who already knew but nodded politely. 'Poor Cherie was there. As we all know, he'd had many girlfriends, but Cherie was the unlucky one to be with him the night of the fatal drive. Barry asked her to go and make us all tea; I emphasise tea, that may surprise you, but he seemed to be making a big thing about them both being sober and drug free. Whilst she was making it, Barry took me into the drawing room.'

'Barry picked up what looked like an old school satchel

from the piano. We sat down and he fiddled the strap buckles undone. He flipped the top back, put his hand in and pulled out a small grey metal box-like thing. I know exactly what it is now, but I hadn't got a clue back then. It was a Walkman; just remember it wasn't going to be invented for another nine or ten years.'

'"This is called a Walkman. It's like a mini tape recorder," he said, squeezing it to make a clicking sound that flipped the lid open. He pulled out the miniature reel to reel, showed me, then slid it back and pushed the lid shut. "The battery may be a bit dodgy. There isn't much life in it and I've kept meaning to find new ones that fit it. Still let's give it a go." He squeezed another button and music came out of it. It slurred very slightly, but it was definitely the tune of 'Shattered Dreams and Promises', but the words were 'Broken Hearted Nobody', and it certainly wasn't Barry singing it.'

'He wanted me to listen to the others, 'Night Club Fight' and the like, but the battery was giving up and you could hardly make out the words, never mind the tune. "Borrow it Shoogs," he implored, and showed me where the batteries went. "Put new batteries in it, you'll find ones that'll fit, no problem." He switched it off and put it back in the satchel, at the same time pulling out an old calendar page from July 1965. It had all our gigs for that month written on the grid. It was the stuff written on the back that was important; all the lyrics and chords to the song he just played me and written above each line, were his lyrics to 'Shattered Dreams and Promises'.'

'I told him I needed time for this to all sink in and for me to hear the tape properly. He came out to my car with me, put his arm around me, gave me a hug and kissed me. "See you Saturday," he said. "Bugger me, I just remembered, it's that dump in Derby, isn't it?"'

Sugarlips put her hand over her eyes, vainly trying to cover the tear that had run down her cheek. 'You know the rest. I never heard him say "Bugger me" again, he never kissed me again, and I was never able to return the Walkman. Three days later they found him and Cherie in the canal.' Carol fumbled with her jacket pocket to get a tissue out.

The back room at the Crown and Anchor fell into silence, as they sat there in their own worlds.

It was Bodkin who spoke first. 'Did you get to play the Walkman?'

Carol had gathered herself. 'Oh yes, but not for some time. Getting to buy new batteries that fitted was one problem, The Bombastics were in turmoil was another; we had to cancel the last two gigs, then there was the funeral. God, that was difficult and me leaving to go to London just added to the confusion. It was weeks before I got round to it; remember I was trying to earn a living and I had to find a flat that I could call home. That took some time. When I heard all those songs at the proper speed, I just knew Barry had to be telling the truth, but who was going to believe such a crazy story?'

Sugarlips picked up her handbag, which she'd placed on the floor beside her. She undid the clasp, reached inside and pulled out the Walkman, wires and all. 'It's just how Barry gave it to me in 1970, except for the batteries, of course. Listen.' She placed it on the table and pressed play.

'I can't believe it's come to this, surely it's not true,
You packed your things and moved away, just how will I get through?
The life together that we planned, has now come to an end,
The hurt begins to know you're in the arms of my best friend.

I'm just a broken hearted nobody, a fool too blind to see,
The truth was there for everyone, everyone but me.

*Broken hearted nobody, broken hearted nobody,
The truth was there for everyone, everyone but me.*

Your cheatin' heart...'

'That must be Robbie Rochester,' said Stan, shaking his head in disbelief.

'Well it sure as hell ain't Barry Harper,' said Frank. 'Let's listen, eh?'

'Bar Room Brawl' followed, then about a third of 'Let's Run Away', after which the sound distorted badly. Sugarlips reached over and switched it off. 'That was always the trouble with cassettes, chewed up tapes, remember?'

Nobody answered.

'That poor bastard,' said Bodkin. 'It wrecked his career.'

'Who, Barry?' asked Gloria.

'No, Robbie Rochester, they were his songs,' answered Bodkin. 'Remember I've spoken to him. It cost him a fortune in damages and legal costs. He could have done with this in court.' He said, pointing at the Walkman.

'What happened Carol? Did you not hear what was going on with Danny and the court case?' said Stan.

Sugarlips looked down at her hands, clearly feeling uncomfortable. 'I was wrong, terribly wrong. Ironically I was in New York City at the time, in Greenwich Village, on the same side of the pond as Danny, but I never heard a thing about any plagiarism case. By the time I did I was back in Europe, first France, then the UK. It must have been nearly two years later. There was a lot of stuff going on in my life, I had Dessie to think about. I was a single mom and it seemed easier not to get involved. Cowardly I know, but maybe I thought after so long it wouldn't make much difference, and then the years passed and I suppose it became easier to do nothing.

'Oh, I've often thought about that incredible journey Barry made to find himself twenty years ahead of all of us. How on earth did that happen?' Then she smiled. 'And I've often thought what the first words Barry might have said when he discovered himself in 1983.'

'BUGGER ME!' shouted Stan, spreading his arms above his head.

They all laughed, but the odd tear fell.

'The silly bugger doesn't realise the problems he's left behind,' said Bodkin. 'I think we owe a certain man in Stechford an explanation, don't you?'

'We do.' Frank was nodding his head, so too was Stan.

'It's spooky.' Sugarlips gave a little a shiver. 'I knew nothing about Robbie Rochester making a reappearance and I certainly didn't know anything about Bod's visit to Stechford, but as soon as I got the call from Mom about this meeting, I just knew I had to find that Walkman. It took some finding too, it was still in the satchel Barry gave me. I found it in one of the enormous cardboard boxes we stuck down in the cellar when we moved in nearly eight years ago; and look at this in Barry's handwriting, it's the lyrics I told you about.'

Carol took a folded dog-eared A4 sheet and passed it to Stan.

He unfolded The Bombastics' bookings for July 1965 and on the other side, written in Barry's hand, were the lyrics to three songs. Lots of words and sentences had been scribbled out and new words written above. Notably, 'Broken Hearted Nobody' changed to 'Shattered Dreams and Promises'. Also scribbled amongst the lines were chord changes and keys.

'Jeeeezus Christ! No doubt about it now!' exclaimed Stan.

'It would seem The Bombastics, and Barry in particular, have benefited from Robbie Rochester and his friends,' said Carol, pulling a sheaf of paper from her handbag and tossing them on the table. 'And look here – betting slips – eight in all; they must be winning bets he never got round to collecting.'

'Blimey.' Stan picked a couple up to study them. 'I bet these bookies aren't even around any more.'

'Why don't the four of us meet up with Robbie?' suggested Bodkin. 'He seems a straight guy, I think we owe him at least that.'

'Aren't you opening Pandora's box?' said Gloria. 'Isn't he going to try and put the record straight, get his money back?'

'If I remember correctly, wasn't it hope that was left in Pandora's box?' said Stan. 'Maybe it's time his hopes were realised; think of it another way, it's Danny fuckin' Hoffman's estate that'll have to cough up.'

'STANLEY!' Elsie gave him a good slap around his upper arm.

'Sorry,' he said.

'Everyone okay for tomorrow?' asked Bodkin. He had his mobile phone in his hand. They all nodded, and Bodkin gave a thumbs-up to everybody before standing up and moving away from the table. As he disappeared out into the garden area he was poking numbers into his mobile.

'Eleven o'clock at his place,' announced Bodkin as he came back through the door. 'He sounded surprised, but I didn't give him a clue. He just thinks you want to meet him.'

'Good, that's sorted,' said Frank, raising a glass.

'Frank, can I ask a question?' said Sugarlips.

'Shoogs, the floor is yours,' replied Frank.

'What was this meeting all about? It seems to have got overtaken by other things.'

'You're right, Carol.' Frank stood up, took a gulp of his red wine and carefully placed the glass back on the table. 'I'll keep this very, very simple.' He hesitated, then announced with a broad grin. 'We've been asked to play Glastonbury.'

'Fuckin' hell!' gasped Stan.

He got another good slap from Elsie.

CHAPTER 25
'A DAY IN THE LIFE'

The Beatles

Barry opened his eyes, his head throbbed, his mouth was dry but there was a stench of whiskey and cigarettes. The recurring nightmare of Janice's eyes glaring hate still pulsating in his brain. He blinked to make them disappear, but he was uncomfortably hot and it felt like his whole body was bathed in sweat. He kicked the sheet and bedcover to one side in an effort to cool down. Instead he felt cold and wet; he began to shiver.

Bugger me, have I pissed the bed?

He turned over and sat on the edge of the bed to check himself in the strands of early morning light struggling to come through gaps around the curtains. Even those half-hearted beams of daylight felt like lasers burning through his thumping head. He was wearing just underpants and a T-shirt, the rest of his clothes seemed to be in a tangle on the floor around his feet. He rubbed his hands into his crotch, around his backside and across the sheets where he'd slept.

Damp, yes, but it's sweat, not piss... Oh God, how cold am I?

He fumbled around amongst his abandoned clothes, but they seemed to be in a knot. Now shivering uncontrollably and starting to feel sick, he yanked the linen counterpane off the bed and wrapped it around his shoulders, clutching it together on his chest. There were pains in his stomach now and the feeling of nausea was beginning to overtake him. He dropped to his knees on the floor, burying his head amongst the sheets left strewn across the bed, as if that would offer relief. It didn't.

He raised his pounding head and his eyes fixed upon the bathroom door, inches ajar, just a few feet away. He was very close to desperate now and crawled across the hotel room, pushed open the bathroom door with one elbow and scrambled the last couple of yards over the lino. Fortunately the toilet seat was up, as he grabbed the porcelain rim with both hands and thrust his head into the bowl, just as his stomach lurched and erupted. He spewed forth a foul-smelling, whiskey-tasting brown liquid, until there couldn't be any more left in his stomach. He groped round for the lever to flush it away and gripped the rim as he watched the clean, fresh water cleanse the toilet bowl.

Thank God that's all out.

He was wrong. He spewed again, and when that was flushed away he threw up again, but this time it was yellow bile which made his brain explode with every retch. Minutes passed and the vomiting stopped. He waited a little longer then pushed himself up, gathered the counterpane around him and staggered back into the bedroom to collapse onto the bed.

He lay there thinking; the feeling of sickness was gone, but the pain in his gut and the throbbing in his head raged on. Bit by bit the previous night came back to him.

I had an argument with Harry Secombe about a bottle of whiskey. Sugarlips paid. I must pay her back.

God I feel like shit!

Sugarlips is leaving us, going to London to play jazz, The Bombastics are over – finished – gone. What was it that artist bloke's been saying? "Everybody will have fifteen minutes of fame." Well artist bloke, whoever you are, our fifteen minutes has lasted nearly an hour, so up yours!

Barry had come to terms with what he called his peak days and his bleak days. Like the girl with the little curl, when they were good they were very, very good, but when they were bad they were horrid. This had already turned into a bleak day.

Jeezus, it feels like I'm going to die!

He suddenly sat bolt upright in bed.

Bugger me, I told her – I told her about Robbie Rochester and 1983!

The only person I've ever told. I remember the look on her face, she didn't believe me, she needs to listen to that tape. I was crying, blabbing like a babby. You're a wimp Barry Harper, a waste of space. God Almighty, my bleedin' head. I swear I'm never going to touch another drop or pop another pill from this moment on.

That wasn't the first time he'd sworn to go clean, nor even the hundredth, this was possibly the thousandth. He turned his head towards the sliding wardrobe where he knew he'd thrown his overnight bag yesterday afternoon. He needed to fix this hangover.

Barry had got himself a routine. Night after night, after The Bombastics had gigged, he drank himself silly. If they weren't gigging, he got paralytic. If he was with the wrong people, there could also be pills and weed. He had a morning cure, a quick fix; cocaine, if he could get hold of it, or acid; Barry always convinced himself he could handle it, he was in control.

Not this morning though, not yet. He rolled across the bed and dropped himself carefully in front of the wardrobe. He slid the door completely open and pulled his black leather hold-all halfway out. He felt for the slider and zipped opened the bag. He pushed his hand inside and felt about. He pulled out his wash bag. He put his hand back inside, rummaging about until his fingers came upon a lumpy polythene package held intact with rubber bands. He grabbed it. Acid.

This is the last time, purely medicinal – after this no more – as God is my witness!

He staggered to his feet, picked up the wash bag and went back into the bathroom. He felt round for the cord and pulled it. The sudden bright light hurt his eyes; he tried to shield them as he tore at the rubber bands on his precious little bundle. He then unrolled the polythene bag as carefully as he could, caught hold of one of the bottom corners and shook it gently until some of the contents tumbled out. Two of the sugar cubes landed in his other hand whilst two more fell into the wash basin. He looked in horror as they spun round the basin, like the silver ball on a roulette wheel. Fortunately, they were far too big to go down the plug hole and he grabbed at them before they changed their minds.

I remember – Andy Warhol, the artist bloke – Andy Warhol.

He popped two of the cubes in his mouth, half-filled one of the two tooth mugs standing at the back of the basin and took a large sip. He watched himself crunching the dissolving sugar cubes in the mirror and raised the tooth mug. 'Here's to you Andy, and just remember for everyone like me who gets more than their fifteen minutes, some other poor bastards get less.' Then he remembered Robbie Rochester and cringed.

He put the two remaining cubes back in the polythene and pushed it into his wash bag taking toothpaste and brush out at the same time. The sugar cubes had got rid of most of the foul taste in his mouth, but this would cleanse it completely. He squeezed a worm of red and white toothpaste onto his brush and scrubbed away at his teeth and gums, finally swilling his mouth clean with mugs full of water.

Bugger me, I need to get back in bed whilst Dr Sugar works his magic.

He turned back into the bedroom, switching the light off and grabbing the counterpane he'd left strewn across the floor. He shook it open, wrapped it around him, flopped onto the bed and cracked his head on something hard where the pillow should have been.

'Bugger me, that's just what I need!' he screamed. He grabbed hold of an empty bottle, pulled it close to his face and in the half-light could see the familiar whiskey label.

'Bushmills, the demon drink!' his father called it. He thought about throwing it across the room, then thought better and let it drop to the side of the bed. He lay back, holding his head and waited.

***

Stan was angry and upset.

'Yet again Barry Harper messes other people about.' He banged his tea cup down a little harder than he'd intended. 'Look, it's nearly ten o'clock and the breakfast room will be closed soon. The others left nearly an hour ago.'

'He'll just have to go without his Sugar Puffs,' said Carol, then she added, rather tentatively, 'he got himself into a right state last night.'

'Huh, what's new? He's out of his brains on booze and drugs most nights,' sneered Stan. 'Well it's a long drive back to the Midlands and I won't be stopping – not unless you want to of course, Shoogs.'

Carol smiled, but Stan was not only angry with Barry, he was angry with Danny Hoffman for buggering off to the States like that; leaving his son Ike to manage them. What a start he'd made to his new role, telling them how difficult it was to get work for has-beens. *Has-beens? The ignorant little bastard!* He was upset too; upset that Sugarlips was seeking pastures new, and upset because The Bombastics' golden years were at an end.

Barry appeared at the breakfast room door.

'He's been at it again, look. He looks like death warmed up, but he's got that stupid grin on his face; that's been put there with chemicals.' Stan snatched his empty cup from the table and walked towards the tea urn, passing Barry on the way. 'It's all about you, yet again. Well take note of this Barry, I have to get back home by two so I leave here in fifteen minutes with or without you, right?'

Barry sat down next to Carol. 'I need a quiet word, Shoogs.'

She glanced furtively over at Stan who was waiting to fill his cup. 'You'd best be quick.'

'The things I told you last night...'

Carol studied him close up. Stan was right, he was on something, his pupils were dilated and his speech almost slurred.

'...You didn't believe me, did you?'

Carol didn't have time to shake her head.

'...Drive over to my place tomorrow night and I'll show you the Walkman and the tapes, certain proof of everything I said.'

'Walkman? What in God's name is a Walkman?' Stan was coming back to the table, so she shut the conversation short. 'I'll be there... about seven.'

Barry didn't want any breakfast and he'd brought his bag down and checked out, so Stan left most of his tea and the three of them set off. To begin with, Barry wouldn't shut up about how he'd taken his last fix, how he was now on the wagon, no more booze, no more weed, no more bad boy.

Stan couldn't take anymore. 'Barry, we've heard all this before, many times; now do us a favour and shut the fuck up, will you? Sorry, Carol, but I can't take much more.'

After that there wasn't a lot said, just Jimmy Young on Radio One.

***

Carol pulled off the narrow country lane that was Cobley Hill and guided her little white Triumph Toledo up the silver birch lined driveway that led to Broad Heath Hall (or Toad Hall as they all knew it). She parked alongside one of the four rampant stone lions that guarded the extensive frontage. One had a red hula-hoop hanging from a front paw, another had three more hula-hoops, yellow, blue and green, tumbled around its hind legs.

A game for the stoned – and I don't mean the lions!

Barry opened the front door as Carol crunched across the gravel.

'Shoogs, you've kept your word, thank you so much for coming.' Barry put his arm around her as they met.

Carol was surprised. Surprised that Barry appeared quite emotional, and even more surprised that he seemed perfectly sober. As they entered the reception hall, they were greeted by one of Barry's girlfriends, Cherie. She was wearing a strapless red dress with her long black hair pulled back in a ponytail. Barry went to introduce her, but

Carol stopped him.

'We've met before, haven't we Cherie?' she said. 'I met you here at one of Barry's parties.'

Cherie looked slightly confused and a little bit embarrassed. 'Oooo, I'm not sure, but I have seen you playing saxophone in Barry's band and...'

Barry came to her rescue. 'We've had a quite a number of parties here, Shoogs, it's a bit like New Street Station at times, eh, Cherie?'

He put his hand gently on Cherie's arm. 'Be a sweetheart, go and make us a nice pot of tea, we'll be in the drawing room.' With that Cherie waddled off in her very tight, very short dress, fish net stockings and a pair of pink bunny-faced slippers.

Barry led Carol through a large pine door, panelled and beaded with large wooden beehive doorknobs. Inside, the room was at once wholly Victoriana and yet highly Sixties. Ornate ceiling mouldings stretched into every corner and inglenook around the room, with a large centre rose the dominant feature; it was decorated with cherubs, flowers, grapes and vine leaves. Everything Victorian had been painted plain white. White emulsion or white gloss paint. The doors, the plaster work, the picture rail, cornices, sash windows, even the mantelpiece and hearth.

Instead of a chandelier hanging below the cherubs, three layered pendant lamps, probably Scandinavian, were suspended. The curtains were black and white Heals prints, large contemporary smudges and splodges that draped from ceiling to floor. Around the walls comic book pop art of every size and colour was framed and hung, with an enormous oil and canvas Roy Race scoring for Melchester Rovers and making a '*THUUUMMMP*' that stretched from his trusty right foot to the back of the bulging net. It took pride of place above the white, white mantle piece.

'Sit down, Shoogs,' said Barry. 'I've got something I promised you.' As Carol sat down on one of the two large black leather sofas, Barry moved over to an upright piano on the far side of the room, picked up a satchel that had been placed on top of it and came back to sit beside her.

She listened in absolute silence as he gave her a detailed account of his 1983 experience, having completely forgotten he'd given her the inebriated man's version two nights before. When he got to the bit about Robbie Rochester's songs, he slid the Walkman out of the satchel, pressed the eject button and pulled out the cassette tape to show her. Carol looked awestruck.

'These aren't on the market yet,' Barry said. 'Just listen to this.' He pushed the tape back in and shut the lid, then he pressed the play button. Immediately she heard 'Broken Hearted Nobody'. She wasn't sure about the words, but she certainly recognised the tune as 'Shattered Dreams and Promises'. The other thing she knew was that it wasn't Barry singing.

The tape started to slur. 'Damn! It's the batteries, they must be on their last legs,' said Barry, showing impatience as he opened the battery compartment and twirled the batteries round in their housing to try and squeeze a bit more life out of them. He pressed the play button again, but got nothing.

Just then Cherie came into the room wheeling a tea trolley laden with cups and saucers, milk jug, sugar bowl, and a large tea pot.

'Here, take it home and listen, you'll find some batteries that'll fit,' he said to Carol, pushing the Walkman back into the satchel that lay open on the sofa next to her. 'Give it me back when you can, but please don't tell anyone, not yet. You are the only one I've ever told, Cherie only knows bits and pieces.'

Cherie gave them each a cup of tea. Carol thanked her,

but clearly still in shock, she put her tea down on the side table. 'I really don't know what to say... time travel? It all seems so ridiculous!'

'Like I said, take it home and listen to it properly.' Barry put his cup and saucer down alongside Carol's, pulled the calendar page out of the satchel and unfolded it. 'Look at this too. Here are the original lyrics and chords I copied down off the tape.' He then moved his finger across the alternative lyrics he'd scribbled above them. These are the words you'll recognise, 'Shattered Dreams and Promises'.'

Carol slowly nodded her head, still shocked.

Barry turned the page over. 'These are the July gigs we had booked in that year. The Twisted Wheel. The Beachcomber, Titan's, La Dolce Vita; four and five a week, look.'

For a few minutes Carol studied it in silence. 'So what happens in 1983 when this Rochester guy realises someone else has already recorded and had a hit with his song?'

'I dunno,' shrugged Barry. 'I've tormented myself with that one for months. It was recorded and ready to go out on Chekka, but there's no such label – not yet! Maybe one of the older guys will recognise the song from our era and stop the release, or maybe it won't get that far and Robbie will think it's an old melody that's got stuck in his brain, the way these things do, and he didn't write it after all.'

'However it turns out, he's in for one hell of a shock,' said Carol, folding the calendar page back up and returning it to the satchel. 'This is a lot for me to take in, I need to think about it, listen to that tape properly on that Walkman thingy.'

Barry lowered his head and clasped his hands between his knees. 'Bugger me, however it turns out I will feel a complete shit. I shouldn't have done it, they were Robbie's songs and he was so good to me. I was totally bewildered, I didn't know where I was or how the hell I'd got there; even the money in my pocket was out of date. Robbie took control, got me thinking straight and eventually helped get me back home. Then I go and do this!'

'Maybe he'll think it was all a dream,' suggested Carol.

'Unlikely. Remember the other guys I told you about. Billy, and Jez, then there was his girlfriend Janice, not to mention Robbie's band. They're not all going to believe they had the same dream at the same time, are they?' Barry picked up his cup and saucer and took a thoughtful sip. 'There is another angle to this, something I can't get out of my head.'

'1983 is getting closer!' said Carol, immediately.

'Bang on, Shoogs, it's only thirteen years away now. Somewhere out there is a young Robbie Rochester, probably still at school, almost certainly playing the hits of the day 'Get Back' or 'In the Summertime' with some mates in his dad's garage and not half bad, if truth be known. Just the same as the Chekka label is going to suddenly appear, so is Robbie Rochester.' Then Barry's face turned glum. 'Problem is I remember him saying he was part of a covers band in the seventies and the name 'The Robbie Rochester Band' was a last minute decision in 1982, when they had their first hit, 'Warwickshire Girls'.'

'Are you thinking of making contact then?' asked Cherie.

'Well it is something I've thought about,' mused Barry. 'Not sure what I would say to him.'

'You'll be nearly fifty by then,' Carol reminded him. 'So what happens when a nineteen-year-old Barry turns up too?'

Barry hung his head again. 'I don't know, I've thought about that too. Sometimes I think my brain is going to burst, but the truth is I don't know how this time travel thing works; does it stop you bumping into yourself?'

Carol stood up. 'Talking of bursting brains, I need to go away and think about all this.'

Barry and Cherie walked Carol to her car. She opened the driver's door and they stood there for a moment, as Barry hugged her and kissed her on the cheek. 'I meant what I said yesterday on the way back from Norwich. We're staying clean, taking it a day at a time.' He put his arm around Cherie and squeezed her. 'No more booze, no more pills, no more funny fags for us.'

Carol caught her last glimpse of Barry through her wing mirror, as she slowly drove round the curve of silver birches.

***

'I'm only staying at Jimmy's party for a couple of hours,' said Barry. 'We got our penultimate gig at Derby tomorrow and I want to be in top condition.'

'What's penultimate?' quizzed Cherie.

'Means there's only one more,' sighed Barry. 'It's the last but one gig, then The Bombastics are no more.'

'You're going to miss it aren't you, Barry?'

'More than you can imagine, but as with everything there's a time to be born, a time to die, turn, turn, turn....'

'What?' Cherie looked through the dressing room mirror where she sat applying make-up.

'Oh nothing, just remembering an old tune.' Barry picked up his car keys.

***

It wasn't so much cold turkey as temptation. Jimmy's house was full, the music was loud and stimulants aplenty. It started as it often does, with just one small drink to be sociable and very soon it was Barry walking round with a whiskey bottle topping up his own glass as well as Cherie's.

Just before midnight, Cherie came back downstairs; Barry presumed she'd been up to the toilet. When she saw Barry she stopped and beckoned him. She turned back up the stairs and he followed. She stood at the top of the staircase with a short blonde girl that Barry recognised as Cherie's friend Maggie. Maggie, with her long hair swept back behind her bare shoulders, stood with her hand on one of the bedroom doorknobs.

'Maggie wants to know if we fancy a threesome,' smiled Cherie. 'The bedroom's free.'

Barry didn't need asking twice. Bottle and glass in hand he kissed Cherie deeply then moved quickly onto Maggie, pressing her back against the doorframe, almost swallowing her.

'Steady on, tiger,' laughed Cherie. 'Let's get inside before they start a queue.'

Maggie slipped her top and jeans off, revealing what looked like, even in the darkness of the room, the skimpiest bra and knickers. Barry levered off his shoes and trod his way out of his corduroy trousers in haste. By the time he'd pulled his shirt, still buttoned, over his head, Cherie was in bed alongside Maggie. He moved across the bed on all fours as they parted and lifted the sheets to let him in between.

'Here's a little something to make the experience even more enjoyable,' whispered Maggie hoarsely, holding her palm upwards. Both Cherie and Barry could just about see a cluster of pills in her hand. Without a word, they each took some and swallowed deeply. Neither would have known how many, and Maggie scooped the remainder into her mouth.

If there was one thing that Barry was good at, it was

removing bras in confined spaces; he was also very experienced at prolonged foreplay. He took turns with each of them and in between they took turns with each other. Over an hour later, the three of them were giggling and kissing as they sorted out their garments and got dressed by the light of the bedside lamp. The alcohol had helped and those little pills (Barry never did ask what they were), undoubtedly kept him stronger, longer.

Downstairs, the numbers had thinned out. The front room was billowing with clouds of marijuana, so Barry made his way through the diner and into the kitchen where the whiskey was still flowing.

'We shouldn't be having anymore, you naughty boy, we're teetottlers – teetollers – whatever,' stumbled Cherie, but she managed to hold her glass still. 'Go on then.'

'We start again tomorrow morning, prompt my girl,' barked Barry like some clockwork sergeant major. Then, both giggling he filled his own glass too.

It was just after three when they both poured themselves into Barry's car and he sped along the main Birmingham Road. It wasn't until he turned north onto the winding country lane that led to Toad Hall, that he realised his headlights weren't switched on.

He'd climbed the hill that led to the canal bridge many times in an assortment of cars, sometimes quite sober, but more often drunk. There had been a number of girls in those front passenger seats; it just happened tonight that it was his current squeeze, the unfortunate Cherie.

It was a clear night, especially now he had his lights on. It was dry and as usual very quiet, the same as it had been on dozens of previous nights. However, tonight there was to be one big difference. A frightened deer.

He accelerated and approached the canal bridge, passing the 'hump-back bridge' road sign at about forty miles an hour (far too fast, but with no headlights coming the other way not much of a gamble. He'd leap it just for the thrill, see if he could get all four wheels off the ground). Cherie was screaming with excitement and holding onto her seat and the dashboard for dear life, about thirteen years before seat belts became compulsory.

To the right a hawthorn bush spread onto the roadway just enough to partly obscure the brickwork of the bridge wall. From behind this bush darted a young Muntjac deer. Barry braked hard and instinctively tried to avoid it by pulling to the left. He skidded violently sideways, hit the deer full in the flanks, cartwheeling it into the air; his onside front wheel smashed against the end kerbstone which marked the entrance to a tiny pathway that walkers, bike-riders and fishermen used to get to the canal towpath. It was a well-worn kerbstone, but it protruded from the Tarmac high enough to flip Barry's car over and with a sickening crunch it hit the brickwork, windscreen first, smashing the two occupants into oblivion against the upper window frame and roof. The car bounced off the bridge, taking two layers of bricks with it, did another half twist and landed upside down on the far bank, its back end and wheels stuck up in the air, it's front end completely submerged under water. A hot cloud of steam hissed into the night sky.

The deer's badly maimed body lay half in the hedge and half on the tiny pathway; it twitched a couple of times, but was killed almost instantaneously with a broken back.

The car sizzled for a few minutes and gurgled escaping air for a few minutes more. Then there was silence.

This part of the canal always remained deserted in the early daylight hours. The first narrow boat wouldn't pass that way until seven or eight o'clock in the morning; it was more likely to be a walker exercising his dog and picking his way along the tow-path. And so it was to be.

As Don South approached from a distance, at first he couldn't make out what the strange black shapes were that he could pick out through the bridge on the far bank. *Large birds? – They weren't moving. Tree branches? – Not that black, surely.* Then as he got nearer... *They're car tyres – it's an upturned car – my God!* He ran under the bridge, not taking his eyes off the submerged wreck. Then his border collie, Bessie, started barking. He looked to his left; she'd found the dead Muntjac deer on the pathway and was barking and sniffing, circling around the corpse. He darted forward and grabbed her, clipping the hook of the lead into the ring on her collar.

Don South stood there for a moment taking in the scene, the dead deer, the broken brickwork and the upturned car. He stepped up the pathway, pulling the dog clear of the Muntjac's body and crossed the canal bridge by the roadway to see if he could get onto the far bank from the other side. There was no way he could get through a thick thorny hedge. *Anyway, what am I going to do if I do reach the car?*

Knowing the area very well, he was aware of a farmhouse, maybe three quarters of a mile down the road. They would have a telephone. He half ran and half walked, with Bessie running alongside, to call the emergency services.

By lunchtime the road was closed and police and ambulance waited by as frogmen broke into the car and recovered two bodies. Both had hideously smashed skulls and severely broken spines; had been underwater for some hours, and were pronounced dead at the scene and taken to the police morgue. Relatives of Barry Patrick Harper and Cheryl Daphne Sissons were notified.

***

The funerals took place seventeen days later. The reason for the delay was the post-mortem findings.

'Suspicious circumstances', the police called it. High levels of amphetamines and alcohol in both bodies led the police to question many people who were in contact with either of the deceased during those last hours. Most of the partygoers, particularly Jimmy and Maggie, had a difficult time, but not as difficult as Barry's mother and father and Cherie's widowed mother who had to identify their children; they were distraught.

Next week the papers were full of the predictable sex, drugs and rock 'n' roll stories, but by then with The Bombastics' star waning, they weren't even a seven-day wonder and it was confined to the inside pages. Unfortunately, Cherie's family – she had two brothers and a number of close cousins – believed the lurid accounts in the red tops and they warned anybody associated with The Bombastics to keep well clear of her funeral in a Redditch churchyard, the day before Barry's. Frank, Stan, Bodkin and Carol were worried they might turn up at Barry's and cause trouble, but they didn't.

Barry was buried at St. Bartholomew's and Fordrough was full of fans, both genuine and ghoulish, and of course the press. Danny never bothered to come over from the States, sending an enormous wreath and letting his son Ike, represent the Hoffmans. After prayers, committal and blessing, the family and close friends went back to Jack Richards' house. He felt it was the least he could do and it was far enough off the beaten track to discourage any unwanted guests. Frank and Bodkin, but Carol and Stan in particular, looked after Barry's parents throughout; it was very, very difficult.

The last gig was cancelled and that was the end of The Bombastics – or so they thought.

CHAPTER 26
'CAN I GET A WITNESS'

Marvin Gaye

'The Bombastics at Glastonbury!' exclaimed Bodkin. 'How on earth did you manage that?'

'I didn't do a thing,' admitted Frank. 'I was doing a cruise ship gig, on at Southampton and round into the Med. It was going quite well, you know, the usual nostalgia thing. It was my last night, I was due off at Malaga next morning to fly back home. So there I was having a drink at the bar when this guy approaches me, he had his wife with him and he said how much they'd enjoyed the show. I thanked him and just hoped he wasn't going to bang on about how he finally managed to get her knees apart listening to 'Teenage Crush' all those years ago.'

'Frank!' protested Sugarlips. 'That's terrible, you're

getting very cynical in your old age.'

'How wrong was I?' Frank continued. 'The next thing he says was that The Bombastics were his mother's favourite band – his bloody *mother* for God's sake!'

They all enjoyed that one!

'I looked at the pair of them again and yes, they were younger than I'd first thought, in their fifties I suppose, so it was very possible his mom threw her knickers at us. Anyway, he takes a business card out of his top pocket and gives it to me. Star Gazers Incorporated, it says across the top. Jerry Dean's his name and he introduces me to Millie, his wife. He then tells me his company helps organise Glastonbury and how they're putting together the line-up for next year's festival and he thinks the old Bombastics would knock 'em dead. The only problem he saw was that it was strictly live and me singing along to backing tapes was not an option. He said it would be great if I could get the original band together and create the old magic, and would I be interested?

'He assured me that modern Glastonbury wasn't all mud, wellies and revolting toilets, with hundreds climbing over the fences to get in for free. A lot of money had been spent improving facilities and tightening up security. Then he began preaching about all the millions Glastonbury donated to charity. His missus started giving me a list of old timers who had appeared there during the last few years. Tony Bennett, Neil Diamond, B. B. King, Kenny Rogers, Shirley Bassey; they'd even had Bruce Forsyth there.'

'What was she trying to say?' laughed Stan.

'That's what I said,' continued Frank. 'She said how well the Rolling Stones had gone down and the rock 'n' roll wrinkly market was alive and well and us lot would be the perfect fit. Well I didn't know whether to be flattered or flattened, but I wasn't going to miss a chance like that, was I? The chance to play in front of over 175,000 people, plus millions watching on telly doesn't come along too often, does it? So I thought, sod the truth, and told him I was still in regular touch with all you guys and that I'm sure we'd all love to play Glastonbury.'

Nobody spoke.

'Hey, c'mon guys, you would, wouldn't you?' Frank started to sound unsure. 'The guy's phoning me next week for an answer when he's spoken to the rest of his team. You're not going to turn it down, are you?'

'No, Frank, not at all,' said Sugarlips. 'It's just a bit of a shock, I think it's stunned all of us, I mean, can we still do it?'

'She's right Frankie boy,' agreed Stan. 'It's over forty years since we played together. I'm up for it, but we're going to have to put some practice in.'

'That shouldn't be a problem, we've got plenty of time for that,' said Bodkin. 'Not having Barry's guitar and vocals is more of a problem. Did you give that any thought?'

'I did,' replied Frank. 'We're gonna have to get someone to stand in. What about the guy I replaced, Martin Wassisname, he was a Bombastic, what's he doing?'

Stan shook his head. 'Martin Spilsbury – poor old Martin's in a care home in Redditch; he's seventy-eight now and probably couldn't tell his slippers from his blue suede shoes.'

'Frank, what about JoJo?' Sugarlips asked hesitantly. 'We always said we'd bring him over to guest with us and well, he was rather special to you, wasn't he? But time slipped by, as it does and then The Bombastics were no more.'

Frank sat back in his chair.

'I have some bad news. I tried to make contact with

JoJo.' He spoke slowly and quietly. 'It was a long shot, but I phoned Chess in Chicago; they're now owned by Universal. I had no problem getting through to someone who remembered JoJo. I spoke to a guy name of Leo Marshall who used to do session work with him. I'm very sorry to tell you JoJo was drafted to Vietnam in 1967 and was killed on the Mekong Delta in 1968.'

'Oh God, that's terrible!' Carol reached out and squeezed Frank's hand. 'What a shocking waste, I am so sorry, Frank.'

'I know I got emotionally involved, but it was that guitar picking of his that I remember so well. Just unbelievable; no wonder my head was turned.'

'It was only three years after he was with us,' said Stan. 'The poor kid.'

'Truly, truly awful, but it's a long time ago and we need to move on,' said Frank. 'I've got a couple of guys in mind, but before I speak to them I just needed to know you lot were up for it.'

They all nodded, but the room had become sombre.

'Ladies and gentlemen, this is a special moment, I think it calls for a celebration drink.' Gloria got up from the table and made her way to the bar, determined to lift the mood. 'Same again everybody?'

Nobody said no.

'There's only one place we can practice, Frankie boy,' said Stan. 'The Fordrough village hall.'

'Couldn't be anywhere else, could it?' said Bodkin.

'Right on,' nodded Frank. 'We're going to need a few gigs too, blow away any cobwebs, get you lot used to a live audience again. You can leave that to me.'

Gloria, with the help of Matt, brought the fresh drinks over.

'Here's to The Bombastics and Glastonbury.' Stan raised his glass.

'And a very belated toast to JoJo, an old and very talented friend,' added Frank. 'Cheers, JoJo.'

'Cheers JoJo.' They all joined in.

'It would be nice if you could do your first gig somewhere local,' said Gloria. 'What about using the village hall? Okay, it's only small, but it could be invited guests only. They could have their pre-concert drinks here, we could even provide a buffet and bring over pre-ordered drinks for all your guests.'

'I can see why old Dennis lets you run the place, you don't miss a trick,' laughed Stan. 'We'll work on that. Now, what about arrangements for tomorrow morning before we get too pissed?'

***

Bodkin picked up the other three. They'd agreed it was appropriate to drive over together in Jezza and by ten o'clock, Bodkin, Stan and Sugarlips pulled up outside Frank's bungalow in leafy Balsall Common.

Stan slid open the side door and took Frank's guitar case off him.

'Thought I'd bring this along,' said Frank, as he pulled himself into the camper. 'It might just come in handy.'

'Don't think you'll get Robbie Rochester jamming,' said Bodkin. 'When I drove over and spoke with him, he said he hadn't touched a guitar in a long time. He looked really hacked off about that, I think there's still a lot of bitterness there.'

'This should make a difference.' Sugarlips half pulled the Walkman out of her bag.

'It'll certainly help change things,' said Bodkin. 'But he'll have had recordings like that in court, it's you Shoogs that's important. Ms Carol Meadowsweet, a.k.a. Sugarlips, witness for the defence. Yes, you are the only one Barry told his story to. If Robbie wants to lodge an appeal against a verdict given over thirty years ago, it seems to me it'll be a case of whether they believe that Barry actually told you. I mean it is the stuff of science fiction, isn't it?'

'There are the lyrics on that calendar too,' said Carol. 'Surely we can match the handwriting to prove Barry wrote it. Maybe it can be carbon dated, or whatever they call it; and, for the record, he told Cherie too.'

'Sorry, Shoogs, I forgot,' said Bodkin. 'Sadly she can't help.'

Stan quickly changed the subject. 'That's the radio at the centre of all this, right?' He pointed underneath the dashboard between Carol and Bodkin.

'Yes, according to the guys that work for Robbie,' answered Bodkin. 'They were adamant that it's the original.'

By this time they were well up the A41 and on their way to Stechford; they arrived at Rochester Classics just before eleven o'clock.

***

'We'll have our chat down here, there's more room,' said Robbie, after he'd been introduced to Frank, Stan and Sugarlips, and he, in turn had introduced Jez and Billy. 'I want my guys to hear what's being said, but at the same time we need to keep an eye on the shop.'

Over on the far corner wall hung a coffee machine, next to which stood a Formica-topped table and two wooden benches. Three chairs had been brought down from upstairs – Bodkin remembered the green upholstery from his previous visit. They were impressed with how neat and tidy everything was; after all this was a workshop with oil and grease, spray paint too, but there was not a smudged fingerprint to be seen. They also noticed Jez and Billy wore clean and pressed overalls with a Rochester Classics logo on the bib – all were freshly laundered. Robbie was wearing collar and tie and a stylish maroon jacket. He was taking things very seriously; clearly this meeting was important to him.

'Do you want to risk a coffee out of our temperamental machine?' said Robbie. 'Or shall I get Billy to nip upstairs and make a pot of tea?'

'Coffee everybody?' Bodkin looked at the other three.

It was thumbs up all round and Billy took charge of the gurgling, hissing machine; also organising milk and sugar.

'Well, where do we start?' said Stan.

'I'll tell you where we start,' burst forth Jez. 'We start with that little time travelling shit, Barry – and I suppose you lot are going to tell me you didn't know what he was up to either?' His eyes blazed.

'Calm down, Jez.' Robbie put a hand on Jez's forearm as if to hold him back. 'You'll have a stroke.'

Jez was still animated. 'But they destroyed everything, they were your bleedin' songs and...'

'We lost that battle over thirty years ago,' said Robbie. 'I get the feeling these guys aren't directly to blame, but after Bodkin and I arranged this meeting, I decided I wanted them to hear our side of events.' He paused and looked at each of them. 'It's an incredible story, so incredible that nobody believed us, they laughed me out of court, down Corporation Street, right across the Bull Ring and all the way back to Solihull, with the media mocking me all the way. Headlines like Time Bandit, Looney Tunes... but hold on, you'll remember all that, you're The Bombastics, it was your songs they said I'd filched.'

'There's something you need to...' Frank began.

Robbie raised a hand to stop Frank. 'Let me have my say, I've waited a long time for this.' He carried on. 'Barry arrived out of nowhere. Billy and Jez thought he was trying to steal our gear, but it soon became obvious that something was seriously out of kilter. The way he was dressed, his driving licence, things he said. He was part of a band and yet he'd never heard of the Jam, punks, nor New Romantics. Big Macs, Maggie Thatcher, parking meters and Gold Leaf cigarettes – they were clearly new to him. When I told Billy and Jez that I thought his story about being from the past might just be true, they thought I was nuts, but in the week he was with us, they started to believe him too.'

'I did,' agreed Jez. Billy, perched on the end of a bench next to Stan, gave a cursory nod.

'During that week, he came to rehearsals, to a couple of gigs, and to our recording session at Chekka. It was at one of these, we gave Barry the Walkman with my new songs on it.'

'That was at the rehearsal at Pandora's,' interrupted Jez. 'He'd never seen a Walkman before, he was like a fourteen-year-old kid after his first wet dream. He couldn't leave it alone.'

'Er, thank you Jez,' said Robbie, looking around and focussing on Sugarlips. 'I do apologise, but believe me, knowing Jez it could have been much worse. Anyway, we thought the best way to try and get him back home was to replicate events that had brought him to us. The lay-by in which he'd taken refuge, midnight the next Thursday, whilst we were still in Aquarius and that radio frequency, Hilversum, that's something I'll always remember.'

'It's on the radio you've still got in the VW outside,' said Billy. 'It's the same radio, we never changed it, just in case we were able to get through to the nineteen forties and strangle the little bastard at birth.'

'And don't think we didn't try.' Robbie's eyes narrowed. 'I can tell you, after the court case we spent a few nights in that Drovers Lane lay-by, waiting for it to snow and scanning the frequencies, but nothing ever happened.'

'The damages I had to pay to that Hoffman character, crucified me. The costs were astronomical too, because I'd tried to fight it. If I'd admitted to plagiarism, and not mentioned Barry's time warp, it would have been over in a couple of days at a fraction of the cost and my career wouldn't have been carted off to the funny farm.'

'What hurts is Barry doing what he did, after all the support we gave him. We took him in, fed him, even clothed him, we straightened his confused head out and helped him find his way back. I thought the trust we gave him was mutual, but it wasn't and as a result I lost nearly everything, my recording career was shattered beyond repair and because of constant hounding of the press boys, I nearly lost Janice, my fiancée.'

'It was a black time indeed, but it was no good wallowing in self-pity so I decided I needed to rebuild my life and three things helped with that process. My fascination and knowledge of vintage cars, my older brother Johnny, who has a very successful import and export company and was able to fund my embryonic customised car enterprise, and these two characters. Like me, they've learned as they've gone along, but I can never repay their loyalty and the successful business you see around you is down to them.' Robbie spread his arms wide.

'I need to speak, Robbie?' Sugarlips spoke as though she was half expecting to be stopped. 'I think there is something here you should see.'

She balanced her large blue handbag on her lap, propped it against the table edge and unclipped the clasp. She pulled out the Walkman and carefully laid it on the table. After untangling the earphone wire, she turned the machine onto its back and squeezed the 'Play' button.

'I can't believe it's come to this, surely it's not true,
You packed your things and moved away, just how will I get through?
The life together that we planned, has now come to an end,
The hurt begins to know you're in the arms of my best friend.

I'm just a broken hearted nobody, a fool too blind to see,
The truth was there for everyone, everyone but me.

Broken hearted nobody, broken hearted nobody,
The truth was there for everyone, everyone but me.

Your cheatin' heart...'

Robbie leant across the table and shut the Walkman off. 'There's nothing new there, we had all that stuff at court thirty years ago. They just said we'd taped that after we'd changed the words.'

'Is that the actual one Barry stole?' asked Billy.

'Yes it is,' said Frank. 'However, before you write it off as unimportant, I think you need to listen to what Sugarlips is going to say.' He half-turned to face Carol.

She coughed gently and pushed the Walkman a few inches towards the centre of the table, 'Barry gave me that three days before he died. He was a bit drunk and very high after pushing pills during the concert we'd just done. He told me the whole story, he was quite emotional, in tears at one point. He'd had this bottled up inside him for nearly seven years, afraid no one would believe him and also ashamed of what he'd done with your music and the consequences it might have.

'I didn't believe him to begin with, it all seemed so far-fetched. He gave me the Walkman, told me to listen to it again and that he'd see me in a day or so. I never saw him again, three days later he was dead.'

'Why do you suddenly believe his story now?' asked Robbie. It wasn't the cool, calm Robbie of a few minutes ago, he sounded agitated.

'There was nothing sudden about it, Robbie, I believed his story then. Oh, I thought about it from every angle, but the one thing I hadn't got an answer for was the Walkman. This was 1970 and Walkmans weren't around for another nine or ten years – even more if you accept Barry brought it back to 1963. It was a no brainier, as they say these days. There was also this.' She handed Robbie the A4 calendar page; July 1965 on one side and Barry's hand-written lyrics on the reverse. He flattened it out on the Formica and studied it.

'The other thing we now understand is how he came by all the money he won betting on the 1966 World Cup. Look, here are a few of his unclaimed betting slips.' Carol placed them next to the lyrics, in front of Robbie. 'He obviously remembered all those results from your time. No wonder he cleaned some of the bookies.'

'The bastard,' cursed Jez.

Robbie put both elbows on the table, head in hands. 'Sugarlips, can I ask you why you never came forward at the time? You would have turned the case upside down.' He peered at her through his fingers.

'I was living in the States when it came to court. There was no coverage of the case over there at the time, certainly none that I picked up,' she whispered rather self-consciously. 'It was a couple of years before I got back to the UK and heard what had happened. By then it was only about Danny Hoffman successfully suing a band who were claiming to have written songs owned by his publishing company. By that time the stories about time travel had been largely forgotten, or dismissed as the ramblings of a crank. Forgive me.' She made eye contact with Robbie. 'I know I should have come forward, but I didn't want any sort of contact with Hoffman, and to be honest, there were quite a few dramas going on in Carol Meadowsweet's life at that time. I'm really sorry.'

'That's it, let's go fuck Hoffman.' Jez thumped the table. 'Get every shekel back that bastard took, he won't be able to show his face in the synagogue again.'

'Don't be a prat,' interrupted Billy. 'The last time Hoffman went to the synagogue, he was in a walnut casket.' He turned to Robbie. 'Wouldn't his estate have to cough up, Robbie?'

Robbie was deep in thought. He got up from the table and slowly wandered around the workshop, hands in pockets, weaving his way between a Fiat 500, a Wolesley Hornet and an Austin Allegro, its windows masked and taped ready for a re-spray. He was on automatic pilot.

Six pairs of eyes followed him. 'It must be a lot for him to take in,' said Bodkin. 'It was all a long time ago; with the help of you two guys he's built a new life, then out of the blue...'

'Flash! Bam! Alekazam! Out of an orange coloured sky,' sang Stan.

'WHAT?' squawked Billy.

'Nothing, sorry, just a daft old song that came into my head.' Slightly embarrassed, Stan stood up. 'Anyone up for another coffee out of Hissing Sid?'

'Better leave those to me,' said Billy, then reaching into the cupboard below Hissing Sid, pulled out a bottle of Bell's whiskey. 'After what I've heard today, I'm gonna liven mine up a little. Anybody care to join me?'

Only Bodkin declined and of course, Robbie, who had

other things on his mind. Bodkin noticed the bottle was only about a third full when Billy stood it back on the cupboard shelf. He wasn't exactly sure how much was in it to begin with, but he guessed the measures had been generous.

Robbie had disappeared outside the Rochester Classic's unit and wandered around the forecourt. He strayed over into next door's car park, talking and gesticulating to himself and probably wouldn't have remembered the bright orange CitiExpress Parcel's van that skidded to a halt just a few yards away from Robbie after driving in far too fast, from the feeder road that curved around the estate. The driver neither blasted his horn nor shouted abuse (an accomplishment perfected by most CitiExpress drivers it seemed), because most of the delivery boys knew, and liked next-door Robbie.

After the best part of half an hour, Robbie came back to the table. In the meantime Hissing Sid had given forth another round of coffees, but this time Sugarlips had joined Bodkin in declining the mixer.

They waited whilst Robbie took his seat. 'I cannot decide whether I want to go through all that court rigmarole again. Okay, it'll be different this time. Hoffman's dead and no doubt the judge and most of the silks will be pushing up the daisies...'

'...And those bleedin' paper artists too!' added Jez.

'Yes, thank you Jez, the paparazzi too,' continued Robbie. 'Particularly that evil old hack from the *Daily Enquirer*. What was his name? Gerald Hackett, but remember a lot of the old Bombastic fans too, will be twistin' the night away with St. Peter and those that aren't probably won't remember Rochester v Hoffman Melodies.

'What if they don't believe Sugarlips and I get humiliated in court again, after all the work we've put in to build this business, this new life? Remember, without the witness statement from Sugarlips and Barry's lyrics, the case falls apart. Carol, are you ready for the shit they're going to try and unearth to discredit your story and are you going to stand by it, no matter what?'

'I am,' Carol whispered gently.

'Robbie, it has to be worth it, they'll have to compensate you for loss of earnings,' said Stan. 'We took that record to number one in a dozen or more countries around the world. You'd have surely done the same. It was only moderate for us in the States, but you might have broken big. Imagine the royalties after being number one on Billboard for six weeks. Then there are the album sales worldwide, not to mention your follow up singles.'

'Yeah right, and don't forget my knighthood for services to Britain's export sales! I think you might be getting a little ahead of yourself.' Robbie gave Stan a wan smile. 'However, you raise a moot point. There's an enormous amount of work that'll have to go into any appeal, the amount of time and therefore money that'll be spent going over statements made thirty years ago, not to mention the new evidence. Is it really all worth it?

'We've got a super little business here, me and the guys. We enjoy what we do, it's a labour of love. We don't owe a penny to anyone, Billy and Jez earn good money, well I haven't heard them complain, anyway. Me and Janice, we have two great kids, Ava has just got a teaching job at a private school in Coventry and young Ben is in his first year at Bristol University reading engineering and economics and we're hoping he'll take over this business in a year or so. We live in a detached four bedroom des res in rural Warwickshire, take two holidays a year with a big daft Labrador named Archie, and have our groceries delivered by Tesco. Why should I want to face all that disruption and possible ridicule again?'

'Do you still play a bit, Robbie?' asked Frank, out of the blue.

'Very little Frank, only for my own pleasure,' answered Robbie, taken aback by the sudden change of subject. 'I did a spot at Janice's mom and dad's Golden Wedding, but that must have been a few years ago.'

'The Bombastics have been invited to play at next year's Glastonbury. The four of us are up for it, but with Barry no longer available, we need a fifth Bombastic who can sing and play a little and I guess it would certainly help if he wrote half the bloody songs we're gonna play.'

There were just a few seconds whilst the penny dropped before the place erupted.

'What a fucking brilliant idea!' screamed Stan shaking clenched fists above his head like the scorer of a cup-winning goal.

Bodkin was on his feet shouting, 'Yeeeehaaah!' and pounding out a rhythm on the table top. Billy and Jez were doing a curious cross between the twist and the dashing white sergeant and Sugarlips was wrapped around Frank, giving him one colossal hug.'

Only Robbie remained seated, his elbows stretched out supporting him, whilst he watched the antics in front of him. Was he going a bit misty eyed?

After a minute or so things calmed a little, and Robbie smiled. 'I'd really love to, but like I said, it's been a long time and I don't want to spoil a special reunion.'

'You won't,' replied Frank. 'We have nearly nine months to rehearse and we've already decided we'll do a few special gigs, to make sure we get it right, because remember we're very rusty too. I tell you what, I've got my guitar in the VW, do you fancy trying something? You can have a plonk if you want to.'

'No need, I've got my Hofner upstairs in the office.' Robbie got to his feet. 'You show me yours and I'll show you mine.'

Frank and Robbie sat on chairs facing each other and after a bit of tuning, Frank said. 'Only one number we can do really, isn't there?'

'Yes, but which version, 'Broken Hearted Nobody', or 'Shattered Dreams and Promises'?' said Robbie.

'Let's try your version, 'Broken Hearted Nobody',' replied Frank. 'If I get a bit tangled up with the lyrics, just plough on, I'll get there. In G?'

Robbie nodded, shaped a G with the fingers of his left hand, and began.

'I can't believe it's come to this, surely it's not true,

You packed your things and moved away, just how will I get through?'

Frank followed and instinctively took the harmonies (Barry's bits) on the hook lines. Bodkin gently rapped out the rhythm with his fingers on Formica. Apart from a few understandable mistakes with the lyrics, it sounded wonderful.

There were ripples of applause from around the table

'That was brilliant boys,' said Stan.

'Yeah, fantastic,' echoed Billy and Jez.

Carol didn't say a word. She'd taken a tissue out of her hand bag and was dabbing her eyes, trying not to smudge her mascara.

The applause continued from the other side of the Austin Allegro. They all turned to see a middle-aged couple beaming across at them.

'That was beautiful, Mr Rochester,' said the lady. 'We came to check and see how our Wolesley was coming along and never expected to be serenaded.'

CHAPTER 27
'ON THE ROAD AGAIN'

Canned Heat

It was mid-afternoon, and raining, as the VW made its way back through Solihull.

'When did you come up with that idea, Frank?' Bodkin was looking at Frank through the rear view mirror. 'Inviting Robbie to be part of The Bombastics was a master stroke.'

'I just knew it was right,' answered Frank. 'After hearing the tape a couple of times, I was impressed. It's a bit of a gamble, I know. Those recordings were over thirty years old, they were also single track and one-take. Well, now you've heard him live, the guy can sing and play, right?'

'Right,' said Bodkin.

'He says he's rusty, but if that's rusty, he's gonna polish up pretty good,' added Sugarlips. 'You just have to sort out between you who sings lead.'

'Easy,' said Frank. 'He takes the ones he wrote and I take the ones I wrote. Any others we play paper, scissors, rock.'

'This isn't going to be without its challenges,' said Stan. 'I don't mean musically. Given a bit of practice, I think we have enough experience between us to come up with a damned good set. No, I mean with the media. Robbie doesn't want to get embroiled with the plagiarism thing again, but it's inevitable he will be, we *all* will, won't we? They'll soon find out that Robbie Rochester was taken to the cleaners by The Bombastics' former manager and now here he is, fronting the band with Frank. There'll be a media frenzy.'

'I'd thought of that,' said Frank. 'And I'm pretty sure Robbie will have too. We're just going to be ready for it; anyway, look on the bright side, it'll certainly get us exposure.'

'I just hope we can handle it,' said Sugarlips.

***

The first rehearsal was at Fordrough village hall, as first suggested. It was without Sugarlips, she had commitments in London both with her family and her jazz engagements, but none of them were too worried about that, in the weeks ahead her diary would get clearer. She was, the others would agree, the most accomplished musician amongst them and was able to reproduce her signature solos perfectly every time, as well as adding her magic to anything new without any difficulty.

They also planned to travel down to her neck of the woods, where the owner of a jazz club at which Sugarlips played regularly, promised they could use the place to practice during the day.

That happened just before Christmas – and so began a chain of events.

***

After three Fordrough village hall rehearsals, it was coming together far quicker than they had dared hope. Robbie was a good musician and his singing was quite superb. Okay, like Frank, with age his voice had dropped very slightly, but it was no problem to change the key, particularly on 'Bar Room Brawl', which even in 1983 had reached the top end of his range.

Bodkin took to his drum kit like he'd never been away, and in a way he hadn't, with the evening class tutorials at the college he was still doing. Stan soon picked up his bass lines, but his problem was more his body than his soul. He was going to the gym every day to try and lose some of his beer belly, so he could roll back the years and let his Fender hang low. His body wasn't too sure about this new fitness regime and what with his aching bones and his painful feet, from standing too long, he spent most of the rehearsals sitting down.

They were so pleased with their progress they decided to give it a go with a low profile concert. They took up Gloria's suggestion and set up an early December concert at Fordrough village hall. The place only held eighty, so it had to be by invitation only and that meant mainly family, friends and selected locals. They had to decide whether to charge for tickets or do it for free. The idea being if they charged, they'd give any profit to charity. In the end they chose to do it free.

'There's not much of an overhead anyway. What'll it be, sixty quid for the village hall?' said Frank. 'If Billy and Jez do the mixing and the lighting, what will they want for that?'

'Don't worry about that,' said Robbie. 'I'll give them a Christmas bonus; anyway they'll see it as doing their bit, and Jez is a whizz on sound.'

Making sure the right people got the tickets wasn't easy. By the time family and friends had taken a share, there were less than fifty left. When word got out in the Crown and Anchor, Gloria was under pressure, but fortunately for her Mavis and Marion Meredith (aka The Dither Sisters) were at hand. They had a pretty good idea of the genuine fans still alive and kicking and living in Fordrough. They'd organised The Bombastics fan club during the band's heyday. Most former 'Bombettes', as the girl fans became known, remembered that address fifty years later: Bombastically Yours, 1 Rose Cottages, Fordrough, Worcestershire.

For 7/6d and a stamped addressed envelope, you got membership, a signed photo of the fantastic five, a monthly update on Bombastic gossip, and news on forthcoming gigs and appearances.

They told Stan, who been pestering Gloria as to who should have tickets and who shouldn't, to sling his hook and concentrate on his guitar, his belly and his bad feet.

Come the night, Gloria had arranged special concert drinks before and after (or cocktails and entrails as Stan later called them onstage), so the Crown and Anchor was packed. The Bombastics had done a sound check that afternoon with Jez working the deck and getting the balances just right, no mean feat in such a confined space. Billy had fixed up some lighting and with the house lights down, everybody agreed it looked pretty good.

There was a bit of clapping and whooping as the house lights went down, Jez dimmed his house music, Billy struck his stage lights and The Bombastics trooped onstage. Frank turned and counted Bodkin and Stan in.

'One, two, three, four.' And off they went into Chuck

Berry's 'Rock and Roll Music'.

It couldn't have been better and the clapping and cheering as they finished, reached a whole new level.

'Thank you – Thank you – Thank you,' smiled Frank, holding his arms aloft waiting for the applause to die down. 'Thank you, you're very kind. I know you were expecting people a lot older, but yes, we are The Bombastics.' There was another short burst of laughing and cheering.

'How time flies. It only seems like yesterday you girls out there were screaming and jumping up onstage. Well, if you want to scream tonight, just let rip, and if you want to jump up on the stage come down to the front and we'll get someone to give you a hand up.'

Cue more cheers and laughter. Then Frank counted in 'Love You Honey', their second hit. It was after the fourth number that Frank introduced the band. 'Ladies first, it's our sexy, sassy saxophonist… Sugarlips!' Carol took a bow to rapturous applause.

'On bass and wearing tartan slippers because of his bad feet.' Frank raised an arm towards Stan. 'Stanley, your mother warned you about wearing those winkle pickers when you were a child of the sixties.' This time there was more laughing than cheering, from Stan's drinking chums.

'And on drums. He's big, he's bad, and he's bald – it's Bodkin!' Bodkin stood up and gave a nod for the applause.

'Finally, on guitar and helping me with the vocals, someone new to The Bombastics. Ladies and gentlemen, can I ask you to give a large Fordrough welcome to Robbie Rochester!' There was enthusiastic clapping, but it quietened in anticipation as Robbie moved his mic stand forward.'

'Thank you Frankie,' he said, turning to acknowledge Frank. 'Here's a number that I know means a lot to you. It also means a lot to me.' With that Frank counted in 'Night Club Fight' and Robbie just prayed to himself that he remembered the 'new' lyrics.

He did, and the audience went wild.

They'd long since decided there would be no mention of song writing disputes or court cases. It was unlikely anybody would know Robbie and people would assume he was just a replacement for Barry. If anybody did recognise him or ask any awkward questions, they'd just have to cross that bridge as and when.

So the concert continued; first Frank taking lead, then Robbie taking lead, and some quite well-constructed harmonies they'd worked hard on. When the inevitable encores came, they'd saved the show-stoppers for last. First they did 'Jive Away the Tears' featuring Sugarlips' raunchy solo, then they finished with a superb bit of harmony on 'Shattered Dreams and Promises' for which Robbie had learned Barry's words.

Afterwards, back in the Crown and Anchor, Sugarlips and the boys were treated like the pop stars they'd once been. Out came the cameras and mobile phones for what seemed like an endless demand for selfie opportunities. All together as a band, each of them individually, perhaps with an arm around somebody's mother or sister and definitely with some father's arm around Sugarlips. They were all given far too many drinks, but Gloria had seen that coming and planned ahead. Her four bed and breakfast rooms were allocated to Frank, Carol and Dessie, Robbie and Janice with Billy and Jez sharing. Stan staggered home with Elsie, supported by Bodkin and Julie. He slept with Bertie whilst Elsie slept in the spare room. Bodkin and Julie shared the guest room.

Next came the promised practice session at the Blue Onion Club, just off Soho. It was primarily a jazz and blues club, and Sugarlips was well known and well-loved there as a guest performer with the resident band, the Larry Powell Quartet. It was she who asked the owner, Jess Reynolds, to let them have an afternoon to rehearse when the club was closed.

The club didn't open its doors until 9 p.m., so it was a bit of a surprise when Jess turned up mid-afternoon, to 'look out some paperwork'. Jess and a fabulous raven-haired, olive-skinned beauty named Alana, who Carol told the boys was his personal secretary (Stan said he thought if she was a touch typist she definitely looked more dirty than qwerty), spent some time upstairs in the office. The Bombastics were loud, no question, and Jess would have heard them going through their set, polishing each number up. It was certainly this that brought them back down to sit at one of the tables facing the stage. Jess sat with his hands in his lap tapping his right foot along to the beat. Alana was a little more demonstrative, her long legs crossed and disappearing into the tiniest black dress, clapping away and singing along with bits that she knew.

Jess waited for them to take five, and called Sugarlips over. He was sharing a bottle of sparkling water with Alana and as Sugarlips pulled up a chair he placed a large stemmed glass in front of her.

'Water?' He held the blue tear-shaped bottle above the empty glass.

'Yes please, Jess.' When he'd finished pouring, she picked up the glass and took a deep guzzle. 'That was thirsty work.' She smiled and nodded hello to Alana, who she knew.

'It was really good Carol,' smiled Jess, a striking black guy, who from the grey curls starting to appear around his temples, Carol would have guessed was in his early forties, but knew he was ten years older than that. 'I've got a proposition for you that could do both The Blue Onion and The Bombastics a bit of good. You know I like to bring the best to The Onion and as long as it's good, my customers don't give a tinker's cuss whether it's jazz, blues, soul or rock.' He opened the desk diary he had brought down from his office. 'You're due to guest here with Larry Powell next Friday, right?'

'That's right,' agreed Sugarlips.

'Well how'd you like to bring the whole band in and do an hour, playing the sort of stuff we've just been listening to?'

'Wow! I think that would be a great idea; just hang on a mo, Jess, let's ask Frank.' Sugarlips stood up and shouted across to the stage. 'Frank, can you give us a minute?'

Frank came over to the table, Carol introduced him to Jess and Alana and he shook hands with them both.

'Jess wants us to do an hour guest spot next Friday,' explained Sugarlips. 'What do you reckon, can we do it?'

'What? The Bombastics brand of rock 'n' roll at the Blue Onion jazz club?' Frank was clearly taken aback. 'How would it go down with your modern jazz aficionados?'

'Just fine,' said Jess. 'You'll go down just fine. The Christmas crowd'll be in and you'll have the place jumping. I know it. How about two grand cash in hand, does that convince you?'

'It sure does,' smiled Frank and leant forward to shake Jess's hand. 'Let me tell the others, we don't want Stan booking a passionate night of bingo with Elsie.'

***

Jess was right, it did go down very well with the Blue Onion regulars, and with the not-so-regulars too. In the days building up to the gig, word got out around other pubs and clubs in Soho that The Bombastics were doing a guest spot at The Blue Onion. By Monday night all tables at the club were reserved, and that included the eight tables on the first floor balcony that circled the room. It was very rare that all of these were taken. Alana was now having to turn down bookings, which made Jess realise he may have people just turning up on the night expecting to get in; normally not a problem. He had a couple of 'Full House' posters put on the street windows and booked a couple of extra bouncers he'd used in the past, just in case anyone got over enthusiastic.

The club was full of Christmas revellers and they really got with it, pushing tables back as far as possible to extend the tiny dance floor, which was packed. Couples were jiving in the aisles and up on the balcony too. By the time the crowd let The Bombastics finish their hour set, it had lasted an extra forty minutes. No complaints from The Bombastics, there was no doubt that Sugarlips and the boys were really enjoying themselves, it was party time.

They did all their Bombastic hits and mixed in a fair few of their rock 'n' roll classics, Frank was even able to go through his repertoire of well-rehearsed jokes and ad libs, including the saga of Stan's tartan slippers (which he wore especially).

Jess had reserved them places at his table for afterwards, so they were all quite relaxed enjoying a drink, chatting with Blue Onion clientele and listening to The Larry Powell Quartet, who seemed so smooth and cool after the throbbing back beat of The Bombastics. Just after midnight, a chubby, balding guy, his forehead beaded with sweat, tapped Robbie on the shoulder.

'Say, I really enjoyed that, haven't danced like that in years – phew!' He patted his ample waistline. 'Yer man introduced you as Robbie Rochester, is that right?'

'That's right,' said Robbie, noticing Chubby's dark blue suit was even darker underneath his armpits and his comb-over stuck up in places like damp couch grass.

Chubby stuck out a chubby hand and introduced himself. 'Roger Devereux,' he said. 'We've met before, but it's a long time ago.'

'Oh, really. You have the advantage over me.' Robbie shook his hand. He remembered Roger and his party sitting at a table next to the dance floor, in fact his was one of the tables that was slid back for dancing space, but as for meeting him previously, he was at a loss.

'I was a cub reporter working with Gerald Hackett for the *Daily Enquirer*,' he grinned; a grin Robbie immediately knew was a problem. 'We covered your plagiarism dispute with Hoffman. Wasn't that one of the disputed songs you finished your session with?' He grinned again.

'It was a long time ago.' Robbie tried to treat the subject with nonchalance. 'A lot of water's gone under that bridge.'

'Haven't any of your little green men brought you any more songs lately?' The grin was more of a sneer now. 'I work for the *Weekly Sketch* these days and we'd be very interested in anything you'd like to say.'

'There's nothing to say, we've all moved on and I'm just enjoying my time playing with Frankie and the gang.' The nonchalance was proving hard to keep up. 'Nobody would be interested in yesterday's news.'

'On the contrary, Robbie.' Devereux's face was now expressionless, as he reached into the top breast pocket of his suit and pulled out a business card between two fingers and slipped it into the top pocket of Robbie's black Lurex shirt. 'The *Sketch* readers would be very interested in an update of your story.'

'There is no story,' frowned Robbie, thrusting out his hand. 'So I'll bid you goodnight, Mr Devereux.'

Devereux gripped his hand and held on. 'No story? Bombastics sue the pants off Rochester. Rochester joins

Bombastics. Glastonbury gig for Bombastics.' Devereux's sneer was back. 'I'll contact you through Rochester Classics, now I'll let you get back to your friends, goodnight.'

He let go of Robbie's hand and moved away.

Robbie stood in shock for a minute. *How did he know about Glastonbury and how did he find out about Rochester Classics? Internet? Oh well, he'll get nothing out of me, but I need a word with the others, this could get difficult.*

Just then a tall lady with big dangly earrings and matching tits, pressed a Blue Onion drinks menu into his hand to autograph and the moment was gone.

***

They'd arranged to kip down at Carol's that night; she lived a ten-minute taxi ride away.

'Two of you can take the spare room and the others can sleep downstairs in the arm chairs and on the settee,' she'd said. 'Two house rules. One, I sleep alone and two, don't expect breakfast in the morning, there's a greasy spoon in the high street just around the corner.'

***

Next morning they sat around a table at the Copper Kettle. It wasn't at all the greasy spoon that Sugarlips had described. Each table wore a green gingham tablecloth, had shiny chrome salt and pepper pots and sugar shaker with six sets of cutlery wrapped in green paper napkins standing in a matching chrome container. They sparkled under the strip lighting. The café was quite busy, but they found a table which the owner cleared for them and then came back for their orders.

The boys (Sugarlips stayed home) all drank either tea or coffee out of green china mugs and all had ham and cheese toasties except Stan, whose Glastonbury diet meant he chose porridge, which he ate with half a spoonful of brown sugar and a grimace.

'Anybody else speak with this chap last night?' said Robbie placing Devereux's business card on the table. Bodkin picked it up and passed it around.

One by one they looked at it and shook their heads or grunted, 'No.'

'He approached me after the set last night,' said Robbie. 'He's on to me, reckons he covered the plagiarism story and was at court throughout. Not only that, he knows about Glastonbury and he knows about Rochester Classics. I didn't like his tone, he was friendly at first, but he became very threatening.'

'Did he say what he was likely to do?' asked Billy, looking at the details on the card. 'I mean should me and Jez pop round to Mill Hill and introduce ourselves?'

'Blimey, no!' exclaimed Robbie. 'The last thing we need is you two rearranging the face of the Sketch's grime reporter.'

'Absolutely,' agreed Frank. 'Until he makes contact with Robbie and makes it clear what he wants, I think we just lie doggo.'

There was a good deal of nodding and munching – and slurping of hot porridge.

***

Just over three months later, Frank sat in his conservatory, enjoying a glass of wine and some early spring sunshine, when his mobile rang on the coffee table beside him. He looked down to see Robbie's name flashing.

'Hiya Robbie.'

'Hi, Frank. The next rehearsal is planned for the week after next. We need to bring it forward to next week, if not sooner.'

'This all sounds very dramatic, Robbie. Don't think there'll be a problem at this end, but we're gonna have to check Carol out, see if she can get up from London next week.'

'I'd thought of that, but it's important she's there. Any chance you could give me her number? For some reason I haven't got it.'

'Not a problem, I'll text it to you,' he paused. 'I tell you what, leave Shoogs to me. I can then organise Stan and Bodkin and book the village hall. I'll get back to you.'

'Thanks, Frank. You've probably sussed that after all these weeks Devereux has been back on. We need to deal with things pretty damned quick.'

'I thought he'd forgotten us,' replied Frank. 'What's been the delay? It was weeks ago.'

'The *Sketch*'s legal people have been checking through the case and then this Operation Yew Tree stuff blew up. That's bound to keep the toe-rags from the *Sketch* busy full-time, isn't it?'

'Too right, Robbie. I'll be back soon.' There was a click and Frank rang off.

Just over an hour later, Frank's name flashed on Robbie's phone.

'Hi, Frank.'

'It's all arranged for next Tuesday. Shoogs will get up here for midday and we can have the village hall any time after two.'

'That's perfect it'll give us a chance to meet at the Crown and Anchor and go over a few things. What I intend to do is phone Devereux back and get him to meet us in the pub about six o'clock.'

'What are we planning, an ambush?'

'Not a bad idea.' Robbie laughed, but it sounded

empty. 'Well done, Frank, I'll see you on Tuesday.'

CHAPTER 28
'NEWS OF THE WORLD'

The Jam

Robbie, Billy and Jez were the first to arrive. Jez was carrying a guitar case. Gloria poured them all drinks. Frank arrived with Sugarlips, then came Bodkin and Stan. Stan stuck to his Glastonbury Diet Coke, the others all had fat Cokes.

'How's it going, gunslinger?' Bodkin joked. 'Can you see your G string yet?'

Stan ignored him, just shot him a look of contempt.

'Thanks for coming, everyone,' Robbie began. 'You probably know that Devereux has been in touch, at last. I was hoping he'd forgotten about our little tête-á-tête at the Blue Onion, but it's quite the opposite. I'm afraid, from what he told me over the phone, he's really sunk his teeth into this one. The *Sketch* are planning to do a spread; would have done so by now if it hadn't been for Operation Yew Tree hogging the front pages. Now they're ready to give it the full frontal and when you hear the headline Devereux's planning, you'll realise it's not going to do me, or The Bombastics any favours. Get this – 'The Man Who Stole Rock 'N' Roll'.'

'The tosser,' cursed Stan. 'Can't we bring out one of those super-injunction things, shut the stupid twat up?'

'Not a chance, it's all been in the public domain for over thirty years,' said Robbie, shaking his head. 'I've given it a lot of thought and it seems we have two choices. One, we let him get on with it and hope any mud he slings doesn't stick, or two, we try and get him onside and see if we can change this into a positive.'

'There is a third option,' said Billy, clenching a fist in front of him. 'Me and Jez go down the Smoke and knock seven shades of shit out of him.'

Amidst some stifled chuckles, Robbie put his hand up. 'That's an option we won't be looking at.'

He then produced a bundle of old newspapers, yellowing with age. He slipped off the rubber band and opened them up. There, on the front page of the *Daily Enquirer* was a picture of a young Robbie pushing his way through a crowd of people; beside him was Billy angrily shoving some unfortunate photographer out of the way with his forearm.

'That was taken outside the court after the guilty verdict. That mob are mostly newsmen trying to get a quote out of me. They got nothing. About ten yards ahead, out of shot, Jez is waiting in my car to get me out of there.'

He tossed the yellowing newspaper onto the bar. 'The *Enquirer* disappeared off the news-stands years ago and Hackett the hatchet man, who did the most scathing coverage, died not long after. This Devereux character, who worked with him, is now at the *Sketch*. He's probably re-hashed most of Hackett's drivel for his new article. Listen to this.' He ran a finger along a section of text he'd highlighted in fluorescent pink. '"...This talentless buffoon has been caught red-handed stealing other people's songs and pocketing the royalties with no shame whatsoever. Write a song? This fool would probably have trouble writing his own name."' Robbie paused and thumped the newspaper with his fist. 'It's that bit of trash that's motivated me, made me decide I'm not going to take this lying down, so here's my plan,' Robbie continued. 'I want us to go over Barry's story again and play him the tape; he's gonna say he's heard it all before, but then he'll listen to Sugarlips; that should stop him in his tracks. Okay, he'll ask the same questions we all did. Why now? Why after all these years? Why not at the trial?

'Then we show him Barry's handwritten lyrics on the '65 calendar and those unclaimed betting slips. Now look at this – Stan's come up trumps; show them Stan.'

Stan pulled a small black notebook out of his coat pocket. 'I borrowed this from Barry's parents, it was very difficult, but I realised how important it was going to be. Paddy showed it to me years ago, but its significance didn't dawn on me until I heard Carol's story. It's Barry's little black book.'

There were some looks of astonishment.

'No, it's not what you're thinking. The only telephone numbers in here are of bookmakers he made his World Cup bets with.' He flicked through the pages. 'It seems to have every bet he made and his winnings. I've even checked the unclaimed slips and they're all in there. The handwriting is identical in all cases. This'll knock Devereux right off his perch.'

Robbie gave a mischievous smile. 'I then want to remind

him of the quote from his old mentor Hackett, "This fool would probably have trouble writing his own name."' Robbie pointed back to the highlighted text. 'I've written a new song. Jez, can you give me my guitar, please?'

Jez undid the catches on the black guitar case that he'd put on one of the tables behind them. He lifted out Robbie's acoustic guitar and handed it to him.

'I originally thought of this idea as a sort of celebration of appearing at Glastonbury, then I thought it was an opportunity to ram those words down Devereux's throat and show him I'm not a talentless buffoon who couldn't write a song; having said that it's been many a year since I wrote a song. I hope you like it.'

Robbie moved his chair back to give himself and his guitar some room. Then he began.

Sunshine over Somerset,
Storm clouds chased away,
Greenfields O Greenfields,
A Glastonbury day.

Your music in my heart,
Your music in my soul,
Glastonbury, Glastonbury,
Let your tale be told.

The sun in all its glory,
Now wore an orange glow,
Dusk crept across the Mendips,
Replaced by night's shadow.

Your music in my heart,
Your music in my soul,
Glastonbury, Glastonbury,
Let your tale be told.

An Avalon moon, round and full,
Bedecked a starry sky,
This summer solstice glory,
Just made for you and I.

Your music in my heart,
Your music in my soul,
Glastonbury, Glastonbury,
Let your tale be told.

Robbie finished with a flourish of chords.

'That's great,' said Frank, giving Robbie a little round of applause; the others all joined in.

'I love the Glastonbury link,' said Stan. 'Put that in your pipe and smoke it, mister gutter press man.'

'After all that was written about me, it was hard at first to write such a carefree lyric with the bitterness I felt, but I'm quite pleased with the way it's turned out. There's a bit of work to do on it with you guys,' said Robbie. 'We need to give it the Bombastic touch, but we've got all afternoon.' He glanced at his watch. 'He's gonna be here at the pub for six o'clock and I've asked Gloria to look after him until I get back, then I'll take him round to the village hall where you lot will be.'

'What we waiting for?' Frank jumped up put his glass on the table. 'Let's get round the corner and get this Glastonbury Tale nailed.'

By three o'clock, they more or less had it done. They tried it a number of different ways, but in the end, Robbie let Frank take lead guitar and with Bodkin and Stan he put down a driving Bo Diddley beat. Robbie let his rhythm guitar hang loose, to hand clap his way through the chorus. Billy and Jez joined in and they continued it through Sugarlips' sax break between verses two and three. It had a wonderful feel good factor about it.

'It sounds really good and a lot different to how I envisaged it,' beamed Robbie. 'That driving beat was a master stroke, Frank.'

'Thank you Bo Diddley too!' grinned Frank.

'It's very catchy, Robbie,' said Stan. 'When they hear that coming from the Pyramid Stage they're gonna love it.'

'Even with you lurking about up there in your slippers?' added Bodkin pointing a drumstick towards Stan's tartans. 'I can see the headlines now; grannies wet their pants over Mr Slippers.'

They all laughed, but Stan stuck a middle finger up towards his drummer. 'Swivel, baldy!' he spat.

They put 'Glastonbury Tale' to one side for a bit and got back to the Bombastic set they'd been working on and developing over the past months. At quarter to six, Robbie put his guitar on its stand and headed for the door.

'Better go round and see if Devereux's arrived,' he said. 'Can't leave Gloria holding the fort for too long.'

'I'll come with you,' said Frank, putting his guitar back in its case, laying open on the edge of the stage. 'For moral support, if nothing else, Robbie.'

When they walked into the Crown and Anchor it was fairly busy. The train from Birmingham had pulled in fifteen minutes before and people were enjoying a drink on their way home. Robbie recognised the figure standing at the bar immediately. Red-faced and chubby, with his comb-over; and was that the same crumpled blue suit? With him stood a tall dark stranger; he had an expensive looking digital camera hanging around his neck. They were drinking what looked like whiskey. Devereux spotted Robbie as they crossed the room.

'Robbie Rochester, you're bang on time.' He shook hands with Robbie. 'Let me introduce you to Jock McGee. As you've probably guessed, he takes the pictures.'

'Let's hope we can give you some good ones,' said Robbie as they shook hands.

'I'm sure you will, I'm really looking forward to it,' replied Jock in cultured English, no hint of the Scottish brogue he'd expected.

Robbie then introduced Frank to them both.

'Frankie Atom, no less!' exclaimed Devereux.

'Frankie Atom onstage, but Frank Richards in the pub,' replied Frank.

'And whilst we're in the pub, can I get you a drink?' Devereux tried to catch Gloria's attention.

'No, not at the moment,' said Robbie. 'We have a little surprise awaiting you, only two minutes from here.'

'Really?' Devereux was surprised. 'I hope it's not those little green men with guitars.' He brayed with laughter.

Neither Robbie nor Frank even cracked a smile, and there was an embarrassed half-smile from McGee.

'When you're ready, we'll leave,' said Robbie.

'Lead on McDuff.' Devereux slugged back his remaining whiskey and McGee put his glass down on the bar, with half a finger of scotch left in it.

The two *Sketch* men were taken aback when they walked into the village hall and saw all The Bombastics there, sound gear and instruments at the ready. Frank did the introductions and then led them both over to a trestle table and chairs they'd placed in front of the stage for the meeting. The others gathered round and sat down, Billy and Jez hoisted themselves onto the edge of the stage.

Devereux took a silver-coloured Sony Walkman Pro out of his pocket and held it up for all to see. 'Meet an old friend of mine. Mind if I make a recording of what's discussed, it's so much easier than scribbling pages of notes?'

'Not at all,' said Robbie. 'It'll ensure there are no misunderstandings further down the line.'

Devereux pressed one of the buttons on the side and placed it carefully on the trestle table.

'Thirty years ago I was ridiculed, laughed out of court, as the saying goes, only in my case it was true.' Robbie directed his words directly at the newsmen. 'It cost me nearly everything, including my career. As well as a judge who refused to believe I'd written those songs, the tabloids did a lot of the damage, with your friend Hackett seemingly bent on my personal assassination.'

'Assassination?' interrupted Devereux leaning forward menacingly. 'I think you'll find the damage was all self-inflicted. Who did you expect would believe some codswallop about a time-hopping robber you'd invented to cover your arse? Nobody, that's who!' He tossed his head back to guffaw. 'You'd have had more chance of convincing the honourable judge that Elvis Presley was riding Shergar in the 3.30 at Uttoxeter.'

'Okay, let's try again,' said Robbie, determined to keep calm. 'You don't believe my story.'

'You're spot on there, Rochester,' scoffed Devereux. 'Some rock 'n' roll greaser jumps out of the radio, twenty years ahead of his time, nicks a cassette tape with all your new songs on it and scarpers back to the sixties. As my old man used to say, do you think I came up the Thames on the last banana boat, eh Jock?'

McGee cringed, glancing around the table. 'Perhaps, 'Do you think I was born yesterday' is more appropriate these days, Roger?'

Devereux tossed his head back indignantly. 'You try and tell us that it was *he* who plagiarised *your* songs and then, guess what? You pick the one member of The Bombastics who can't dispute your wild claims because he's dead. How very convenient!'

Robbie smiled and continued, speaking quietly. 'There's been a fundamental change since the judge made his decision, something that changes everything,' said Robbie. He looked across the table at Sugarlips. 'There is now a second member of The Bombastics who can validate my story.'

Devereux was stopped in his tracks.

'That'll be me, gentlemen.' Carol who was sat next to Devereux, opened her handbag, took out the grey Walkman II and pushed it forward onto the table. 'Here is the very tape of which you spoke. This is the tape and the Walkman with Robbie's songs on it, that Barry brought back from 1983.'

Devereux waved his hands dismissively. 'We've listened to that rubbish before. As the judge and many other people pointed out at the time, that was recorded later, when Rochester got found out.'

'If you'll listen me out,' said Sugarlips calmly. 'You will now hear that is not the case, and you will also see some new evidence, that may cause you to think again.'

Devereux turned to face her, sat back and gave a shrug. 'Go ahead.'

Sugarlips also sat back, gave a little tug to her skirt with both hands and crossed her shapely legs. Devereux's left eye twitched, but he swallowed hard and held her gaze.

'Three days before he died, I was alone with Barry in a hotel lobby in Norwich,' she continued. 'We'd just done a show at The Electric Room during which he'd been popping pills; not at all unusual for Barry in those days. He then started drinking whiskey, which I guess is what loosened his tongue. He spilt out the whole story; the snow storm, the radio, being transported into 1983 and meeting Robbie and these guys, Jez and Billy. He got very emotional when he confessed to stealing Robbie's songs and then, after getting back to 1963, pretending they were his.

'Like you, I just could not believe him, told him it would all look different when he sobered up, and with the help of the night porter, bundled him off to bed. Next morning during breakfast, he invited me round to his place to substantiate what he'd told me the night before. I went round to meet him, and before I go any further, there are two things you should know. There were no drugs or drink involved, and no, he wasn't going to try and screw me; his girlfriend was there and in any case, he'd been refused that privilege many years before.

'He showed me the Walkman. I'd never seen anything like it before.' Sugarlips held up the Walkman II she'd put on the table. 'Then again nobody had, it wasn't launched by Sony for around another ten years.' She slid it along the table up alongside Devereux's Walkman Professional. 'On it were the three songs that became part of the dispute.'

'Why the hell didn't you come forward at the time?' said Devereux. 'It all seems very strange this should all come out thirty years later.'

'What are you saying?' burst in Bodkin. 'Are you trying to say Carol is lying?'

'I'm saying nothing of the sort, Sir Galahad,' answered Devereux. 'But surely you can see evidence like this would have changed the whole course of events, not to mention opened up a whole new altercation on time travel.'

'I was in the States when this all blew up,' said Sugarlips, putting a calming hand on Bodkin's shoulder who was seated the other side of her. 'I'd left the Bombastics in 1970. In fact one of the last things I was involved in was Barry's funeral. I eventually came back to Europe and was living in Paris for over twelve months before I finally got to hear about it. Very selfishly, I decided I had enough problems going on in my life at that time. I just didn't think about the chaos it had caused other people. I have apologised to Robbie, who I met for the first time only a few months ago. There is something else you need to see, Mr Devereux.' Sugarlips took Barry's lyrics from her handbag and passed it to him.

Devereux unfolded and studied the scribblings; he then turned it over to look at what was printed on the reverse. He glanced at the Bombastic group picture and then studied the July 1965 calendar grid. He spent a few minutes reading the theatre and club venues Barry had written in, to remind him of The Bombastics bookings all those years ago.

'I've managed to get this off Barry's parents.' Stan pushed the notebook in front of Devereux. 'Barry won an absolute fortune on 1966 World Cup results he found out from Robbie. In this book he recorded all his World Cup bets and winnings. There are even betting slips he never cashed in.'

Stan took one of the slips and smoothed it flat next to the open notebook. 'Look, here's one from a bookie in Newquay, we obviously didn't get back to play down that way again. Just compare the handwriting on both, and then on the calendar; it's Barry's, there's no disputing that.'

Devereux studied the three lots of handwriting, flicking through a few of the pages of the notebook, making careful comparisons with the slips and Barry's lyrics. He leaned back on his chair, ran his hand across his forehead and patted his comb-over, taking care not to disturb it. He was fully aware all of them awaited his reaction.

'Looks like we've got a bigger story here than we reckoned on, Jock,' he said without looking at his photographer.

He stood up, hands in pockets and wandered slowly away from the table deep in thought. Then he turned. 'Have you considered lodging an appeal?' he asked Robbie.

'Oh, I've thought about it a long and hard; it's nagging away non-stop, to be honest,' replied Robbie. 'Chances are, I'll let things stay as they are. I just don't want all that stuff and nonsense resurfacing again. All that personal abuse.'

'Are you crazy? Things cannot stay the same,' said Devereux. 'I'm just one news reporter, the *Sketch* is just one newspaper, wait until the others pick up on the story. It'll be like the runaway train that went over the bleedin' hill!'

'Right, Robbie,' said Stan, slapping the table and standing. 'Let's move on. One of the comments that really irked Robbie was that he was called a talentless fool who would have trouble writing his own name. We want you to listen to a song he's written especially for our June appearance at Glastonbury. He brought it with him this morning. We only heard it a few hours ago and now it's your chance. See what you think of 'Glastonbury Tale'.'

The others didn't need any prompting, they were up and over to their instruments and fine tuning. Jez was behind the mixer in an instant.

'As Stan said.' Robbie spoke into the mic. 'This one I wrote for Worthy Farm, Pilton. I hope you like it. One – two – three – four,' he counted, and in came Frank, Stan, Bodkin with that driving Bo Diddley beat.

Sunshine over Somerset,
Storm clouds chased away,
Greenfields O Greenfields,
A Glastonbury day.

Your music in my heart,
Your music in my soul,
Glastonbury, Glastonbury,
Let your tale be told...

Billy did his clapping routine on the chorus. He walked over to Devereux and McGee and by the second chorus had them clapping too.

When they finished the song, Devereux rose to his feet and his clapping changed to applause. McGee joined him. They walked the few steps to stand in front of the band.

'That was a bit special.' Devereux smiled to Robbie and the rest of them. 'Wonderful, in fact. It would seem I've got a spot of rethinking to do; let's talk.' He gestured towards the trestle table and Robbie, Frank and Carol made their way back to the table.

'Maybe it would be better back at the Crown and Anchor,' said Frank. 'It lends itself to a more convivial chat.'

'You lot go on ahead,' shouted Stan. 'I'll help Bodkin,

THE MAN WHO STOLE ROCK 'N' ROLL

Billy and Jez break down the gear and load up.'

Devereux picked up his Walkman, switched it off and slipped it into his jacket pocket. 'Before you pack everything away I'd like a few snaps of you all. Some nice group ones with your instruments, and one of all you guys around Sugarlips,' said McGee. 'A few individual ones too, we're going to need them for quotes.'

When all was done they left Stan, Bodkin, Billy and Jez breaking down and departed for the pub.

***

'All seems very cosy,' remarked Gloria as Frank came over to the bar to get drinks. 'I was a bit worried sparks were going to fly.'

'I think we may have changed his mind, let's see.' Frank picked up the tray of drinks. 'I'll let you know.' He winked.

Devereux was holding court when Frank returned.

'This story is going to take some careful handling, it'll be the proverbial shit being introduced to the fan when it breaks and I'd like *The Weekly Sketch* to be in charge. I'll have to scrap the story I'd written, we've got something a lot bigger here.'

'So the headline 'The Man Who Stole Rock 'N' Roll' goes?' said Robbie.

'Sadly, yes. I was quite pleased with that,' smiled Devereux. 'Still, it shouldn't take us long to come up with another. In the meantime we need a media blackout. I want exclusivity from the moment I break the story, coverage of Glastonbury and any subsequent court case, should you decide to go back for your compensation.'

'Exclusive photos, too,' added McGee.

'Exclusivity? How much do you pay Robbie and the rest of us for that?' asked Frank. 'Gotta be worth a few quid.'

'Ha, ha, ha!' laughed Devereux. 'You didn't come in on that banana boat either, did you Frankie Atom?'

McGee cringed again.

'I'll need to speak to my editor about that, but worry not, we'll look after your best interests,' said Devereux. 'I've just thought, we need to keep it off Facebook, Twitter and the like, it'd go viral. Are any of you on those social networking sites?'

'I've got a Facebook account, so has Dessie,' said Carol. 'Dessie tweets too, and young Mikey is bound to.'

'I'm on Facebook, but don't tweet,' added Frank.

'We have Rochester Classics on Facebook,' said Robbie. 'Purely for business, and Billy and Jez know nothing about tweeting.'

'You need to check with Bodkin and Stan, this is very important,' warned Devereux. 'Every member of your families and anybody who knows about Carol's new evidence must be sworn to secrecy. We need to throw a blanket over the whole thing.'

***

Roger Devereux worked closely with Robbie Rochester and Carol Meadowsweet over the next few days, going over their stories again, sifting through old photos and photocopying Barry's calendar and World Cup records and betting slips. He set about writing a completely new story.

Looking rather sadly at his laptop screen, he said, 'This original article could still come in handy. Many of our readers won't have a clue what this is all about and even the ones old enough to remember the case, will have forgotten most of it. I can adapt what I've written to remind readers how unfairly Robbie Rochester was treated. Then we can come up with this sensational new twist and absolutely knock their socks off.'

Devereux spread his arms. 'We shall right the wrongs! We've done lots already, look!' he continued. 'We've pieced together Sugarlips' American jazz adventure, and that Greenwich Village poster you got from her mother and the photos, old and new, will help make a great story.'

Robbie and The Bombastics were amazed how a cynical hack had transformed into a born-again investigative journalist who championed his cause. Devereux had made a leap of faith.

'No matter how we do this,' said Devereux, at one of his parleys with Robbie, 'when the story breaks and they read my article and see the pictures you'll have the media camped on your doorsteps, paparazzi, TV cameras, the lot! The other problem you'll have to face is when the other newspapers and TV companies find out *The Weekly Sketch* has exclusivity; expect a backlash of jealous scepticism. You're going to be in the spotlight, no question about that, and it would be better to embrace it rather than fight it. Try and get out of it what you can.'

'You've certainly put my car business in the spotlight with the photo of Billy, Jez and myself posing in the VW Devon,' laughed Robbie. 'I ought to put you on commission. One thing I did think about, what about Ike Hoffman, do we make contact before the story goes out?'

'Naaah, bugger him!' snarled Devereux. 'Let him find out when everyone else does; he'll shit himself.'

'One thing I have given a lot of thought to,' said Robbie. 'Can we hold the article back until the first week of June?'

Devereux raised his eyebrows in surprise. 'June? That's weeks away! Are we sure we can maintain radio silence until then? Remember the five figure remuneration my editor has agreed depends upon exclusivity. It only takes one tweet.'

'Don't worry, the hatches are securely battened down,' replied Robbie. 'My reasoning behind that request is there'll only be three weeks to Summer Solstice and Glastonbury. Think of the maximum publicity that'll bring.'

'Blimey, you really are embracing it,' chuckled Devereux. His face then turned serious. 'You have to understand this is difficult for me, Robbie. The story is my baby and like any expectant father I want to see it spring into life without delay, but I'll go along with you. June it is.'

***

The article finally appeared in *The Weekly Sketch* on Wednesday June 4th 2014.

The centre-fold headline read, 'BOMBASTICS' TIME HOP.' Devereux had reluctantly dropped his original, 'THE MAN WHO STOLE ROCK 'N' ROLL', but he felt this new one fitted the bill perfectly. The sub-heading read, 'Convicted song thief is innocent'.

The copy told the story from beginning to end, featured Sugarlips' witness statement and the reasons for her delay in coming forward, the shame and misery Robbie Rochester had gone through, the change of direction his career had taken, and then the fortuitous meeting up with The Bombastics; all because of a VW camper. It told the readers that Robbie would be up onstage at Glastonbury with The Bombastics later that month, singing the songs that he'd written and had been hits twenty years before their time. Jock McGee's photographs enhanced the storyline. Everybody loved the group shot around Jezza.

Devereux was right, the world turned upside down for The Bombastics and for Robbie Rochester in particular. As soon as the story hit the news stands, the world press swarmed into town, trampling the local press underfoot. The national red tops held the advantage, but the foreign journalists were only hours behind. By the following day

TV cameras, presenters and their soundmen from all over the world; radio cars, newspaper reporters and photographers were soon encamped outside Robbie's home and Rochester Classics in Stechford. They hunted down Frankie Atom in Balsall Common, Sugarlips at The Blue Onion and much to Bodkin's amusement, Stan at the Crown and Anchor. Bodkin was the most elusive, but the Dither Sisters spilt the beans and gave away his address for a couple of gin and tonics.

They gave their interviews and stuck to the script they'd agreed with Devereux, which was basically all contained in his *Weekly Sketch* article. If anything new transpired, it was his and his alone.

Frank got a call from Chekka records; it was some guy calling himself Dixie Maynard. Frank had never heard of him and told him so. Dixie had heard about the new song Robbie had written and was keen to talk to The Bombastics about possibly cutting and releasing it as a single; maybe there was an opportunity for more than that, maybe an album. Frank reminded him that Chekka had ditched The Bombastics over forty years ago, but said he'd talk to Robbie, whose song it was anyway, see what the rest of the band thought and get back to him. He put the phone down and laughed to himself. *We'll also check out other labels, see what they want to offer, so up yours Chekka!*

The real success story was social media. Devereux told the others how he'd tried so hard many times to get stories of his to go viral, with very little success. This time without any effort whatsoever, his 'Time Hop' story exploded worldwide. Twitter, Facebook, Flickr, you name it! Even some old Bombastics and Robbie Rochester videos on YouTube were getting thousands upon thousands of hits.

***

The week before Glastonbury they had a gig at the Beachcomber in Shanklin. Frank had done his one man show there a few times and had got to know the owner, Ade French very well. A few weeks before, when he told Ade about the Glastonbury gig and asked if they could do a dress rehearsal at his club, neither had any idea of the madness the *Weekly Sketch* story would create. Well before the exposé had hit the streets, Frank had posted it on his Facebook page as a Bombastics reunion, he didn't even mention Glastonbury. After the newspaper article, demand for tickets for, what was after all, only a Tuesday night, was unprecedented, certainly in Ade's tenure. People were phoning from the mainland trying to reserve and pay by credit card for tickets. Within hours of the article, the gig was a sell-out.

The concert couldn't have gone better, every number was greeted with clapping and cheering, but it was the audience reaction to the final two numbers of their encore that stole the show, 'Glastonbury Tale' and 'Jive Away the Tears'. Up onstage all The Bombastics were laughing; Frank could hardly get his words out when the dancers began.

It was a middle-aged couple at the front who started it; by the time they were halfway through 'Glastonbury Tale' and then all the way through 'Jive Away the Tears' everybody on the dance floor had joined in what became known as the 'Time Hop'. All hopping to the left together, all hopping to the right together, waving their arms together. It was wonderful.

'Never seen so many silver-haired pogoers,' Frankie said to the others afterwards. 'It was like a punk version of The Rocky Horror Show out there.'

Glastonbury was less than a week away.

CHAPTER 29
'YESTERDAY ONCE MORE'

The Carpenters

It hadn't been the most idyllic of summers. In fact the days preceding Glastonbury, although mild were mainly overcast, and the Friday before their Saturday afternoon appearance, it rained quite heavily. Not that rain ever discouraged a Glastonbury crowd.

The plan was to travel down to Somerset on Friday and lie low in a hotel they knew, hidden away in the sprawling countryside on the outskirts of Weston-super-Mare; then travel to the helicopter transport near Glastonbury on Saturday morning.

Easier said than done!

The media machine had been out in full force since the story broke and getting out of the Midlands without the paparazzi in tow was going to be difficult. Each of them was being door-stepped, particularly Robbie and Frank, and it was going to take some careful thought to make a clean break.

It was Stan and Bodkin who came up with the master plan, but even they couldn't have counted on the heavy thunderstorm that would help their subterfuge. Bodkin, Julie and Wally, and some of Stan's mates from the Crown and Anchor congregated at Stan's house that Thursday night, on the pretence of a pre-festival knees-up. The comings and goings of people and cars confused the little knot of reporters and the next morning, thunder rolled across dark Fordrough skies and rain falling in sheets. From under their umbrellas and cagoules it certainly looked like Bodkin and Stan getting into Jezza, and the chap loading guitars and drums into the back was probably a roadie.

Wally was delighted with the storm. Julie and Elsie had threatened to shave his head to make him look even more like his brother, but now a waterproof beanie, a stick on goatee with a touch or two of non-drip mascara and he was good to go. Two of Stan's drinking pals made up the party. Dougie Jones shoved a cushion up the front of his anorak and pulled the hood low over his head to look like Stan, whilst Benny Watson also in a hoodie loaded guitar cases on board Jezza. Off they set and the newshounds gave chase.

It was still raining heavily when Wally drove The VW camper up Frank's driveway. The pursuing pack joined those already camped outside the automatic gates. In Frank's kitchen, it was quick change time for Benny Watson. Benny had been chosen because he had Frank's stature and he was still a child of the seventies with his long greying (and thinning) hair. He quickly slipped into Frank's denim jacket and jeans, whilst Frank himself pulled back Benny's hair into a tight ponytail. The final touch was the Frankie Atom sunglasses. He even gave the crowd a wave as he and Wally and Dougie Jones got back into the VW to drive off, hotly pursued by cars, motorbikes and TV vans. Frank laughed to himself from behind the bedroom curtains.

Picking up Sugarlips was going to be a more of a challenge. The press had sussed out she was staying at her mom's in Solihull. Mary's drive wasn't as long as Frank's, so things had to be slick. Wally drove through the growing mass of scribes and snappers, to park as near to the front door as possible. Mary opened the door and out stepped Carol with her long blonde hair bunched to one side, her white gabardine mac belted loosely and the collar up high. She opened her umbrella for the short walk to the car, and she too gave her audience a wave, as she climbed into Jezza. The others had wanted Carol to wear sunglasses, but she was adamant; she never wore celebrity sunglasses and she was confident Dessie could pull it off without them. And so it turned out.

Meanwhile, Robbie had arranged to be at Rochester Classics with Janice as well as Billy and Jez, for what seemed the normal start of business hours on a Friday morning. The trick here was Robbie's older brother Johnny, and his partner Steph, arriving incognito to pick up a VW Beetle they'd supposedly had freshly sprayed in bright metallic scarlet. Robbie made a big thing of shaking hands in the open doorway of the unit with Johnny and Steph, clad in matching purple designer jackets and Harris tweed trilbies. When they disappeared upstairs 'to finalise things' they quickly swapped jackets and hats and Robbie and Janice swished away in the rain in their scarlet Beetle. The posse of journos waited.

About three quarters of an hour later, Wally drove in off the feeder road and parked Jezza outside Rochester Classics. Their paparazzi tail also ground to a halt and gathered around as they watched Wally, Dougie, Benny and Dessie being joined by Johnny, Steph, Billy and Jez to line up and take a bow, like the cast of some provincial pantomime after a wet Wednesday matinee.

'Sorry we can't make you all a cup of tea,' beamed Billy, unable to suppress his delight. 'We haven't got enough cups and, anyway, the milk's gone off!'

There was a lot of grumbling and cursing from the dripping masses, as they dispersed in different directions.

Billy and Jez then used Jezza to pick up Carol, Frank, Stan and Bodkin, dropping off the decoys as they went. They met Robbie and Janice at Strensham Services on the M5, where they also arranged for Johnny and Steph to bring Robbie's Jag and take the Beetle.

That night at the Webbington Hotel there was a lot of laughter as they enjoyed reliving the highlights. Stan didn't think the cushion up Dougie Jones' anorak was necessary and therefore didn't qualify as a highlight. Bodkin disagreed and when Billy and Jez sided with him, Stan threw a tantrum. Cue more laughter.

Saturday morning was cloudy. The Bombastics thought it appropriate to drive the rest of the way to Somerset in Jezza, with Robbie following in his Jag with Billy and Jez.

'And don't get messing with that radio dial,' joked Billy. 'We don't want Robbie at Glastonbury and you lot at Woodstock in 1969.'

They all laughed in the VW, but nobody touched that dial and they all felt a little happier when Frank plugged in his iPod and The Eagles joined them on the A371. After a few miles it started to rain, only lightly, but there were some long faces.

They arrived at the heliport in plenty of time; they were billeted in a six berth motor home, it was a bit tight on space, but as they didn't plan to stay overnight it mattered not, at least they were in the dry.

They resigned themselves to a few hours ensconced in the motor home. Sugarlips made a large pot of tea and produced a big bag of donuts which she set out on a glass cake stand she found in one of the cupboards.

'My Glastonbury diet finished at noon today,' announced Stan. 'So keep your thieving hands off my donut.' With that he snatched back one of the two donuts that Bodkin had claimed.

'You've done quite well, lardy boy,' scoffed Bodkin. 'Where are you wearing your guitar today, above or below the belly button?'

'I've lost nearly a stone, I'll have you know,' retorted Stan. 'Today, I shall be the mean and moody gunslinger my fans know and love; I shall be breaking hearts like they're mere playthings.'

They were all laughing now.

'Mean and moody? Breaking hearts? In your tartan slippers?' Bodkin slapped the table, almost choking on a mouthful of hot tea that went down the wrong way.

Stan bit into his donut and squirted jam up his nose.

Carol had to look the other way.

'There's enough blue sky to make a sailor a pair of trousers,' said Robbie suddenly.

The others gave him a puzzled look. Robbie was sat on the window seat, holding slats of the Venetian blind open with two fingers and staring skywards.

'It's something my old dad used to say when the weather perked up,' he added. 'Look, it's stopped raining, most of the clouds have disappeared and the sun is trying to come out.'

Frank pulled the cord to open the blind on the window next to where he and Billy were sat, so they could all see. 'Hey, the sun is out! It's a good omen, it's gonna be a bostin' day. The crowd are going to love us, I just know it.'

'Let's go and have a drink in the bar,' suggested Robbie. 'It's still nearly two hours before they fly us in.'

'Good idea,' laughed Bodkin. 'Give Stan a chance to get some Dutch courage inside him before we go hedge hopping.'

'Dutch courage?' asked Robbie.

'Take no notice, he's taking the piss,' said Stan.

'He used to have a problem with flying.' Bodkin was trying to keep a straight face. 'But now he wears incontinence pants.'

'We just have to make sure he tucks his trouser legs in his socks,' hooted Frank.

Sugarlips wrinkled her nose. 'You men don't get any better, do you?'

'They think they're so funny.' Stan opened the motor home door. 'C'mon Shoogs, c'mon Robbie, I'll buy you that drink.'

At three o'clock precisely the first of the two helicopters arrived to whisk Carol, Frank, Stan, Bodkin and their instruments over to the Pyramid Stage. They climbed aboard the bright yellow ROTO-bird, strapped themselves in and hopped over the trees and hedges to arrive backstage. By the time Robbie, Billy and Jez arrived in ROTO-bird two, the press were upon them.

They'd been very relieved that their arrival at the heliport was so low key; they were big news now for things other than their music and had expected a media scrum. Using clandestine methods to sneak out of the Midlands was one thing, but expecting to arrive at such an iconic festival unnoticed, with headline news clattering all around them was another thing altogether.

Once it was known they were there, the texts and tweets

started and everything changed. They wanted to enjoy the atmosphere before their set, but they were soon overwhelmed by TV cameras, men and women pointing microphones and cameras at them. Fortunately, Devereux, with his 'Access All Areas' wristband was at hand and soon had the Glastonbury marshals restoring some sort of order.

In no time at all, Billy and Jez were onstage making final adjustments ready for the grand entrance. They were announced. 'Let's give a big Glastonbury welcome to Frankie Atom and The Bombastics, with guest star Robbie Rochester.'

As they took to the stage the final wisps of cloud had gone and the bright sunshine lit up the hundreds and thousands of faces that disappeared into the distance. Flags of many nations and football clubs atop long poles fluttered in the gentle breeze. Messages daubed on large pieces of cardboard were all around. 'BEAM ME UP SCOTTY' said one right in front of them, and another to their right read, 'LET'S DO THE TIME HOP'.

There were Dr Whos, Captain Kirks and Mr Spocks everywhere. There were Buzz Lightyears and Darth Vaders too. The atmosphere was electric, this crowd wanted to party. It was just like the old days – yesterday once more.

Right from the off, starting with The Bombastics' old favourite 'Rock and Roll Music' the crowd went wild. Three or four Tom Bakers with permed hair and long knitted scarves, were hoisted on shoulders near the front and an inflatable ET was being bounced around by the enormous crowd. Every song in their repertoire had the fans singing and clapping. They thumped out all the hits, 'Teenage Crush', 'Little Bit Crazy', 'Love You Honey'. Robbie took centre stage to sing 'Warwickshire Girls', 'Bar Room Brawl', and his version of 'Broken Hearted Nobody'. They saved 'Jive Away the Tears' and a rousing version of 'Glastonbury Tale' for the inevitable encores.

It started at the front amongst a section of tightly packed, happy sardines, who did a sort of pogo hand-jive routine. The crowd around soon picked up that it was a version of the Time Hop and it spread like wildfire, thousands upon thousands of pogoers. The Bombastics watched, almost in awe as bouncing heads and dancing hands disappeared into the faraway.

As they stood on the stage, arms around each other, taking their final bows in the afternoon sunshine, Frank shouted in Robbie's ear, 'We must do this again sometime.'

'We must,' Robbie mouthed back.

***

Back at the Crown and Anchor, Gloria had persuaded Dennis Jenkinson, the gaffer, to hire a wide screen television for the Glastonbury weekend. In the end they hired two, one for the lounge bar and another for the beer garden which was placed under cover, in case the clouds didn't roll back. Television in his pub was not what old Dennis did, but he could hear the tills ringing as beer and spirits (not to mention food and snacks) sales went through the roof.

Gloria put the word out, sticking posters in shop windows and on notice boards around the village, and the Dither Sisters arranged for tickets for The Bombastics' performance on Saturday afternoon, even borrowing chairs from the village hall.

It turned out to be a warm, sunny day in Worcestershire and the good people (and the not so good), of Fordrough turned up in their droves. Every chair was taken outside and it was standing room only inside; if any of the villagers had had their noses put out by not getting a ticket for the original village hall dress rehearsal, it certainly didn't show that afternoon.

Carol and Dessie didn't think Glastonbury was quite

the place for a ninety-two year old great-grandmother, although she was game! So Mary Meadowsweet, Dessie and young Mikey, were front row guests of honour at the Crown and Anchor for the live TV coverage.

Jack and Doris Richards, both alive and well and still living in Little Barnham opened their home to family and close friends; sister Suzie (now grandma Suzie) and her brood, along with Elsie and Julie. Wally and Bodkin's mom, still the only living person to call him Duncan, settled down with a couple of gin and tonics and had to be woken up by Wally when The Bombastics came on.

One sensible thing Barry's fortune had done, was to make provision for his mom and dad. They were now being cared for at The Elizabeth Shaftsbury Residential Home in nearby Ashton Fells. They were both far too frail for the Crown and Anchor, or Little Barnham. Both in their nineties, in his dad's case against all odds, they had never got over the death of their son. Stan had kept in touch, particularly with Barry's dad, and without realising it, had got him to open up about his wartime experiences more than anybody else had ever done before. Stan took Carol, Bodkin and Frank round to see Paddy and Martha, realising it would be difficult for them all, but feeling it was the right thing to do at such a time. Mom got very emotional and Dad, very poorly and now in a wheelchair, still referred to Barry as 'that feckin' eejit', for which he got told off by Martha. The four of them spent some time with Barry's parents, remembering the good times, but unable to avoid the sad ones. Stan gave the staff of The Elizabeth Shaftsbury, the times and channels of The Bombastics' Glastonbury appearance. Mom and Dad declined the chance to watch.

***

The media scramble descended into pure insanity, as hordes of journalists stampeded to take their places for the post-performance interview. Roger Devereux placed himself alongside the band, partly to guard his own interests and partly to field any difficult questions. The hack pack were having none of it.

It started off quite gently. What was it like to be back together again after all these years? How had they enjoyed the Glastonbury experience? Were they surprised by the love and enthusiasm the crowd gave them? Did they enjoy the crowd's version of the Time Hop? Would they be performing together again? Was there any plan to release 'Glastonbury Tale' as a single?

Then, inevitably, the mood and the questions changed.

How come this time travel story wasn't headline news in 1963 when Barry Harper got back home? Did any of you try to follow his trail back in time and go looking for him? Did he steal anybody else's hits from the future? Robbie, are you going to get the case re-opened? Is this some outrageous publicity stunt to resurrect your careers?

They stuck to the Devereux script as best they could, answering the serious questions honestly and laughing at the daft ones.

Was it true that time travel buttons were now fitted in all VW campers? Was Robbie Rochester considering becoming the next Dr Who?

Soon it was time for ROTO-birds to shuttle them back to the heliport, and none too soon either; Roger Devereux stood up, spreading his palms high and wide, waiting for a good two or three minutes before he could get a word in edgeways.

'Thank you. Thank you ladies and gentlemen. Thank you. You've listened to Robbie and Frankie and The Bombastics play their music, now it's time for you to listen to all the other amazing artists at this wonderful festival. Any further questions are for another time and another place.'

He turned towards the others, anxious to lead them away, when just for a fleeting moment there was silence; enough silence for a young denim-clad reporter in the front row to shout forth a question that stopped Robbie in his tracks.

Bespectacled Jenny Pargeter from Focus South West, her straw-coloured hair pulled back in a loose bun and secured with a knotted pink chiffon scarf, was heard loud and clear.

'Robbie, how come you didn't know The Bombastics had recorded your song?'

She looked around self-consciously, all eyes upon her. 'After all it was a big hit twenty years before you released it, you must have heard it?'

Devereux's heart sank. 'I've tried to explain...'

'I'll answer that,' interrupted Robbie, looking at Devereux, and he sat back down in front of the mic. 'Jenny, I've spoken to a number of people about that very subject. To be honest it, was something that drove me insane to begin with.'

The press tent was hushed, you could have heard a pin drop, if it hadn't been a grassy field.

'First you must understand that when Barry left us and returned to 1963, we were on the brink of recording 'Broken Hearted Nobody' and it was released within a month to become a hit around the world; even the album with 'Bar Room Brawl' and 'Running Away' on it was in the shops before the summer of '83.

'Meanwhile Jenny, at the time Barry returned to 1963 with that cassette tape, The Bombastics hadn't yet got a recording contract and remember, Barry said nothing to anybody about his time with us. So from the dates we now know, he didn't claim to have written my songs for over two years.

'Just put the twenty year time gap to one side for a moment. I released that song over two years before The Bombastics. It sounds crazy just saying it, but it does it make sense, doesn't it?'

Jenny Pargeter nodded her head, and everybody waited for more.

'So for those two years, The Bombastics' recording never existed. Nothing in the archives of the BBC, nor the music papers, not in the Guinness Book of Records, not in anyone's memory or on any DJ's playlist.'

'Now comes the difficult bit. I sometimes wonder if I really understand this myself, but let's try.' Robbie looked Jenny right in the eye. 'One of the guys I spoke to, Andrew Hamilton, or Professor Andrew Hamilton to give him his proper title, said he believed the Butterfly Effect would apply even more profoundly, should time travel ever be possible.'

Jenny Pargeter looked puzzled.

'You will be aware of the Butterfly Effect? Whereby a very minor event in one part of the world, like a butterfly landing, can have an immense, even devastating, effect tens of thousands of miles away; like an earthquake or tsunami. Well, Professor Hamilton's belief was that anybody travelling back in time and changing the events of history, even just tinkering with it, didn't reckon with the consequences it could have over the ensuing years. You can see from our own example that what Barry did was not just dishonest, it was life-changing. When 'Shattered Dreams and Promises' was released, it caused havoc for other people all those years later. Some we know about, but hundreds, maybe thousands, we don't and probably never will. As George Michael once wrote, 'Turn Another Corner'. Wham! And who knows what the future could have held.'

'Hey, hey,' butted in Roger Devereux. 'Our time is up,

the helicopters are waiting. I think we should leave talk of butterflies and tsunamis for another day.

***

'Glastonbury Tale' was released as a single on the Chekka label. Despite Frank's early reservations, in the end Chekka's offer was by far the best. The CEO himself handled the deal and everyone was pleased with three singles and an album on a one-year, rolling contract. Robbie also signed a contract for songs he'd written, or would go on to write, with the publisher Frank had been using since his escape from Hoffman's clutches.

The single just couldn't fail, it was number one on the download charts within hours and stayed at number one on combined record and download charts for seven weeks. With the international interest in their story, 'Glastonbury Tale' started to appear in charts all around the world, including the Billboard charts in the States, and for a few mad months, the Time Hop became the favourite dance in clubs all over the free world and maybe in the not so free world too!

The Bombastics were hot tickets once again, hotter than the first time around. Robbie Rochester was even hotter, if that was possible. Roger Devereux made the most of the *Weekly Sketch* exclusivity deal and sold their story and pictures to newspapers and magazines around the world. They even set up a Time Hop website, which crashed dozens of times during the first week as millions hit it.

However, it was the demand for TV and films that started to take on gigantic proportions.

They appeared on all the top shows and chat show hosts both sides of the Atlantic clamoured for an appearance from them. Offers of in-depth documentaries, even fly-on-the-wall exposés poured in.

'What if Jeremy Kyle's people get in touch?' joked

Frank.

'We'll send Billy and Jez,' grinned Robbie.

It was Robbie who received a film script from an American literary agent. 'Once Upon A Time Hop' was the working title. 'It's garbage, I didn't get past the first act,' he told the others. 'Put it like this, I don't expect Steven Spielberg to be pestering us to shoot it!'

It was after an appearance on Graham Norton that Carol asked if they could discuss the future and get some sort of order into where they were headed. Within an hour they were in an exclusive little Italian restaurant she knew in Knightsbridge.

They ordered their food and wine, then sat back to discuss things.

'The last few weeks have been a whirl,' began Carol. 'We've never been so popular, it's sheer madness and I'm not sure it's for the best musical reason, and now Frank tells me we could be filling two diaries, seven days a week with the demand we're getting.'

She sipped her wine and looked at each of them before continuing.

'This isn't working out for me. I'm not sure I want to be travelling around the country doing gigs again at my age. I'm settled in London, and Dessie, Tom and Mikey wouldn't consider living anywhere else. I intend to visit Mom in Brum more regularly; she's never complained about her daughter neglecting her, but it's something I feel very guilty about. I have my jazz dates too; as many as I want, if I'm honest. I am not going to lose contact with you boys again and I certainly wouldn't mind getting together to do odd dates throughout the year, but being perfectly truthful, that's as far as I want it to go.'

'You don't fancy another trip down Route 66 next winter then?' asked Frank.

'We were a generation too early on that trip,' said Stan. 'Look what we missed out on – stadium concerts, non-stop coverage on MTV.'

'Not to mention throwing televisions out of Holiday Inn windows,' added Bodkin.

The laughter died down as Robbie spoke. 'I'm thinking along the same lines as Carol; I'm not prepared to neglect the business I've built up with Billy and Jez. We've all learned that pop music in all its forms is a transitory thing and when this immediate flurry of fame is done with, we'll become yesterday's news – chip paper. I also think we ought to be very selective with the work we do.'

He held up his hand to hold back Stan.

'If I can add one thing. I'm looking forward to writing songs with Frank, see if we can inspire each other. Remember we have a recording contract to fulfil.'

'Me too,' said Frank. 'There's an album to put together, not to mention follow up singles, but I agree, we ain't nineteen years old anymore. Listen guys, I'm used to life on the road, I've been doing it on and off for fifty years. Ironically, this may be an opportunity for me to slow down. I can understand some disappointment, but surely at our age and with this success we find ourselves in the middle of, we go along with Robbie's suggestion, be selective and play when and where we want.'

Stan at last got his say. 'So my chances of being a born-again rock god are going to be shackled, then; I can more or less hang up my rock 'n' roll shoes.'

'Tartan slippers, more like,' grinned Bodkin. 'Your feet were bigger news than your belly.'

Stan threw a thick slice of ciabatta across the table at Bodkin. It hit him on the arm and finished up in his Pinot Grigio.

'One thing I would request is a bit of a jam session at

our Golden Wedding in three years' time. Yes, me and Elsie, hearts entwined for fifty years.'

There was some light-hearted barracking, but those around the table knew it was true.

'I was only looking at the old diaries from the time I used to get all the bookings. You'll remember The Bombastics used to go out for fifteen quid; well I've had a word with our Elsie and we're willing to push the boat out and pay fifteen guineas.'

This time the slices of ciabatta came flying through the air in his direction.

'I'm happy to play drums whenever you want me,' said Bodkin. 'I also intend to continue giving tuition at Redditch College. It would be a pity to waste such God-given talent.'

'God-given?' laughed Stan. 'What was it John Lennon said when he was asked if Ringo was the best drummer in the world? "He's not even the best drummer in the Beatles." Ha! I'll say no more.'

'Going back to anniversaries,' said Frank. 'In December my mom and dad, Jack and Doris Richards of this parish, celebrate their platinum wedding anniversary. It's two weeks before Christmas and they've booked the Shillingworth. Nearly a hundred guests, dinner and The Johnny West Quintet providing the music. You're all invited of course, and I'd like us to do a spot. Only forty-five minutes or so, any longer could be a little too much rock 'n' roll for a couple celebrating seventy years of married bliss.'

'We could learn a few numbers from their era,' said Carol. 'I've got a few arrangements of songs like 'Pennies from Heaven', 'Zing Went the Strings of My Heart' and 'Blue Moon'.

'Why not?' enthused Bodkin. 'I don't get to use my

brushes too often.'

'Consider yourselves booked,' laughed Frank.

The antipasto arrived.

***

A few days later Robbie, Billy and Jez had stopped work for a few minutes to have coffee. Despite Hissing Sid letting forth steam, Robbie heard his mobile ringing and vibrating on the table top. Roger Devereux's name lit up.

'Robbie, I've been in touch with Ike Hoffman.'

'What for?'

'You know exactly what for, Robbie; we've heard absolutely nothing from that quarter.'

'We weren't likely to either, not until you started poking around, anyway.'

'C'mon, Robbie I'm a newsman, it's my job. I wanted to know if he was shitting himself.'

'Why should he be shitting himself, I've done nothing about re-opening the case, have I?'

'That's exactly what he said. Reckoned you hadn't got the balls to do anything about it.'

'Robbie… Hello… Hello… Robbie… Are you still there Robbie?'

Printed in Great Britain
by Amazon.co.uk, Ltd.,
Marston Gate.